No Boundaries

No Boundaries

TRANSNATIONAL LATINO GANGS AND AMERICAN LAW ENFORCEMENT

Tom Diaz

With a Foreword by Chris Swecker

THE UNIVERSITY OF MICHIGAN PRESS | ANN ARBOR

First paperback edition 2011

Copyright © by the University of Michigan 2009

All rights reserved

Published in the United States of America by

The University of Michigan Press

Printed and bound by CPI Group (UK) Ltd, Croydon, CR0 4YY

2014   2013   2012   2011   5   4   3   2

A CIP catalog record for this book is available from the British Library.

Library of Congress Cataloging-in-Publication Data

Diaz, Tom.

   No boundaries : transnational Latino gangs and American law
enforcement / Tom Diaz ; with a foreword by Chris Swecker.

    p.   cm.

   Includes index.

   ISBN-13: 978-0-472-11629-4 (cloth : alk. paper)

   1. Hispanic American gangs—United States. 2. Gangs—Latin
America. 3. Gang prevention—United States. I. Title.

HV6439.U5D53   2009

364.106'608968073—dc22   2008051144

ISBN-13: 978-0-472-02198-7 (e-book)

ISBN-13: 978-0-472 03468 0 (pbk. : alk. paper)

To Ana Mateo and Daniel Ochoa

FOREWORD

There is a cliché about today's news media that says, "If it bleeds, it leads." By that standard, the highly publicized Latino gang Mara Salvatrucha, or MS-13, has earned its place in the nightly news reports. It has even exceeded that low standard. If we considered only MS-13's gratuitous violence, lack of respect for authority, and utter disregard for human life, it would be hard to distinguish it from many other violent gangs in America. Tom Diaz's account of Latino gangs goes far in understanding why MS-13 is different and was labeled by *Newsweek* magazine in September 2005 as "the most dangerous gang in America." Diaz's work is no esoteric analysis of this transnational gang but, rather, a gritty, real-life look at a menace that most people thought was a big-city issue that did not impact their "safe" bedroom communities. Diaz very effectively traces the origins of this brutish criminal network and the efforts of law enforcement to hold the line against a threat that resides just outside our front doors. As a former law enforcement insider who worked gangs as a street-level FBI agent and, later, as an FBI assistant director ultimately responsible for all FBI gang investigations, I can attest that the most unsettling aspect of this book is that it is 100 percent accurate. Diaz's research is impeccable, and his insights are spot-on.

During my twenty-five-year tenure in law enforcement, I saw an alarming increase in gangs and gang membership across the country. According to recent surveys, more than twenty thousand gangs are active in the United States, with over 780,000 members. It is important to understand that gangs like MS-13 and 18th Street are different from traditional criminal "syndicates," such as La Cosa Nostra or Russian organized crime, whose "families" are highly regimented, hierarchal, and almost businesslike. Street gangs are less evolved on the criminal ladder. They are criminal networks whose structure is more informal and less disciplined. Like a cancer, their particular brand of brutality and random violence demoralizes and erodes entire communities.

True law enforcement professionals—that is, detectives, street cops, and federal agents—know that in the evolutionary hierarchy of criminal organizations, gangs occupy the lowest rung of the organized crime ladder. That makes them very dangerous to the average citizen and law enforcement. More sophisticated criminal organizations focus on money-producing crimes and use violence as a tool to enforce the "business" of crime. That does not make them less of a threat to society, but when it comes to gratuitous violence, targeting innocent citizens is bad for their "business." These criminal organizations hide their affiliations with crime families and shun the spotlight. In contrast, gangs use violence to intimidate the public and establish their identity. They publicly display their criminal affiliation through visible tattoos, hand signs, tagging of their turf, and special greetings. Much of their recruiting efforts are directed toward juveniles as young as age thirteen. Their initiation rituals involve violence or forced sex on aspiring members and the verified commission of violent crimes against "civilians." They will rob, kill, and maim simply to gain "respect." They relish the spotlight. The risk of treating gangs like MS-13 as usual threats is that when they do evolve, ditch the tattoos, take up more sophisticated tactics, and become a less visible criminal organization, they will be too entrenched to eradicate. A bad example of this level of entrenchment is the development of the crime families of La Cosa Nostra from the 1920s through the 1960s. These families essentially had a forty-year head start before law enforcement, particularly the FBI, acknowledged their existence and attacked them as organized crime. It took the next thirty-five years to reduce their presence from over thirty active families to less than a dozen.

Diaz very effectively traces the roots of MS-13, which seemed to burst on the scene in 2004, after a series of well-publicized brutal assaults and homicides took place in the quiet, orderly suburbs of Northern Virginia, in the shadow of our nation's capitol. Particularly shocking was the gang slashing of a pregnant sixteen-year-old federal witness whose mutilated body was found near a tranquil stream in the Shenandoah Valley of Virginia. Overnight, the media and the American public awakened to the presence of a machete-wielding criminal network that hit uncomfortably close to their suburban homes.

Ironically, the presence of MS-13 in America is a self-inflicted disease. As Tom Diaz's research points out, the gang has its roots in the Rampart area of South Los Angeles but proliferated through the policy of deportation of these convicted criminals to what one member described to FBI MS-13 Task Force agents as a "paid vacation" in prisons in El Salvador, Guatemala, or Honduras, where they thrived. These facilities are nothing more then gang-controlled universities and training camps. In these "prisons," networks are solidified, members are recruited, doctrine is established, and leaders consolidate their power. During the year 2000, a monthly average of three hundred violent Salvadorian criminals were deported from the United States to El Salvador. Most were MS-13 or 18th Street members. Many of the original Salvatruchans had military training and combat experience as members of the Farabundo Martí National Liberation Front, a Salvadoran rebel group. Upon release, these hardened and better-networked criminals quickly and easily slipped back into the United States and fanned out, establishing new footholds in communities thriving on such industries as meat packing, agriculture, and construction. The story of the notorious MS-13 butcher "El Culiche" (the Tapeworm), is not unusual. He reentered the country after deportation no less then five times, at least twice after killing twenty-eight innocent men, women, and children in an ambush of a busload of passengers traveling the Salvadoran countryside. A State Department report places the number of individual MS-

13 cliques at more then 250, concentrated in the United States, El Salvador, Mexico, Honduras, and Guatemala. Aggressive government crackdowns like the Mano Dura and Super Mano Dura in the Central American countries had the effect of pushing even more gang members to cross into the United States.

Reading this book from a law enforcement perspective, it is clear that Tom Diaz has worn out some shoe leather—much like a good detective—in gathering facts, not myths or urban legend. As a result, he has produced an accurate and comprehensive look at a grave and present danger to our society. In the three Central American countries of El Salvador, Honduras, and Guatemala, MS-13 has evolved from a criminal network to a destabilizing force, threatening the very rule of law in those countries. Inability to take control of the streets and protect the public from intimidation is a characteristic of a failed nation-state. Unfortunately, in the United States, arguably the most advanced country in the world, there are far too many failed neighborhoods and communities because of gangs, drugs, and violence.

The challenge of reducing gang violence is formidable, and at times, it seems like the government cannot get out of its own way. Diaz effectively exposes the bureaucratic infighting between federal agencies, as well as the administrative obstacles and congressional lethargy in funding coordinated antigang efforts. Part of the infighting stems from a lack of Executive Branch and congressional leadership in addressing the wasteful and counterproductive overlap in the missions of the FBI; the U.S. Bureau of Alcohol, Tobacco, and Firearms; the Drug Enforcement Administration; and the U.S. Bureau of Immigration and Customs Enforcement—all of whom claim a mandate to address gangs. Despite these conditions, Diaz reveals that, regardless of agency affiliation, the line is held by a handful of dedicated state, local, and federal investigators and, of course, street cops. Their efforts, while heroic, needed a cohesive national focus. The impact of going after a transnational criminal network like MS-13 by arresting them one by one is minimal. Only a well-resourced, fully coordinated national effort focused on digging the network up by the roots will have true impact. That was the basis for the formation of the FBI's MS-13 National Gang Task Force, which has already seen dramatic results with racketeering prosecutions of entire MS-13 cliques in New York, Baltimore, Los Angeles, and Charlotte, essentially neutralizing their presence. These indictments typically include twenty or more defendants and charge an array of felonies committed over many years, including multiple homicides. The RICO statute and the enterprise investigative strategy is a proven tool to dismantle networks like MS-13.

As the head of the FBI's Criminal Investigative Division for over two years, my experience, from many visits to Capitol Hill to inform staffers and testify about gangs, was that, aside from the strong and persistent efforts of U.S. congressman Frank Wolf, there was a plethora of talk but little action in supporting a sustained effort at attacking gangs in general. While federal law enforcement resources "refocused" on the terrorist threat, local officers were left with a multijurisdictional, international criminal threat that is responsible for far more deaths then the 9/11 terrorist attacks. Unfortunately for local law enforcement, government funding like COPS and Bryne grants, which funded more cops on the street, were cut dramatically over the last seven years. At the same time, over two thousand FBI agents were diverted from criminal investigations to counter terrorism. In a shell game, Congress has failed to fund adequate terrorism resources, forcing the FBI and other agencies to cannibalize seasoned investigators from long-established squads on gangs, narcotics, and organized crime, at a time when gangs were committing mayhem in cities throughout the United States.

Tom Diaz has produced an incredibly incisive work that reads like a novel. Unfortunately, it is an accurate portrayal of a very real and growing threat. The presence of MS-13 has been reported in 147 cities across the United States. It is no longer confined to big cities like Los Angeles, New York, Chicago, and Miami. The cities infected now include Fairfax, Virginia; Charlotte, North Carolina; Tulsa, Oklahoma; Alpharetta, Georgia; and Colorado Springs, Colorado. There is not much time. Every U.S. congressman and senator should read this book. We ignore its warning at our peril.

Chris Swecker, former assistant director
of the FBI's Criminal Investigative Division

ACKNOWLEDGMENTS

The problem with acknowledgments is that there is always someone left out who feels that they should have been included. To that someone I apologize. My thanks go to all of the men and women of state, federal, and local law enforcement who agreed to share their stories, observations, and hard-won knowledge with me. I am especially grateful to those who gave me key documents about their cases. This is invaluable grist for any writer's mill. Unfortunately, there were many more stories than I had room to tell in this book, so some people whose insights were valuable are not mentioned by name.

Angela Bell of the FBI's Office of Public Affairs was a blessing, a cheerful and knowledgeable guide whose response to my queries was never no but always "Let me see what I can do." Among the people I write about in this book, four merit special thanks: FBI agent Bob Clifford; former assistant U.S. attorney Bruce Riordan; Kevin Carwile, chief of the U.S. Department of Justice's Gang Squad; and Sgt. Richard Valdemar, retired from the Los Angeles County Sheriff's Department. Each helped me or sent me off in an especially valuable direction at one or another critical juncture in my research. There are a few others whose names must remain unwritten for reasons of discretion or personal safety. I am also grateful to Roseanna Ander of the Joyce Foundation, who suggested that I submit the proposal for this book to the University of Michigan Press, and I thank Jim Reische, who read the proposal, encouraged me, and offered invaluable advice on ways to make it better.

It goes almost—but not quite—without saying that this book would not have been possible without the tolerance and encouragement of my wife and my family. They are getting back a dining room.

CONTENTS

Force has no place where there is need of skill.

—HERODOTUS

INTRODUCTION

The moon was brand-new in Houston on the night of Thursday, November 3, 2005, a tiny sliver in the big Texas sky. The night was pitch-black, save for wavering illumination from scattered streetlights and the passing beams of a few cars. It was dry and cool. The thermometer was headed down to a low of forty-four degrees from a high of eighty during the day. As the clock crept past 10:00 p.m., agents of the FBI, including members of the local SWAT team, and officers of the Houston Police Department's Narcotics Division quietly checked their weapons one more time. They were waiting in deep concealment just across the street from 5709 Liberty Road. The neighborhood in that part of Houston is run-down. A railroad line runs along the far side of Liberty Road. The houses and yards are big, but they have been battered by time's indifferent passage. Some former dwellings have switched to commercial use. Others are abandoned or devoted to hidden enterprise on the underbelly of society. A heavily laden freight train lumbered by. A dog barked.[1]

FBI supervisory special agent Brian Ritchie checked his watch and ran the sting operation through his mind one more time. Ritchie was the case agent on the gang Mara Salvatrucha, or MS-13, in Houston. He was in charge of this dark night's operation. Working with the local police, his squad had learned of a violent group of gangsters who had taken to ripping off local drug dealers. The MS-13 crew's method of operation was to declare themselves to be FBI agents and police as they smashed through the doors of startled dealers, scooping up drugs, money, and whatever else of value they could grab. It was a recipe for a violent disaster, so the FBI and Houston police set in motion an elaborate plan to snare the gangsters. Undercover "negotiations" ensued for a proposed sale of drugs. The gang was led to believe that a particularly rich store of cocaine was being held in the big old house at 5709 Liberty Road, across the street from where Ritchie now waited. The FBI wired the building with cameras and microphones. Now the team of FBI agents and Houston police officers were waiting to see if the gangsters would take the fictional bait and raid the house.

At about eleven o'clock, the law enforcement team's earpieces murmured to hushed life. A muffled voice advised that three men were approaching through the darkness on foot. The natural rush of adrenaline that coursed through the officers and agents was controlled, channeled, and contained by years of experience and hundreds of hours of training. Shortly thereafter, a car—later determined to have been stolen— stopped in front of the bait house. Two more men got out. All five were wearing baseball hats with the letters *FBI* on them. The sixth man drove off and began making wide circles around the neighborhood. The trap was about to be sprung.

But there was something ominous and disturbing about the gangsters' behavior. They exchanged no words at all, using only infantry-style hand and arm signals. They moved as a unit and with the precision of a well-planned military exercise. One was armed with an AK-47 military assault rifle. Before they entered the house, they did a precise reconnaissance of the grounds. "They never spoke until they were inside the house," says Agent Ritchie. "They knew exactly what they were going to do. The guy circling in the car was doing countersurveillance. Any patrol officer who happened upon this team would have been completely outmaneuvered and outgunned."

What happened next was brief, shocking, and violent. "Four of them went in, and one stayed outside as a sentry. They kicked in the door and started yelling, 'FBI! FBI!'" Ritchie recalls. "They went right to the fake drugs. We approached the house and identified ourselves. The individual outside turned with a weapon as if to engage us. He was told to drop the gun, did not comply, and died in the yard. The other four opened fire on us from inside the house."

When the shooting stopped, Jose Antonio Pino, the lookout, lay dead outside. Another gangster, Juan Antonio Bautista, was dead inside the house. No law enforcement personnel were hurt. The remaining gangsters were arrested and successfully prosecuted on various charges. The episode, however, took on much greater significance within the FBI than a random shootout. Earlier in the year, the bureau had formed a new unit, the MS-13 National Gang Task Force, to coordinate investigation of this rapidly expanding transnational gang. To the leader of that task force, FBI supervisory agent Bob Clifford, the military precision with which the gangsters in Houston operated was evidence that the MS-13 gang was becoming increasingly efficient and dangerous.

"Our worse suspicions about MS-13 have been confirmed," he said of the incident. Clifford knew the gang was violent. Now he worried that gangsters were bringing paramilitary training into criminal operations.[2] These gangsters were also more sophisticated than old-style gangbangers, who covered themselves with tattoos and openly challenged society. The Houston crew seemed to be of a new generation. Having learned that tattoos brought unwanted attention from law enforcement, they adapted and kept their body art to a minimum. What bothered Clifford most of all was that law enforcement in the United States had no coordinated plan for dealing with a gang that had exploded from a ragged bunch of dope-addled "stoners" in Los Angeles into a nascent criminal coalition that ignored borders. Every local, state, and federal agency was chasing its own vision of how to deal with Latino gangsters.

This book tells the story of the birth, growth, and maturation of MS-13 and a few other major Latino gangs. It examines what law enforcement is doing about them. It also seeks to suggest their potential impact on the future of American society.

This is first and foremost a journalistic book. It is not an academic work of sociology or criminology. Nor is it an encyclopedia of Latino gangs in the United States. It is the tale of a journey into darkness, an attempt to explore an exceedingly violent land-within-a-land of which most Americans have only recently become vaguely aware. It aspires to illuminate that turbulent land through the stories of real people. A subtext is the contrast between the character and values of the gangsters and those of the men and women of law enforcement to whom society has handed the job of containing gang violence. This book is built around actual cases in which the criminal actions and motivations of gangs and gangsters were documented beyond cavil in the adversary forum of a criminal trial. Priests, social workers, and politicians may yet hope, pray, and advocate for the redemption of the gangsters whose stories are captured in these cases. But the record is clear, and final judgment has been rendered in the courts of earthly justice.

If there is a single postcard to be sent from this frightening land, its message would be that the historical and social forces that carved the cruel terrain of the Latino gang and molded the Latino gangster are wide-ranging and complex. Perhaps those forces can be adequately described only in academic tomes and government studies, of which there are legion and from some of which this work draws. But the warp and woof of Latino gang life can be summed up in two words—heartless violence. This is simply what street gangs ultimately do in real life. Gang life may include hours of ethnic and brotherly bonding, days of chemically assisted partying, and weeks of listless hanging out. Some observers of gangs find this social matrix of gang life charming in a countercultural way, even positively good. After all, the heartless greater society, "the system," cannot or will not provide the family and economic means that the gang affords dispossessed youth. But sooner or later in gang life, there erupts the bloody assault, the brutal murder, and the casual death of innocent bystanders. Every gangster is capable of such violence. Indeed, each is expected to step up to commit violence when the "shot callers" decide that it is needed. All the rationalizations, justifications, explanation, and finely tuned ethnic politics in the universe cannot change that brutal fact.

Latino criminal street gangs are not merely transient phenomena of youth, ethnic culture, and violent crime. They are all of that. But they are most importantly markers of vast changes that have swept over the United States and the world. These changes continue to trouble Americans and unsettle political life in the United States. They include economic restructuring, globalization, migration patterns that defy national borders and ignore immigration laws, transnational crime, and the federalization and growing internationalization of law enforcement. These challenging and bitterly divisive changes and the struggle to fashion humane, rational, and effective political responses to them are woven deeply into the story of Latino street gangs.

The economic change from smokestack manufacturing industries to service and information industries was an unforgiving crucible in which many Latino gangs were transformed and hardened. Many gangs went from traditional local "fighting" associations to enduring, institutionalized, and irreducibly violent alternative societies for the most marginalized youth within marginal communities. The largest of these gangs have become well-organized criminal enterprises. Latino street gangs today are family, mistress, employer, and nation to that small fraction of immigrant and especially second-generation youth—the children of immigrants—who are most alienated and least capable of adapting to the majority population's social, cultural, and economic norms. In an earlier era, unskilled, poorly educated youth without language ability might have pulled themselves up from poverty on assembly lines, at the furnaces of steel mills, or in tire plants. Now, they find it harder to get a hand on any rung—much less a ladder—to a better life.

Globalization writ large fueled this harsh and indifferent process. Jobs went offshore, and sweatshops came onshore, as the bottom line of profit dictated. Global transportation and communications networks fed other trends, including the growth of transnational criminal organizations and the deep human urge to wander in search of livelihood. The lure of work across borders became stronger as the world shrank to the size of a television screen and as transportation networks made any migration dream feasible. Transnational criminal organizations, such as the powerful Mexican drug-trafficking organizations, are exploiting the street gang as a source of muscle and connectivity to communities all over the United States. The gangs themselves are becoming better organized, intuitively adapting to law enforcement pressure and searching for a structure that will ensure that they survive and thrive. Some Latino gangs have become nothing less than ongoing criminal enterprises whose rationale is no longer neighborhood or ethnic identity but raw criminal profit. The worst now operate throughout the United States, Mexico, and Central America and appear to be spreading to other regions, including Canada and Europe.

These changes are putting stress on federal, state, and local law enforcement agencies. International borders mean nothing to the most dangerous gangs, such as MS-13. For decades, they and their members have been invisible to the dominant society. Latino gangsters live within communities of "aliens" whose language and culture, if seen at all, is perceived by the dominant society mostly as a cultural and existential threat to the nation. Entire geographic regions of Anglo law enforcement cannot communicate with—much less understand the underpinnings of—the gangs, the gangsters, and the communities from which they come. Absence of perceived evidence has become evidence of absence in these jurisdictions. This becomes, in turn, grounds for denial that a gang problem exists, and denial makes it possible for gangs to take root undetected and unmolested. Stresses on law enforcement agencies have been increased by the diversion of resources from traditional crime fighting to "national security," counterterrorism, and, latterly, mortgage fraud, public corruption, and other white-collar crimes.

The American people and most politicians have defined the Latino gang problem as a law enforcement problem whose solution is "gang suppression." Gangs are to be stamped out by force—arrest, imprisonment, deportation, and the creation of seamless international borders. It is no coincidence that the evolution of street gangs into hardened criminal enterprises coincided with the rise of mass imprisonment in the United States, driven in turn by the primacy of law and order exemplified in the criminal justice policies of the War on Drugs. The state of California alone imprisons more people today than any country in the world except China. The United States has the highest incarceration rate in the world.[3] Neither gangs nor mass imprisonment caused the other, but each has a noxious influence on the other. Imprisonment has become a rite of passage for many gangsters. Prisons have become institutions of higher criminal learning and centers of command and control for some of the worst gangs.

Yet in the course of three years of talking about Latino gangs with law enforcement personnel and prosecutors across the United States, I never met a single one who would say that the problem of street gangs is solely a law enforcement problem. "We cannot arrest our way out of this" is a commonly expressed sentiment. It may be clichéd, but it is accurate. There is absolutely a need for strong law enforcement suppression of criminal street gangs and gang violence. That enforcement is what this book is principally about. But if there is to be any hope of a lasting solution to the Latino gang problem, intelligent programs of prevention and intervention are also important. Moreover, one can hardly imagine a comprehensive solution that does not include a rational immigration policy.

Another point must be made, underscored, and capitalized. Only a small minority of Latino youth—perhaps 10–12 percent in threatened communities—are actually drawn into gang life. Most of these young people are not immigrants but the children or grandchildren of immigrants. The overwhelming majority of the Latino populations, even in the most marginalized communities, are hardworking, productive people. They are decent human beings with human hopes, aspirations, and values. Parents work against all odds to keep their children out of gangs and to give them tools for success in the United States. The cruelest lash of all is that these good people are not only preyed on by the gangs but suffer the scorn and approbation of the dominant culture, which projects outlandish stereotypes onto them and caricatures the negative qualities of the gangsters. This has been true of all immigrant waves, but the needle seems to be stuck in the groove for Latinos because of the proximity of the southern border. A cottage industry of "gang workers" and professional handwringers too often subsidizes this injustice by making it appear that gang membership is inevitable, the pregnant negative being that there are no "good kids" left who can resist "the system." On the contrary, there are lots of Latino kids who reject gangs, and some of them take voice in this book.

The question of ethnic adjectives naturally arises when one presumes to survey a subject as intimately involved with national origin as that of this book. Is *Hispanic* or *Latino* a better generic term? Neither term adequately captures the complex mosaic of peoples from south of the border—the history and cultures of Peruvians, Mexicans, Cubans, and Puerto Ricans, for example, are different in many important ways. Nor does either term sufficiently recognize that immigrants and their children tend to think of themselves not generically but specifically. When asked about ethnicity, people usually reply in terms of the specific country from which they or their forebears came. If you ask a person whose grandparents were from Dublin what their ethnicity is—as opposed to their current "American" nationality—they are less likely to answer "European" or "Anglo-Saxon" than "Irish." Just so, someone whose parents came from Oaxaca is more likely to label themselves "Mexican" than either "Latino" or "Hispanic."

Hispanic is a word invented by federal bureaucrats. It has oozed outward from the Census Bureau and infiltrated virtually all government discourse. In the process, it has acquired a sort of political correctness. Street cops, federal agents, and Census Bureau enumerators all tend to use this term because it has come to populate every piece of paper they touch and every seminar on community relations they attend. *Hispanic* has also come to be seen as a linguistic safety zone, a marshmallow word that the Spanish-speaking person you just arrested may never have heard of but by which he cannot legally be offended. The word derives from the Latin *Hispania,* the Roman name for the rich province located in much of what is Spain today. *Hispanic* strongly connotes the Spanish conquest of most of Latin America (and a great part of North America). It tends to raise hackles among those from regions whose European roots are not Spanish but Portuguese (and German, and Irish, and so on). Those who identify with the indigenous Indian people see the Spaniards (and Portuguese) as unwelcome conquerors and brutal despoilers. They prefer not to wear the hair shirt of a name derived from their oppressors.

Latino has broader roots in the predominant Romance languages used officially throughout Central and South America, all of which derive from Latin (although there are many regions in which indigenous languages predominate). Since *Latino* has no direct connection to the Spanish conquest, it does not carry the baggage of an implied subservience. Nor, frankly, is it as lifelessly gray a word as *Hispanic*. For some complex of reasons, it has become the preferred word for many who wish to convey a commonality of culture and feeling beyond what is conveyed by the terms *Mexican* or *Guatemalan* but who prefer not to use a word so drained of passion as *Hispanic*. In the end, there is no final arbiter. The choice between the two terms boils down to individual preference, and I prefer to use *Latino*.

The linguistic swamp gets darker and muddier when one tries to parse the words that connote the potent combination of ethnicity, nationality, and legality of immigration status. When does a Mexican gangster become a Mexican American gangster? How many of either are there? The plain fact is that nobody knows. Despite all manner of official and putatively precise emissions about the numerical and ethnic composition of Latino gangs, nobody really knows how many members are native-born, how many are immigrants, and how many among the immigrants have legal status. Virtually every statement about the ethnicity of gang membership, the immigration status of gang members, and the proportion of crimes committed by legal immigrant residents and illegal aliens is based on pure guesswork—estimation derived from emanations from the penumbra of the seat of the pants of law enforcement officials. There is no convenient set of census-style boxes to be checked on field interview or arrest forms to provide the raw material from which real data and general conclusions based in hard fact could be drawn.

The same disability applies to questions of how many gangs, how many gangsters, and how many gang crimes there are. The authors of one academic text exclaimed, "There are as many estimates as there are estimators!"[4] In the mid-1990s, for example, estimates of the number of all gang members in the United States ranged from 660,000 to 1.5 million.[5] Citing a 2007 national survey of law enforcement officials, the U.S. attorney general reported in April 2008 that there were "more than 20,000 gangs, consisting of an estimated 1 million members."[6] Thus gang membership has either increased by half or declined by a third over the last decade. Skeptics have observed that the police agencies from which such reporting is drawn have a vested interest in qualifying themselves for federal gang-fighting funds. If there are no gangs, there will be no funds.

Local estimates vary just as wildly. A senior law enforcement official in Los Angeles told me that according to CalGang—the official and widely criticized gang database for the state of California—there were 7,703 gangs in California as of June 2, 2008, with 223,828 members. But Los Angeles city attorney Rocky Delgadillo was reported to have stated in March 2007 that there were 3,700 gangs in California, with 150,000 members.[7]

These disparities are inevitable. There is no universal definition of what constitutes a "gang" or gang membership. Even if there were, there is no consistent, uniform, well-maintained system for recording data about gangs and gang members. What constitutes a gang crime is defined in significantly different ways by different jurisdictions. Yes, computerized information systems such as CalGang exist as useful tools for "gang intelligence"—pointers as to which gangs are operating where. But they are hopelessly inadequate to the production of solid, fact-based, and current quantitative data. Therefore, with very few exceptions, the numbers about gangs, gang crimes, and gang membership that one hears tossed around in congressional hearings and on Lou Dobbs's CNN news and entertainment show, *Lou Dobbs Tonight,* or reads in newspaper articles and anti-immigrant rants are extraordinarily soft estimates hardened into concrete as they progress up the information chain. They remind one of the infamous "body counts" of the Vietnam War.

This raises at least the possibility that the United States may be in the grip of a "moral panic" about Latino street gangs, "a situation in which public fears and state interventions greatly exceed the threat posed by the targeted groups."[8] Like an old-fashioned magic lantern show, we may be projecting onto the national consciousness a vastly inflated image of the Latino gang "problem." This could, in turn, be a function of the proposition that "a necessary, but not sufficient, condition for a moral panic is some level of public fear toward certain minority groups."[9] After all, most motorcycle gangs and most hate gangs advocating "white power," populated by white Americans born and bred in the United States, are as violent as Latino gangs and are involved in most of the same criminal activity, yet they have not ignited the same level of popular concern or captured the imaginations of the media, the chattering class, or government bureaucracies from which all funding flows. If we are indeed in a moral panic, it would not be the first time a "crime problem" has been so inflated. The country has only recently been able to deal with the question of crack cocaine versus powder cocaine in a way that actually takes into account hard data about their relative effects.

Nonetheless, a wealth of anecdotal and court-derived evidence supports the conclusions that Latino gangs in fact exist, are extremely violent, and are growing in size and dispersion along with the Latino population generally. It should be remembered that it would have been just as difficult to quantify the emerging problem of the Mafia—La Cosa Nostra—in the early years of the last century. Gangsters generally do not carry identification cards or keep public membership registers. Yet, with the notable exception of the FBI, law enforcement agencies who had to deal with the mob's violence had no doubt that something organized and evil existed and was growing. Even J. Edgar Hoover's reluctance to admit the Mafia's existence was probably more a matter of bureaucratic politics than factual denial. It was easier to count bank robberies and car thefts than to chase Italian mobsters. Today, local, state, and federal law enforcement agencies, prosecutors, and courts are similarly grappling with a phenomenon that most know is undeniable—the rise of the Latino street gang.

These children are easy to ignore.

But that won't be true when they are older.

—DR. SPENCER ETH

1

LOS ANGELES AND POINTS SOUTH

At precisely 10:30 a.m. on the morning of March 30, 2001, Juan Antonio Martinez Varela, a major general in the Salvadoran Air Force, stepped smartly from his limousine at the foot of the Pentagon's River Entrance. A select honor cordon of U.S. soldiers in dress uniforms stood in two ramrod-straight lines along the broad riser of steps. Martinez Varela, El Salvador's minister of defense, ascended through a blustering early spring rain. When the general was exactly three feet from the U.S. secretary of defense, Donald H. Rumsfeld, the cordon commander barked an order, and the soldiers snapped a crisp salute in perfect unison. They held their salute until the two ministers of defense entered the pharaonic headquarters of the mightiest military power the world has ever seen. At a strength of somewhat less than fifteen thousand, including uniformed and civilian members, the armed forces of El Salvador are a hair on a gnat on the hide of the U.S. military elephant, some 1.3 million men and women.[1] Nonetheless, protocol is protocol. General Martinez

Varela was greeted with a traditional River Entrance ceremony similar, if not identical, to that accorded during March 2001 to other ministerial worthies from Turkey, Georgia, NATO, Great Britain, Germany, and Bulgaria.

It would be a serious mistake, however, to regard the meeting between the two men as a mismatch between a slickly powerful American government wizard and his "little brown brother" from a banana republic.[2] The U.S. military establishment and the ruling elite in El Salvador have been intertwined in a sinuous history that winds back at least until the middle of the last century. At this writing, El Salvador is the only country in Latin America that still has troops in Iraq supporting the American war. Moreover, the Martinez Varela family is one of those that ordinary people speak of in respectful whispers in El Salvador. Its sons, like General Juan Antonio Martinez Varela, have had a more or less continuous grip on the country's most important offices— including the powerful ministry of the interior, the ministry of defense, the leadership of the military academy, presidential secretary, various ambassadorial posts, and more—since the military seized power in the 1930s.

The only public record of the actual meeting is a Pentagon publicity photograph in which General Martinez Varela, with an amiably distinguished mien and only a hint of bemusement, appears to be listening respectfully to a discourse from Secretary Rumsfeld, whose back is to the camera. Their conference at the Pentagon was held almost six months before al Qaeda terrorists crashed an airliner into that very building, so it is doubtful that the agenda included the War on Terror, much less the current war in Iraq. It was also some four years before the FBI created a special national task force that thrust Mara Salvatrucha, or MS-13— the violent transnational street gang born out of the misery of refugees from the Salvadoran civil war in the 1980s—into the public eye. So the "war on transnational street gangs" was also not a likely topic. Most likely, the two men exchanged the usual pleasantries of military diplomacy. General Martinez Varela no doubt thanked the United States for the military helicopters and other aid recently sent to help El Salvador recover from an earthquake and massive mudslide.

What is almost certain is that there was no discussion of the general's family, most particularly a young man who variously calls himself Nelson Martinez Varela Comandari and Nelson Agustin Varela Comandari, among other names. By whatever name, Nelson Comandari—now thirty years old—was, at the time, an important leader of the transnational MS-13 gang. He was also a fugitive from the FBI and the Los Angeles Police Department. In fact, it is highly unlikely that Secretary Rumsfeld or anyone in his vast entourage had ever heard of Nelson Comandari or knew him to be the scion of a long-fractured union between two of El Salvador's most influential families. Nelson was born in 1977 of a marriage between the Varela and the Comandari clans, the latter a transplant from the Palestine of the 1920s and also powerful in El Salvador in its own, less savory way.

While Nelson awaits trial in New York on federal charges of drug trafficking, family members on either side do not wish to discuss publicly the enigmatic criminal career of the product of their union. Nor, it turns out, do senior officials of the FBI and the U.S. Department of Justice. Public information about Nelson Comandari's criminal case is in lockdown, and I was subtly warned more than once about writing about it. It is no doubt merely coincidental that Nelson's uncle, Franklin Varela, aka Frank Varelli, was one of the most disastrous informants the FBI ever employed. Varelli, or Varela, was at the very heart of a 1980s scandal under the Reagan administration, involving an abortive and embarrassing FBI "counterterrorism" investigation into a left-wing domestic grassroots political group called CISPES (the Committee in Solidarity with the People of El Salvador).

The story of Latino street gangs in the United States begins in Los Angeles, often called the "epicenter" of America's gang problem. An epicenter is "the part of the earth's surface directly above the focus of an earthquake."[3] The earthquake analogy makes some sense, as the rapid growth of violent street gangs in recent years has shaken America. Tremors radiate from the epicenter of an earthquake, and much of the gang problem in America radiates from Los Angeles. Many of the largest and most violent gangs in the United States started in the City of Angels—Latino gangs like Mara Salvatrucha (MS-13) and 18th Street and black gangs like the Crips and the Bloods. These gangs or the artifacts, attitudes, and lifestyles associated with them spread eastward and brought trouble to cities and towns all over the United States. "If you want to know what's going to happen with Hispanic gangs in your hometown two years from now," a gang expert advised his audience at a 2006 gang summit in Virginia, "find out what's happening now in Los Angeles."[4] That expert is from Scarsdale, New York, an affluent suburb of New York that one might incorrectly think is a cozy, gang-free zone.

The Los Angeles Police Department (LAPD) invented the specialized "police gang unit" in the 1980s as an innovation in its long-running guerrilla war with gangs.[5] They ended up calling it the CRASH unit. The acronym stood for "Community Resources against Street Hoodlums," an aptly in-your-face name for a department known for its aggressive policing. If Daryl Gates, a controversial former chief of police, had prevailed, the unit would have been called the TRASH unit, with the tougher acronym standing for "Total Resources against Street Hoodlums" and intended "as a way of demeaning gang activity." But Gates reports that the latter name was considered "unseemly" because "we were dealing with human beings out there."[6] Whatever it may be called, the LAPD gang unit, located at the "epicenter" of gang violence in America, is now the most widely used model for local law enforcement response to gang violence throughout the country.

The epicenter model has a flaw, however. It conjures up an inanimate, Newtonian world governed by the laws of physics, a world in which action and reaction may be more or less predictably charted by formulas: if you apply force X to intersection Y, for example, consequence Z will result. But gangs are not inanimate. They are complex organisms populated by human beings who react to interference in unforeseen ways. Thinking of gangs as organisms invokes mutation and adaptability. It acknowledges the fluidity of their structures and the ambiguity of how best to deal with them. It recognizes the uncertainty of intervention and the possibility of unintended consequences. An examination of the history of MS-13, thought by many to be the most dangerous gang in America today, reveals that unintended and undesirable consequences caused by national policies—including some that, on their face, have nothing to do with gangs—have been the rule, not the exception.

At the dawn of the 1980s, two young psychiatrists at a children's out-patient clinic in Los Angeles, Spencer Eth and William Arroyo, began to see a disturbing pattern of symptoms among a cluster of children referred to them. Their investigation into that cluster would mark an important turning point in the history of child psychiatry. It would also lead one of them to make a strikingly prescient forecast in 1983 about gang violence within the growing Salvadoran community in Los Angeles. Today, that prediction is playing out in big cities and tiny hamlets all over America. It has been confirmed in the explosive growth of MS-13, a criminal street gang that started on the street corners of the Pico-Union neighborhood of Los Angeles and is now pandemic in the United States, international in its reach, and barbaric in its violence.

At about the same time that Eth and Arroyo were studying these children, a young infantry officer hundreds of miles away was beginning to work his way through the U.S. Army's toughest training, including the legendary Ranger School. Brian Truchon is the youngest son of a blue-collar family. Raised within strict Roman Catholic values, Truchon had faithfully watched enough of Efrem Zimbalist Jr. in the ABC hit television series *The F.B.I.* to have already decided that his ultimate ambition was to become an FBI agent. It was not a bad fit—tall, dark-haired, carefully spoken, with a clear-eyed and steady gaze, Brian Truchon looks a good bit like Zimbalist, the icon of the ideal FBI agent. In 1985, after completing his army tour, Truchon graduated from the FBI Academy, became an agent, and embarked on the peregrinations that make the career paths of the FBI's brightest talents. He and MS-13 were destined to meet head-on twenty years later.

Dr. Eth recently recalled the specific incident that sparked his interest in studying more closely the backgrounds of the children he was seeing: "I was evaluating a young child who had witnessed his mom's murder, and in trying to understand what happened, I spoke to the police officers who had investigated the crime. 'What a horrible story,' I said to the officers. 'But at least it doesn't happen very often.'" The response of the police officers shocked Eth, now a professor of psychiatry at New York Medical College and medical director of behavioral health services at St. Vincent Catholic Medical Centers in New York: "They said, 'What do you mean? It happens all the time.'"[7] That matter-of-fact response about the nightmare of a child witnessing the murder of a parent determined Dr. Eth, joined later by Dr. Arroyo, to look more closely into what he was seeing among certain children referred to the clinic—those who had witnessed the murder of a parent. (Another colleague, Dr. Robert Pynoos, was interested in similar problems among children who had witnessed the suicide of a parent.) What they saw in these children looked very much like a form of anxiety disorder that—amid some controversy—the American Psychiatric Association (APA) had only just recognized in 1980 as a mental illness. It is called post-traumatic stress disorder, or PTSD.[8]

The hallmark of PTSD is the patient's exposure to a catastrophic trauma, something beyond the range of the ordinary stresses of daily life. Such traumas include wars like those in Vietnam and Iraq, natural disasters like Hurricane Katrina in 2005, or terror attacks like those on the World Trade Center and the Pentagon on September 11, 2001.[9] Events like these, in which life—of the subject or others—is dramatically threatened, may generate a range of symptoms of anxiety among some of the victims or witnesses. (Not everyone exposed to the same trauma will develop PTSD.) Some relive the terrible event, suffering flashbacks, hallucinations, and other disturbing recollections. They may try to block out reminders by avoiding certain places, activities, or people that might cause them to recall the catastrophe. Symptoms include emotional detachment from other people, inability to form loving relationships, sleeplessness, a sense of one's being inevitably doomed and thus excluded from the possibility of a normal future, extreme vigilance and irritability, and the inability to control impulse and anger.[10]

The newly recognized ailment was professionally memorialized in the bible of the American psychiatric profession, the APA's *Diagnostic and Statistical Manual of Mental Disorders (DSM)*.[11] Curiously, however, the *DSM* did not include any recognition that PTSD might occur in children. Most professional and popular attention about the newly recognized disorder was directed to Vietnam War veterans.[12] Recognition of the new diagnosis by the APA and the U.S. Veterans Administration meant that veterans diagnosed as suffering from PTSD could get such benefits as disability pensions.[13] The newly recognized ailment replaced the terms *shell shock* from the World War I and *combat fatigue* from World War II. Some experts estimated that as many as 1.5 million veterans suffered from it.[14] PTSD began being offered in the courtroom as a defense to a variety of criminal charges,[15] including murder. It was called "the Vietnam defense."[16]

"This was a new condition and there had not been a lot of work on kids in this field at the time, "said Dr. Eth. "There were very few articles about childhood trauma, and most of these were wrong. So it is not surprising that there was no reference to children in the *DSM*."[17]

Not only was there no reference in the *DSM*, but according to another professor of psychiatry at the University of Michigan, "it was difficult for professionals to accept that traumatic events, caused by fellow humans, in the lives of children might color and shape their lives for years to come."[18] In brief, many professionals accepted the folk wisdom that children simply "roll with the punches" and glide relatively unscathed through horrors that warp their elders. Eth and Arroyo set out to challenge this Mary Poppinsish view of childhood trauma—the comforting but erroneous perception that a spoonful of sugar and a tousle on the head made the trauma go down in a most harmless way.

The clinic in which these doctors treated children was not a boutique for the pampered progeny of Lotusland. It was part of the twenty-story Los Angeles County–University of Southern California Medical Center (LA-USC). Housed in a massive, Stalinesque edifice, LA-USC stands like a fortress athwart the gang-infested Lincoln Heights and Boyle Heights neighborhoods of East Los Angeles. The hospital, Dr. Eth notes dryly, was "surrounded by violence, a natural place to study trauma."[19]

In fact, LA-USC lay in the eye of a storm of violence that, as terrible as it was then, was to become even more furious over the coming decade. Between 1984 and 1995, gang-related homicides in Los Angeles County increased fourfold, from 212 to 807.[20] That murderous hurricane was to be driven in part by implacable social and economic forces and in part by evolution among the gangs and within their distinctive form of urban warfare. Children like the young patients that the team was seeing helped feed the storm.

Dr. Arroyo, fluent in Spanish, is now director of children's mental health services for Los Angeles County and a clinical assistant professor of psychiatry at the University of Southern California School of Medicine. His language facility gave him a unique insight into the children of an immigrant population that was expanding rapidly in Los Angeles. These were the children of refugees from wars in El Salvador and Nicaragua.[21] "You can always tell where the revolution is by our patient population," an LA-USC staff member remarked in 1985.[22]

The doctors in the hospital's emergency room had a name for the grisly fraternity of the maimed and the dying propelled through their doors by the violence of East Los Angeles. They called it the "Knife and Gun Club." The mayhem sometimes burst into their very medical haven—in 1984, a security guard in the emergency room shot to death a patient who reached from a gurney and grabbed another guard's gun.[23] The doctors at LA-USC and other hospitals serving the gang-tortured neighborhoods of Los Angeles were forced to refine their specialties in order to treat the endless torrent of victims. Orthopedic surgeons who once devoted their talents to repairing bones snapped in football games or crushed in automobile crashes now had to adapt their skills to deal with a new class of injuries, the shattering effects of multiple gunshot wounds. As the decade of the 1990s unfolded, the armed services began sending their surgeons to these inner-city hospitals. They were, after all, the best places to learn how to treat wounds that the military doctors would otherwise see only in the urgent confusion of the battlefield.[24]

"This is a war zone," said the chief of orthopedic surgery at Martin Luther King Jr./Drew Medical Center, a hospital (now closed) across town from LA-USC, on the edges of Watts, a neighborhood also plagued by gangs. "We're getting injuries worse than in World War I and World War II. This is Vietnam-era stuff. It's the same weapons, AK-47s, M-16s. It's the same injuries."[25] FBI agent Brian Truchon witnessed the violence of the Watts gangs firsthand. Assigned to the Los Angeles field office in 1991, he arrived just before the riotous explosion of civil disorder—some called it an insurrection—that erupted in 1992 when several LAPD officers were acquitted on charges stemming from the beating of a black man, Rodney King, after a high-speed chase and traffic stop. In the wake of those riots, the FBI set up in Los Angeles its first gang units ever. Truchon headed one of the four new units, the South Central unit, investigating the black gangs in Watts and Jordan

Downs. At the time, Truchon had never heard of Mara Salvatrucha, or MS-13.

The military teaching tradition at LA-USC continued as the armed services capitalized on the classroom of inner-city combat. In 2003, the U.S. Navy opened its Trauma Training Center there, just as the Bush administration ramped up to wage war on Iraq. LA-USC was chosen over sixty-two other hospitals that competed for the program to train navy personnel in "salvage surgery."[26]

The bloody preeminence of Los Angeles directly results from the city's gangs. Almost 57 percent of the ten thousand gang-related youth homicides that occurred in California between 1981 and 2001 happened in Los Angeles. "This extraordinary disproportion cannot be explained by LA's large population, nor by its age, racial or ethnic composition," according to California's attorney general.[27] The authors of a study that examined those homicides concluded that "what truly sets Los Angeles apart from the remainder of California is not a general propensity for violent behavior, but rather the existence of a specific milieu that has fostered the development of a violent gang culture unlike any other gang culture in the state."[28]

"It's a shame that Los Angeles has so much violence," Lt. Cdr. John Newman, a surgeon, observed in 2003. "But from a training standpoint—fantastic."[29] Since Vietnam, there had been "no big wars except in our cities, where AK-47s and M-16s were being used increasingly by drug dealers and gang members," said Dale Smith, chair of the medical history department at the Uniformed Services University of the Health Sciences in Bethesda, Maryland.[30] Another navy surgeon remarked that the LA-USC emergency room was "as close as you'll get to a combat situation."[31] Sister programs were established for the U.S. Air Force in Baltimore and for the army in Miami.[32]

Eth and Arroyo, of course, were not healing shattered bones and shredded flesh. They were tending to less obvious but equally grievous injuries to children's minds and souls. "These children were being exposed to the broad range of violent acts that one may see certainly in Los Angeles but also in other parts of the country where there is a lot of gang-related violence," says Dr. Arroyo. "It started to become apparent that an increasing number of children coming from Central America had the same symptomatic picture as kids being exposed to violence here in Los Angeles who were native to Los Angeles. For all intents and purposes, all of these kids looked the same from a clinical perspective."[33]

In short, from the point of view of child psychiatry, metaphors about gang "wars" on the streets of America are not mere literary devices—they are literal descriptions of these children's lives. Similar observations were being made in other parts of the United States to which large numbers of Central American refugees immigrated. In the nation's capital, a third of the refugee children were estimated in 1985 to have emotional or mental problems stemming from their war experiences. "We're bringing people from a war situation to a place of peace, but mentally they are still at war," said an education official in Washington, D.C.[34]

Psychiatric history was made by these young doctors after they presented their findings to a symposium at the APA's annual meeting in Los Angeles in May 1984. According to Dr. Eth, "It all confirmed the strong impression that PTSD did occur in children and that it looked similar to what occurred in adults—in the same way that children and adolescents have major depression just like adults."[35] He and Dr. Pynoos edited an influential book on the subject, *Post-Traumatic Stress Disorder in Children* (1985), which included a paper on the work of Dr. Arroyo among the Central American children.[36] All of this "set the stage for revision of the *DSM,* which for the first time included PTSD in kids," says Dr. Eth, looking to the future. "We could move on to the point where we are not debating the symptomology of kids but, rather, focusing on better treatment."[37]

There was more to be said, however, about the future effects of this childhood trauma. Better treatment for PTSD may have been on the horizon for some children. But for the refugee kids from El Salvador and the children native-born to the gang-wracked streets of America's inner cities, treatment of any kind was a mirage. Few of them would receive any psychiatric treatment at all, which, even in the best case, would have been only part of a complex overall solution.[38]

These children were born in the United States or washed up on its shores precisely at the time when a bitter convergence of social and economic developments was eroding important parts of the system of care and conditioning on which modern societies depend to "socialize" their children: schools, early employment, and public health services.[39] One such development was a "taxpayer revolt" that was sweeping the nation, spawned in California by the 1978 passage of a Constitutional referendum called Proposition 13. The popular measure slashed and capped the property taxes out of which many social services are funded. The taxpayers had been given a taste of the War on Poverty, an ambitious concept proposed by President Lyndon B. Johnson in his State of the Union address in 1964. After a decade of mounting middle- and upper-class backlash under Proposition 13—backlash fueled in the 1980s by President Ronald Reagan's apocryphal and dishonest stories of "welfare queens" driving "welfare Cadillacs"—the taxpayers decided to quit the battlefield.[40] Bleeding hearts for bleeding kids were one thing. Bleeding wallets were quite another. One prominent civil rights attorney and advocate in Los Angeles claims that one billion dollars in funding for gang prevention has been lost every year since the passage of Proposition 13.[41]

California and the nation essentially dumped the gang "problem" into the laps of law enforcement agencies. The cops were expected to do whatever was necessary to contain gang violence, primarily by means of suppression. They were to beat back the most visible forms of gang-related street crime, "assaults, drive-by shooting, drug sales, and graffiti." That, for all serious intents and purposes, is where the problem has remained ever since, as "policy makers no longer believe that the social intervention approaches of the 1960s and the 1970s are successful in dealing with gang problems."[42]

This was the incipient state of affairs in 1983, when Dr. Eth assessed the phenomenon of the children he was seeing and described it as "an enormous public health problem."[43] He made a somber and uncannily accurate prediction. Without treatment, these war-scarred children from El Salvador were "a danger to all of us." Such a child, he said, could "grow up to abuse his own children or join a gang where he may be the one to commit the crime." He concluded, "These children are easy to ignore. But that won't be true when they're older."[44]

Dr. Eth was precisely right. PTSD may not "cause" gangs any more than it causes unemployment or fractured families. But its existence in some children almost certainly predisposes them to the sort of emotionally detached violence that is characteristic of the Los Angeles gang culture. At the very moment Dr. Eth spoke, some of the refugee children of El Salvador's wars were forming what would be called, twenty years later, the most violent street gang in America: Mara Salvatrucha, which, as a result of the California intergang pecking order, would later become known as MS-13. Of all the criminal street gangs in the United States, it is the only one to which the FBI has dedicated a separate headquarters unit, the MS-13 National Gang Task Force. FBI agent Brian Truchon was destined to head that task force.

There was a small and industrious Salvadoran community in Los Angeles before 1980, and it was not plagued by gangs. What changed that community and ultimately the United States was the unintended, unforeseen, even irrelevant consequence of a civil war in a tiny nation that, overnight, became the focal point of the American foreign policy of containing Communism. In the 1980s, El Salvador became "the site of America's most prolonged and expensive military endeavor in the period between the Vietnam War and the Persian Gulf conflict."[45] The collateral damage of that war was the children who washed up onto the corners of Pico-Union. To understand their behavior in Los Angeles and the behavior of their children and grandchildren throughout the United States, one must start with their experience in El Salvador.

The etymology of the name *Mara Salvatrucha* begins in entomology. *Mara,* Central American slang for "gang," is derived from *marabunta,* a Spanish word used regionally for the fierce army ants (*Eciton burchelli*) found throughout much of Latin America.[46] *Marabunta* may also be used to mean "horde"[47] and "disorder and destruction."[48] *Salvatrucha* is a neologism formed by combining the slang word *salva*— short for *Salvadoreño,* or *Salvadoran*—with *trucha,* which literally means "trout" but has the additional slang meaning of "watch out" and may symbolize the hazards and difficulties of a life spent swimming upstream against the current.[49] Early in its Central American usage, *mara* apparently meant nothing more than the benign English phrases one might use to describe a group of youthful pals, such as "our crowd" or "our set." Later, however, it took on more sinister overtones, connoting violence, tumult, and delinquency, and became associated specifically with violent street gangs.[50]

The marabuntas—*Eciton burchelli*—have inspired several B movies: *The Naked Jungle,* starring Charlton Heston in 1954, and *Marabunta,* originally a TV movie titled *Legion of Fire: Killer Ants!* in 1998.[51] Not surprisingly, these movies exaggerate the danger to humans from army ants. Nevertheless, as scientists have explained, army ants on the march present a fearsome mass: "Very few animals, large or small, can withstand the approach of the *Eciton* army. . . . The victims are trapped, stung and torn to pieces, and carried to the rear of the phalanx along the feeder columns to the bivouac, where they are soon eaten."[52]

For centuries, impersonal economic and cultural forces have submerged the great mass of the Salvadoran people in poverty, presided over by a privileged elite. This elite is sometimes referred to as "the Fourteen Families." In reality, it is an oligarchy of several hundred families. The Martinez Varela clan is among them. The Salvadoran military, supplemented by private armies and secret "death squads," has been the oligarchy's scourge.[53]

These impersonal forces are the instinctive and deeply ingrained way of corporatism—the merger of government and commercial power—that has characterized much of Latin America and certainly El Salvador throughout their histories. One expert reported to the House Committee on Armed Services, "Youths growing up in such cultures feel frustrated without knowing why. Instead of promoting independent thinking, parents, churches, and schools encourage accommodation to the way things are. The name for this is corporatism—an antique belief that everyone has a fixed station in life."[54] Through hundreds of years, whenever the poor attempted to change the fixed station assigned to them, the Salvadoran elite has responded with force, sometimes savagely, to preserve its privileged station. The horror of it has been the elite's historical compulsion to punish collectively tens of thousands of persons perceived to be "the enemy." The punishment has most often been death, delivered in the most violent ways imaginable, accompanied by torture, and visited upon man, woman, and child alike.

El Salvador is the smallest state in Central America, about the size of Massachusetts, with little in the way of precious metals or mineral deposits. Its population density of 825 persons per square mile is among the highest in the world and is by far the highest in Central America. By comparison, the next most densely populated Central American state, Guatemala, has a density of about 350 persons per square mile; that of the United States is about 80 persons per square mile.[55] It is not surprising that the defining social, political, and economic issues in El Salvador have centered on control of the land.

Since the time of the Spanish conquerors, El Salvador's land has been dedicated to the cultivation of a single crop for export: first cacao, then indigo, and lastly coffee. Plantations suit such monoculture. (When a patriarch of the Palestinian clan of Comandari—gangster Nelson Comandari's maternal forebear—emigrated from Bethlehem in the 1920s, coffee was among the businesses his progeny got into.) As the small elite of coffee plantation owners consolidated their holdings at the expense of ancient communal holdings, the poor were pushed off the land, creating "a legacy of the landed and the landless—an economy in which laborers could be hired and fired at will without consideration of working conditions or a livable wage."[56] Antivagrancy laws ensured that the peasants were always available when the plantations wanted them for work. "The people live as appendages to coffee growers," a priest observed.[57] The consequences of this system were harsh: in 1961, the poorest 20 percent of the population earned 6 percent of El Salvador's total national income, while the wealthiest 20 percent earned 61 percent of the national income, a distribution that the U.S. Agency for International Development reports has changed little since, despite economic diversification.[58]

The masses of El Salvador have not been entirely passive in seeking a more equitable distribution of land and the income from it. They have pushed back, at times violently, provoking even harsher retaliation from the oligarchy. Landowners crushed an Indian uprising in 1833. Almost a hundred years later, the worldwide depression knocked the bottom out of the coffee market. Export prices fell 54 percent between 1928 and 1931. Plantation owners cut wages and laid off workers proportionately. Supplies of food, imported because coffee production had forced out subsistence farming, also fell. In 1932, following a military coup and the annulment of municipal elections, an abortive peasant insurrection was mounted. The revolt, planned under the leadership of Agustín Farabundo Marti, the Marxist scion of a wealthy landowning family, was betrayed. Marti and other leaders were arrested four days before the insurrection was scheduled to begin. The revolt nonetheless went ahead. It was crushed within three days.

Military reprisals then began on a mind-numbing scale. The rebels themselves had killed perhaps a hundred civilians and military personnel combined. In response, the military executed as many as thirty thousand peasants—2 percent of the population. The precise number is not known. Communists and peasants who wore traditional dress or spoke ancient languages (i.e., Indians) were especially targeted. The carnage demonstrated that the military was in absolute control. It was known thereafter simply as La Matanza, "the Slaughter." A firing squad executed Marti. After La Matanza, the military did not give up its control of the government until the first free election in 1994.

In the latter third of the twentieth century, popular support grew for the militant Left. Marxist hopes were buoyed by successes in Cuba in 1959 and in neighboring Nicaragua in 1979. Unrest was fueled by unalleviated economic oppression and by the constant theft of elections by the oligarchy, in concert with the military.

The Left's growth alarmed the establishment, which panicked after the fall of Nicaragua's regime to Marxist Sandinista rebels. Mass demonstrations were regularly met with gunfire. Secret death squads murdered, tortured, and "disappeared" persons labeled "traitors" and "subversives," among them opposition political leaders. Left-wing terrorism also broke out, including kidnappings, assassinations, and bombings. The spiral continued. By 1980, the tiny country was a madhouse of violence. In March 1980, the archbishop of San Salvador, Oscar Arnulfo Romero, was shot to death while celebrating a Holy Week mass. He had called regularly for an end to the violence and had urged soldiers to disobey immoral orders. Demonstrating mourners at his funeral were shot down on the steps of the National Cathedral. Four American churchwomen were murdered in El Salvador in December 1980.

In 1981, the political parties of the Left united with guerrilla groups to form the Farabundo Martí National Liberation Front. A rebel military offensive began in January. The rebels gained control of some parts of the country, and El Salvador was plunged into a brutal civil war, the savagery of which defies summary description. One can merely hope to capture a shadow of this "convulsion of violence" in the passionate words of the 1993 report of the UN Truth Commission, after its investigation of thousands of atrocities committed by both sides.

> Violence was a fire which swept over the fields of El Salvador; it burst into villages, cut off roads and destroyed highways and bridges, energy sources and transmission lines; it reached the cities and entered families, sacred areas and educational centres; it struck at justice and filled the public administration with victims, and it singled out as an enemy anyone who was not on the list of friends. Violence turned everything to death and destruction.[59]

If life was hell for the adults of El Salvador in the midst of this orgy of death and destruction, what is left to describe the experiences of their children? In every corner of the country, children were unceasingly exposed to monstrous events. Some saw the grisly results of decapitations and armed combat.[60] Others slept under their beds for fear of gunfire. When some saw the mutilated bodies of people they knew, they were forced to remain silent and hold in their tears, lest they become the next target.[61] Children were raped, were subjected to aerial bombing, witnessed brutal raids and murders of neighbors, and were conscripted to fight.[62]

There are many who would lay blame for these horrors at the feet of the Reagan administration, because of the aid it gave to the Salvadoran military regime. In fact, however, "this pact with the devil was made not by the Administration of the aggressively anti-Communist Republican Ronald Reagan but by that of the moderate Democrat Jimmy Carter—ironically a president deeply committed to emphasizing human rights in his foreign policy."[63] Certainly the Reagan administration expanded military aid and dissembled about human rights progress in El Salvador. But the fact remains that "despite the obfuscation engendered by the ensuing decade of bickering between Congress and the Administrations of Reagan and George Bush, and between Democrats and Republicans, this was the outline of what amounted to a bipartisan policy."[64] There is also the fine question of whether a different U.S. policy would have made any difference in the human toll, the Salvadoran elite having proven throughout its history a penchant for the nonchalant slaughter of innocents.

These are profound questions for history's judgment. What is indisputable is that many of the children who endured the Salvadoran civil war and came to the United States were deeply scarred emotionally. Some were trained and experienced in warfare. Those who came to California as refugees were an organic catalyst, an unforeseen and unpredictable force. Two powerful and conflicting armies—the cops and the gangsters—waited in Los Angeles to ignite the force of these children.

Southern California is man-made, a gigantic improvisation," Carey McWilliams, a trenchant observer wrote. "Virtually everything in the region has been imported: plants, flowers, shrubs, trees, people, water, electrical energy, and, to some extent, even the soils."[65] Humans, of course, are the region's only murderous import. From the moment a wandering Spaniard first set eyes on a resident Indian, human imports—migrants—have clawed at each other, some seeking to dominate, others merely to survive. El Salvador's refugee children came late and were handed a cruel menu of harsh facts from the moment they set foot on the streets of Los Angeles.

The first was that they were unwelcome. The U.S. government had—at a minimum—stirred the toxic pot of Central American violence. Yet the administrations of Ronald Reagan and George H. W. Bush wanted little to do with the hundreds of thousands of Salvadorans who fled to the United States during the 1980s. American foreign policy in the region was defined by the perception that the United States was engaged in an epic contest between good and evil forms of government—the Soviet "evil empire" versus the American "shining city upon a hill."[66] The war in El Salvador was seen not as a struggle among Salvadorans but as a war between surrogates of the two superpowers fighting a hot version of the cold war, right in America's backyard. The bright line of American policy would have been blurred by acknowledging that the suffering of the migrant masses who fled El Salvador was in large part a consequence of that very policy.

Salvadorans and other Central Americans have migrated to the United States in several waves since the middle of the nineteenth century. Before the 1980s, most Salvadoran immigrants entered the country legally. They were largely members of the middle and working classes who emigrated for economic reasons. There was also a sprinkling of political dissidents, many from upper-class families, who fled specific conflict with one or another of the region's oligarchic, militaristic governments.[67] The profile of Salvadoran immigrants changed markedly in the late 1970s and throughout the 1980s. Most were refugees in fact, if not under U.S. law, and most entered the country illegally. The brutality of the conflict forced many to flee because they were in the crosshairs of one side or the other—there was no neutral political ground in El Salvador. Death squads operated on both sides. Some who fled were combatants, soldiers, and guerrillas tired of fighting. Many more were civilians physically displaced by the fighting, often forcibly relocated by the military to places in which it was impossible to find work. Others simply wanted to get away from the capricious and ubiquitous violence.[68] For all of these reasons, a million Salvadorans fled their country during the decade of the 1980s. This amounted to about 20 percent of the population.[69]

The Reagan administration and its conservative supporters saw immigration policy as an important weapon in the fight against the evil empire. Those who fled Communist regimes or other nations especially hostile to the United States, such as Iran, were freely admitted to legal status under U.S. refugee laws.[70] But those who fled El Salvador and Guatemala, whose governments the United States supported against insurgencies perceived as Communist-inspired or supported, were denied legal refugee status, and only a "handful" of asylum applications were granted.[71] The U.S. government approved more than thirteen thousand of about one hundred thousand asylum claims filed by Nicaraguans, whose Marxist Sandinista government the United States worked to topple. Of a roughly equal number of claims filed by Salvadorans, only fourteen hundred were approved.[72]

Nelson Comandari's family was among the Salvadorans who fled the turmoil. His paternal grandfather, Col. Agustin Martinez Varela, was former minister of the interior. The colonel—known in his youth as a sizzling baseball pitcher nicknamed "the Pharaoh of the Mound"—also held posts as chief of the national police force, commandant of the military training academy, head of the national firefighting force, director of social security, and ambassador to Guatemala and to Egypt.[73] On the morning of April 2, 1980, a hellacious gun battle broke out at the colonel's home as it was attacked by a team of insurgents. The fight lasted twenty-five minutes, with the colonel's wife, Aida, passing ammunition to the colonel and his son, Franklin, as they fought off the attack. Three weeks later, most of the family flew to Los Angeles.[74] There, Franklin became Frank Varelli and an FBI informant. His three-year-old nephew Nelson was destined to become an MS-13 gangbanger.

It is impossible to state with any certainty how many Salvadoran refugees-in-fact ended up in the United States, because so many of them entered illegally. Some analysts contend that Salvadorans are grossly undercounted in the U.S. Census Bureau's official figures. They argue that undocumented immigrants are generally not likely to cooperate with government enumerators and, if they do, are likely to give false information for fear of being betrayed to immigration authorities. Thus, although the Census Bureau counted some 709,000 Salvadorans in the 2000 decennial census, some analysts estimate the actual number to be as high as 1,118,000.[75]

Likewise, it is impossible to state how many Salvadoran refugees went to Los Angeles. It seems undisputed that by far the greater number of those who came to the United States settled in the Los Angeles metropolitan area. In 1987, the Urban Institute was reported to have estimated that there were between 500,000 and 850,000 Salvadorans in the United States. Of these, the institute estimated that between 250,000 and 350,000 lived in Los Angeles.[76] Other observers of the Los Angeles community estimate that the number of Salvadorans living there at the end of the 1980s was around 500,000—a vast increase from the 43,400 counted in 1970 and the 147,500 counted in 1980.[77]

However many new Salvadoran immigrants there were in Southern California, they faced another harsh fact. Neither California nor its subordinate local governments were in a welcoming mood. The refugees would only add more stress to the structure set up for the Golden State's social services, a structure shrinking inexorably under the mandate of Proposition 13 and the crabbed worldview of the tax revolt.

The economy of Southern California was undergoing a vast transition. Smokestack industry was dying, as it was all over America—a condition that would affect a growing volume of Latino immigrants elsewhere as well. The blue-collar jobs in manufacturing that had been a reliable first rung on the ladder up the socioeconomic scale for previous generations of unskilled immigrants were disappearing. For example, 75 percent of workers in such heavily unionized industries as automobile manufacturing, tire production, and steel were laid off between 1978 and 1988, just as the Salvadorans were arriving. At around the same time, the lower-paying garment industry generated some eighty thousand new jobs.[78]

Defense-related industries would thrive during the military buildup of the Reagan presidency, "a free-spending crusade that lifted the nation's military industry out of the doldrums after the Vietnam War."[79] Defense spending peaked in 1987, and much of the money flowed to the Los Angeles area. Other jobs would grow out of the expanding service economy. But the better of these jobs—those with any kind of future—demanded more education and skills than most of the refugees brought with them. One group of researchers reports, "The undocumented status of the more recent immigrants and the fact that many of them did not speak English meant that the majority were relegated to low-wage service or manufacturing jobs."[80] The Salvadorans were welcomed only where there was a demand for cheap and docile labor, the historic labor market in California for immigrant masses from south of the border. These economic stresses affected not only Salvadorans. A dramatic increase in Mexican immigration to Southern California had been going on since the 1970s.

Traditionally strong and well-networked Latino families were often fractured in the migration, crippling an important resource that earlier waves of Salvadorans relied on. Children were sometimes left behind by parents and sometimes sent ahead to relatives. Parents were often split apart by the vagaries of war, the vicissitudes of illegal transit, and the stresses of being strangers in a strange land. The adults went to work as nannies, custodians, nighttime cleaning crews in skyscrapers, landscaping hands and backs, construction muscle, day laborers, and hunched toilers in the sweatshops of the booming garment industry. The children were often left to make their own way on the streets.

The streets presented a new cruelty. In the dilapidated neighborhoods in which most of the children found themselves, the streets were controlled by violent youth gangs. More precisely, they were controlled by Mexican (or, if one prefers, "Mexican American") street gangs, long institutionalized as an enduring fact of barrio life. The members of these gangs did not think of themselves as sprung from the notional vanilla "Hispanic" ethnicity to which the bureaucracy, academia, and political correctness seek to reduce the complexity of the Latino presence in the United States. They were emphatically Mexican, and they had been dug in for decades. The new kids from El Salvador were interlopers in the fiercely defended barrios, or neighborhoods, about which the gangs were organized. The Salvadorans represented only one thing to the gangsters—prey.

In the beginning, the safest place on the street for Salvadoran youth was off it—inside a tenement or on the rooftops. Many early pictures of the Salvadoran teens who clumped together in groups—usually as "stoners" doing powerful drugs and listening to heavy metal music—were clearly taken on rooftops. However, it did not take the Salvadoran kids long to learn how to play the street game in their new home. After all, enough of them had been real soldiers in a real war. When they finally got their own street gangs together—Mara Salvatrucha preeminent among them—they burst onto the streets with a vengeance. "In their countries, they're used to bombs and decapitated bodies," a gang worker said in 1989. "They laugh at drive-by shootings."[81] That violent attitude brought the new Salvadoran gangs face-to-face with another harsh fact. The LAPD saw nothing to laugh about in drive-by shootings. In fact, it was under heavy community pressure to do something about them.

Past epochs never vanish completely, and blood
still drips from all their wounds, even the most
ancient.

—OCTAVIO PAZ

2

CRUCIBLE: GANGS AND THE STRUGGLE
FOR CULTURAL DOMINANCE

The rise of Mara Salvatrucha did more than any other factor to thrust
Latino gangs into national notoriety. The gangs have become a stalking
horse for everything opponents do not like about immigration from
Latin America. "Gang members from Mexico and Central and South
America are crossing the Mexican Border to commit all kinds of may-
hem," warns Christian conservative leader Paul Weyrich.[1]

Statements like this gross generalization, unmoored from the facts,
have wrapped Latino gangs firmly around the axle of the national immigration debate.

"In the absence of rigorous empirical research, myths and stereotypes often provide the underpinnings for public policies and practices," the authors of a detailed 2006 study of immigration and crime
observed. These myths and stereotypes "are amplified and diffused by

the news media, and shape public opinion and political behavior." Almost three-quarters of Americans surveyed in 2000 thought immigrants were linked to higher crime rates—less than the 60 percent who thought immigrants caused Americans to lose jobs or than the 56 percent who thought immigrants make it harder to keep the country unified.[2]

Immigration hard-liners hold out Latino gangs, MS-13 in particular, as an example of cultural change that they argue will engulf the United States—some say that it has already done so—if its immigration laws are not fiercely strengthened and its borders tightly sealed. In a long article in *American Spectator,* for example, an author who claims that he was formerly pro-immigration assesses crime and gangs as net negative results of Latino migration: "Hispanic crime is high because Mexican and other Central American immigrants have brought with them a gang-ridden culture."[3] Conservative commentator, immigration opponent, and former presidential candidate Patrick J. Buchanan argues for the "systematic and public deportation of felons and gang members who are not U.S. citizens," claiming that "tattooed thugs being put on planes in cuffs will do the GOP and nation a world of good."[4]

But some senior federal and local law enforcement officials insist that precisely such hard-line immigration enforcement aimed at "criminal aliens" during the 1990s had the unintended and ironic effect of creating the worst of the Latino gang problem. The gang culture did not come to the United States from the south. On the contrary, deportees from the United States took the Los Angeles gang culture south with them. With no skills and no prospects in poor countries shattered by wars, they re-created the LA gangs in San Salvador, Tegucigalpa, and Guatemala City. Mara Salvatrucha and the 18th Street gang mutated into transnational criminal enterprises and are now "blowing back" into the United States.

Putting aside the problem of gangs and crime, another, more purely cultural argument lurks as subtext throughout the immigration debate—the fear that Anglo-Saxon culture is being overrun by Latin American culture. "I think you're risking having happen to our Southwest what happened to Texas when the Mexicans lost it, and what happened to Kosovo," Buchanan argues. "Not militarily or politically, but culturally, ethnically, linguistically, I think you're seeing the possible Reconquista of the Southwest. The Mexican folks talk openly about it. Why we don't wake up to it escapes me."[5] This "culture war" argument squarely connects with the fact that the rise of Mexican American gangs and the history of cultural conflict in the Southwest are intimately related. The Latino gangs of Los Angeles did not simply fall out of the sky. Nor are they a passing phenomenon—they are deeply rooted, institutionalized, tightly woven into the culture of the barrio. That barrio culture is in part a result of the history of the American West, "a continuing contest for cultural dominance between Anglos and non-white minorities."[6] The complex socioeconomic forces out of which the Mexican gangs of Los Angeles emerged and that feed the Latino gangs of today were shaped by the violent history of that struggle for dominance.

The struggle for cultural dominance in the Southwest is not over. Mexicans, albeit a relatively small population in California, were expelled or forcefully subordinated to Anglo-American cultural, political, and economic dominance during the latter half of the nineteenth century. By 1900, there were no more than fifteen thousand Mexicans and Mexican Americans among the 1.5 million residents of California, roughly 1–2 percent.[7] The old Mexican culture was all but extinct, superseded by Anglo-American culture. Today, the trend has reversed. Latinos are reasserting themselves in Southern California, politically, economically, and most powerfully through the force of demography. The U.S. Census Bureau estimated that of the almost 10 million persons living in Los Angeles County in 2006, slightly more than 4.7 million were Hispanic, the largest Latino population of any county in the United States.[8]

The wonder is not how many Salvadoran children in Los Angeles in the 1980s became gangbangers. It is how many did not. In 1989, the LAPD was reported to have variously estimated Mara Salvatrucha's membership at 150 and 500.[9] This is an infinitesimal percentage of the Salvadoran population in Los Angeles, even if one takes the greater gang estimate (500) and the lower end of the Urban Institute's 1987 population estimate (250,000). Looking at the smaller cohort of Salvadoran youth, James Diego Vigil, a longtime academic observer of Latino gangs, estimates that 2–10 percent of the Salvadoran youth joined street gangs.[10] Put another way, 90–98 percent did not become gangsters. It is the extraordinarily violent behavior of MS-13, not its numbers, that has propelled it to international notoriety.

Likewise, Vigil estimates that only 4–10 percent of Mexican American youth in most Los Angeles barrios are "affiliated" with gangs, including hangers-on and marginal participants.[11] The same is true of Latino gangs and the youth populations from which they are drawn throughout the United States. A ruthless willingness to use lethal violence is the lever by which a relatively small number of gangsters are able to intimidate the larger community, achieve their criminal designs, and enforce discipline within their organizations.

These proportions suggest another conclusion. A minority group's getting the short end of the socioeconomic stick may create the conditions from which gangs are likely to emerge. But that condition alone demonstrably does not "cause" one to become a gangster. If there were such a direct cause and effect, there would be many more Latino gang-bangers, by an order of magnitude, than there actually are by any estimate. That raises one of the most puzzling aspects of Latino gangs. How is it that two kids from the same disadvantaged ethnic and socioeconomic milieu, from the same run-down block in the same blighted barrio, and even from the same struggling family can each take a different path, one choosing gang life and the other rejecting it against all the furies?

There are as many different pieces to that puzzle as there are gang "experts." Sociologists, criminologists, ethnologists, community activists, gang detectives, clergy, artists, authors, politicians, and gang members, past and present, all have their own views. It is possible, however, to put together a broad picture that includes elements of life in the barrio, the greater American society, and the human soul itself.

Frank Flores has a simple answer that is as good a place as any to start examining the conundrum of who does or does not become a gangbanger. "You make a choice," Flores says. "You take personal responsibility for your life." Flores was born in 1974 into the difficult circumstances of barrio life in East Los Angeles, the very heart of Latino gangs.[12]

Amorphously defined, East LA spreads out from the Los Angeles River and the railroad tracks alongside. It is a major gateway into the United States for Latinos from Mexico and Central America. It is also called "the Eastside" and "East Los." Its boundaries depend on the person defining them, sometimes including only a district within the city limits of Los Angeles and sometimes including a larger area that spills across the city line and well into Los Angeles County. The latter area is policed by the Los Angeles County Sheriff's Department, the LAPD's longtime sibling rival. East LA is one of America's "most mythologized barrios" and "constantly vies with Spanish Harlem in the American pop imagination as stereotype of the Latin."[13] Life in East LA has inspired films and television portrayals ranging from the somber 1992 gang movie *America Me* to the buffoonery of the 1987 comedic film *Born in East L.A.*

With perhaps more gangs per square mile than any other part of the United States, it is also the birthplace of hundreds of thousands of Latinos who have lived quiet lives of hard work. Generations have moved up and out of East LA to better neighborhoods. Individuals from there have risen to positions of prominence in politics, the professions, and the arts. The latter include, for example, Antonio Ramon Villaraigosa, the first Latino mayor of Los Angeles since 1872, and award-winning actor and director Edward James Olmos. "You never hear about the doctors and lawyers from East LA," Frank Flores says. "Only the gangsters." Even so, those who make it up the ladder and out of the poorer barrios like East LA and Boyle Heights are more than replaced numerically by the steady flow of poor and unskilled immigrants pouring in from the South. As early as 1980, when Frank was six years old, 45 percent of the adults in Boyle Heights and 35 percent of the adults in East LA spoke no English.

Flores's grandparents came to Los Angeles—legally, he emphasizes—shortly after World War II. They came from Ciudad Juarez, Mexico, across the border from El Paso, Texas. Juarez was then a small town of little note. Today, it is the location of almost three hundred maquiladoras (foreign-owned assembly plants) and is a job magnet for workers from all over Mexico.[14] Some argue that the maquiladoras have sucked jobs out of the United States. Juarez is also notorious for the unsolved murders of hundreds of women raped, killed, and dumped in the nearby desert.[15]

The home in which Frank was raised—at East Second and South Mott streets in Boyle Heights—lays at the heart of territory that had been staked out since the early 1940s by the White Fence gang, one of the oldest and most deeply rooted of the Mexican American gangs in Los Angeles. The story of Boyle Heights itself is inextricably intertwined with a 150-year history during which a conquering tide of Anglo occupiers and European immigrants pushed vanquished Mexicans out of the city's center and into cracks and crevices at its margins. The neighborhood was once the center of Jewish life in Los Angeles and a polyglot mix of European ethnics and Japanese.

Young Frank was burdened from infancy with one of the classic "risk factors" that some experts opine drive children into street gangs. He was raised in a single-parent household. "It was not the best environment," he says in his characteristically matter-of-fact way. "My mother pretty much raised me on her own. My father was not in the picture." Gang life surrounded the young man at every step of his growth into adulthood. "Two of my uncles were gangbangers," he volunteers. "They belonged to the Spiders clique of White Fence." The Spiders, active in the 1950s and 1960s, were one of a series of age-based cohorts—called *clicas,* or "cliques"—characteristic of earlier Mexican American gangs.

In secondary school, classmates peeled off around Frank Flores. The kids that he played with at First Street Elementary School began making fateful decisions at Hollenbeck Middle School. By the time Frank got to Roosevelt High School—an enormous failure factory, with more than five thousand students who drop out at a rate twice the state average[16]— the hard core had slipped into darkness. They were drawn into various local cliques among the pulsing welter of gangs in and around Boyle Heights—White Fence, Lorena, and Evergreen were just a few among them. Gangs in East LA range from microorganisms clinging to life on a single block or street corner to sizable appendages tied to gangster conglomerates that are morphing into national and transnational criminal enterprises. The youngsters themselves took gang nicknames like "Gyro," "Scooby," and "Trigger." These are real nicknames of kids

Flores knew before they were gangsters, when life was sweet and they were all innocent moppets. The brief lives and violent deaths of some of them are chronicled in *East Side Stories: Gang Life in East LA,* a 1998 book featuring a photo essay by Joseph Rodriguez and Ruben Martinez.[17]

Flores made different choices than Gyro, Scooby, Trigger, and scores of others. He got his first job when he was twelve years old, helping a mother who made ends meet with any jobs she could find. They ranged from domestic cleaning to managing a small shopping center. Frank set his sights early on being a cop. "All I can ever remember wanting to do was to be in the LAPD," he recalls. "I took the test as soon as I was old enough."

Today, Frank Flores is an experienced LAPD gang detective and an internationally recognized expert on the MS-13 gang. He has testified in federal racketeering cases against Mara Salvatrucha in the East Coast and lectured at conferences of international gang fighters in Central America. He keeps a well-worn copy of *East Side Stories* behind his desk. It is readily at hand to educate others and perhaps to remind himself of how far he has come.

Flores has a boyish face, a friendly demeanor, and the broad shoulders of a weight lifter, which he protests he is not. He has an engagingly mild, matter-of-fact manner of speaking. His opinions on life, gang life, and gangsters are fully formed, hard-core, and brightly polished. He is not the least bit puzzled by the questions of why he rejected gang life and why he became a cop. Indeed, to hear him tell his story, there could have been no other path. The system of values that was early and constantly inculcated in him propelled him to where he is now.

Like other Latino youth, Flores was sometimes bruised by the proactive muscle behind the LAPD shield that he wears proudly today. But what he saw the gangsters doing to his life and to the lives of members of his family and community outweighed the annoyance of what he writes off as simple police incompetence rather than deliberate harassment. Two incidents illustrate the balance.

When Frank was about ten years old, he and his older sister were walking to the Benjamin Franklin Branch Library at 2200 East First Street, a community institution since the late nineteenth century. The books on Benjamin Franklin's shelves have changed with the history of

Boyle Heights. In 1915, the Los Angeles library system's entire stock of Russian-language books were moved to Benjamin Franklin, along with a substantial collection of books in Yiddish for the Jewish community. By 1927, most of the Russians and Jews had moved to the Westside. More than half of the Russian and Yiddish books had been moved along with them, back to the central library branch. In 1942, the library suffered a loss of patrons with the transport of Japanese and Japanese Americans to concentration (or "internment") camps. Today, the library serves the Latino community with books in Spanish.

"We were crossing with the light at First and Soto," Flores recalls. "That light really changes fast. When we were halfway across, it started blinking, meaning pedestrians should not cross. An LAPD officer happened to see us. He wrote me and my sister a ticket. That caused my mother to have to take time off from work." Flores reflects on the incident, which was humiliating and costly. "Come on," he says. "Common sense tells you that giving a couple of kids a ticket was not the best thing that cop could have been doing with his time. As I grew up, I never forgot that incident. I thought I could do better than that. I wanted to wear that uniform and serve my community."

At about the same age, Flores was walking on the street with his mother when a gangster snatched her purse. He was enraged. "I saw these people stealing from each other," he remembers, "stealing from their own, stealing from people who don't have anything." He does not conceal his contempt for the gangster life. "These people are just into immediate gratification, the impulse of the moment," he observes.

Flores's attitude toward these incidents illuminates a moral code based on free will and involving personal responsibility, respect for one's family and community, and the power of personal redemption. " 'I had to steal to feed my baby,'" he mocks. "If I've heard that one once, I've heard it a thousand times. These gangsters are people who are ripping off ice cream vendors, stealing from poor people living on the edge. Sure, there are lots of things to blame for their choice to do bad things. Weak-minded people are always looking for an excuse, for something other than the fact that you can choose to be in the gang life. But once you do, it's your choice, nobody else's."

Flores is plainly repulsed by the suggestion that given a slight cali-
bration in his life one way or another, he might have followed his
friends into the gangster underworld. One thought was constantly on
his mind: "I'm going to break my mother's heart if I do something to
disrespect her or to disrespect myself." He dismisses the notion that
broken families push kids into gangs. "It's not that the parents are not
there," he says. "I can show you lots of families where the parents are
there. They're at home. They don't work nights. But their kids still end
up in gangs. It's a question of good parenting skills. I can show you parents who spend quite a lot of time with their kids who are worse than
no parent at all—the kind of parent who smokes pot in front of his kids.
No parent, an absent parent, is better than a bad parent like that in the
picture." Flores acknowledges that gangs are a lure to kids on the street.
"It's impossible to keep kids indoors 24/7 and there are lots of things
that compete with the family structure," he concedes. "So parents have
to teach their kids personal responsibility. You can't just let kids man-
age themselves."

Flores insists that there is more than one source of values that com-
pensate for a missing parent. In his own case, in addition to his mother,
he credits his grandfather and even his gangster uncles. "Respect in my
house was a big thing," he explains. "I would never have talked back to
my mother. And if I had, my uncles would have beat the shit out of me."
How did he learn positive values from his gangster uncles? "In those
days," he explains, "even the old gangsters had values—they had jobs,
they dressed cleanly, and they respected the family. They took pride in
themselves. They were nothing like the gangsters of today. I could see
the changes happening in gangsters throughout my own life. I lived it."
Flores's grandfather was another strong influence. "My grandfather
was very proud that he followed the rules and came into this country
legally," he says. "He was proud of the fact that he made a better life for
his family. He loved this country and he taught us to respect it and to respect ourselves. 'In Mexico,' he used to say, 'You can work all day and
get nowhere. America is a land of opportunity. Here you can work hard
and make something of yourself.'"

Asked whether illegal immigration contributes to the gang problem in Southern California, Flores answers elliptically. "I have no problem with anyone coming here to get the same opportunity my family had," he says. "But there has to be some order. And that's what I do. I keep order." What about redemption? Is there a way out of gang life? "Sure," Flores says. "You make one bad choice at first. Then you make another. Then you continue to make bad choices. But they are your choices. You can hit the brakes at any time. At every point, there is a place where you can stop."

Frank Flores's views are a concise expression of what might be called the law-and-order approach to gangs. According to advocates of this approach, society does not create gangs; gangsters do. If you do the crime, you do the time. It is your choice. Proponents of this view do not necessarily dismiss the need for prevention and intervention programs. On the contrary, many law enforcement personnel repeat the bromide "We can't arrest our way out of this problem." At the same time, many are skeptical about the efficacy of such programs once a kid fully commits to the gang life, and all are realistically resigned to the fact that no matter how much politicians talk about gang prevention and intervention programs, they are rarely willing to fund them adequately. Coddling "juvenile predators" does not play well at election time.

A harsher variant of this view—articulated to me over lunch by an expert from a think tank in Washington—sees gangsters as the result of a kind of predestination that virtually precludes redemption. This view holds that in any given society, there will always be some proportion—say, 10 percent—who choose lives of crime simply because that is the kind of people they are, inherently and irrevocably flawed. At the other end are the 10 percent who would never knowingly commit any crime. The other 80 percent are in play. Those born to privilege and opportunity among the criminally inclined 10 percent will become white-collar larcenists and con men, like the notorious congressional bribe artist Jack Abramoff. Those born to lesser circumstance and restricted opportunity will happily choose to be violent thugs. They are gangsters precisely because they want to be. In this view, the best that can be hoped for is to control the criminal element by vigorous police action and by building a strong cultural disapproval of crime among the ambivalent 80 percent. But some argue that the puzzle is more complex.

To see the whole picture, one needs more pieces than the bad choices of individual gang members. How did this peculiarly violent institution of Latino gangs happen? What keeps it going? Lack of good values and strong moral fiber are not enough to explain why gangs exist and why some youths join the gang life. The truth must lie somewhere between "Just say no to gangs" and the claim that the devil of an uncaring society made them do it. "Macho conservatives wave the flag of self-reliance," while liberals blame society, "their patronizing hearts bleeding for the ghetto dwellers"—so Ruben Martinez complains in *East Side Stories,* the book that detective Flores keeps behind his desk. "If there has been a failure of will in the barrio," he continues, "it has been matched by a failure of society to entertain any solutions other than gang-sweeps and prison-building."[18]

James Diego Vigil, a professor in the Department of Criminology, Law, and Society at the University of California, Irvine, has studied and written about the gangs of Los Angeles for decades. His books and writings advance the theory of "multiple marginality" to explain why gangs emerge and why some families and children fail and others do not. Vigil and others have drawn on observations in the barrios to fill in the theoretical outline with historical, sociological, and anthropological detail. They describe tipping points that they argue condemn a minority of Latino kids to the seductive hell of gang life.

Street gangs, Vigil posits, are "an outcome of marginalization," which is "the relegation of certain persons or groups to the fringes of society." These marginalized persons are made powerless by "pressures and forces in play over a long period of time," operating at many levels grand and small. "The phrase 'multiple marginality,'" he explains, "reflects the complexities and persistence of these forces," which are both "macrohistorical" and "macrostructural" in nature. Specific forces include discrimination and segregation in low-income neighborhoods, poverty, poor schooling, minimal parental supervision, and distrust of law enforcement. The confluence of these forces results in "communities whose members face inadequate living conditions, stressful personal and family changes, and racism and cultural repression in schools."[19]

When the "primary agents of social control"—schools, families, and law enforcement—fail to adequately provide means for meeting the needs of marginalized youth and bringing them to maturity as socialized members of society, some of the youth turn to gangs to fill the empty spaces in their lives.[20] As Ruben Martinez explains, the gang then becomes "the 'family' of last resort . . . when the parents are absent, abusive, or just worn down by the pressure of barrio life," and it becomes "a school when public education disintegrates."[21] In short, concludes Vigil, "street socialization" takes over, and in the particular case of the barrios of Los Angeles, that process has firmly "rooted the quasi institution of the street gang."[22]

The pressures of marginalization fall most heavily on the second generation—the children of immigrants—who find themselves alienated from the old culture of their first-generation immigrant parents and from the new culture of the dominant Anglo society in the United States, which has historically rejected them.[23] The relationship between crime and immigration is precisely the opposite of what one would expect based on popular wisdom and the prattling of Paul Weyrich, Patrick Buchanan, Lou Dobbs, and the like. In fact, immigrants of every origin have a much lower crime rate than their second-generation children (measured by their rate of imprisonment for criminal conduct). Foreign-born men are institutionalized at half the rate of non-Hispanic white native men. Among Latinos, the lowest incarceration rates are found among Salvadorans, Guatemalans, and Mexicans—the groups identified as "most stigmatized as 'illegals' in the public perception and outcry about immigration."[24] To a considerable degree, it is "Americanization" on the streets, rather than immigration, that leads the children of immigrants into higher rates of crime. "By the time these children of immigrants reach adulthood," researchers argue, "the impediments and opportunities faced as adolescents solidify."[25]

But the children of all immigrant groups, including the vast majority who do not join gangs, have suffered from similar pressures. So where is the fault line that distinguishes between the children who end up in gangs and the ones who do not? Vigil suggests that "while almost all immigrant families had to cope with stresses of economic pressures and cultural change, some families were strained even greater." Thus, while most families (like that of Frank Flores) "gradually acquired a stable, if not prosperous, status," others spiraled downward into "long-term poverty and were left behind."[26] A "considerable number" of the children of these families "are unable to devise a smooth, consistent strategy of adaptation." In the barrios of Southern California, these "losers" are called *cholos,* an alienated status that may continue well into adulthood.[27] They become another subculture—the underclass of the underclass—who are most likely to turn to street gangs for the human identity that neither their families nor the agents of the greater society can provide them.

Faced with public demands to control gangs and contain the violence they cause, politicians and government functionaries are often impatient with academic analysis and abstractions, such as macrohistorical factors. "We don't want to understand the problem, we want to stop it," one city official told Vigil.[28] But to understand the origins and perverse persistence of the Latino gangs of Southern California, a survey of historical forces is in order. The story of these forces is intimately bound to the story of the American West's struggle for cultural dominance. It starts with a mean little war whose echoes still reverberate across every inch of the U.S.-Mexican border.

The history of the Mexican American community in Southern California begins with the Mexican-American War, waged between 1846 and 1848. Historians from the past portrayed this war as a righteous conflict between a vigorous young democracy and a backward, corrupt country reeling drunkenly from dictator to dictator. Some more recent historians tend to put most of the blame on the United States for this short, brutal war of aggression.[29] Driven by America's hunger for western lands, the conflict ended in a humiliating defeat for Mexico. The peace treaty of Guadalupe-Hidalgo forced the defeated nation to surrender, for a trifling sum, more than five hundred thousand square miles of land—roughly half of its territory—in what then became the American Southwest, including California. If the area of Texas, whose previously disputed independence Mexico formally recognized, is included, the total amount of land Mexico lost exceeds one million square miles.[30] There followed what historian Manuel Gonzales describes as the "sad and depressing" story of a "small and powerless" Mexican population, "despised and oppressed by mainstream society."[31] The treaty guaranteed U.S. citizenship to Mexicans who chose to stay in the territory ceded by Mexico. For most of them, however, the rights of citizenship were illusory. Successive waves of "Anglo-Saxon" settlers pushed the "greasers" aside.[32] First they took their land. Then they reduced them to an inferior "racial" minority.

This bloody and unseemly business of empire building from the nineteenth century seems remote from the gritty reality playing out today on the streets of twenty-first-century Los Angeles. In one sense, it absolutely is remote. There is virtually no direct ancestral or sociopolitical (as opposed to cultural) connection between the Mexicans in California then—the Californios—and Latinos in California today. Mexico had gained its own independence from Spain only in 1821. Before the Mexican-American War, it had shown faint interest in developing California or in providing for its defense. It did only so much as it thought necessary to control the Indians and check English and Russian ambitions.[33] There were relatively few Mexicans in California at the time of the U.S. conquest. The non-Indian population of California in 1848 was about fifteen thousand. Of these, a "few thousand" were European Americans—drifting misfits and restless opportunists, the outliers of a horde yet to come—and a "smattering" of other Europeans. The rest were Mexicans.[34] Moreover, Alta California was no paradise for ordinary Mexicans. The Californios were organized in a feudal ranchero society in which a privileged few at the top, holding vast land grants, reaped the benefits of the laboring masses at the bottom. A contemporary observer compared the social structure to that of the Deep South. The criollo landowners, mostly of Spanish descent and born in the New World, were the plantation owners; the Indians were the slaves; and the Mexican laborers, derisively called by the derogatory name *cholos,* were the "poor white trash."[35]

The number of Mexican Americans in California today who can trace their lineage directly to any of these preconquest Californios is thus insignificant. The fate of the preconquest aristocracy, which had virtually disappeared by 1900, is not a matter of burning interest to most California Latinos. "The old displaced Ranchero elite held no importance in the starkly racialized, working-class experience I knew as a child," writes scholar Tomas Almaguer. "No one lamented the regrettable fate of Don Camillo or Don Ignacio del Valle."[36] Only with the so-called Great Migration of the second and third decades of the twentieth century did the Mexican and ultimately Mexican American population mushroom and again become a significant factor in California.

But despite the lack of such a direct link to today's Mexican Americans, the history of the latter half of the nineteenth century is important for several reasons. No matter how indifferent the majority of Latinos may be to the fate of the Californio elite, political and cultural developments after the war "left a lasting impression among Mexicans," and "the period was a crucible upon which the modern Mexican American has been forged."[37] The racial attitudes of the white majority and the rules they mandated during this period defined social and economic boundaries that relegated Latinos to the margins of society. For Mexican Americans and California Latinos generally, these realities of life "set the stage for a twentieth-century experience qualitatively different from that of the nineteenth."[38] The complex interethnic and racial dynamics of California continue to play out on that stage. Rancor occasionally shows through. "Ever since the first conquistador bedded an Aztec maiden," an *LA Weekly* columnist fumed in 2007, "*Gabachos* [whites] have viewed Mexicans as only slightly more respectable than a taco."[39] Some gangs—notably the powerful prison-based Mexican Mafia—have molded the conquest story into an idealized racial myth, justifying their predations as "political resistance." A small irredentist movement also exploits this history, equating the part of Mexico taken by the United States after the war with Aztlan, an ancient land said to be the source of the original Aztec migration in Mexico. In any case, the story deserves recounting on its own merits in any discussion of Latinos in Southern California, for "history tells us that no more sorry record exists in the Union of inhuman and uncivil treatment toward minority groups than in California."[40]

A variety of factors—agrarian, commercial, and shipping interests; raw greed; and concern for national security—drove the United States and Mexico to war in 1846. What bound them into an irresistible force was the American concept of Manifest Destiny, based on belief in Anglo-Saxon racial superiority.[41] Manuel Gonzales explains, "The second half of the nineteenth century witnessed the rapid growth of racism throughout the Western world, and the United States was no exception."[42] By the middle of the nineteenth century, it was widely accepted in the United States that it was the right—indeed, the duty—of the white nation to subordinate inferior races and put to productive use the land those races "held captive" and selfishly squandered.[43] There was some principled opposition to the theory of racial superiority. After all, it flew in the face of both Enlightenment thought on which the young nation was founded and Christian doctrine of the equality of God's human creations. But expediency and the pressures of the frontier prevailed. Racial destiny neatly justified ethnic cleansing of the Native American population and the theft of their lands.

In the heated international elbowing leading up to the Mexican-American War, the noxious flower of racial superiority burst into full bloom in the United States. The term *Manifest Destiny* was fashioned. "In confronting the Mexicans," notes one scholar, "the Americans clearly formulated the idea of themselves as an Anglo-Saxon race."[44] Yet the very idea of an Anglo-Saxon "race" was necessarily flexible and vague, founded as it was on historical fictions and flawed science. "An Irishman might be described as a lazy, ragged, dirty Celt when he landed in New York," explains one scholar, "but if his children settled in California, they might well be praised as part of the vanguard of the energetic Anglo-Saxon people poised for the plunge into Asia."[45]

At first, the question of precisely how Mexicans fit into the California racial pecking order was especially dicey. The old elite, ostensibly of Spanish descent, were reluctantly allowed to be considered "white." Many of them intermarried with powerful "white" families, sometimes as a deliberate survival strategy. It would not do to classify these Mexican relatives of white folk the same as the dark-complexioned greasers, the mestizos whose blood was mixed with that of the despised "savage" Indians.[46] A Texas farmer summed up the situation with respect to the mestizos when he said, "We feel toward the Mexicans just like toward the nigger, but not so much."[47] The question of how to "racially" classify Mexican Americans and other Latinos vexed the U.S. Census Bureau well into the twentieth century.[48] "Mexicans" were classified as "white" in the 1920 census but were reclassified as a separate race in the

1930 census.[49] Finally, there was the annoying fact that Mexicans of all hues were guaranteed the option of U.S. citizenship under the treaty of Guadalupe-Hidalgo. Blacks, Indians, and Asians enjoyed no such legal buffer. They suffered the full weight of discriminatory legislation and state action from which Mexican Americans were to some degree spared.[50]

Eventually, however, California Mexican society was homogenized. The criollo elite all but disappeared, and all remaining Mexicans were treated as racially inferior by the dominant society. One scholar observes, "Racial rhetoric tended to become particularly explicit whenever Mexicans and whites competed for control of vital economic resources such as land or labor."[51] In fact, the next 150 years of relations between Anglos and Mexicans in California can be divided roughly into two great struggles: the first fifty years over the land and the last century over labor.

The loss of land—and, with it, power, status, and dignity—suffered by the Californios was a "transaction by demography."[52] In the wake of the war, an "overwhelming horde" of Anglo-Americans "took possession of the land and made things over to their own taste."[53] The change was rapid in Northern California, ignited by the discovery of gold on January 24, 1848, at Sutter's Mill, near Coloma (just northeast of Sacramento). Gold fever followed, as reports of the bonanza crept eastward, setting off a massive immigration that was "dominated by white Americans."[54] There had never been many Mexicans in the north, and those few were soon immersed "in a sea of foreigners."[55] By 1849, there were one hundred thousand argonauts in Northern California.[56] Things went more slowly in Southern California—traditionally defined as the land south of the Tehachapi Mountains, which fall across the state transversely, just north of Santa Barbara.[57] As late as 1854, Los Angeles was a predominantly Mexican pueblo. Out of a total of five thousand residents, three thousand to thirty-five hundred were Mexicans; the rest were Anglo-Americans.[58] Even so, Los Angeles changed more quickly than the basin around it. By 1880, the town's population had grown to more than eleven thousand. Over the same period, the Latino population shrank to around two thousand.[59]

In the north, envy, racism, and economic competition quickly inspired discriminatory laws and violence against Latinos in the goldfields. Experienced miners from Mexico and the Andean highlands of South America were among the most successful in the earliest days of the Gold Rush. They arrived before the bulk of the Anglo prospectors, who could get to California from the East Coast only by one of three slow ways: by making the arduous and dangerous overland trek; by sailing around the horn of South America; or by sailing to Panama, slogging across the jungles of the isthmus, and continuing up the Pacific coast by sea. All of these routes took more time than it took for the Latino miners to hear about and get to the goldfields. Moreover, scholars observe that "the Spanish-speaking miners knew how to mine gold, worked hard, lived frugally, were often successful, and in this way acquired the resentment of the Yankees, who were inexperienced, required more amenities, and had poorer returns as a group since there were more of them."[60]

What followed was a template for the broader Latino experience in the new California. Some Latino and Chinese miners were forcibly expelled from the goldfields. All of them became the butt of discriminatory laws, first a rash of exclusionary mining codes in individual camps and then the Foreign Miners' License Tax, enacted by the California legislature in 1850. The tax was not levied on Europeans, only on Latinos and Asians.[61] Ironically, local white merchants suffered an object lesson in practical economics. The foreign miners were not exporting American wealth, as tax advocates had argued to support their discriminatory legislation. The Latinos were in fact spending their profits locally on food, clothing, gambling, and entertainment. Business suffered. The tax was hastily repealed in 1851. But most of the Latino miners were gone by then.[62]

Inevitably, the goldfields were exhausted or taken over by industrial miners. The immigrant horde then turned its attention to the real wealth of California, the land. Largely devoted to grazing livestock, the abundant and fertile land seemed vacant to them. The governments of Spain and Mexico had parceled it out in vast land grants—two hundred families owned fourteen million acres.[63] The newcomers fell onto these estates like locusts. Some newcomers simply grabbed land by squatting and violently resisting efforts to expel them. Others exploited more so-phisticated means, such as litigation. The latter often was as effective as squatting in taking possession and yielded bigger blocs of land. The fed-eral government established a board of three commissioners, sitting in San Francisco, to hear and decide conflicting land claims. The process required that landowners hire platoons of lawyers—some of whom had their own designs on the land. Rich in land but poor in cash, many of the rancheros traded land for litigation expenses. By the time the com-mission finished its work five years later, the landowners had been over-whelmed. Immense amounts of lands changed hands in payment of fees, lost defense of arcane Spanish and Mexican grants, and outright fraud.[64]

The ranchero system was crushed, and with it collapsed the eco-nomic niche of the Mexican workforce. But their troubles were not over. Mexicans became a "favorite target" of the vigilante justice that ruled much of California during the 1850s and 1860s.[65] "Mob violence became a common method of Anglo settlers," reports one scholar, "as they sought to secure their control over the incipient capitalist economy of the southwestern states."[66]

The English word *vigilante* is borrowed from the Spanish word meaning "watchman" or "security guard."[67] Vigilantism was common throughout the frontier. In 1854, the mayor of Los Angeles quit his office to lead a mob that seized a suspect from jail and summarily hung him. The mayor was promptly reelected to office.[68] Vigilantism has its ro-mantic modern defenders, who argue that it was better than anarchy and the best system of justice available until a formal legal system could be established. That might have been true among Anglo peers. But there seems to be no question that, "given the intensity of racist sentiments at this time," Indians, Asians, and Latinos suffered inordinate unfairness under the ministrations of vigilantism.[69]

In California, at least 163 Mexicans were lynched between 1848 and 1860. Vigilante committees continued to take violent actions against Mexicans long after formal legal systems were in place. A comprehen-sive survey of lynching of Mexicans in the Southwest found that "only a small number of Mexican lynching victims—64 out of a total of 597—met their fate at the hands of vigilantes acting in the absence of a formal judicial system." "Most," the survey reports, "were summarily executed by mobs."[70]

The rate at which Mexicans were lynched is nothing short of astounding when compared to the rates of black lynchings. Between 1848 and 1879, Mexicans in the Southwest were lynched at a rate of 473 lynchings per 100,000 of population. The rate of black lynchings in Mississippi—the state with the worst record—during their peak years, from 1880 to 1930, was 52.8 per 100,000. The Mexican lynching rate fell to 27.4 lynchings per 100,000 during that period. This compares to the rates of black lynchings during the same period in North Carolina (11.0), South Carolina (18.8), and Alabama (32.4). Carey McWilliams was not exaggerating when he wrote, "The practice of lynching Mexicans soon became an outdoor sport in Southern California."[71]

Mexicans suffered other legal disabilities under the formal legal system. For example, nonwhites were not allowed to be witnesses in cases against white defendants. In 1857, the rule was applied against Manuel Dominguez, a prominent Mexican American. Dominguez, a wealthy landowner and Los Angeles County supervisor, had been a delegate to the California constitutional convention in 1849. He was also a mestizo of Mexican and Indian ancestry. Called as a witness for the defense in a civil case, his "Indian blood" was enough to bar his testimony.[72] Another example of white legal hostility was the formal title of an 1855 state antivagrancy law—the "Greaser Act."[73]

Not all Mexicans and Mexican Americans went quietly into the night of Anglo domination. "Naturally," writes Manuel Gonzales, "the vast majority of Mexicans came to resent the arrogance they encountered."[74] Some resisted in violent ways, and an "unofficial, undeclared war between 'lower-class' Mexicans and Anglos" was waged in the latter half of the nineteenth century.[75] On one front, this low-grade guerrilla war was nothing more than plain old horse stealing, highway robbery, and assault, rationalized as a form of protest by people who "resented their status as a conquered people."[76] Foremost among these "social bandits" was Joaquin Murrieta (whose name is spelled variously), on whose story the legend of Zorro was based. Murrieta (or Murieta) was most likely a mythologized composite of a number of real-life bandits. But his legendary feats struck a psychic chord among the Mexicans. Gonzales observes, "It provided the marginalized Mexican population with a much-needed symbol of resistance against oppression, a function the myth continues to perform today."[77]

If there ever was any chance for full assimilation of the conquered Mexican population, the harsh encounters between the two cultures during this period snuffed it out. The final conquest was sealed in Southern California with the arrival of the railroads and the land boom of the 1880s. The railroads "functioned as a pipeline, picking up white middle-class Protestants in their home territory in the east and Midwest and pumping them out at the other end into the formerly remote regions of the West."[78] With the arrival in force of middle-class white America, the Mexicans withdrew or were pushed into rural *colonias* and barrios—often called "Little Mexicos" by Anglos—where the native-born and the immigrants merged into a common community. They "remained Spanish-speaking, continued to think of themselves as alien or Mexican, and were increasingly removed from vital contact with the dominant culture."[79]

If the history of Mexican Americans in California had ended in 1900—as many Anglos assumed then that it had—there would never have been a Latino gang culture. The hucksters who built Los Angeles out of the desert were happy to exploit the gauzy Hollywood memory of a mythical and romantic Spanish mission period. Street names and exotic movie plots alike conjured up images of dashing caballeros and swooning senoritas—often played by Anglos against the comic foil of stereotypic "Mexican" buffoons. But the moguls of the ascendant culture assumed that the real-life greasers would simply fade away, out of sight and out of the way of progress.

History did not end in 1900. On the contrary, the "most persistent dynamic of the border" kicked into action—"the dependence of American business on Hispanic labor."[80] The growth of agribusiness in California brought with it a demand for cheap, unskilled, and docile labor. Between 1900 and 1930, that demand was met by an explosion of Mexican immigration. The gangs of California were born among the children of that "Great Migration."

If things were so bad for Mexicans in California, it is fair to ask, why did so many of them come to California during the Great Migration, and why have they kept coming ever since? One reason is that life is and always has been a hell of a lot worse in Mexico than virtually anywhere in the United States. Mexicans have been pushed out of Mexico by poverty, political turmoil, and violence, as well as pulled into the United States by jobs and opportunity. Another reason is that, in the early twentieth century at least, Mexicans—especially those of the northern border states—considered themselves to be indigenous to the Southwest. They felt at home in an area that had until recently been part of Mexico. The climate, terrain, language, and face of the people were similar to Mexico's. Proximity was yet another reason. It was harder to put together the immigrant passage from Hamburg, Kiev, or Naples than it was to ride a railcar or walk across an imaginary line in the sand. More than anything, however, Mexicans came north because the jobs were there and because employers wanted them.[81]

The immigrant stream started as a trickle. Only about 24,000 Mexicans entered the United States between 1900 and 1910. The trickle turned to a river between 1910 and 1920. Mexican immigration increased by a factor of ten during that decade, as 225,000 Mexicans entered the United States. The river became a flood in the next decade. About 500,000 Mexicans came across the border between 1920 and 1930. Most of them entered illegally or "at least through irregular channels."[82] A broad pattern of Latino immigration was set in place during these decades. When Mexicans were a glut on the U.S. labor market, as during the Great Depression in the 1930s, they were subjected to harsh exclusionary measures and deportation. Some U.S. citizens who had the inconvenient misfortune to "look" Mexican were scooped up and hustled "back" to Mexico in that era's immigration sweeps. When labor was sorely needed, as during World War II, Mexicans were welcomed. Starting in the 1970s, welcome or not, the migration north became a permanent facet of the geopolitics of the Western Hemisphere. It has been a volatile and growing political problem in the United States ever since.

By 1930, the population of Mexicans in California had rebounded to 368,000, far exceeding the population of roughly 15,000 during the putatively halcyon days of Mexican California. The cohort of 1920s immigrants that contributed the most to that population balloon is crucial to the story of Latino gangs. "By 1940," reports Carey McWilliams, "a large second-generation group had reached the threshold of maturity, American-born children of the immigrants who had crossed the border after 1920."[83] It was among these children that the first durable gangs were formed.

The flood of Mexican immigrants was drawn primarily by the remarkable transition of southwestern agriculture—including that of California—to agribusiness and factory farming. Three factors contributed to this transition: hard-nosed facts of the farming business, the growth of the railroads, and the institution of irrigation. In general, California's farms were huge, agricultural reincarnations of the old rancheros they replaced. The owners of these farms found that they could not effectively compete with the wheat production of family farms in the Midwest, which enjoyed better rainfall and lower transportation costs. However, vast capital-intensive irrigation schemes subsidized by the government made the cultivation of fruits, vegetables, and some other crops, such as cotton, possible in California. The growth of the railroads and the invention of refrigerated railcars around the turn of the century made transportation of produce to eastern markets feasible. All that was lacking was cheap, docile seasonal labor. Mexican migrants—hardworking, unorganized, and fearful of deportation—fit the bill perfectly. The magnates of factory farming could do pretty much whatever they pleased with these brown backs and arms.[84] If the Mexicans did make problems, the bosses, well organized through various industry associations, did not hesitate to call in the dutifully compliant forces of law and order, including the LAPD, to keep them in line.

Not everyone thought this migration of Mexicans was a good idea. The issue was joined in debates over immigration law and policy in the early twentieth century. The rhetoric seems only slightly more crude than the discourse of today. There were warnings that the negative "race value" of dark-skinned Mexicans would threaten "mongrelization"—the "mixture of white, Indian, and negro blood strains." This dreaded development, it was announced by a professor of economics at a southern university, would create "a race problem that will dwarf the Negro problem in the South" and end up in "the practical destruction . . . of all that is worthwhile in our white civilization." Proponents of immigration, working largely on the side of agricultural interests, conceded that Mexicans were racially inferior. But they argued that the Mexican's natural "homing instinct"—like that of a pigeon—would draw him back to Mexico during the off-season. In addition, one mouthpiece for Arizona industry scoffed, "Have you ever heard . . . in the history of the human race, of the white race being overcome by a class of people of the mentality of the Mexicans?"[85]

In the event, most of the "homing pigeons" working in California preferred to "winter" in the barrios of Los Angeles or the *colonias* of the then-rural San Fernando Valley. Meanwhile, the Los Angeles boom was hailed as a miracle by Anglo America. Los Angeles County grew from a population of 12,000 in 1887—when the railroads arrived—to 120,00 in 1900. The city's population doubled every decade until 1940, and by 1970, it was the second largest city in the United States, outnumbered only by New York. What got much less publicity was the invisible growth of the Latino population. By 1970, there were 1.25 million Mexicans and Mexican Americans in Los Angeles, more people of Mexican descent than in any city in the Western Hemisphere except Mexico City and Guadalajara.[86]

This teeming milieu is the business end of any macrohistorical survey of the causes of street gangs. Mexican youth gangs—at first relatively benign by today's standards—began to take root in the barrios of Los Angeles when the children of the Great Migration of the 1920s reached early adulthood—in the early 1940s. Over the next several decades, they evolved into deadly fighting gangs, each generation more violent than the one before it. The gangs went to war with each other and with the LAPD, and they eventually spread into cities, suburbs, and rural hamlets across America.

The consensus is that no more than five to ten people in a hundred who die by gunfire in Los Angeles are any loss to society. These people fight small wars amongst themselves. It would seem a valid social service to keep them well-supplied with ammunition.

—JEFF COOPER, *GUNS & AMMO* COLUMNIST

3

SMALL WARS:

THE RISE OF MEXICAN AMERICAN GANGS

The attack on Juan Romero was swift, vicious, and bloody. Details of the assault can be found among a long line of gangster melees and murders that shuffle like a chain gang through the opinions of California's appellate courts.[1] The human stories in these cases strike the reader at first as shocking, then as banal, and finally as theater of the criminally absurd. Nonetheless, they are invaluable sources—more reliable than media reports, less passionate than the apologetics of gangsters and youth workers, and more vital than the opaque scribbling of many social scientists. Cops, priests, academics, do-gooders, and moralists pontificate about many issues concerning gangs, including why they emerge, what compels young people to join them, and the precise nature of "gang activity." But a vein of unalloyed truth runs through these court reports. Here are hard facts, cast in the contest of trial by jury and refined in appellate argument. The plain truth emerges that whatever else Latino street gangs may be or do, they are relentlessly and consistently violent.

Juan Romero suffered fifteen torturous minutes of that violent truth at about 10:30 p.m. on the night of July 14, 2005. Romero was standing on a sidewalk in the city of El Monte, located in the San Gabriel Valley east of Los Angeles. The city's only claim to fame is that it was once the site of Gay's Lion Farm, the former home of the MGM lion. White flight drained El Monte's diversity in the 1950s and 1960s. Today, at least 75 percent of the city's population is Latino. Sixty percent of its residents claim to be of Mexican origin. Another 15 percent cite Central American or "Hispanic" descent. The remainder of the population is mostly Asian, leavened by a tiny sprinkling of non-Latino white and black residents.

The court's opinion does not reveal what Romero, a member of the eponymous El Monte Flores gang, was doing on the street that night. Perhaps he was just hanging out, enjoying a pleasant evening. The midday heat, which had reached the high nineties, had cooled by that time. The balmy night turned into hell for Romero when Antonio Carreto Leon and another young man identified only as "Victor," both members of the Los Angeles-based 38th Street gang, walked up and hurled the standard gangster challenge "De donde eres?"—literally translated "Where are you from?" but meaning "What gang do you claim?"

Words to that effect—or the equivalent in gang "signs" that are "thrown" with fingers contorted into the shape of letters and numerals signifying the gang's name—have been the opening volley in thousands of Latino gang murders. This ritualistic challenge is the human equivalent of dogs sniffing each other with their fur raised, already committed to fight. To back down from the challenge is to disgrace oneself and one's barrio, the inseparable dual identity Latino gangsters carry with them wherever they go.

Before Romero could reply, the two men pounced on him like angry young lions. "Fuck El Monte Flores gang," they yelled. "38 Street fuck EMF." Leon produced a screwdriver and stabbed Romero with it. Again and again it fell in a savage arc, slamming holes through Romero's skull. The assailants pummeled their victim to the ground, pounding him with their fists and feet. The scene was pandemonium. Romero was screaming in pain. He tried to get to his feet and defend himself but kept fading out of consciousness. Women were yelling at the assailants, begging them to stop. One shouted for someone to call 911. Suddenly, it was over. The two 38th Street gangsters broke off their attack and faded into the night. Romero crawled to the nearby driveway of a residence, leaving a slimy trail of gore from the puncture wounds in his head. He lapsed into convulsions. The owner of the home applied pressure to the back of Romero's skull, preventing his bleeding to death.

Romero survived the attack. But four months later, at Leon's trial, he claimed that he could recall nothing of that night. Leon was convicted by other testimony. The case of *People v. Leon* then took its humble place in the archives of gang ritual—challenge, response, mayhem, and death. It stands out only because Romero's assailants used a screwdriver instead of a gun, the most common tool of gang violence. "Each gang will have a certain number of guns, mostly owned by the gang," Joseph Rodriguez observed while gathering materials for his book of photographs of gang life in East Los Angeles. "They're kept stashed and taken out when they sense the need for protection, or for a party to make a show of bravado by shooting at gang rivals' cars or into the air. The younger kids treat them like toys."[2]

The 38th Street gang from which Leon and "Victor" hailed dates from the 1920s and is notorious today in Los Angeles. It has an estimated 350 members in its core neighborhood. They are said to deal drugs, extort money from small businesses, mug passersby, and run a sophisticated auto theft ring.[3] The gang's name appears only infrequently in the pages of the *Los Angeles Times*. However, the opinions of California's appellate courts document years of the gang's violent encounters with its rivals—attempted murders, murders, countermurders, and counter-countermurders. Among its targets are the Florencia 13, Barrio Mojados (BMS), and "All for Crime" (AFC) gangs.[4] Innocent bystanders are regularly killed and injured in these incidents, victims of indiscriminate shooting. A 38th Street gang member, Rodolfo Diaz, was added to the LAPD's list of ten most wanted gangsters in July 2007. Diaz was accused of shooting his girlfriend's mother to death in 2002.[5] In August 2004, a civil injunction—an innovative Los Angeles antigang tool growing in favor elsewhere—was issued barring the gang's members from associating with each other. It restricted their public activity within a "safety zone" of almost four square miles.[6]

Things were not always so predictably deadly among the Mexican American gangs of Los Angeles. Early gang fights involved mostly fists and rarely ended in death. But one of the most famous crimes in the history of Los Angeles involved a murder in which alleged members of the incipient 38th Street gang were implicated. The story provides a point of departure for a look into the birth of the Mexican American gangs, their growth into deeply rooted institutions of criminal violence, and the contentious relationship between law enforcement and the Latino community.

At 1:30 a.m. on Sunday, August 2, 1942, Jose Diaz was found lying facedown in a dirt road, unconscious and gurgling blood. The rutted lane skirted a small reservoir as it cut a lazy S shape through an agricultural tract in southeast Los Angeles called the Williams Ranch. The reservoir was nicknamed "Sleepy Lagoon," supposedly after a hit song recorded by popular bandleader and trumpet player Harry James, released in the spring and later rereleased by a variety of popular artists.

The son of ranch workers who lived in a nearby bunkhouse, the twenty-two-year-old Diaz was raised in the United States. Born in Durango, Mexico, he was exempt from the military draft and had a job packing vegetables at the Sunny Sally Packing Plant. Nevertheless, the young man—like thousands of other Latino immigrants—volunteered to serve. He was to report for induction into the army the next day, Monday, August 3. He never made it. Diaz had been severely beaten and twice stabbed between the time he left a neighbor's birthday party and the time he was found lying in the lane. Taken to a hospital, he died within hours. The evidence was that Diaz had fought furiously with his attacker or attackers. His fatal injury was determined to have come from a blow to the head from a blunt object, likely a wooden club.

Diaz's family were migrant workers. His father and younger siblings were picking prunes in Northern California when he was killed. Ordinarily, he would have been just another stiff in the Los Angeles morgue. But the Los Angeles law enforcement establishment was under heavy public and political pressure to take effective action against what was perceived to be a wave of gang crime. Scarcely two months earlier, on June 12, the LAPD had been unable to control a riot that broke out after a fight between two Mexican American gangs. The incident started after an all-city track meet at Los Angeles Memorial Coliseum. The leader of one gang, nineteen-year-old Frank Torres, was shot in the head by a rival gang member. A melee between the two gangs soon drew in hundreds of other youth and turned into a riot and looting of nearby businesses. Order was restored only when the U.S. Army was called in.[7]

In what was to become a predictable pattern during its decades-long guerrilla war with gangs, the LAPD responded to media pressure and public outrage by announcing a "crackdown." The murder of Jose Diaz provided a suitable moment to show the public that the cops meant business. It became a spark that ignited a racial and social fireball, fueled by the pressures of war and a paranoid suspicion that persons of Mexican heritage were no more to be trusted than those of Japanese descent, who were being rounded up in 1942 and sent off to camps. There was even public speculation that the "Mexican gang problem" was part of a Nazi plot to undermine American unity. The investigation of the "Sleepy Lagoon murder" quickly set off a frenzy among politicians, law enforcement, and the news media. Over the next few weeks, the LAPD cast a "dragnet" over the barrios and swept up more than six hundred youth. Most of them were Mexican Americans, indiscriminately labeled "zoot-suiters." All of them thereafter bore the stigma of an arrest record, albeit on trumped-up charges that went nowhere. Politicians, including the governor, hyperventilated about the "Mexican problem." A hysterical news media trumpeted concern about the crimes of the zoot-suiter "gangs" alleged to be rampaging through the streets of Los Angeles.

Police soon announced that the Diaz murder had been solved. The deed was pinned on twenty-four young people—all but one of whom were Mexican American—affiliated with what authorities called the "38th Street gang." Two of the accused hired private counsel and were quickly dismissed from the case. Trial of the rest began in October 1942. The prosecution's theory was that Diaz died as a result of a conspiracy among the gang members. Regardless of who among them struck the fatal blow, the state argued, all the conspirators were equally guilty of the murder. In January 1943, the jury acquitted five of the defendants and found seventeen guilty on several counts. Twelve were convicted of murder.

The trial, however, was deeply flawed. In October 1944, an appellate court reversed the convictions. The court's opinion systematically flayed the prosecution's handling of the case and Judge Charles William Fricke's supervision of the trial. The accused had been held incommunicado beyond the time at which they should have been arraigned, advised of their constitutional rights, and given access to counsel. Incriminating statements at trial had been beaten out of some of the defendants. No properly admissible evidence linked any of the defendants to the fatal assault on Diaz. Judge Fricke ran roughshod over defense lawyers, refused to let them communicate directly with their clients during the trial, and allowed prosecutors to skirt the rules of evidence to slip in damning statements.[8]

The accused were never retried. Whoever beat Jose Diaz to death that night got away with murder, thanks to the blinkered bungling of the cops and prosecutors. Judge Fricke shrugged off the higher court's scathing criticism and went on to enjoy a successful career as the doyen of tough law enforcement in Los Angeles.

The Sleepy Lagoon case was a turning point in the relationship between Mexican Americans in Los Angeles and the dominant culture, especially the LAPD. One researcher notes, "The absurdity of the case sent shockwaves through East Los Angeles. It was as if the community had been indicted with the boys."[9] Civil libertarians and community leaders organized the Sleepy Lagoon Defense Committee to appeal the flawed rush to judgment. Orson Welles, Anthony Quinn, and Rita Hayworth lent Hollywood star power. It was "the first effective mobilization of the Mexican Community in Southern California."[10] The affair is often cited as a civil rights and political landmark. It has inspired books, plays, movies, lay screeds, and scholarly articles.

The two prime corollaries of received civil libertarian wisdom about the case are that the defendants were railroaded and that there was no such thing as a "38th Street gang"—or, for that matter, any real Mexican American gangs—in 1942. The "gang," it is claimed, was the hyperbolic invention of racist cops and prosecutors, a sinister characterization of a bunch of kids just hanging out together in a loose affiliation. Eduardo Obregon Pagan asks the central question: "Were these young men and women 'baby gangsters' who organized for nefarious purposes, as the state of California . . . contended, or were they merely a casual group of acquaintances joined by circumstances?"[11] Of the railroad, there can be no doubt. The trial was a travesty by any measure. The "halo effect" of denying the existence of gangs in general and the 38th Street gang in particular, however, is contradicted by the studies of law enforcement and academic experts alike. The fact is that being railroaded and being a gang member were not then (and are not now) mutually exclusive conditions.

No matter how poorly handled or how racist the investigation and prosecution, no matter how innocent the youth were of this particular crime, there was something more than casual encounter going on in 1942 among the youth of the Thirty-eighth Street area. That something was the early incarnation—the embryonic form—of the Mexican American gang. The gangs of the early 1940s were, at a fateful moment, transitioning from youthful annoyances to hard-core trouble.

The Mexican immigrants of the Great Migration from 1900 to 1930 came primarily to work in the fields and orchards of big agriculture. But demand for agricultural labor was seasonal, based on the distinctive rhythms of planting, care, and harvest of each crop. When agribusiness needed labor, it needed it in enormous numbers of cheaply paid and easily dismissed temporary workers. The immigrant families therefore settled down in convenient places where they could find off-season work and from which they could get to the fields when their labor was demanded. For hundreds of thousands of Mexicans—like Jose Diaz's family—this was the Los Angeles basin.

Mexicans who came to Los Angeles were attracted to the tightly drawn insularity of the barrios by both affinity and exclusion. Living conditions there were harsh. Housing, water, power, sanitation, and other public services ranged from nonexistent to marginal. But like other waves of migrants throughout history and the world, Mexican migrants were most comfortable in neighborhoods where the people, language, and culture were familiar. Life in the barrio offered "a multi-tude of positive features," including "the kind of security that immi-grants and their children could find in no other place."[12] In any case, the migrants were excluded from "white" neighborhoods by the high cost of housing and by restrictive covenants and other legal and extralegal practices intended precisely to keep Mexicans, blacks, and Asians out. The hucksters who were boosting Los Angeles toward status as a world-class city quite openly envisioned it as a white paradise. John Clinton Porter, an Iowa native who was mayor of Los Angeles between 1929 and 1933, called it "the last stand of native-born Protestant Amer-icans."[13] The "greasers" had their place, all right, but it was offstage and out of sight.

More prime real estate was needed as the city grew. The site of the original pueblo—the old central plaza—became the downtown business district. The Mexicans were shoved out, their barrios pushed eastward. Within that general eastward thrust, Anglo developers claimed the bet-ter ground (like Boyle Heights) for the more affluent. "When the sur-rounding bean fields gave way to expensive housing tracts," notes re-searcher Joan Moore, "the barrios simply became the lower class part of town."[14] Mexicans and other poor immigrants cobbled their com-munities together in less-desirable ground—putting up shacks in the flood-prone gullies and ravines between the heights, for example. Black communities took hold in Watts and South Central. Development of public transportation opened more options for the Mexicans, who es-tablished barrios at available places along the line and were able to commute to some jobs. The real estate chessboard in Southern Califor-nia has been in play ever since. Whites have moved west to the ocean, north to the San Fernando Valley, and east to the desert, leapfrogging East Los Angeles, abandoning it to the resurgent Latino tide. In later years, whites fled to exurbs as the brown tide lapped at their suburban refuges in San Fernando and elsewhere.

Although net immigration was effectively suspended during the pe-riod of the Great Depression in the 1930s, it resumed as demand for la-bor rose during World War II, and it has continued almost uninter-rupted ever since. The "pipeline" pumping white Protestants into the Los Angeles basin has been replaced by a largely underground line pumping in poor, unskilled Latino immigrants from the south. Joan Moore, who has studied and written about the barrio gangs for decades, observes, "New waves of Mexican immigrants have continued to settle in poor Mexican barrios, as those barrios were vacated by upwardly mobile residents."[15] This continuous flood has had two principal impacts on the barrios of Southern California.

One impact is economic stagnation. While a steady stream of Latinos and their families have climbed out of poverty and its associated effects, the overall Latino community, taken as a statistical whole, remains mired at the bottom of the ladder. Why is this? The "standard explanation," writes historian Manuel Gonzales, is that "Anglos have consciously kept [Mexican Americans] in a state of subservience."[16] But Gonzales points to "a more basic problem," namely, "the gigantic influx of Mexican immigrants into the United States." As long as this immigration continues on "the same massive scale," he argues, the Mexican American community as a whole "will continue to occupy a position at the lower end of the American socioeconomic spectrum."[17] Joan Moore reaches much the same ultimate conclusion, writing that "the influx meant that [East Los Angeles] continued to be very poor."[18]

In addition to economic stagnation, Vigil notes that the "continuous waves of immigrants ensure that there is always a large pool of second-generation Mexican-Americans"—the very group among whom risks of gang involvement are greatest—and have kept the Los Angeles barrios "more culturally distinct."[19] Another researcher observes that, historically, "immigrants living in Southwestern enclaves often found it unnecessary to learn English or to adapt to American customs in food or clothing."[20] Moreover, many Mexicans in the Great Migration "were very reluctant to take on U.S. citizenship, often feeling that they would not gain much in a discriminatory society and would lose the protections that Mexican citizenship afforded them."[21]

This milieu of socioeconomic stagnation and cultural inertia—perpetually reinforced by illegal immigration—is the compost in which the Mexican American gangs rooted themselves and, over decades, grew into institutions inextricably intertwined with barrio life. It accounts for their stubborn longevity and immunity to "quick fixes." Gangs have always been a problem during large-scale immigration. In fact, the earliest youth gangs in Los Angeles were a "mixed bag" of Mexican, Irish, and Russian immigrants.[22] In the 1920s, East Los Angeles was a California version of New York's Lower East Side.[23] "Within a generation or two," however, most other immigrant groups "stabilized themselves": problems like youth gangs "were worked through and became less serious as each group acculturated."[24] The relatively swift acculturation that other immigrant groups experienced in the United States eluded the barrios of Southern California. "Mexican neighborhoods . . . saw gangs grow," reports one scholar, "while other cultures that began to thrive economically, namely the Irish and the Russian-Jewish, saw gangs dissipate."[25]

As early as the 1920s, some children of the Great Migration, the second generation, began to coalesce into informally organized social networks. These prototypical forms can hardly be called gangs in the sense of today's street gang, which is consistently directed toward violence and felonious criminality. They were, rather, "unsophisticated clutches of teens"—the police called them "tomato gangs," because their fistfights were often preceded by exchanged volleys of fruits and vegetables stolen from vendors' carts.[26] Some of these groups were originally sponsored by churches or social outreach organizations. Others were evocations of a Mexican tradition of male youth hanging out together in groups called *palomillas*.[27] "In Mexico, it's expected that young bucks will hang around and do daring, aggressive things," Vigil told the *Los Angeles Times* in 1988. "It's a cohorting tradition . . . common in all classes."[28]

Regardless of the impetus or exact shape the protogangs took, they were usually organized around a single barrio (in the 1930s, barrios came to include separate tracts of subsidized public housing) and often in age cohorts. Membership was informal and did not require the violent entry ritual common among later gangs—beating and sometimes commission of a criminal act, including murder, to prove one's steel. Neighbors did not call them "gangs" but referred to them in benign terms as "the boys from the barrio."[29] The 38th Street gang first appeared during the 1920s, along with others, such as the Alpine Street, Dogtown, and White Fence gangs.[30]

Eventually and perhaps inevitably, fighting gangs emerged in the late

1930s and early 1940s. Their members were drawn from the ever-expanding pool of marginalized youth who were estranged from the culture of their parents, rejected by the dominant society, and often left largely on their own. As communities grew and interacted, youth gangs rubbed against each other. This was often the result of members of different gangs being cast together in "alternative" or "special" schools, to which troublemakers and problem students were transferred. The schools were called *escuelas de burro,* or "dumb schools" (literally, "donkey schools"), by the kids, some of whom deliberately got themselves transferred to the schools because the curriculum was easy.[31] Rituals of marking one's territory and traditions of aggressively defending one's neighborhood and its synonymous gang developed. In some cases, as in the earliest days of the White Fence gang, schoolboys had to fight their way through hostile gang turf on the way to and from school. "Jumping in"—a short but intense beating at the hands of members to prove one's toughness and reliability in a fight—came to mark the moment of passage into the gang.

Barrio and gang became one in the minds of the gangsters, and for many, that merged notional thing also became their only meaningful internal identity. "My gang is my barrio," thought the gangster, "and my barrio is me." Joan Moore explains of the gangsters, "They were committed to one another, the barrio, the families, and the gang name in the status-setting fights that occurred in school and on the streets. They were bound by a norm of loyalty."[32]

In these formative years, gangs fought within the confines of a code of informal but widely accepted rules. For example, women, children, and families were not to be attacked or involved in violence. If a gang member had a beef with a member of another gang, it was more manly to call him out when he was not with his family, wife, girlfriend, or child and to duke it out man-to-man in what was known as a "fair fight." One's fellow members provided backup as necessary—for example, if the opponent's fellow gang members tried to interfere. Primary weapons were fists. Moore elaborates, "The fair fight established a pecking order, both within the gang and between groups, and did so in a highly personal tradition that tested the mettle of the fighters in a way that guns cannot do."[33]

In the late 1930s, arsenals were expanded to include sticks, clubs, chains, and knives. At this point, use of guns in gang altercations was rare, and those used were usually homemade zip guns.[34] The White Fence gang was apparently a leader in escalating the violence and may have been the first to regularly use commercially made guns.[35]

Gang life was fundamentally changed in the 1940s. For one thing, the violence became more lethal. Teenagers began to be killed in inter-gang clashes or other gang-related violence. Nobody called them "tomato gangs" any more. They became known as "boy gangs," and they increasingly attracted the attention of the police.[36] A deeper force was at work, however, as two widely different cultural streams came to-gether and created a powerfully defiant cultural amalgam. One was the pachuco culture adopted by some alienated Mexican American youth. The other was the jazz culture, particularly the clothing style that grew out of it—the so-called zoot suit. The resultant youth culture—one part fashion and one part personal style—repulsed the "good people" of the barrios, inspired fear and loathing within the dominant community, and eventually provided a powerful role model for young gang members.

A sea change swept over Mexican American society in California in the late 1930s and early 1940s. The population changed from immi-grants to children of immigrants. Far-reaching currents flowed beneath this fundamental change. Members of the second generation were more assertive politically than their parents, although it would be a while be-fore they organized an effective voice.[37] Families were stressed as the traditionally unquestioned right of the Latino male to rule dictatorially was undercut by the different family mores of the dominant culture and by opportunities for women outside of the home, which accelerated during World War II.[38]

Most important for gang history, Mexican American working-class youth became "increasingly estranged from a society unable to provide adequate jobs or education."[39] They chafed at the insular barrio bonds of custom and community that had comforted their parents. Were they Mexican, American, Mexican American, or none of the above? One an-swer for these youth was what Vigil calls "choloization," a sort of de-liberate embrace of marginal style in dress, language, and outlook, neither Mexican nor Anglo-American. A relatively small number of these youths embraced yet another, even more marginal subculture, that of the pachuco. The pachuco subculture was marked by a deliberately confrontational style in dress and mannerisms—indeed, in every way in which the pachuco interacted with both Mexican American and Anglo society.[40] "The message," explains Moore, "was that if the young Chicano was going no place in Anglo society, at least he would not be caught in the dreary grind of the past."[41]

Though "never very numerous," pachucos "exerted an enormous influence on a whole generation" of Mexican American youth through the 1940s and into the 1950s.[42] Everything about them was distinctive and a rebuke to the conventional, including personal bearing, hairstyle, language, and clothing. Male pachucos combed their hair smoothly back along the sides and tucked it into a "ducktail" in the rear. Female pachucas favored heavy makeup, short skirts, and exaggerated pompadour hairstyles. Distinctive tattoos came into vogue, most commonly the *cruz del barrio* (cross of the barrio) on the web of flesh between the thumb and forefinger.[43]

Pachucos and the mainstream Mexican American society held each other in mutual contempt.[44] In the schools, pachucos constantly challenged the masculinity of their "square" male peers by brazen acts, such as stealing lunches.[45] The pachucos boldly confronted the norms of segregation and marginalization. This cheeky behavior challenged social compromises that the mainstream Latino community had learned to live with. It also threatened efforts of community leaders to polish up the image of Mexican Americans.[46]

The cultural rebels adopted a syncretic language, Calo (the roots of which extend back to Spain and the exotic intersection of the worlds of bullfighters and the wandering Roma people), and modified it to their own ends. The use of Calo was partly a natural consequence of a generation caught between lost Spanish and inadequate English-language skills and partly cultural defiance, since "speaking *gabacho* was viewed as disloyalty" among the pachuco.[47] Calo later became a hallmark of the cholo subculture and an underground patois or criminal argot used by Latino gangs as a crude code and counterintelligence screening device to expose would-be infiltrators.

What came to symbolize the pachuco lifestyle more than anything else, however, was a distinctive male outfit called the "zoot suit"—high-waisted pants baggy at the knees; a long, loose-fitting coat; and a broad-brimmed, feathered hat. The entire ensemble was set off by a dangling watch chain. The basic style could be seen in Hollywood movies and high-fashion magazines of the day, but the pachucos pushed it to the extreme. The origins of the zoot suit are unclear. Some Latino chroniclers suggest that the style originated as a native costume in the town of Pachuca, Mexico, and was brought to Los Angeles by a gangster named Mickey Garcia. But this is most likely an ethnic urban myth, since there is neither evidence that such a Western suit was worn by the natives of Pachuca nor that Mickey Garcia was a real person. A more likely and better-documented trail leads to the suit's origins in black culture. It then gained national popularity as it was introduced by touring jazz musicians. The pachucos added their own distinctive flairs to the basic design.

In any case, not every pachuco wore a zoot suit, not every Mexican American who wore a zoot suit was a pachuco, not every pachuco was a gangster, and not every gangster was a pachuco. In fact, the gangsters of White Fence scorned the pachucos. But pachucos, gangsters, and zoot-suiters became conflated, and their numbers were greatly exaggerated. Law enforcement officials estimated that as many as two-thirds of working-class Mexican American young men wore the "drape," as the zoot suit was called in the argot of Los Angeles.[48] But more levelheaded contemporary estimates were that no more than 5 percent actually were zoot-suiters. For one thing, the suit was relatively expensive.[49] For another, wartime regulations rationed cloth to amounts suitable for more streamlined forms. This drove the sale of the popular zoot suits into the black market and "bootleg tailors."[50]

The reason for the dominant society's conflation and exaggeration of the pachucos, gangs, and the phenomenon of the zoot suit is clear. The zoot-suiter was a tangible, insolently open, and willfully subversive force that threatened everything America the Beautiful stood for in its hour of existential crisis. In a country mobilized for global war, immersed in racism, and awash with propaganda stressing the need for social conformity to advance the common effort, the zoot-suiters' outlandish garb mashed the dominant culture's rage button and held it firmly down. Conventional patriotic wisdom—expressed in art as well as political bombast—demanded conformity to its vision of "a homogenous nation of hardworking, church-going, white, middle-class people of middle American values."[51] The zoot suit became identified with those who wore it, and they were precisely the opposite of the idealized American patriot. They were brown and black men, perceived as damned well uppity, almost certainly raging criminals, and no doubt draft dodgers to boot. One researcher explains, "Like rock and roll a decade later, and the Panthers and hippies a decade after that, the zoot suiters seemed a direct assault on Anglo-Saxon America, on all that was straight and white and therefore good."[52]

The pachuco phenomenon had deep and long-lasting effects on Latino gangs and law enforcement alike in the Los Angeles area. Many of the barrio gangs' older boys, who had been a moderating influence as they matured, went off to war.[53] (Contrary to the period's poisonous myth that Latinos were draft dodgers, they in fact volunteered and suffered casualties in disproportionate number.) This left a vacuum of leadership. The younger gang cadres turned to the coolly in-your-face pachuco as a role model. The pachuco model then developed into the equally composed challenge of the "cholo style" that became associated with California's Mexican American gangs—khaki pants, plaid Pendleton shirt, polished shoes, and watch cap, bandana, or short-brimmed hat.[54] Like the pachuco look, the cholo look would be seized upon by many in the dominant Anglo culture as prima facie evidence of gangster involvement.

The police had their own pressures to contend with. Southern California boomed as the aircraft, shipbuilding, and other defense-related industries took off during the war. Police had to deal with a rapidly growing population and chaotic traffic. But they had likewise seen many of their more experienced and moderating officers off to war. Hastily recruited "war emergency officers" were rammed through an accelerated six-week training course and hurried out onto the streets. One researcher observes, "These were men unfit for military duty. It became commonplace for officers with limited physical or mental skills to respond to calls for service."[55] It is little wonder that something fundamental in the way cops looked at and interacted with Mexican American kids changed in this period. The maddening image of pachucos as wanton criminals mocking the war effort, informed through the racist lens of the day, slapped inexperienced cops right in the face. It left beat cops and supervisors alike frustrated, aching for chances to break heads and clean house. They got both, first in the Sleepy Lagoon murder case and then in the Zoot Suit Riots, which followed fast on its heels.

The site of the Williams Ranch is now an industrial area in the city of Bell. The water hole known as the Sleepy Lagoon has long since been paved over. In 1942, the irrigation reservoir was a swimming hole by day for Mexican American kids, who were barred from public pools, and a lover's lane by night. Some time before that, it had been the site of the exclusive Laguna Duck Club, a hunter's haven established by Henry W. O'Melveny, who founded Los Angeles's third-ranked power law firm, O'Melveny and Myers.[56]

Henry O'Melveny's career is a fine metaphor for the boom days of Los Angeles. He was born in Central City, Illinois, in 1859 and migrated with his family to Los Angeles in 1869. Following his father's professional footsteps, he became a successful lawyer. In 1906, he started a partnership that would eventually become O'Melveny and Myers. When Henry O'Melveny was not out hunting ducks on Sleepy Lagoon with his wealthy pals, he was busy making money with them. The O'Melveny firm prospered by representing the rich and powerful—the flint-eyed businessmen who cannily created the water and hydroelectric power systems that made the boosters' dream of Los Angeles possible; the farmers supplying factories with sugar beets, who coveted the backs and arms of Mexican laborers; and the bankers who kept the money flowing. Today, O'Melveny and Myers has an international practice. Former secretary of state Warren Christopher is its senior partner. The firm grossed $372.5 million in 1999.[57]

O'Melveny's world might as well have been on the far side of the moon for the farmworkers who came to celebrate a birthday party on the ranch the night Jose Diaz was beaten to death. The party was at the home of Amelio and Angela Delgadillo, in honor of their daughter, Eleanor. It was a typical fiesta, with a small band, dancing, good food, and alcohol. About twenty youth from the nearby town of Downey—most of them apparently Anglo kids—crashed the party. When the beer ran out around 11:00 p.m., they became unruly and were thrown out. The Downey crowd left angry and vowing to get even.

Meanwhile, an entirely separate group of young Mexican Americans from the Thirty-eighth Street area had driven in two cars out to the Sleepy Lagoon, which lay to the north of the cluster of bunkhouses that included the Delgadillo residence. As the Downey boys drove out on the rutted ranch road, they passed the Thirty-eighth Street group. Epithets in English and Spanish were exchanged. The young men from Downey appeared to move on, and the Thirty-eighth Street group dispersed into moonlit trysts. Half an hour later, shouts and groans shattered the quiet. The boys from Downey were back and proceeded to beat up the hapless Thirty-eighth Street lovers. For the Thirty-eighth Street victims, "there was little question about what they would do next: they drove straight back to their neighborhood."[58]

Within an hour, they had assembled a caravan of eight cars and some forty compatriots from the Thirty-eighth Street barrio and headed back to the lagoon. The water hole was deserted, but the youth could hear the sound of the Delgadillo birthday party, which was breaking up by then. About half of the Thirty-eighth Street group headed for the party, purportedly on the theory that their attackers from Downey might be there.

At this point—just as the avenging crowd arrived at the bunkhouse—two women from the Thirty-eighth Street group found Jose Diaz lying in the road. The main body of the group went on to the Delgadillo home, where they provoked a brawl and attacked the remaining partygoers with fists, feet, and sticks. The assault lasted about ten minutes, after which the Thirty-Eighth Street crowd left and repaired to their barrio to savor their misdirected "revenge." One of their number paused long enough to kick the supine Diaz, giving him a few licks with a stick for good measure. Nevertheless, the appellate court found that there was no admissible evidence linking any of the Thirty-eighth Street defendants to Diaz's fatal blow.

So how did Jose Diaz die? A posthumous confession emerged in the 2002 PBS television documentary *Zoot Suit Riots*. According to this version, a young man named Louie Encinas confessed early on to his sister that he had been thrown out of the party for causing problems, stayed behind with a few friends, and attacked Diaz as he drunkenly stumbled home. Louie Encinas was swept up in the LAPD dragnet but released. He committed suicide in 1972 during a botched bank robbery. Encinas's sister died in 1991, having never come forth with her brother's confession. But she did tell it to her daughter. All of the principals having passed on, Louie Encinas's niece related the story of the confession to PBS.[59] Eduardo Obregon Pagan doubts the credibility of this version. He concludes that Diaz was the victim of a simple mugging.[60]

Were the events that bracketed the unsolved Diaz murder—the sequence set in motion by the Downey boys' assault at the former duck pond—an early episode of 38th Street gang violence? Pagan argues that "the young men and women of 38th Street were clearly not a gang." For him, the persuasive evidence is that they "had no leadership hierarchy to speak of, no cash-flow operations, no initiation rites, uniforms, hand signs, or any other public displays of group membership."[61] But, assuming this was so, absence of evidence is not evidence of absence. The modern gang indicia that Pagan cites were only just developing in the early gangs of 1942. Historian of Chicano culture George Sanchez calls the group the "38th Street Club." He writes that it was "one of at least thirty-five 'gangs' in Los Angeles during the early 1940s" and that "these gangs differed from the complex east-side gangs that have operated in Los Angeles in recent decades." He notes that most of the defendants had already been in trouble with the law, although many of the incidents were minor.[62]

Moreover, the ability of the Thirty-eighth Street group to return to their neighborhood at midnight and assemble a force of eight carloads of youth ready to go back to the Sleepy Lagoon and seek out a fight—indeed, to force a brawl on an entirely innocent party of working people—is strong evidence that something more than a casual relationship existed among these youth. The sequence calls to mind a test for identifying whether a gang exists that is described by Fairfax County, Virginia, juvenile official David Rathbun: "If it walks like a duck and quacks like a duck, it's probably a duck."[63] The "duck test" can lead to dangerous stereotyping when it is applied to individual appearance ("he looks like a gangster, therefore he must be one"), because subcultures can overlap in dress and mannerisms. The cholo style of dress, demeanor, and even autos that is associated with Latino gangsters is widely popular among many law-abiding Latinos and some Anglos, as "the gang culture is diffusing into the middle class."[64] Vigil warns, "Even among the ducks, you have Daisy Duck, Donald Duck and Daffy Duck."[65] But concerted violent actions are a different matter, and here the deliberate acts of the Thirty-eighth Street group look and sound like the gang "duck," what has since become the lethal ritual of challenge, attack, and counterattack, often at the expense of an innocent bystander's life. It is beyond dispute that the violent 38th Street gang of today is real: witness the screwdriver rammed into Juan Romero's skull. That gang grew from something, and the trace of that something in 1942 is the embryonic fighting gang.

The Sleepy Lagoon episode marked a turning point in the relationship between the Mexican American community and law enforcement. What followed was a period during which the relationship changed "from one in which neither side had a particular view of the other one to one in which both sides viewed the other with deep suspicions and hostility."[66] This would have serious consequences for how the community and police dealt with the gangs flourishing in their midst. As the gangs got stronger and more violent during the 1950s and 1960s, community cooperation with the police waned.

Before the 1940s, the LAPD was generally not interested in devoting more than a bare minimum of resources to the barrios. "Other than hiring a handful of Mexican American officers to patrol the barrios," reports one researcher, "the department . . . had no specific policy for handling Mexican crime."[67] Throughout most of the first four decades of the twentieth century, the LAPD was deployed by the city's establishment as a head-cracking blunt instrument to keep organized labor out of Los Angeles and other troublemakers in line. It "protected friends and punished enemies of the machine in power," while it "gained the reputation of being one of the most corrupt police forces in the nation."[68] Under these conditions, the LAPD's interactions with Mexicans and Mexican Americans often distinguished the police either as head-cracking, strikebreaking enforcers or as shakedown artists. Gang members, like other Mexican American youth, were harassed by police when they ventured out of the barrio into white areas, but police did not routinely engage in mass enforcement actions within the barrios themselves. "All this was to change during the pachuco incidents," notes Joan Moore, "and there was soon a climate of suspicion and hostility between the barrios and the police."[69]

The pachucos and the increasingly visible gangs were not the only factors contributing to tensions. Nationwide, reform efforts to clean up police corruption were changing the very way police saw their role in society. The LAPD and other big city departments were moving from being passive reactors to working as paramilitary units proactively fighting crime. In 1938, reform efforts got a boost in Los Angeles when an investigator working for a reform coalition was seriously injured by a car bomb. Suspicion fell on a red-baiting intelligence unit of the police department. A recall election put reforming judge Fletcher Bowron in office as mayor. He sacked more than 150 corrupt or incompetent cops and nudged the LAPD to take its first sustained steps toward reform. Although the department would not institute comprehensive reform until the 1950s, it did adopt the idea of "police professionalism" that progressive reformers had been pushing nationally since the turn of the century.[70]

Implementing the progressive police reform agenda nationwide was like herding cats, given the lack of a uniform national police force and the independence of municipal departments. The first wave of reform focused on breaking the control of corrupt political bosses over the police. Reformers argued that police should be professionals, hired and judged on merit, not through patronage jobs doled out by political hacks. Reformers decided that the military, perceived as politically incorruptible, was the ideal model for police agencies. This fit in well with the view, widely accepted by the 1930s, that the country was engaged in an all-encompassing war on crime. "Criminals were the enemy, lawyers were their diplomats, policemen were the main line of defense, and civilians were combatants in the struggle"—under these conditions of total war, "no holds were barred, no tactics ruled out, no rights respected, and no mercy tendered."[71] Although the early reformers also believed that police departments could prevent crime as well as fight it—through such things as assigning police to work with juveniles through welfare bureaus and special courts—the thrust was to get the troops out onto the streets in hand-to-hand combat with the criminals. This push would inevitably lead to the presence of more police in the barrios, where the gangs were ensconced.

Another source of stress—exposed during the Sleepy Lagoon murder investigation—was a vein of raw racism that was apparently widely held within the Los Angeles law enforcement community, although perhaps not official doctrine. In August 1942, Lt. Edward Duran Ayres, chief of the Foreign Relations Bureau of the Los Angeles County Sheriff's Department, testified before the Los Angeles County Grand Jury on the causes of the "great proportion of crime by a certain element of the Mexican population" in the United States. His testimony became known as the Ayres Report.[72]

Lieutenant Ayres, who may have been of Latino descent himself, started his report with the reasonable observation that among a "number of factors" contributing to Mexican American crime were "economics, lack of employment, and small wages." He also sympathetically noted that Mexicans "are discriminated against and have been heretofore practically barred from learning trades," and he enumerated "segregation as evidenced by public signs and rules such as appear in certain restaurants, public swimming plunges, public parks, theatres and even in schools." After half a dozen opening paragraphs in this vein, however, Ayres dismissed them with a rhetorical wave of the hand and turned to the "basic cause that is even more fundamental than the factors already mentioned." The "biological basis," he argued, was "the main basis to work from."

Citing the difference between wild cats and domesticated cats ("while one may be domesticated the other would have to be caged to be kept in captivity"), Ayres opined, "Basically it is biological—one cannot change the spots of a leopard." The biological taint is the Indian blood in the Mexican, which is essentially "Oriental" in origin. In August 1942, it was not necessary to connect the dots between the evil characteristics of "Oriental" blood and the infamous Japanese attack on Pearl Harbor of December 7, 1941. Ayres explained, "The Caucasian, especially the Anglo-Saxon, when engaged in fighting, particularly among youths, resort to fisticuffs and may at times kick each other, which is considered unsportive, but this Mexican element considers all that to be a sign of weakness, and all he knows and feels is a desire to use a knife or some lethal weapon . . . to kill, or at least let blood."

Ayres's testimony stunned community leaders. Almost a century after the United States conquest, the racist underpinnings of Manifest Destiny were revealed to be deeply imbedded in the police forces of Southern California. Moreover, the Ayres report was the bellwether of a branch of "scientific" criminology that had developed over the several preceding decades. It held that Mexicans were not merely racially inferior but inherently—genetically—criminal.[73]

In June 1943, whatever fragile remnants of comity remained between the LAPD and the Mexican American community were shattered with the sledgehammer blow of the so-called Zoot Suit Riots. Hostility had been growing for months between Mexican American youth and the thousands of predominantly white servicemen stationed in Southern California. The rancor was punctuated by fistfights and skirmishes between small groups. Such friction between local youth and servicemen is not uncommon where a military base abuts a civilian population. But "it is hard to imagine two lifestyles so completely at odds" as that of the middle-American white boys with short hair and crisp uniforms enduring the rigors of boot camp and preparing for combat and that of the nonconformist brown-skinned Mexican American boys wearing zoot suits.[74] One scholar identifies it as "a textbook case of race and loathing rubbing up against each other."[75]

On June 3, after a clash on May 31 left a sailor with a broken jaw, a group of about fifty servicemen—mostly sailors and marines—armed themselves with belts and clubs and went to town, looking for Mexican Americans wearing zoot suits. The ensuing riots grew to involve thousands of servicemen and civilian allies. Their targets soon broadened to include any young Mexican American of either gender in the path of the rampaging soldiers, sailors, and marines. Boys wearing zoot suits were beaten, stripped of their clothing, and left bloody and dazed, but other Mexican Americans were beaten up simply on principle. The LAPD deliberately looked the other way while the riots raged, moving in only to arrest the beaten Mexican Americans. The riots were brought under control only when President Roosevelt—under diplomatic pressure from Mexico, which had just declared war on the Axis powers—ordered the military to restrict the servicemen to their bases.

The fallout from the Sleepy Lagoon murder case and the Zoot Suit Riots for the future of Latino gangs was enormous. The gang mythos was inflated from common criminality to the heroic proportions of common defense. "It is difficult to imagine what might have happened to these gangs if the zoot suit persecutions had not occurred," writes Joan Moore. "The boys that fought the marauding sailors in East Los Angeles were seen by their younger brothers as heroes of a race war."[76] The conduct of the LAPD and the governing establishment it represented was hardly such as to inspire respect for the rule of law in the barrios. The convicted gangsters from Thirty-eighth Street, however, became folk heroes. It was legend on the streets that, even though cruelly abused, they conducted themselves with dignity and stoic resolve while in prison. "This behavior set a new standard for Hispanic gang members who were subsequently sent to jail," according to Al Valdez, a former investigator for the district attorney's office in Orange County, California. "They demonstrated a type of gang pride and resolve that had never been seen before."[77]

By the end of World War II, many barrio kids had the mentality that "gangs were there for protection, although no one could define what that meant."[78] Moreover, community cooperation with police in investigating gang violence began to evaporate as the attitude developed that "the departed's homies would take care of it," so there was "no need for police."[79] Gang homicides escalated during the 1950s, as drugs and drug trafficking became an increasing part of the gang scene. State and federal drug investigations sent growing numbers of gang members to prison.

A vicious cycle was started as "the larger gang subculture began to incorporate mythologies about coping in prison, and these stories became a part of gang tradition for young gang members."[80] Going to prison became another rite of passage, accepted as a "normal" part of gangster life. In 1953, Deuel Vocational Institute opened as a model for progressive rehabilitation schemes for youthful offenders. The juvenile offenders quickly banded together to protect themselves from adult sexual predators, with whom they were mixed during shower times. A few key members of this informal band were impressed by the methods of the Italian Mafia and the respect its incarcerated members got in prison. They organized their own Mexican Mafia, which later became known as La Eme (Spanish for the letter *M*), or simply Eme. By 1967, the Mexican Mafia was a powerful force and controlled a number of prison yards. Its bloody command over what happened in prisons enabled it to extend its reach out into the streets, and within a few decades, La Eme controlled important aspects of drug trafficking in Southern California.

At about the same time that the Mexican Mafia was germinating in the California prison system, a new kind of Latino gang was hatching in Downtown Los Angeles, around Eighteenth Street and Broadway. It grew out of the discriminatory policies of the Clanton Street gang, then one of the most powerful gangs in the city. The Clanton Street gang limited its membership to candidates who could prove that they were of 100 percent Mexican ancestry. The youngsters who were turned away by Clanton eventually organized their own gang and called it the 18th Street gang. But organizing was one thing. Solving the problem was another. "They were getting their asses kicked by Clanton," says LAPD gang expert Sgt. Frank Flores. "So they opened the books to non-Mexicans."[81] The move was dramatic for a Mexican American gang, directly contrary to the temper of the times. It was an era of rising Chicano consciousness, during which the Mexican American gangs developed aggressive hostility toward immigrants from Central America and elsewhere. Opening its books gave the struggling 18th Street gang a massive infusion. One researcher reports, "The lax requirements led the gang to spread like wildfire among immigrant and disenfranchised kids, especially those tired of Clanton."[82]

The hybrid 18th Street gang would become the biggest street gang in Los Angeles and one of the most violent in history. Like Mara Salvatrucha, it would also be transplanted to Central America by deported criminal aliens (as Barrio Dieciocho and M-18) and then blow back all across the United States. In 2007, the FBI would add the 18th Street gang to the mandate of its MS-13 National Gang Task Force (although it would not change the unit's name).

While the street gangs of the 1950s and 1960s were mutating into the violent forms of today, the LAPD got serious about reform. It recast itself into a professional model that would be the envy of the police world. The department's first specialized gang squads were sent into the barrios in the 1950s.[83] They were dispatched by William H. Parker, whom the department's history describes as its "most distinguished Chief."[84] Parker Center, the LAPD headquarters, is named after him.

Parker was a leader among the "second wave" of police reformers, who rejected the earlier idea that police could prevent crime by attacking its root causes through welfare and recreational programs. He and others argued that the "thin blue line" could "contain but not convert criminals, repress but not prevent crime."[85] A corollary was that police should go on the attack with aggressive measures known variously as preventive patrol, stop-and-search, stop-and-frisk, and field interrogation. Police departments sought quantitative measures to evaluate officer aggressiveness. Everything an officer did was counted, weighed, and ranked. The department valued felony arrests more highly than responding to a radio call, a moving traffic violation more than a parking ticket. Researchers explain that "highly productive officers were the ones who generated the most felony arrests."[86]

These ideas were all wrapped up in the LAPD's proactive policing package, which aimed to "stop crime before it happened," according to Daryl Gates—a controversial chief brought down in 1992 by the Rodney King sociopolitical melodrama. The cops "knew who the troublemakers were" and did not hesitate to put them under close scrutiny. "If someone looked out of place in a neighborhood," said Gates, "we had a little chat with him."[87] One of the department's sternest critics, University of Southern California journalism professor Joe Domanick, described proactive policing sharply: "You had to hit the street hard and be aggressive."[88]

Proactive policing was not merely an academically good idea for the LAPD. It was a necessity. In the words of current chief William J. Bratton, "the LAPD is one of the most understaffed police departments in the world . . . half the size of what it should be to police Los Angeles."[89] In 2003, the LAPD had 9,307 full-time sworn personnel, making it the third largest police department in the nation, after New York (with

35,973) and Chicago (with 13,469). It ranks considerably further down a list scaled by the ratio of full-time sworn personnel to hundred thousand residents. The LAPD's ratio was twenty-four per hundred thousand, compared to Chicago's forty-seven and New York's forty-five. Washington, D.C., with 3,632 sworn officers, had the highest ratio, at sixty-five.[90] The LAPD also has a larger area to police with its smaller force. The city of Los Angeles covers 498 square miles, New York City 301 square miles, and Chicago 228.[91]

In comparison, the Miami-Dade County Police Department covers 2,100 square miles—four times the area of Los Angeles—with 3,178 sworn personnel at a ratio of only fourteen per hundred thousand residents in 2003. The force was even smaller in 2008, reporting 2,900 sworn officers.[92] The ability of the Miami-Dade department to operate at a much lower staffing level may reflect more than a difference in police administration. It is also likely an artifact of the fundamentally different ways in which the Latino communities in the two metropolitan areas see themselves, their histories, and their relation to their police forces. Patricia Nelson Limerick's observation that "a minority by conquest is not the same as a minority by immigration," although made with specific reference to American Indians, is, in important ways, just as cogent to the difference between the Latino communities in Los Angeles and Miami.[93]

Given the LAPD's thin staffing and the sprawl of Los Angeles, backup for an officer in trouble "is likely not around the corner and is probably a long time in coming," according to Bratton. The LAPD has had two practical choices on the street. It could stay out of trouble by ignoring or dodging it, or it could deflect problems in the first place by projecting an intimidating aura of mastery over every situation—touting the stereotypical street cop with the silvered sunglasses, bulging biceps, and kick-your-ass attitude. Reinforced by the tenets of the police professionalism reform movement, the LAPD in 1950s chose the latter course and has ever since utilized "a uniquely proactive style of police work."[94]

But proactive policing had its downside, reinforcing the deleterious effects of the department's historical role as an occupying force deployed to ensure untroubled rule by the white elite. In the opinion of journalist Lou Cannon, the "racist nature of the LAPD reflected the attitudes of the society it served."[95] The LAPD was not alone in this regard. In addition to society's general tenor, police recruiting in the early 1960s favored men with military backgrounds and the sons of police families. These recruiting biases "basically filled America's police departments with fairly well-disciplined white males."[96] The recruits, who often pulled the weekend and night shifts shunned by veteran officers, had little understanding of or sensitivity to the problems of black and Latino communities to which they were deployed. "By the end of the 1960s," researchers report, "police had basically become an occupation force for high-crime, inner city neighborhoods."[97]

The new police patrol practices aggravated racial and ethnic tensions in minority neighborhoods, not only in Los Angeles, but all over America. They rarely caused problems in white neighborhoods, because "few whites used the streets in ways that aroused the suspicion of the patrolmen."[98] But preventive policing ran head-on into cultural conflict in minority neighborhoods where teenagers and young adults spent much of their time on the streets and stoops, sometimes out of tradition and sometimes out of necessity. Aside from whatever biases individual officers had, even neutral attempts at stop-and-search and field interrogations were bound to fall heavily onto a broader spectrum than the criminal element at which they were aimed. "To the dismay of some blacks, Mexicans, and Puerto Ricans," notes one scholar, "these changes seriously threatened their life styles and the values, attitudes, and customs underlying them."[99]

In the proactive world of the LAPD, Latinos found "out of place," in white neighborhoods, were "spotted, circled, checked out and 'moved' every few blocks, moved back to where they belonged." In their own neighborhoods—their own proper place in the suspicious scheme of proactive policing—minority youth were subjected to "constant mind games, hassles, intimidation and shakedown by the cops."[100] Young black and Latino males complained that police—regardless of the officers' race—often stopped them for minor traffic violations or for no apparent reason at all. They were then made to "prone out"—lie facedown, spread-eagled.[101]

Gang enforcement programs developed in the 1970s and 1980s inevitably increased the abrasive contact between police and youth in minority neighborhoods. Young blacks and Latinos precisely matched the demographics of the street gangs. From the cops' point of view, one of the more effective ways to root out the gangsters and understand their networks was to use a technique that the LAPD's CRASH antigang units called "jamming," a system of deliberately confrontational contact intended to generate intelligence and suppress gang activity. One "jamming" technique was hostile field interrogations—stopping people who looked like gangsters, asking them a lot of questions, and saving the information for later analysis or leads in gang-related crime cases. Another was to confront the ones they knew to be gangsters—the ones who "looked like ducks, walked like ducks, and talked like ducks"—to get across the message that they were being vigilantly watched. According to one CRASH sergeant, "jamming" reminded gangsters that "they don't rule the streets."[102]

"We were harassing the gangs," said former LAPD chief Daryl Gates. But Gates scoffed at suggestions that the harassment violated the civil rights of the targets of jamming: "No one seems to talk about the civil rights violations of the good people out there . . . that are caused by gangs. . . . All we talk about is how we violated the civil rights of these idiot gang members."[103] Thus, for decades, there has been high-voltage tension in Los Angeles between, on the one hand, the thin blue line of iron-jawed cops whose mythos is that they hold back chaos by getting in its face and not yielding an inch and, on the other hand, the sullen pushing back of the underclass against the perceived arbitrariness of proactive authority.

Notwithstanding the LAPD's reforms, gang violence continued to accelerate. Although it moved in fits and starts—up one year, down the next—the overall trend of violence and increased lethality was up. California has experienced three periods during which its overall homicide rate steadily increased to new peaks, fell back briefly, and then rose again—from 1965 through 1988, from 1989 through 1993, and from 1999 to the present.[104] Part of this phenomenon reflects similar national trends. Over the last twenty-five years of the twentieth century, the increase in homicides in the United States was so great that it became a major public health issue.[105] But a substantial part of the increase in California was driven by gang homicides, especially in Los Angeles County.

By the mid-1970s, "guns were normal, and a fair fight (one person on one person without weapons) was fairly unusual"; the old gang code was junked as gangsters started shooting into houses where mothers and other "noncombatants" lived.[106] The practice of drive-by shootings—blasting away with a firearm from a moving car—started in the 1970s, and real guns (as opposed to the old zip guns) were used to kill and maim enemies, rather than scare them off.[107] One explanation for the increased gun violence was the tendency for each generation to try to outdo the preceding generation of gang members in *locura*, or crazy behavior. But another was a significant increase in the number of handguns on the civilian market during the 1970s.

Of 27,302 homicides in Los Angeles from January 1979 through December 1994, law enforcement determined that 7,288 (26.7 percent) were related to gang activity. In 1979, gang-related homicides accounted for 18.1 percent of all homicides in Los Angeles County. By 1994, they accounted for 43 percent. A detailed study of more than five thousand of these gang-related murders found that 56.6 percent of the victims were Latinos, 36.7 percent blacks.[108]

After a decade of escalation during the 1970s to a peak in 1980, Latino gang murders in East Los Angeles suddenly dropped significantly. The Los Angeles County Sheriff's Department counted seventy-one in 1980, forty-three in 1981, and twenty-nine in 1983.[109] Optimists thought that the key to gang violence had been found in various "outreach" programs and police gang suppression. Other observers were focused on black gangs, such as the Crips and the Bloods. Los Angeles was one of the first cities in which crack cocaine appeared, and it became a national gateway for the drug. Violence soared among black gangs as guns were used to "rationalize" the new drug market and allocate turf among gangs.

For a time, the focus of public and media attention on the crack wars masked the fact that Latino gang violence bottomed and began to soar again in the latter 1980s. The increase was partly caused by the return to the streets of veteran gang members who had been imprisoned under tough new laws in the 1970s. They were hardened and eager to take control again. Younger gang members were willing to start the killing again to prove that they were even more loco than the *veteranos*. Another factor was the mass marketing of high-capacity semiautomatic pistols during the 1980s. Known as the "wonder nines," these nine-millimeter guns quickly became gang favorites. The proportion of Los Angeles gang homicides in which semiautomatic pistols were used skyrocketed after 1987.[110] Armed encounters were more lethal—more likely to result in death—because more rounds of ammunition can be carried in a semiautomatic pistol (from ten to as many as nineteen) and because rounds can be pumped out faster than through the old-fashioned six-shot revolvers that dominated the century before the 1980s. This amount of firepower dramatically increases the likelihood that someone, not necessarily the intended target, will get hit by one of the rounds sprayed out during the increasingly popular drive-by shootings.

It was during this period that the Salvadoran refugees landed in the midst of territories controlled by the Mexican American gangs. Although some of the Salvadorans joined the "open-book" 18th Street gang, others preferred to form their own gang, Mara Salvatrucha. The leadership of the Mara Salvatrucha gang regarded the Salvadorans who joined the 18th Street gang as traitors. Bad blood quickly developed. A war broke out between the gangs for control of the Rampart area of Los Angeles. The war continues today. Members of both gangs—from San Salvador to Boston—are sworn to attack members of the other gang on sight.

The LAPD reacted with an iron fist under the leadership of Chief Gates as the Latino gang wars spiraled into waves of bloody violence. Meanwhile, the federal government remained deliberately aloof from the bloody fray. The Justice Department, the FBI, and other federal law enforcement agencies regarded gangs as a local "street crime" problem. None of them were about to send their highly skilled investigative agents out into the streets to arrest common hoodlums. But that was all about to change. The Feds were going to be dragged into the fray by the scruff of their necks.

People, I just want to say . . . can we all get along?

Can we get along?

—RODNEY G. KING, MAY 1, 1992

4

AFTER THE RIOTS:

THE DAWN OF FEDERALIZATION

The sun rose over Southern California at 6:04 a.m. on the morning of Thursday, April 30, 1992. It had cleared the San Gabriel Mountains to the east by 6:30 a.m., when FBI agent Brian Truchon left his home in Agoura, an unincorporated community in the Conejo Valley. That valley is one of a series that undulate through the mountains north of the Los Angeles basin. Predominantly white suburbs branch out from the main roads into the nooks and crannies of these rolling valleys.

Beyond the Conejo Valley, over the Simi Hills in Ventura County, lies the city of Simi Valley, home since 1991 to the Ronald Reagan Presidential Library. When the area was developed in the 1950s, signs warning "No niggers or dogs allowed" were commonly painted on its rock formations.[1] A local newspaper editor candidly described Simi Valley in 1992 as a "lily-white community," with most of its residents coming from Los Angeles, "escaping the big city and its problems."[2] Several hundred Los Angeles Police Department officers lived in Simi Valley. This was not unusual. About 83 percent of the force lived outside the LA city limits.[3] But Simi Valley was special. It was rated the second safest city of one hundred thousand or more in America, for good reason. The town liked cops, and cops liked the town. Local prosecutors described the Simi Valley Police Department as having a "heavy badge," meaning it took a hard line on crime and no sass from suspected criminals.[4]

Simi Valley was on Brian Truchon's mind that morning. At 3:15 p.m. the preceding afternoon, a Simi Valley jury lit a fuse. Hearing a case moved to Ventura County from Los Angeles County on fairness grounds, the jury acquitted four LAPD officers on felony charges of assault with a deadly weapon and using excessive force under color of authority. The charges grew out of a thrashing they gave a black man, a convicted felon on parole, Rodney Glen King, in the course of his arrest after a high-speed midnight chase. By 5:00 p.m. on Wednesday afternoon, word of the acquittals hit the highly charged streets of South Central, originally a black enclave, but now increasingly mixed with Latino immigrants. All hell broke loose. That explosion of racial violence is said to be "the worst single episode of urban unrest in American history."[5] The fallout changed the then thirty-one-year-old Truchon's life, thrust him into a new assignment, and pushed the FBI to shift its efforts against street gangs into high gear. It marked the dawn of the federalization of gang enforcement. Acrimony in the riot's wake left the proud LAPD shattered, at war internally, and drifting like a ship without a rudder.

Six-feet-three FBI agent Truchon looks back with fondness on the time he spent in Los Angeles, between 1991 and 1996. "I loved every minute of it," he says. "Except the traffic. Eventually it just became too much and I had to get out of there."[6] That April morning, he guided his silver Ford Thunderbird, a take-home "bucar" (FBI jargon for "bureau car"), onto the Ventura Freeway, drove east to Interstate 405, and headed south. He passed the Sherman Oaks Galleria shopping mall—erstwhile icon of the San Fernando Valley's suburban culture, memorialized in 1982 in Frank Zappa's song "Valley Girl" and the film *Fast*

Times at Ridgemont High—and cut through the Santa Monica Mountains to the exit at Wilshire Boulevard in West Los Angeles. The FBI office is on the upper floors of the federal office building that rises above the southeast corner of that intersection. The building—dismissed by one critic as "a steel cage with a glass skin in a white corset" and a "pasty white pie"[7]—offers a commanding view of Los Angeles, splayed out to the east and south.

"Surreal," Truchon says of his commute that morning. "Very surreal." The freeways were deserted. The empty highways were an eerie contrast to Wednesday evening's nightmare, when it seemed that "everyone in the whole world" was clawing frantically to get away from the violence and out of Los Angeles. Densely packed traffic moved by inches over hours. Even on an ordinary day, the commute could be a nerve-racking grind. In 1992, 80 percent of those who commuted from Truchon's neighborhood drove into the city alone.[8] A one-way trip to or from Agoura took forty-five minutes at best. With the slightest problem, the trip doubled to an hour and a half. Truchon made it in twenty minutes on that Thursday morning.

"I distinctly remember thinking of the Omega Man," he recalls. In the opening moments of the 1971 movie *The Omega Man,* Charlton Heston—as Col. Robert Neville, apparently the only human survivor of a biological war—drives a convertible through deserted Downtown Los Angeles. The reference is evocative. In Boris Sagal's dystopian vision of Los Angeles, Heston embodies Western culture and ultimately becomes a bathetic Christ figure. He makes an armed last stand against fatally infected albino mutants seeking to destroy all scientific knowledge and level society to brutish medievalism. Some today see the struggle against Latino gangs in equally apocalyptic terms, as Anglo-Saxon culture's last stand against a tidal wave from south of the border.

Feeling as alone as the Omega Man, Truchon parked his car in an empty lot, walked through the silent lobby, and took the elevator to the tenth floor. The agent he relieved, his supervisor, had been up all night. He greeted Truchon with a new assignment that would morph into a whole new job for Truchon and become the FBI's first major foray into the world of Los Angeles gangs.

The day before, Truchon and the other agents of the Los Angeles field office had a front-row seat as the disorder unfolded in what he calls "an LA moment." Such moments include earthquakes, fires, mudslides, high-speed chases, celebrity murders, and now this incident—all covered live in minute detail by one of the most aggressive TV markets in the world. Take your pick of what to call it: the Rodney King Riots, the Los Angeles Riots, the Rodney King Uprising, or the 1992 Insurrection. It was the worst of a series of race-related disorders that had wracked the city periodically since the United States seized it from Mexico.

The LA field office is one of the FBI's great fiefdoms. It has the third greatest number of agents among the bureau's field offices. Its jurisdiction covers seven counties: Los Angeles, Orange, Riverside, San Bernardino, San Luis Obispo, Santa Barbara, and Ventura. Eighteen million people live within the forty thousand square miles of its province.[9] Truchon came to Los Angeles from Salt Lake City, one of the smallest offices, where he spent his first four years after graduating from the FBI Academy in 1987. In Los Angeles, he was assigned to the Joint Terrorism Task Force. He spent most of his time with local cops and other federal agencies investigating skinheads and domestic terrorists.

The FBI had already begun refocusing its efforts as the cold war wound down. Over the long history of that standoff, the FBI devoted a substantial part of its resources to foreign counterintelligence—hunting down spies. Although the number was secret, it was commonly estimated at the time that out of a total of 10,350 agents, about 2,500 were assigned to foreign counterintelligence. On January 9, 1992, Attorney General William P. Barr told a press conference that he was asking Congress to approve "the largest single reallocation of resources in FBI history."[10] About three hundred agents would be reassigned from foreign counterintelligence duties to a new program announced by FBI director William B. Sessions on the same day—the Safe Streets Violent Crimes Initiative.[11] "Call it a peace dividend," one official was quoted as saying.[12] Driven by the crack cocaine phenomenon of the previous decade, the Safe Streets Initiative was to focus on violent crime, particularly street gangs. It would bring to bear the expertise that the FBI had developed in using sophisticated investigative techniques and tough federal sentencing laws to take down organized criminal enterprises like the Mafia, or La Cosa Nostra—the LCN, as the FBI prefers to call it. To this day, the Safe Streets Initiative remains the basic architecture of the FBI's antigang programs.

The "largest reallocation" in FBI history was in fact a modest staffing change. No new agents were hired. No players were added to the board; the pieces were just shifted around. Indeed, Sessions had argued only months earlier that the bureau needed more, not fewer, foreign counterintelligence agents. His theory was that foreign spying was as big as ever but had shifted from military to economic targets.[13] Nevertheless, the Safe Streets Initiative was a genuine effort to deal with the challenges of a changing world. The three hundred reassignments for foreign counterintelligence agents slowly trickled down to FBI offices across the nation. The LA field office announced in February that twenty-two agents would be reassigned to focus exclusively on gangs.[14] In San Francisco, ten agents were moved.[15] The pace was measured, if not downright leisurely. In Los Angeles, the bureau began the new initiative by convening a series of meetings with other law enforcement agencies and community groups to decide how best to use the agents.

None of the change had yet affected Brian Truchon. He was hitting his stride as an experienced FBI agent, working in a city he loved, among people whose competence he respected.

Brian Truchon's dad was bitten by the gold bug in the early 1970s. The result was an excellent adventure. Brian was born in 1961 to classic midwestern stock—hardworking, blue-collar parents—in the Chicago suburb of Evergreen Park. His father never made it to high school. Driven by necessity, he dropped out of school and became a welder. He was also handy at repairing mechanical things. "I never saw a repairman in our home," Truchon says. "My dad fixed everything in our house and did all of the work on our car." The handyman gene carried over into Brian. "Much to my wife's dismay," he jokes, "I do all the home repair stuff." Truchon's mother was a licensed beautician who ran a one-chair beauty shop in the family basement. He remembers seeing "little old ladies with their hair pulled through that funny plastic hat" and can still recall the distinctive odor of the chemicals his mother used to treat their hair with permanents and dye jobs.

Brian was a "later-life child." He arrived eighteen years after his brother and sixteen years after his sister. Raised, in effect, as an only child, he was steeped in the traditions of a world deeply committed to old-fashioned values. He learned the reality and merits of hard work from the object example of his parents' daily toil. His elementary education at Evergreen Park's Most Holy Redeemer religious school added another dimension. "The students are well behaved and there is no use of profanity," a student's parent enthused in a comment posted on the school's Internet Web site in 2003. Young Brian became a voracious reader. "I read everything I could get my hands on in every spare moment," he recalls.

His parents instilled two other qualities in Brian. One was the value of bettering himself through education, using the lever of learning to lift himself beyond the daily grind and limited horizon of their lives. "You can do it our way, the tough way," he recalls them saying during their constant life mentoring. "Or you can go to school, get an education, and do it a better way." Another inspiration was the worth of the noble quest. "My dad was a dreamer," Brian explains. "He loved the pursuit of ideals. He was a Don Quixote, always chasing windmills."

One such windmill appeared on the Truchon family horizon in 1971, when Brian was ten years old. It was the legend of the Lost Dutchman Gold Mine. Some dismiss the legend as pure fabrication. Others insist that it is true. Truth or fancy, the basic story goes something like this: Sometime around 1860, Jacob Waltz, a German immigrant miner, claimed to have found an incredibly rich vein of virtually pure gold. The lode was hidden somewhere in the Superstition Mountains east of Phoenix, Arizona. The mine was so well hidden among rugged natural features that one could walk right over it without seeing it. Waltz (whose name is spelled variously) tantalized his contemporaries by disappearing into the desert wilderness from time to time, carefully covering his tracks, then popping up with just enough gold to sustain his credibility. He supposedly revealed the location on his deathbed in 1891. But those who heard his description were never able to find the lode.

Since then, hundreds of "authentic" maps have drawn tens of thousands of prospectors into the Superstitions. Known as "Hell's Backyard," the harsh, furnace-hot mountain desert is bone-dry and teems

with the venomous Gila monster, scorpion, and rattlesnake. The Superstitions have been the site of mysterious deaths (including rumored be-
headings), disappearances, and reports of alien abductions. None of
that deterred Brian Truchon's father. "When my dad became aware of
the legend, he was totally dialed into it," Truchon says in a recollection
half pride and half nostalgia. "He thought he had as good a chance as
anyone else to find it. He really believed that if you worked hard at
something, you can do it."

For two summers in a row, the Truchons piled into their 1967 Dodge
Coronet and drove from Evergreen Park, on the old U.S. Route 66 ("the
Mother Highway"), to the middle of the Arizona desert. There they
were magically transformed into prospectors. It was a perfect and exotic match for a boy of Brian's age. A car trunk stuffed with pickax,
shovel, and the essential miner's gold pan; wandering through rock
hounds' stores, bulging with the very stuff of legend, in search of the ultimate map; the strange and dangerous desert environment—his young
friends back in Chicago could only read about such things. "Everywhere we went in the desert area we ran into rattlesnakes coiled up under bushes and rocks, scorpions that scampered across our path, and on
several rare occasions a sighting of the Gila monster," Truchon remembers. "My dad took it all in stride. But my mother was not a big fan of
reptiles of any type. Rattlesnake sightings kept her on constant watch."

Brian was assigned the task of map reader for the expedition (a skill
that served him well later as an army pathfinder). He was just as "dialed
in" as his dad. "I was convinced that, hey, we can do it," he recalls. Like
the thousands of others who pried at the desert, however, they never
found the mine. He remembers finding "more than our share of iron
pyrite," a crystalline mineral also known as "fool's gold" because it is
often mistaken for the real thing by amateur miners.

In 1973, the Truchons retired and moved to Phoenix. Brian went
from winters playing ice hockey on the frozen surface of a flooded ball
field to the perennial heat of the desert. "I came to know the desert, and
I really fell in love with everything about being there," Truchon says. "I
have always been a fan of the Old West. Even as a kid in Chicago, I read
a lot of the old gunfighter books. I loved [director] John Ford's movies
and John Wayne movies. One of my favorite movies is *Gunfight at the*

O.K. Corral, with Burt Lancaster and Kirk Douglas. And then I was actually there. You could drive off the main road a little bit and see it exactly as it was hundreds of years ago. It was just the way I had imagined it, even in the images of the black-and-white movies."

These were the early foundations of Brian Truchon's life, youthful experiences that imbued specific qualities that serve him well as an FBI agent. His intense practicality about the hard edge of life, tempered with belief in the worth of ambition, is accompanied by a commitment to a system that rewards true merit. All this is fueled by his intellectual curiosity. Yet, when watching him in the midst of an international conference about violent street gangs, it is easy to believe that part of his mind is thinking of the peaceful solitude of the Arizona desert.

L os Angeles is a tough place to be a police officer," says Truchon. He worked closely with local law enforcement, first on the Joint Terrorism Task Force and then on one of the FBI's first antigang task forces. "The LAPD and the Los Angeles sheriff's office are some of the best I have ever worked with," he continues. "But Los Angeles also has some of the best TV coverage in the world. They focus on the LAPD like a laser beam. In my experience, police in Los Angeles were absolute professionals. But they were in a no-win situation. One little slipup, and that's all you need."

On the night of March 2, 1991, Rodney King provoked a historic "slipup." Near midnight, after hours of heavy drinking, King led California Highway Patrol officers on a five-mile chase along the Foothill Freeway at speeds that reached 115 miles per hour. The chase began near exit 11 at Sunland Boulevard, where the 1978 flick *Corvette Summer* was filmed. (It starred Mark Hamill, who went on to fame as Luke Skywalker in the *Star Wars* movie series.) King left the Freeway at exit 6A, where the highway action scenes in the NBC television series *CHiPs* (1977–83) were filmed. When he finally stopped, King was in LAPD territory, just east of the city of San Fernando.

His two passengers obeyed police commands, exited the car, lay facedown, and were handcuffed. In contrast, King originally refused to leave the car. When he did, he engaged in bizarre behavior, shaking his butt at a female highway patrol officer and jabbering nonsensically.

LAPD sergeant Stacey Koon, who had taken command of the scene, hit King with darts fired from a Taser gun. The gun's fifty-thousand-volt charge will normally immobilize a person. King was hit twice to no apparent effect. After that, at the command of Sergeant Koon, three officers struck King a total of fifty-six times with steel batons. Exactly why the attack was ordered, why it continued so long, and where the blows landed became the subject of fierce controversy that divided even the LAPD.

Unbeknownst to any of the participants, a man named George Holliday was filming part of the confrontation with a new video camera. He sold the tape to local television station KTLA, which edited a clip from Holliday's film and shared the edited segment with CNN. It quickly became one of the most widely broadcast vignettes in electronic media history. "Television used the tape like wallpaper," a CNN executive vice president was quoted as saying.[16] Rodney King became a media cliché, the one-dimensional, hapless black motorist beaten senseless by a racist gang of white cops.[17] "A firestorm immediately developed in the Los Angeles area," the California Court of Appeal for the Second District wrote. "Minority Black and Hispanic citizens came forward proclaiming the incident was not an isolated one, but conduct all too often occurring in their own communities."[18]

Koon and three other officers were indicted on felony charges of assault with a deadly weapon and using excessive force under color of authority. But there was a crucial fact that the public did not know. Among the thirteen seconds that KTLA cut from the Holliday tape were three seconds at the beginning that appear to show King charging at one of the police officers. The defense lawyers skillfully used the entire tape in the Simi Valley trial to eviscerate the excessive force charge. "It was the most powerful evidence we had," a juror said, "but most of America saw only part of the tape."[19] Combined with the officers' testimony of King's weird behavior, it was enough to convince the jury a year later that "King had it in his own power to prevent what happened to him."[20]

The officers' acquittal was a complete surprise to the news media. The significance of the missing seconds of video, the effect of the complete tape, and the powerful thrust of the defense team's strategy had sailed over the heads of the "legal analysts" and crime reporters covering the trial. The needle of conventional wisdom was frozen on the Rodney King cliché. The news media, Los Angeles, and the LAPD were caught flat-footed when the acquittals were handed up on April 29, 1992.

No one in the FBI field office expected the acquittals either. "Someone came into the squad area and said, 'Hey, the jury's coming back,'" Truchon remembers of that afternoon. "People were stunned when they learned the verdict." The verdict was announced at 3:15 p.m. "Within an hour," says Truchon, "we could see visible evidence, looking out from the south side of the building toward the South Central area, that something was happening. We could see smoke rising. Then it seemed like it was just one thing after another."

By 3:45 p.m., a crowd of more than three hundred peaceful protestors had massed at Parker Center, LAPD headquarters. As the afternoon wore on, the crowd changed, and the mood got ugly. Some began to throw things at the police line outside. "We're going to tear this motherfucker down right here!" one shouted. "That building's gonna come down!"[21]

Sometime between 5:00 and 6:00 p.m., about two dozen LAPD officers faced an angry crowd at the intersection of Florence and Normandie avenues. The cops were outnumbered to begin with, the crowd was growing into a mob, and the mob was howling mad at the police. An LAPD lieutenant, Michael Maulin, made a tactical decision that would cost him his career in the orgy of retrospective finger-pointing that followed the riots. He ordered the police officers to withdraw. The hard-charging, in-your-face, proactive thin blue line faded like a gaggle of Las Vegas showgirls at curtain time. "It was widely believed in South Central that the LAPD did not want to protect the city's poor, minority neighborhoods," journalist Lou Cannon observed. "The shocking reality was that the LAPD was unable to provide that protection."[22]

Within an hour, an appalling television image—soon to be joined at the hip with the video of King's beating—would be broadcast live. At about 6:45 p.m., white truck driver Reginald Denny stopped at the intersection. Dragged from his truck, he was beaten to within an inch of his life, his head split open with a concrete block. Denny's life was saved by four black residents who saw the assault on TV, rushed to the scene, and rescued the truck driver at the risk of their own lives.[23] Other motorists, among them Asians and Latinos, were beaten similarly, but their agonies were not played out under the eyes of live television.

Notwithstanding the horror of these images, the problem that afternoon did not seem to Truchon to be a matter that would much involve the FBI. "I thought it was still a local police problem when I went home that night," he recounts. "I thought that the LAPD would get it under control and the city would right itself." After grinding his way through the nightmare commute to his home in Agoura, Truchon got a different and ominous picture. He called one of the LAPD officers assigned to the terrorism task force. The officers on the task force customarily worked in street clothes. Truchon learned that his friend was frantically trying to assemble a complete uniform. He had been ordered to report for duty on the boiling streets. "I can't find my holster, I don't know where my belt is, and I don't think I can even fit into my uniform any more," the officer said.

By the next morning—the time of Truchon's Omega Man commute—it was clear that the city was not righting itself. The riots were not under control. They were getting worse, spreading north and west, lapping at the edges of Hollywood and other centers of elite power. Washington was rattled. President George H. W. Bush—who had built much of his domestic policy around law and order and who was facing a general election in November—wanted something done. For the FBI, the riots officially became a case of "civil unrest," in which the FBI's duty was to "respond and protect." Civil unrest cases were a matter for the domestic terrorism squad. "Brian," his weary supervisor told him that morning. "This case is assigned to your squad. You're going to be the case agent."

Brian Truchon was now the FBI's point man on the riots. He opened a case titled "Respro," for "respond and protect." Over the next few months, Truchon's assignment would meld into the FBI's first concentrated program against the gangs of Los Angeles. That program marked the pivot of "federalization"—the federal government's direct involvement—in what had previously been considered a local crime problem.

The Rodney King Riots "made the 1965 riots in Watts look like a minor street disturbance," wrote Sergeant Koon.[24] Estimates of the dead range between fifty and sixty, depending on which deaths one attributes to the riot. More than two thousand were injured. Property losses exceeded $880 million and may have topped $1 billion, as 1,100 buildings were destroyed.[25] There was going to be hell to pay politically. The postmortem began while Los Angeles was still sprawled out and smoking. Politicians and community leaders went at each other with rhetorical chain saws, assigning blame and cutting off careers. Chief Gates was battered into retirement. The LAPD slipped into autopilot under a series of cautious chiefs.

Brian Truchon's job initially involved setting up a command post and coordinating the FBI's role and presence with a patchwork quilt of other federal, state, county, and local agencies suddenly involved in trying to suppress the riots. The bureau flew in experts to enhance the videotape of Reginald Denny's beating and help identify his assailants.[26] Its new gang squads, working with LAPD gang cops, quickly identified four black men—said to be members of the Crips street gang—who were arrested and charged with the attack on Denny. The special agent in charge of the LA field office opined that the investigation and arrests could be a model for future FBI cooperation with local law enforcement agencies.[27]

Truchon soon found himself working on another matter that alarmed law enforcement officials. "In the middle of all that mayhem," he recounts, "someone broke into the biggest gun store in town and stole thousands of guns." As many as seventeen hundred guns and the ammunition to go with them were stolen from the Western Surplus store. The owner of Westside Loan, a pawnshop, also reported that at least fifteen hundred firearms—maybe three times that many (he was not sure)—had been stolen from his shop. Moreover, in the weeks after the riot, the *Los Angeles Times* randomly polled ten other pawnshops in the riot area and learned that every one of them had been looted.[28] The stolen guns disappeared like quicksilver. Although no major cache was ever found, some guns were recovered, and arrests were made from time to time for crimes in which guns stolen during the riot were used.[29]

"That case just morphed into the formation of about half a dozen or so gang squads in Los Angeles," recalls Truchon. The FBI concluded that much of the riot damage was caused by gangs. Building on its new Safe Streets Initiative, the bureau decided to make gangs a central part of a joint federal, state, and local strategy for reducing violent crime in the Los Angeles region. The strategy would target "violent gangs in neighborhoods with high rates of violent crime."[30]

By July, a senior agent in the field office described the FBI's Los Angeles antigang offensive as "the biggest effort ever, federally."[31] The bureau took the lead in organizing the multiagency Los Angeles Metropolitan Task Force on Violent Crime. In addition to the FBI, original members included the Bureau of Alcohol, Tobacco, and Firearms; the Immigration and Naturalization Service; the Los Angeles County Sheriff's Department; and the Compton, Inglewood, Long Beach, and Los Angeles police departments.[32] Street crime was entirely new ground for the FBI. The Los Angeles antigang task force was one of only two such joint FBI-local antigang task forces at the time. The other was in Washington, D.C.

The Justice Department announced also that it was sending in a hot gun from the U.S. attorney's office in Chicago. Assistant U.S. attorney William Hogan was credited with breaking the back of Chicago's notorious El Rukn street gang, skillfully using the RICO antiracketeering law that was devised for and had been successful in cases against the LCN. Hogan was going to show the federal prosecutors in Los Angeles how it was done.[33]

In October—with Bill Clinton hot on Bush's heels scarcely a month before the presidential election—Attorney General Barr announced the award of a three-million-dollar federal grant to the Los Angeles antigang task force. A formal agreement was signed among the task force members. The U.S. attorney said that the task force hoped to develop a "surgical approach" in attacking gangs. The special agent in charge of the LA field office laid out the Feds' new approach. "We are looking at determining the leadership of the gangs," he said. "We will try to apply federal (antiracketeering) statutes, take them on as an enterprise, rather than just as individuals."[34]

The federal "enterprise theory" is the means by which a criminal organization's "entire structure is brought within the investigation's cross-hairs." Applied to well-established criminal street gangs that have "a hierarchical structure and multiple gun and drug connections," the goal is "to incarcerate as many of its key members as the evidence allows."[35] Federal prosecutors and Congress have developed and refined three major aspects of the enterprise theory over three decades of hammering the Mafia. The first is the statutory anvil—the several criminal laws that define as federal crimes the major kinds of bad conduct in which organized criminal conspiracies engage. The second is the vise—investigative techniques, tools, and supporting statutes that enable the federal government to get deeply into a criminal organization, grasp its entire structure, and slam it down on the anvil. The third is the hammer—the harsh penalties the law provides for offenses under the organized crime statutes.

The statutory anvil is built on two pillars. The first pillar combines two similar but slightly different statues aimed at "broad based, violent, and entrenched enterprises."[36] These are the Racketeer Influenced and Corrupt Organizations Act (*U.S. Code* 18 [2006], §§ 1961–68) and the Violent Crimes in Aid of Racketeering Act (*U.S. Code* 18 [2006], § 1959). The foundational element in each of these—known in practice as RICO and VICAR, respectively—is the existence of an "enterprise" (or a "group of individuals associated in fact") including a structure for making decisions and a core of persons who function as a continuing unit. Given this foundation, the key elements are a variety of "predicate acts" in which are embodied the continuing criminal activity of the enterprise. RICO requires proof of two acts from its more general list of racketeering acts. VICAR requires proof of only one from a more specific list of violent acts. The other pillar of the statutory anvil applies "where the gravamen of the gang's activity involves a coherent drug distribution conspiracy."[37] This scheme is used when the group exists generally only to "make weight" or move drugs. Members of the organization may carry guns and commit other crimes on occasion, but the group is in essence simply a network for drug distribution.

Investigating organized criminal conspiracies and getting them firmly in the law's vise poses singular difficulties. They are secretive by definition. They are often composed of persons closely related by blood, race, ethnicity, or language and in such a way that infiltration by outsiders is difficult. Many such organizations employ sophisticated and often expensive means, including the use of cutting-edge high technology, as counterintelligence and counterinvestigation tools. The conspirators often seek to mask their criminal operations behind a facade of legitimate enterprise.

The federal government has developed a bundle of specific tools to overcome these obstacles. They are designed to be used by a cadre of experienced prosecutors and investigators dedicated to rooting out organized crime under the broad supervision of the Justice Department's Organized Crime and Racketeering Section. The tools include the use of confidential informants ("snitches" or "rats"), wiretaps and other sophisticated means of surveillance, undercover agents (where possible and where informants are not sufficient), the federal witness protection program (to encourage cooperation by informants and witnesses), and asset forfeiture laws (to deprive the enterprise of its operating wealth).

Not everyone agreed that the federal enterprise theory of investigation and prosecution would work in the case of Los Angeles gangs. One of the more outspoken critics was Sgt. Wes McBride of the Los Angeles County Sheriff's Department, president of the California Gang Investigators Association then and for many years after. McBride, an amiable but salty marine, was a member of the task force. He had already locked horns with Truchon and the FBI and was not reluctant to express his doubts publicly. "You can't go to any of our gangs and say, 'Take me to your leader,' because there isn't any leader in any of the gangs," McBride barked.[38] The difference in approach still divides the FBI from some other federal agencies—particularly the Bureau of Alcohol, Tobacco, Firearms, and Explosives—and some local police agencies, who argue that developing big cases against gang leaders takes too long and has little lasting effect.

The matter of the imported legal gunslinger William Hogan also rankled some in the U.S. attorney's office. Professional hackles were raised at the thought of being lectured to by a man one former prosecutor described as "the poster boy of the Safe Streets Initiative."[39] Aside from ruffled feathers, the old bulls in the U.S. attorney's office had a substantive disagreement with Hogan. They agreed with Sergeant McBride that RICO simply would not work in the context of Los Angeles gangs, which were not like the highly organized (virtually bureaucratic) gangs in Chicago.

"The old-timers said, 'We don't do gangs that way,'" recalls Bruce Riordan.[40] An intense man with the athletic frame of a long-distance runner and given to expansive gestures and facial expressions, Riordan was in his first year as an assistant U.S. attorney. He was on "Rookie Row," learning to be a federal prosecutor—immersed in a kaleidoscope of fast-moving trials, motions, and on-your-feet decision making. "The organized crime section rejected the idea of using the enterprise theory and RICO, because they said Los Angeles gangs had no organizational structure," Riordan says. "They were partly right. Some of the gangs, especially the black gangs, didn't. But they missed the mark when it comes to the Latino gangs."

Riordan would eventually prove the graybeards wrong in a spectacular RICO case against the Mexican Mafia and the 18th Street gang. But that was years to come, and he put his finger on a peculiar aspect of the federal effort as it rolled out in 1992. Latino gangs had been growing in power in Los Angeles since the 1940s. Within the last few years, they had erupted into a major surge in violence. Moreover, it was clear that once the riot, which had started in a predominantly black area, had gotten underway at full steam, more Latinos than blacks were involved.[41] Most of them were immigrants, about a quarter newly arrived.[42] But the new federal antigang effort focused almost exclusively on black gangs—the Bloods and the Crips. "The voices of people who were concerned about Latino gangs were drowned out," Riordan says. This exceptional focus on black gangs is explained in large part by the curious history of the so-called crack epidemic of the 1980s. This phenomenon shaped—and, some would argue, distorted—federal law enforcement policy for decades.

Crack is a solid, smokable form of cocaine. It consists of small "rocks," broken off from a dried paste or crystalline residue. Its origins are obscure. It was developed as a safer extension of a method of producing smokable cocaine known as "freebasing," a complicated and dangerous process. At some fateful juncture in the early 1980s, the supply line of a glut of powder cocaine and the demand line for cocaine in a readily smokable form crossed.[43] Crack was "cheap, simple to produce, ready to use, and highly profitable."[44] A "marketing breakthrough" had been achieved, and "for several dollars, an intense smokeable cocaine high could be obtained."[45]

The marketing of crack started at a crawl in several "gateway" cities and then broke into a race across the United States. It appeared in Los Angeles as early as 1981. The first "crack house" was uncovered in Miami in 1982. In 1983, crack was discovered in New York City. In 1986, "crack distribution and abuse exploded," and the drug was ubiquitous by 1987.[46]

The news media paid little attention to crack until 1986. Then, there was "a virtual flood of media attention," and "the public was bombarded . . . with dire reports."[47] In the view of some observers, the intense media coverage set off a form of social hysteria—a "moral panic"—that coincided with a period of increasingly conservative social and political views.[48] The 1980s had become an era of terrifying epidemics that raised in common the specter of the undoing of the blissful world of the 1970s flower children—the utopian meadows of the sexual revolution and do-your-own thing, turned-on and tuned-in tolerance. First came herpes, then AIDS.[49] Now this monster drug purportedly snatched its victims into deep addiction practically on sight and left hopelessly addicted "crack babies" in its ruthless wake—there would be as many as four million by 2000, the March of Dimes warned.[50] In fact, the crack epidemic eventually receded, following a pattern typical of new drug use.[51]

But at the time, breathless media coverage created a scramble in which powerful political figures postured and jostled each other to prove their toughness on crime. Members of Congress raced to support a law that imposes a hundred-to-one penalty ratio on possession of crack versus powder cocaine. Ten years of imprisonment without parole was prescribed for possessing five thousand grams of powder cocaine or fifty grams of crack. The U.S. Sentencing Commission tried to narrow the disparity in 2007, after decades of criticism that the sentencing scheme was racially discriminatory because crack was primarily a drug of the black inner city while powder cocaine was a drug of the white suburbs.[52] Local politicians also played the crack card. In July 1986, for example, Manhattan district attorney Robert M. Morgenthau blasted U.S. attorney Rudolph W. Giuliani, former U.S. senator Alfonse M. D'Amato, the FBI, and the federal government generally for confronting the crack problem with a merely "cosmetic" approach with only "minimal effect." It was no coincidence that Giuliani and D'Amato had made a media show just the day before by venturing into drug-infested Washington Heights to buy crack.[53]

Elbows were being thrown in the Washington law enforcement establishment as well. A 1988 law tackling drug abuse—the centerpiece of a national "crackdown" on drugs—created the White House Office of National Drug Control Policy, a cabinet-level office. The first incumbent, William J. Bennett, informally called the nation's "drug czar," proposed moving FBI and DEA agents into the cities to work with local cops in fighting the "drug war." That would not do at all according to Attorney General Richard Thornburgh and various anonymous minions of the FBI and DEA. An aide to Thornburgh huffed that such a radical proposal would be "a major shift in federal anti-drug strategy, which has traditionally targeted drug traffickers." The agents were "trained for major drug trafficking and money-laundering cases . . . not for handling street crime."[54]

That Olympian view sounded fine in Washington. But it did not play well among panicked politicians in the war zone that America was becoming. Crack was an eminently retail drug, a trade that was easy to get into. The natural economic result was an explosion of competition. The scramble for crack markets came just as the civilian gun market was also exploding, making firearms easily accessible to gangs fighting local wars for control of market territories. What changed in this period, according to former LAPD chief Daryl Gates, was "not only the proliferation of guns, but their sophistication." A flood of high-capacity semiautomatic pistols—the so-called Wonder Nines—poured onto the streets. "These semiautomatic guns expended bullets faster and required less skill to use," Gates wrote. "They were priced within reach of even low-level criminals." It got worse as "the less expensive but just as deadly AK-47 [semiautomatic assault rifle] became the weapon of choice among the drug-dealing gang members in south central L.A."[55] The same escalation in firepower went on all over America, wherever the crack wars were fought. As a consequence, the crack epidemic "is associated with a doubling of the number of murdered black males aged 14 to 17, a 30 percent increase for those aged 18 to 24, and a 10 percent increase for those 25 and over."[56]

In 1989, Thornburgh's Justice Department issued a report that would eventually have precisely the result he had argued against the year before—a "major shift" in federal strategy that put FBI agents on the streets of Los Angeles, working with local police. The product of a year's work by the government's ninety-three U.S. attorneys, the report was called a "Dun and Bradstreet" of the nation's drug problem. It labeled Los Angeles as an "epicenter" of the problem and fingered the Bloods and Crips street gangs in particular as "one of the most menacing developments in drug trafficking." More than ten thousand Los Angeles street gang members were said to be actively involved in the crack cocaine trade, controlling it with "murderous violence." More ominously, it warned that "the LAPD has identified 47 cities from Seattle to Kansas City to Baltimore, where Los Angeles street gang traffickers have appeared."[57] Given this official obsession with the Bloods and Crips and their perceived power over the business of crack cocaine, it is no wonder that once the Los Angeles federal task force got up to speed, it concentrated primarily and almost exclusively on black gangs. Meanwhile, the LAPD and the Los Angeles County Sheriff's Department were in a slap-down wrestling match with what would prove to be a bigger problem by far in the long term—the Latino street gangs.

The LAPD and the Los Angeles County Sheriff's Department (LASD) are like stubborn, strong-willed, competitive siblings. They share the task of policing Los Angeles gangs. Each thinks it does a better job. The rivalry has at times been less than friendly. Both started their first intensive antigang efforts during the gun-driven violence of the 1970s. Each took a different approach. The LAPD went for smashmouth patrol tactics, saturating gang areas with the goal of suppressing them by brute force. The LASD operated more like a team of snipers, identifying and then taking out key members who drove each gang's inner being. Since then, however, the LASD has come to operate more like the LAPD, relying less on finesse and more on roving applications of concentrated force.

Gang expert Richard Valdemar—who retired from the LASD in 2004 after thirty-three years of service—thinks that has been a colossal mistake. He has no doubt about what has caused the current Latino gang problem and how to fight it. Valdemar was present at the creation of the LASD's original antigang unit, Operation Safe Streets (OSS), in 1978. An outspoken man with a quiet manner of speaking and the round, bearded visage of an amiable prophet, Valdemar tirelessly advances a gospel with two main rubrics. One is that illegal immigration is not only the root, trunk, and branch of the Latino gang crisis in the United States but also corrupts the entire system of American justice. The other is that the original version of the LASD's Operation Safe Streets was the Camelot of gang enforcement, the only antigang program that really works.

Valdemar was a teenaged Latino activist during the fiery days of the Chicano political awakening in the 1960s. Today, he thinks illegal immigration threatens the Latino culture he advocated for in that era. "The three Super Gangs spawned in the streets of Los Angeles—Florencia 13, 18th Street, and Mara Salvatrucha—are composed primarily of illegal immigrants," Valdemar asserts. "These are not the poor working people of twenty years ago. These gangs are growing and migrating into cities and towns across the United States. Their aim is to first seduce and then destroy our children and our way of life."[58]

Valdemar's assertion that the three gangs are composed "primarily of illegal immigrants" is impossible to prove. He and others who hammer on the element of illegal aliens in gangs are links in a long and complex chain of people inside and outside of law enforcement who pass such assertions on to each other on the Internet, in statements of congressmen, through rants on blogs, and via news media entertainment shows. They often cite each other as "sources." The whole edifice, however, is built on a flimsy foundation of opinion, rump surveys, and speculation. "Other than anecdotal information, no one is tracking this stuff," FBI agent Brian Truchon says when asked about the proportions of aliens and illegal aliens in criminal street gangs. "There are no hard numbers available that I know of."[59] Retired LASD sergeant Wes

McBride, who created the first gang information system in California and is the intellectual father of gang information systems in the United States, agrees. "I don't believe those numbers exist," says McBride, who is now the executive director of the California Gang Investigators Association. "Most agencies, if any, do not routinely keep such statistics. LAPD is not allowed to ask, and most others don't bother."[60]

One number frequently cited is supposedly from a "confidential" California Department of Justice study that is said to have reported in 1995 that 60 percent of the members of the 18th Street gang in Southern California were illegal immigrants.[61] "California Department of Justice has never had a realistic number for anything," retorts McBride. "So I would not accept their number." Another source sometimes cited is McBride's own organization, the CGIA, which supposedly found that 20 percent of Latino gang members are illegal aliens. He explains the genesis of that number. "In a very unscientific manner our association asked our membership once—and in a discussion with a group of Hispanic gang investigators—what they thought the number was," he says. "We all agreed that about 20 percent of Hispanic gangsters were illegal. I think it differs as to where the gang is. Some cities along the border that number may be higher, or certain neighborhoods, but over all I bet that 20 percent is not far off."

There is no doubt that there are many illegal aliens among Latino gang members. In two RICO investigations of the 18th Street gang in Los Angeles, says FBI agent Jim Wines, fifteen out of twenty-six charged defendants in one case and twelve out of eighteen in another were illegal aliens. When Wines projects from his experience, he ends up with estimates closer to Valdemar's. "Whatever the percentage is," he concludes, "in terms of 18th Street and MS, I would think you could safely say that it is well above 50 percent due to the large number of Central American members of both gangs."[62] But McBride replies that most 18th Street gangsters in Los Angeles are not illegal aliens. As to Mara Salvatrucha (MS), he argues that the growing number of gang members drawn from "anchor babies" (second-generation children born in the United States) is changing the ratio. "I do not think there is a definitive source on this issue," sums up Kevin Carwile, chief of the U.S. Justice Department's Gang Squad.[63]

In 2005, Richard Valdemar took a turn helping the controversial Minutemen "guard" the Arizona-Mexico border.[64] Although President George W. Bush originally denounced the Minutemen as "vigilantes," the head of the U.S. Border Patrol later suggested that the agency would look into establishing a civilian volunteer auxiliary.[65] Valdemar compares the border watch carried out by armed civilian volunteers to the civil rights sit-ins of the 1960s. He says he found the Minutemen to be not "whackos" or racists but "ordinary, very level-headed people frustrated by their government's policy on immigration." He has also advised anti-immigration congressman Tom Tancredo on the relationship between illegal immigration and crime.

Valdemar has no problem reconciling his hard-line immigration stance with his own heritage, including the fact that his grandparents immigrated from the state of Chihuahua, Mexico. Both of his grandfathers were miners who fought in the Mexican Revolution—Chihuahua was the home base of revolutionary warlord Pancho Villa—and later settled in Arizona copper-mining country. He underscores that his grandfathers came to the United States legally.

Valdemar emphasizes that illegal immigrants do not bring the gang culture with them from Latin America—they gravitate to it once they get into the United States. At the same time, their unacculturated influx helps to perpetuate the barrios' socioeconomic marginality, which breeds gang cadres. "We Hispanics should be the first to speak out against this perversion of our culture," he asserts. "The ugly backlash against this lawlessness will result in social repercussions against both legal and illegal immigrant Hispanics in the United States and more racism."

Born during the baby boom, in 1947, Richard Valdemar grew up in Willowbrook, an unincorporated area wedged between Watts to the north and the frighteningly violent city of Compton to the south. He was born and went to high school in Compton. Nearly the dead center of Los Angeles County, Compton was once a poor, mostly black city riven by gang violence. The city and its bloody gang culture were catapulted to national notoriety with the birth of gangsta rap—a genre created by N.W.A.'s 1988 album *Straight Outta Compton*. The blockbuster album, which sold half a million copies in its first six weeks, included the inflammatory cut "Fuck tha Police," a mock trial of police featuring rapper Ice Cube.[66] Today, Compton is demographically a predominantly Latino city. It is still ravaged by gang violence. In 2005, it was reported to have fifty-seven street gangs active within its ten square miles.[67] Only the complexion and the language have changed. The city was abandoned in the 1960s by whites and the black middle class and devastated by the passage of Proposition 13 in 1978, and its tax base has long since evaporated. Strapped for cash, Compton disbanded its police force in 2000 and contracted with LASD to do the job.[68] Forty of the Los Angeles County's eighty-eight cities have similar contracts with the sheriff's department.

When Valdemar's parents moved to Willowbrook from Arizona after World War II, developers were offering tract housing affordable to veterans. By the time Valdemar was a teenager in the 1960s, Willowbrook was transitioning from a mixed rural, suburban community to an urban and poor area. "There were a lot of gangs around," he recalls. "And there was a lot of radicalism, movement toward a revolution in the streets." The Latino gangs had names like Compton Varrio Tres and Tortilla Flats. Piru Street—where the Piru Street Boys formed, hung out with the Crips for a while, then broke with them and became the Piru Bloods—was only a few blocks away from the Valdemar residences at 2121 Oris Street and, later, 1611 Largo Avenue. A Black Panther Party headquarters was close by, on Stockwell Avenue.

Strongly influenced by his parents, Richard Valdemar had no sympathy for gangs, gangsters, or the gang life. Both of his parents had run-ins with gangs in the 1940s and conveyed their strong disapproval to young Richard. His mother was born in the copper mining town of Miami, Arizona, on the eastern side of the Superstition Mountains (where Brian Truchon and his father searched for the Lost Dutchman Mine). In the 1940s, Miami was the segregated Mexican satellite of Globe, where the white miners lived. During World War II, Valdemar's mother became a "Rosie the Riveter." She got a job on a wartime production line in Mesa, near Phoenix. While there, she witnessed a violent crime by a gang member. Despite threats to her life, she refused to back down and testified against the gangster. Valdemar's father participated in the Zoot Suit Riots—on the other side of the race line. A soldier on his way to the war in the Pacific, he regarded the zoot-suiters as criminal punks and went after them with his buddies. Valdemar himself dismisses the conventional narrative of the Zoot Suit Riots as so much liberal prattling, the misguided defense of a bunch of criminals who more or less got what they deserved. But the teenaged Richard did have empathy for the poor and the plight of the Latino community. He looked for a way to make a difference and became a self-described liberal activist with the help of the Catholic Youth Organization and the local branch of the Federation of Settlements and Neighborhood Centers. At seventeen years of age, he became the director of the teen center at the Sagrado Corazon (Sacred Heart) parish church on North Culver Avenue, just around the corner from his home.

Almost 20 percent of Americans lived in poverty at the time. Few were more miserable than the urban poor in the ghettos and barrios clinging like orphans to the city's eastern and southern legs—East Los Angeles, South Central, Watts, and Compton. In 1960, 34.7 percent of nonwhite families in Los Angeles County had a family income of less than four thousand dollars, the official poverty line, as did 25.7 percent of families with Spanish surnames.[69] In January 1964, President Lyndon B. Johnson announced in his State of the Union address to Congress that it was time to do something about it. He grandly declared the War on Poverty, the keystone of his vision for the "Great Society." The War on Poverty would be butter to the guns of the Vietnam War, whose volume Johnson would crank up to nation-splitting levels the following year. Before he was twenty-one years old, Richard Valdemar would get a taste of both.

In August 1964, Congress passed the cornerstone of Johnson's War on Poverty, the Economic Opportunity Act of 1964. But in Los Angeles, the war bogged down while the public service community's field marshals maneuvered among themselves for the new federal funds. Meanwhile, young Richard Valdemar was selected to attend a 1965 international conference of Spanish-speaking activists in Puerto Rico. Having just graduated from Compton High School, Valdemar was one of the youngest delegates. He recalls telling the conference about the dire conditions in Los Angeles among the poor and warning of the possibility of riots. "The people in the community felt like they were under occupation by the police," he says. "There was no effective program for young people, not even a decent recreational facility."

Many of the other youth delegates went on to Fidel Castro's Communist Cuba to cut sugar cane, a gesture fashionable among the era's militant Left. Valdemar returned to Willowbrook. His prediction unfolded before his eyes. On August 11, 1965, a routine California Highway Patrol traffic stop escalated into a six-day riot that consumed the city of Watts and much of the surrounding area. The toll staggered the country: thirty-four dead, 1,032 injured, 3,952 arrested, two hundred buildings destroyed, four hundred damaged, and losses totaling $183 million.[70] The shock moved everything off dead center. As funds flowed, new programs opened up. But the riots left Valdemar disillusioned. Advocating for change through traditional channels seemed to be trumped by violence in the streets. As the movement shifted further left, Valdemar gradually swung right, bothered by the collapse of order.

He enlisted in the U.S. Army in 1966, where he spent three years as a military policeman. He was assigned to the military police school, the only one open at the time. His first thought was that it was "a joke—I had no love of police." Moreover, the military police were effectively segregated. "There were no blacks, no Jews, and only a few Hispanics" in his class, he recalls. But there were a few good cops, and Valdemar came grudgingly to admire them. "It was the first time in my life I could identify with a police officer," he recalls. He was sent to Vietnam with the 504th Military Police Battalion, where he saw furious combat at Nha Trang during the 1968 Tet Offensive. Valdemar returned as a sergeant and finished his enlistment with two years at Fort Huachuca, Arizona.

When he came back to Los Angeles in 1970, he found the economy changing and permanent jobs hard to come by. Valdemar's father had been a steelworker. But the industrial economy that had sustained Los Angeles for three decades—comprised of smokestack plants of General Motors, Firestone, Bethlehem Steel, Goodyear, and others—was shutting down, just as it was all across the American Rust Belt. The demise of the industrial economy and, with it, entry-level jobs for the unskilled and undocumented during the 1970s was an ominous curtain-raiser to the coming crack epidemic, Latino immigration surge, and gang eruption of the 1980s. Valdemar got a temporary job as a "bumper man" at a Dodge assembly plant, but he knew that he was going nowhere fast.

There was, however, something he already knew how to do: police work. When a buddy suggested taking the LASD entrance examination, Valdemar went along. He passed and promised his family and friends that police work would be a temporary job for him until something better came along. In 1971, while he was attending the Los Angeles County Sheriff's Academy, he was pulled out for a special assignment—working undercover. "The sheriff's department found out that I was a former activist and liberal sympathizer, so they pulled me out to infiltrate groups like the Revolutionary Communist Party and the Brown Berets," recalls Valdemar. "I just walked in cold and told them I was an AWOL soldier. I knew what to say and how to act, and reported what I learned to my contact in the sheriff's department."

Valdemar dreamed of a career in police intelligence after he graduated from the academy. But like every other newly minted LASD deputy, he was assigned to duty in the Correctional Services Division. The division runs the Los Angeles County jail system, the largest in the nation. Of its average inmate population of more than eighteen thousand, at least 20 percent are gang members, and 90 percent are waiting trial on felony charges.[71] Valdemar was frustrated and annoyed. He wanted to get out on the streets, like his peers in the LAPD who went straight from the same academy to patrol duty. Being a jail guard, he thought, "was a waste of my talent." He learned, however, that the experience was invaluable when he finally did get on the streets four years later.

"It's one thing to be out driving around in a car, with a gun and backup available," he says. "It's another to be alone inside a module with no gun, no nightstick, no weapons, and outnumbered by rule breakers and outlaws who you are trying to get to obey the rules of the jail." In time, Valdemar learned to use his "primary weapon," his brain, and his "secondary weapon," his mouth, effectively. "You learn to talk to people to get them to do what they need to do for their own good." The tour in the county jails is a maturing experience for young deputies. Valdemar says it makes them better street cops than their peers on the LAPD, who go straight to patrol from the military boot camp environment of the law enforcement academy, taking a hard-edged attitude with them. "Working in the jails smooths our edges down," he explains.

Valdemar got another valuable lesson during his tour in the county jails. "It was my first exposure to gangs," he says. "And I learned that the gangs run the jails. They control everything up to the walls." He saw in particular the power of the prison gangs, especially Eme, the Mexican Mafia. "The prison gangs set the code of conduct in the jail," he explains. "Whoever controls custody controls the streets, because sooner or later most gang members end up in jail, where the prison gangs have the ability to murder them if their gang has not cooperated on the street."

These were not easy lessons. Valdemar admits that he was doing everything wrong at first. Then an elderly trustee, a veteran gangster in jail for killing a police officer, took the young deputy aside and explained to him how things really worked in jail. "You're doing such a bad job running the module," the trustee explained, "that we can't get any business done here." It was in everybody's interest to get things in Valdemar's module under control. The counseling opened Valdemar's eyes to the fact that two worlds existed in the jail: the overt world he could see and a parallel covert world in which the gangs operated. "Nothing was going on among the inmates without a reason," he explains. "Somebody mopping down a hall? He's not just pushing a mop to keep the place clean. He's doing something else, something secret at the same time. Maybe he's delivering a message or an extortion demand. Or maybe he's moving drugs or a weapon." From that moment on, Valdemar says, "I became a different kind of deputy." He learned to spot the covert behind the overt, how to get the inmates to work with him in keeping order to their mutual benefit, and how to spot the signs of pending trouble or danger to himself. His nickname soon became "Super Val." A supervisor once joked, "Valdemar finds so much drugs and so many weapons that you have to wonder whether he brings them in himself."

In 1974, Valdemar was assigned to patrol duty, first in East Los Angeles and eventually in Willowbrook. At the time, LASD was doing gang suppression with the saturation method. "Patrol-heavy presence," Valdemar says, "That's exactly what started Watts. It doesn't work, never has worked, and never will work. All it does is turn the community against the police. Saturation patrol is like saturation bombing was in Vietnam. You take a hill and leave. The enemy comes right back. It didn't work in Vietnam and it doesn't work on gangs." But in 1978, Valdemar was among twelve deputies who were handpicked to start a "revolutionary" pilot project in gang suppression, Operation Safe Streets. Funded by a federal grant, it was an expansion of a successful concept developed by LASD Sgt. Curtis Jackson against a gang called the Hickory Street gang. "Instead of saturation patrol, we concentrated our attention on one gang at a time," Valdemar remembers. "We built up all the intelligence we could about every member of that gang and every victim of that gang. We wanted to know everything about it, who the leaders are and what gives them the ability to do what they do."

Valdemar explains that the Latino gangs of Los Angeles are "democratic gangs." They are not "structured" like the gangs in Chicago or New York, with a pyramidal organization and designated leaders. "Here you have different people in different leadership roles in each clique, depending on their personalities and the gang's needs," he says. "One might be charismatic, good at motivating people, another good at dope dealing, and another more violent, a shooter. Some gang members just want to kill cops. Instead of saturation bombing, we wanted to use smart bombs to take out the key members and weaken the gang." Valdemar explains the OSS approach as follows: "Every gang has two arms. One arm is the violent arm. The other arm is the moneymaking arm that makes possible what the violent arm does. If you cut off only the violent arm, it will grow back because there are plenty of younger gang members to take the place of the ones you eliminate. You have to also take out the other arm. So, once we knew everything there was to know about our target gang, we started taking out the most violent members and the revenue makers." As a result, Valdemar says, the gang gets "weaker and weaker" until it gets so weak that its traditional rivals are emboldened to attack it. "Then we go after them," he explains. The process clears an ever-widening circle of gang power. "Once you take a territory, you never give it back," says Valdemar. "The safe zone just keeps getting bigger and bigger."

The OSS program had such success that "it attracted the attention of the politicians." That was not a good thing, he explains: "The politicians did not understand the concept. They pulled us out and started moving us around, so we were forced to give up the safe zones we had secured, and go into areas where we did not have the intelligence we needed." The result, he says, was that OSS was effectively gutted. It lost the ground it had gained and could not meet expectations elsewhere. Eventually, the LASD slipped back into the saturation methods of the LAPD.

The LAPD's first intensive antigang program started in 1977. It was supported by a federal grant funding a special unit of forty-four officers in the Hollenbeck Division of East Los Angeles. Originally to be called TRASH—Total Resources against Street Hoodlums—the unit's name was changed to CRASH, substituting the word *Community* for *Total,* after civic leaders objected to the implication that human beings, even gangsters, were no better than trash. Intended to target the worst gangs, the technique had some initial success. In 1979, the city took over funding. But CRASH officers were soon spread thinly across the city. Their primary method was the classic LAPD thin blue line—hitting gangsters hard in operations that had names like Operation Hammer, interrogating people who looked like gangsters, taking an endless series of hills and eventually giving them back.[72]

By the end of the 1980s, both agencies were claiming success, but at the same time, they were crying for help. "What was wrong with the crime-solving equation," argues Gates, "wasn't the police. It was the money to fund the police—and the laxity of the criminal justice system after the police had done their job."[73] The police came to feel like they were on an endless treadmill, chasing an endless supply of gangsters. "It seems like we're putting out one fire after another," a CRASH officer complained in 1991. "Gangs that have been very quiet, all of a sudden they're involved in a shooting. Things go crazy. It goes in cycles."[74]

Mara Salvatrucha and the "open-book" 18th Street gang had grown into major problems by the end of the 1980s. The "enormous number" of undocumented aliens "continued to stump us," Chief Gates complained. Many were from El Salvador and elsewhere in Central America. "Our lack of control over these criminal immigrants became an almost insurmountable obstacle," continues Gates. As many as

30 percent of the department's arrests were undocumented aliens. "No sooner had we identified them and they would be out on the street," says Gates, "on bail, with a new name."[75]

Sometime around July 1986, an LAPD lieutenant named Robert Ruchhoft headed the gang detail and observed what he called "a dramatic increase" in crime by street gangs made up of illegal aliens. He thought things over and came up with a bright idea. "Street gangs are our number one crime problem," he reasoned. "And we have become increasingly aware over the last two or three years of a dramatic increase in illegal aliens involved in criminal street gangs." At least half a dozen gangs—including Mara Salvatrucha and 18th Street—were thought to be made up primarily of aliens, most of them Latinos. The LAPD itself had no authority to act on a person's immigration status. But from the sum of information available to the police, it was often clear which gangsters were in the country illegally. "Why not enlist the aid of the federal Immigration and Naturalization Service?" Ruchhoft thought.[76] The federal agency clearly had the authority and the means to take the alien gangsters off the streets of Los Angeles and send them back to where they belonged.

Ruchhoft contacted the local INS representative, who sent the plan up the agency chain of command. Headquarters enthusiastically endorsed the idea. Within two months, INS assigned a four-agent team to work with the LAPD CRASH unit, joining gang expertise with immigration authority. "We know who they are, and where they are, and the criminal activities in which they are taking part," Ruchhoft said at the time. Once the alien lawbreakers were identified and located, INS could take action to deport them. By early September 1986 as many as sixty gangsters had been "shipped back" to their homelands through the program. Most of them were Mexicans, Ruchhoft said, "but we are now working on a Salvadoran gang."[77] The press reported episodically on a moderately growing number of deportations over the next several years. In April 1989, the task force claimed to have "decimated" the leadership of Mara Salvatrucha with the deportation of more than twenty key members of the gang. They were among 175 criminal aliens deported in the first four months of the year, after federal funds for the program were increased and eight INS agents were assigned to the effort.[78]

Meanwhile, FBI agent Brian Truchon had been assigned as the case agent in charge of going after a black gang known as the Grape Street Crips. Truchon got his man and left Los Angeles in 1996 to a new assignment as chief of the Safe Streets Initiative headquarters unit in Washington. He had been thoroughly immersed in the world of the black gangs of Los Angeles. Yet he had never heard of Mara Salvatrucha. In fact, aside from the INS program of criminal alien deportation, MS-13 was hardly a blip on the federal radar screen.

It would become clear that MS-13 was far from "decimated" by twenty deportations. But Bob Ruchhoft had indeed planted a seed that, within a decade, would grow into a major federal program. Congress would give INS (succeeded by U.S. Immigration and Customs Enforcement) new authority and new funds for a massive program of hunting down and deporting criminal aliens—those who commit serious crimes while in the country illegally. In September 1986, it all seemed like a grand idea. "It is too early to tell whether it will result in a big decrease in crime," Ruchhoft said at the time. "But it can't hurt."[79]

5

DEATH, TREACHERY, AND TAXES

Ramiro Valerio knew that someday they would come for him. He just did not know who it would be, and he did not know whether they would put handcuffs on him or give him a "birthday hug"—that is, kill him. Valerio was in a bad spot in the summer of 1997 when the knock on his door finally came.

Also known as "Greedy" and "Ojos" (Eyes), young Valerio led a fast, drug-pushing, double-dealing life in the shadow of violent death. Now it was catching up to him. Three years earlier, he had been a "shot caller" for the Columbia Lil' Cycos (CLCS) clique of the 18th Street gang. After it opened membership to all comers, 18th Street grew to be the biggest Latino gang in Los Angeles. It was built on scores of cliques based on territory. The gang now blanketed Southern California and was spreading rapidly into neighboring states. Founded in 1985, the Lil' Cycos controlled a swath of territory around MacArthur Park in West Los Angeles. Its name derived from a combination of location—Columbia Avenue—and attitude, a transliteration of the slang word *psycho,* meaning "loco" or "crazy."

As one of the clique's shot callers, Greedy was an important boss to whom income and obedience were owed by CLCS soldiers. He was first among equals with three other shot callers, "Lefty," "Coco," and "Termite." That, however, was then. This was now. Lefty was dead. His own homies killed him. Greedy was hiding from two gangs—the Mexican Mafia (Eme) prison gang and his own, once-beloved CLCS street gang. Leaders of both gangs had "green-lighted" Valerio. A green light is a various thing. It can mean death or injury, depending on the offense. In this case, Greedy was under sentence of death, what Eme calls "hard candy." Greedy was a mild, nerdy-looking guy who wore thick eyeglasses. Hence his other nickname, "Ojos." Eme mockingly called its plot to murder Valerio "Operation Coke Bottle."

Local law enforcement—the LAPD and LASD—were also interested in Greedy. Some of their investigators thought he was "good for" a couple of murders. If he had not participated directly in them, he likely had ordered them. "You cannot rise to the level of shot caller unless you do some serious violence," says retired LASD gang expert Richard Valdemar. "If you only order violence and don't participate, you appear to be a coward. No coward is going to be accepted as a member of one of these gangs, much less rise to the level of leadership."[1]

Neither stupid nor overly macho, Greedy had gone to ground like a rabbit. The knock sounded again. He heard a polite voice in Spanish say, "FBI, Mr. Valerio. FBI. Please open the door, we just want to talk to you." Greedy may or may not have been happy to hear the dread name of that federal institution at his door. But once he opened it, there would be no turning back. The two agents were bringing him an offer he could not refuse.

Three years earlier, on the morning of Monday, September 5, 1994, the *Los Angeles Times* briefly noted the murder of an unnamed man and woman, "killed early Sunday when automatic rifle fire from the sidewalk riddled their passing car in a drug-and-gang-infested area near Downtown Los Angeles." The note of one hundred words, deep in the paper's Metro section, reported that police "knew of no motive in the killings."[2] But from the moment he arrived on the scene at 4:20 a.m. Sunday morning, veteran LAPD homicide detective Robert Bub suspected that the carnage was a gang hit somehow connected to the Lil' Cycos.

The crime scene stretched for a block and half along Burlington Street, between Fifth Street and Maryland Avenue, at the intersection of which a brand new Chevrolet Suburban sport-utility vehicle had jumped the curb, crashed into a utility pole, and come to rest. The street along that valley of death—a residential area of faded apartment buildings and duplex apartments—was littered with 7.62 × 39 mm shell casings. The thirty-four casings police recovered were later determined to have come from two different AK-47 rifles. Brain tissue and pieces of skulls and other body matter were mingled in among the casings. More than twenty-five rounds had slammed through the vehicle, ripping holes in the steel body like buzzing can openers. The occupants were slumped in the awkwardly grotesque postures of violent death. The driver, Carlos Alberto "Truco" Lopez, twenty-six, a "bagman," or extortion collector, for the Mexican Mafia, had been hit three times in the head. He lay against the door, his mouth slightly open as if he were asleep and snoring. His passenger, Donatilla Contreras, fifty-seven, a midlevel drug wholesaler, was hit eight times, once in the head and seven times in other parts of her body. Her matronly corpse slumped forward, face hard against the dash. "The sheer firepower was one of the worst I've seen, almost akin to the old Chicago gangland killings," Detective Bub told the *Los Angeles Times* a few years later.[3]

A number of facts pointed to the 18th Street gang. The location was in the heart of CLCS territory. The crime scene was awash in spray-painted gang graffiti, including "XVIII" sprayed on the power pole and the scrawled nicknames of several CLCS members, among them shot callers Coco and Termite. No one needed to tell any residents who came to their windows that night who or what was behind the killings, and the residents did not need instruction on the risks inherent in talking to police. "Are you kidding?" an LAPD detective exclaimed in 1992 while refusing to be interviewed by the *Los Angeles Times* on the subject of witness intimidation. "If we put out that our witnesses are getting killed, nobody will cooperate with us."[4]

Gang violence has a powerful multiplier effect on infected neighborhoods. "What you get from gangs like 18th Street, on a large scale basis, is fear . . . an army in the community," a Los Angeles County assistant district attorney assigned to gang cases said in 1996.[5] When someone is shot dead on the street of a nice suburban neighborhood, the residents are properly fearful until the case is solved and the miscreant removed. Things then return to normal. In a gang-infested neighborhood, there is no return to normal. Life is marked by a steady drip of "low-level" violence and threats of violence, occasionally punctuated by a dramatic killing. A case of gang violence might or might not be "solved." No matter what happens, the gang is always there. Its menace permeates the neighborhood through graffiti, hard-eyed stares, and violent lessons. This is why so-called victimization studies—surveys asking people if they have been victims of specific crimes—underestimate the reach and impact of gang crime. Unlike random street crime, gang crime is multiplied by the pervasive presence of the organization itself. One does not have to have been an actual victim of gang violence to get the gang's message.[6]

Nevertheless, for this hit that went down at 2:30 a.m. on a Sunday morning, one witness was willing—at least temporarily—to cooperate. Juana Gutierrez was returning home from a party when the street erupted into the distinctive booming sound of AK-47 rifle fire, the sound of breaking glass, and the collision of metal. Gutierrez identified several gang members from a "nine pack," an array of photographs Detective Bub showed her. The police brought several suspects in for questioning. One was CLCS shot caller Anthony "Coco" Zaragoza. Another was Juan Manuel Lopez Romero, also known as "Termite" or "Feo" (Ugly). A third was Ramiro "Greedy" Valerio.

Coco Zaragoza was a hard case—bullet-necked, "tatted up," defiant, and brimming with attitude. He claimed to know nothing, and if he did know anything, he was not going to share it with the cops. This is no doubt a wise course for a blood-drenched gang enforcer with a history like Coco's. Ironically, Coco's penchant for incautious tough-guy talk would later be instrumental in bringing down the leadership of the Lil' Cycos. For now, Detective Bub and the entire LAPD could go pound sand until Coco's silk-suited mouthpiece arrived to spring him. Coco's homey Termite also clammed up, perhaps a bit more smoothly, but just as tightly.

Greedy Valerio was not made of such steel. "Greedy was the brains of the CLCS," according to FBI special agent Carl Sandford, who later would come to know Greedy very well. "Greedy was a negotiator and he tried to resolve disputes by talking and not like Coco by shooting. Arresting Greedy was like arresting Al Capone's bookkeeper." Sandford contends that, contrary to Valdemar's expert opinion, Greedy never directly participated in any violence, as far as the FBI knows, although he may have ordered it done now and again.

Detective Bub and his partner Chuck Salazar "sweated" Greedy about the Truco murder. The classic law enforcement interrogation is a poker game, a blend of fact, bluff, and illusion that goes something like this: "You don't know what we know, but we know a lot more than you think we know. So, if you lie to us, we're going to know that you're lying. And lying is not good for us. But mostly it's bad for you." In Greedy's case, the police were able to drop a couple of hard facts, inconvenient things that made sweat beads break out like spring rain on Greedy's forehead. One was that an eyewitness placed Greedy at the scene of the Truco murder. "Remember the lady in the party dress?" they asked. "She identified you." The other was that the Mexican Mafia—which has an extraordinary intelligence network—had already learned that Greedy was under arrest. Operation Coke Bottle was in motion. The Eme chiefs planned to murder Greedy even while he was in custody. It was not the first time such a thing had been done. It would not be the last.

Ramiro "Greedy" Valerio was in a pincer. The cops had done their duty and warned him of the Eme plot. If he lied to them now, they could shrug and cut him loose. Then he would have to deal with Operation Coke Bottle on his own. "Once the LAPD squeezed him on the Truco murder, Greedy tried to do everything to save himself, especially when he knew that he did not pull the trigger," says Agent Sandford. "He thought LAPD would protect him if he cooperated."

In order to thwart the Eme hit, the LAPD arrested Greedy and held him in "protective custody." Greedy started to talk. He did not "flip" at this time. He did not agree to become an active informant. But he did talk, carefully distancing himself from the Truco murder. More important for the long run, Greedy described an elaborate criminal enterprise that put the Columbia Lil' Cycos right in the middle of a vast drug-trafficking and extortion system overseen by the Mexican Mafia prison gang and implemented by the street gang. The LAPD homicide detectives were not disinterested in this part of Greedy's story. But their job was to solve a murder, a specific murder, the killing of Truco Lopez and Donatilla Contreras. It was not their job to get bogged down in the morass of an investigation of drug trafficking. So nothing much came of Greedy's story at the time. A few years later, however, Agent Sandford and federal prosecutor Bruce Riordan would learn of what Greedy had described. They would be very interested.

Being put into protective custody automatically made Greedy a pariah to the 18th Street gang. They knew of no specific evidence—yet—that he had ratted them out. But informants commonly are placed in protective custody to keep them from being killed. So the status of being in "PC" was enough to put Valerio under suspicion, strip him of his position as shot caller, and start the gang's search for "paperwork"—proof that their erstwhile shot caller had become an informant, a snitch, a rat. "They usually try and get paperwork on people that they say that they're snitching or they said something to incriminate somebody," a CLCS member explained in trial testimony. "And once they get the paperwork, they place a green light on the person."

A huge problem lurked for Greedy in terms of "paperwork." An LAPD tape recorder captured every word of his interrogation. Taping interviews was standard procedure for gang homicide investigations. No special precautions were taken to protect the tape. It was just another piece of evidence filed away in the LAPD system. The "Greedy Tape" was a time bomb, waiting to be found by the Lil' Cycos gangsters.

Street gangs are the primary retail distributors of illicit drugs in the United States. They are becoming increasingly involved in wholesale trafficking as well, through their growing connections with transnational criminal and drug-trafficking organizations (DTOs).[7] If there were no other reason to be concerned about Latino street gangs, these facts alone would be enough.

The abuse of cocaine, heroin, marijuana, and synthetic drugs afflict over 35 million Americans, resulting in over 20,000 deaths in the United States in recent years. The total economic cost of drug abuse in the United States—defined . . . as negative health and crime consequences, as well as loss of potential productivity from disability, death, and withdrawal from the legitimate workplace—was estimated to be approximately $180.9 billion in 2002.[8]

Of course, there are many more reasons to worry about gangs. Drugs and drug trafficking did not cause the rise of Latino street gangs. Nor would street gangs completely dry up if illicit drugs were no longer contraband and thus lost black-market value. Latino street gangs engage in many other kinds of crime. There is also the random violence stemming from their commitment to a gang ethos that breeds rivalries, murderous raids, and a preening demand for "respect." But since the crack boom of the 1980s, drug trafficking has been a force that sustains many street gangs, contributes to their unremitting violence, and drives their expansion. Many gangs are little more than violent criminal enterprises in drag, wearing the comradely neighborhood clothes of an earlier era. The clever and ruthless few who seize the leadership of such enterprises reap enormous profits. Their loyal and poorly compensated foot soldiers—in thrall to deeply rooted concepts of manhood, pride, and loyalty to one's barrio and homies—eagerly provide the muscle through which the enterprise asserts its control over markets and disciplines those who participate in them. Instead of toiling in garment-industry sweatshops, these tattooed minions work in drug-industry sweatshops.

Transnational Latino gangs, such as 18th Street, are particularly well placed for this illegal trade, since "Mexico is the conduit for most of the cocaine reaching the United States, the source of much of the heroin consumed in the United States, and the largest foreign supplier of marijuana and methamphetamine to the U.S. market."[9] The Mexican DTOs that effect this conduit historically operated in the southwestern United States but now "are rapidly increasing their influence over drug distribution in all regions of the country," according to the Justice Department's National Drug Intelligence Center. The center reports that

"Mexican DTOs exert greater influence over drug trafficking in the United States than any other organizations" and that "their influence is increasing, particularly with respect to cocaine and methamphetamine distribution."[10] Mexican DTOs are wresting control from old-line Colombian and other criminal organizations in East Coast drug markets. They are also strengthening their relationships with major Latino gangs, which they use to smuggle and distribute drugs, collect proceeds, and serve as enforcers and other forms of criminal muscle.[11]

Los Angeles is today "the most significant illicit drug distribution center in the United States," the only U.S. city that serves as a "national-level drug distribution center for all major drugs of abuse—cocaine, heroin, marijuana, and methamphetamine," as well as other drugs, such as MDMA and PCP. Southern California draws its unique status as a center for drug distribution from "its proximity to the California-Mexico border, sizable Mexican population, elaborate multimodal transportation infrastructure, and expansive rural areas."[12] The alliances that street gangs based in Los Angeles have formed with Mexican DTOs and other criminal groups, combined with the gangs' spread across the United States, have helped drive increased distribution of drugs throughout the country, including expansion of suburban and rural drug markets. These alliances have created long-term criminal networks available for all sorts of dark enterprise beyond drug trafficking, including smuggling of humans and guns. The Columbia Lil' Cycos clique was an early, innovative, and violent contributor to the creation of the Los Angeles system of drug distribution.

The street gang is a reservoir of vast potential energy. That energy—the sum of the testosterone, adrenaline, brains, muscles, vision, and life force of its members—is made kinetic by doing what gangsters call "putting in work for the neighborhood." To the gangster, working for his neighborhood does not mean sweeping sidewalks, cleaning up parks, or painting schools. It means committing crime on behalf of the gang. Members of the CLCS clique testified in a federal trial about their "work" in a chillingly literal and ethically tone-deaf manner. They appeared to lack awareness of, much less appreciation for, the moral and social implications of what they were describing in such matter-of-fact tones.

"It's like going and do drive-bys to another gang, write on the walls," shot caller Juan Manuel Lopez Romero, "Termite," replied when he was asked about work for the neighborhood. His answer implicitly equated murder and vandalism as just so much gangster clock punching. "Well, sometimes they tell you to, for example, sometime they tell you've got to go do a drive-by because homeboy got shot by MS [Mara Salvatrucha] or whatever gang," said CLCS gangster Ismael "Loner" Jimenez. "And so we go, they pay people or sometimes there's volunteers and you just go and do the drive-by."

Anthony "Coco" Zaragoza's lawyer strained to elicit some sympathetic motive to justify his client's having joined the gang and done its "work." "Was there a purpose in joining 18th Street?" the lawyer asked. "To protect yourself and your family from others?" he helpfully suggested. Coco would, however, have none of the rationale, favored among gang apologists, that gangs comprise defensive neighborhood leagues. Zaragoza's reply exemplified LAPD detective Frank Flores's view that gangsters are gangsters because they choose to be, not because they have to be. "Not really," Zaragoza blustered. "It's not just protection, you know what I mean. I was associated with them and, you know, I would participate with them. You know, do drugs with them. And eventually they asked me to join 18 and I did."

Coco bluntly described the nature of the 18th Street gang's relationships with its rivals: "Yeah, we fight each other, shoot each other, stab each other, kill each other. All that." "Was there some benefit in terms of protection in your being part of CLCS?" the frustrated lawyer tried again. "No, Sir," Coco replied obtusely. From the time he was thirteen years old, Coco explained, he "participated in all the gang activities, shooting, vandalism, fighting, everything."

The motives for doing "work" are acceptance and promotion to positions of leadership or better income. "You make a name for yourself in that as time goes by, they start noticing you," Ismael Jimenez explained. "And that's when they say, oh, he's pretty good and I guess you work your way up." Lopez Romero offered a more detailed explanation. "I want to be part of the gang. . . . I want to show them that I can do things that they do so they can accept me," Termite said. "That gives you more power. They start to recognize you more for doing that. The more you do, the more they think about you like being a good guy to hang around with."

This macabre recitation of routine violence contrasts starkly with pieties uttered by gangsters in their private communications. Lil' Cycos enforcer Coco Zaragoza, for example, wrote in a letter from prison that he hoped the recipient—a female gang associate intimately involved in violent criminal activity—was living in a world "blessed with peace, love, happiness, joy and under the protection and guidance of the big man above us," an apparent reference to God. Similarly, in a wire-tapped telephone conversation, another female associate offered pious advice that could have come from the mouth of a priest. "Have faith in God," she urged the gang's leader after a federal raid. "Everybody. Stop. Relax. Have faith in God."

Around 1988, shortly after the CLCS clique was founded, the gang's shot callers sent their foot soldiers out to do a new kind of "work for the neighborhood." A rapacious idea occurred to the leadership of the Lil' Cycos. Drugs, lots of drugs, were being sold in their territory. An existing staple of 18th Street crime was extorting sidewalk vendors, who operated illegally in an informal market.[13] Why give the drug dealers a free ride? The gangsters' new neighborhood "work" was to tell the drug dealers that henceforth they would give up a percentage of their drugs to CLCS members. The gangsters themselves would then sell the narcotics. The sellers had no more alternative than did the sidewalk vendors. Any who resisted were first warned, then beaten up, then whacked if they persisted. What were they going to do, complain to the police?

For a while, Lil' Cycos members sold drugs on the street. It became clear, however, that selling drugs on the street was an unnecessarily risky business. It was too easy to get nailed in a "buy-bust" police sting. It would be safer and more profitable to let the dealers sell the drugs. The gang would extort from them a percentage of their sales in cash, rather than in kind. In addition to giving the dealers the right to sell in CLCS territory, the gang would protect them from competition and violence. A system of "tax" or "rent" on drug sales thus came into being.

By 1989, a weekly collection system was fairly well organized. Each of the shot callers, the clique's leaders, was assigned a specific street or area within the territory, within which to extort "rent" or "taxes" from drug dealers. The shot callers did not collect the taxes themselves. Each had a subordinate team of "backup men." The backup men collected the taxes, patrolled their assigned streets to keep out *piraterias* ("pirates"—persons selling drugs without permission), and prevented unsanctioned violence. Random street crime drew police attention. That was bad for business. Some of the dealers tried to avoid paying rent to CLCS by moving further west, into the territory of another 18th Street clique, the Hollywood Gangsters, or HGs. The Lil' Cycos explained how *renta* worked to the HGs, who set up their own extortion system.

The enterprise worked so well that it soon attracted the attention of the Mexican Mafia, which many would argue is the most powerful prison gang in the United States, certainly in the Southwest. Eme was formed in the late 1950s by young Latino gangsters from Southern California incarcerated at the Deuel Vocational Institute in Tracy, California. Their intention was supposedly to protect themselves from older inmates, including more hardened Latino inmates from Northern California's rural communities and members of white and black prison gangs. The founders were hard cases from a variety of street gangs. They would have been at each other's throats outside of prison. But they were remarkably successful in putting aside their parochial interests and forging a common organization. A smaller number of prisoners from Northern California formed a rival group, Nuestra Familia, whose name means "our family." An attempt to merge the two into a common front failed. Instead, a spectacular prison war broke out between the two Latino gangs. They are now bitter enemies. Each has joined forces with allies among white and black prison gangs—Nuestra Familia with the Black Guerrilla Family and Eme with the Aryan Brotherhood.

Eme imposes strict discipline on its own members and demands ethnic loyalty of all Latino prisoners. The cardinal rules of conduct for Eme members forbid homosexual relations, cowardice, informing on one another, admitting the gang's existence to outsiders, "politicking" against other members, and, in some versions, poaching on another member's wife or girlfriend. All Latino inmates are expected to obey other Eme rules covering personal hygiene, appearance, prison etiquette, and the duty of standing up in ethnic solidarity when interracial prison combat breaks out. Latino prisoners flaunt these rules at the risk of death or serious injury. Unlike some eastern gangs, the Mexican Mafia has an egalitarian, horizontal structure. Leadership is shared among respected *veteranos,* but there is no one chief. The votes of three Eme members are required to authorize the killing of a "made" Eme member and to admit new members from among hopeful hangers-on known as "associates." Such candidates for membership are required to demonstrate their loyalty by committing acts of violence. "If the mafia has any enemies . . . they're also my enemies," Ernesto "Chuco" Castro—a former senior Eme member and one of only a few ever "flipped" by law enforcement—explained in federal court testimony. "So long as I take care of them by stabbing them, then that would deem me eventually a member."

When California's correctional authorities woke up to the gang's presence, they inadvertently aided Eme's growth. In an attempt to break up the gang, they dispersed its leaders throughout the state prison system. This was casting seeds to the wind. Wherever they landed, the leaders organized Latino prisoners. By the late 1980s, when the Columbia Lil' Cycos were setting up their system of taxing drug dealers, Eme's membership was about two hundred or three hundred men. However, its discipline, organization, and willingness to use lethal violence built the gang into a powerful criminal force inside California's prisons. It soon controlled drug trafficking, gambling, smuggling, and prostitution within the walls. Prison officials admit that Eme runs a parallel government. Eme members communicate by talking face-to-face in the exercise yard, passing small notes called "kites" or *wilas,* and using visitors and inmates being transferred to other prisons to carry *wilas* and oral messages to the outside and other prisons. Wives, girlfriends, even mothers are used as channels of communication by the Mexican Mafia.

The gang's reach soon extended outside the prison system. Its leaders deliberately emulated the criminal activities and style of the Italian Mafia, La Cosa Nostra. Mexican Mafia members released from prison carry missions for the gang, including names of persons green-lighted for murder. Specific tasks are handed off to the street gang from which the Eme member originally hailed. With but few exceptions, the street gangs cooperate with the Mexican Mafia. They understand full well that Eme controls inmate life in California's prisons and the Los Angeles County jail system, where most street gangsters sooner or later end up. Anyone who disobeys an order from the Mexican Mafia—whether it be a single gangster, a clique, or an entire gang—will almost certainly be green-lighted.

Apart from going into "administrative segregation," there is no place to hide in prison from an Eme assassin, likely an eager associate seeking to be made a full member. Homemade knives, called "shanks," and other ingeniously crafted weapons are ubiquitous inside the walls. Administrative segregation units are used to isolate inmates who are in danger from other inmates. But life for the protected inmate is grim, and some prefer to take their chances. The California Office of the Inspector General reports, "Unlike general population inmates, those in administrative segregation and security housing units are confined to their cells almost around the clock, including for meals, and are shackled and escorted by guards whenever they leave the cell for showers, exercise, or other reasons. In contrast, inmates assigned to general population housing eat meals in dayrooms and dining halls and spend a substantial portion of the day outside their cells."[14]

The CLCS shot callers cooperated, therefore, when Vevesi "Vesi" Sagato, an Eme member and former 18th Street gangster, showed up in 1990 and announced that the Mafia was taking a cut of the taxes collected by the Lil' Cycos. Treachery and greed followed. It took several years and considerable violence for things to settle down. For one thing, the Lil' Cycos lied at first about how much they were raking in. Eme's men easily found out the truth by going to the dealers. In 1991, Sagato brought in another Eme member, Frank "Puppet" Martinez, an illegal immigrant from Mexico just released from imprisonment for a 1982 voluntary manslaughter conviction. Martinez started as Sagato's bagman, but took over in 1992 when Sagato was sent back to prison. When Puppet Martinez found out that the Hollywood Gangsters were also collecting drug taxes, he expanded his extortionate empire to include them.

Perhaps inspired by the success of the 18th Street gang's tax system, the Mexican Mafia made dramatic moves in 1992 and 1993. Its representatives fanned out and held a series of mandatory mass meetings, usually in public parks, with the leaders of all of the Latino gangs in

Southern California. Shot callers from rival street gangs who would ordinarily have opened fire on sight stood side by side and listened quietly and respectfully. One such meeting was held only a few dozen yards from the LAPD Academy in Elysian Park.[15] The message from the gang of gangs was twofold. First, Eme wanted all of the gangs to tax drug dealers in their territory and remit a cut to the Mafia. Second, the street gangsters were ordered to stop doing drive-by shootings.

Many among the political and social service *nomenklatura* swooned and wildly misinterpreted Eme's motives for the second rule. Concluding that the gangs really wanted to stop the killing, they thought they could lure them out of darkness and mold them into responsible political organizations. "It's none of my business why it happened, but I think it's beautiful that the killing has stopped," said one "anti-gang activist."[16]

The truth was that Eme had no problem with the killing. Its move was entirely self-serving. It wanted to stop drive-bys because they often end in the death of innocent bystanders, which attracts the attention of the police and news media. This attention is bad for business. The word went out that anyone wanting to kill someone should do a walk-up, not a drive-by. "I'm all for peace, but what we're really looking at is the beginning of organized crime," Lt. Sergio Robleto, an LAPD gang homicide commander, said at the time. "I just don't believe that a pact between people who are rapists, murderers and robbers should be hailed with accolades of peace."[17]

The Eme edict led to legalistic hairsplitting worthy of a congressional ethics ruling. The impulse to jump in a car, drive by, and kill someone is deeply ingrained in the gang culture. Some gangsters tried to push the edge of the Mafia's new envelope. Eme's leaders were forced to parse the taxonomy of autoborne death dealing to define exactly what is and is not a "drive-by." Reportedly, the Solomonic decision came down that stopping the car and putting at least one foot on the ground was enough to meet Eme's ukase.

The business of taxing illicit drug dealing was big money. Suddenly, control over scores of millions of dollars was in play. Not surprisingly, a classic intragang struggle broke out within Eme and raged over the next several years. CLCS found itself in the middle of the turmoil, not least because of the greed and dishonesty of its own leaders.

Frank "Puppet" Martinez was the Mafia kingpin overseeing the Lil' Cycos and using their shot callers to act as bagmen funneling tax revenue to him. In 1993, however, Martinez was arrested on a gun possession charge. He turned to his longtime girlfriend, Janie Maria Garcia, and used her as his principal conduit to and from the CLCS clique. In addition to other nicknames, Janie was known as "Mom" and Frank as "Dad" among the CLCS shot-calling bagmen. Lil' Cycos shot callers were instructed to deliver Frank's share of the taxes to Janie. They were to take their instructions from her, relayed from Frank.

In the spring of 1993—while Martinez was incarcerated on the gun possession charge—trouble showed up in the form of several Mexican Mafia members not from the 18th Street gang. These interlopers on Puppet's turf announced that henceforth they were taking a cut of the tax collections. When asked by his shot callers what to do, Puppet Martinez told them to play along with the poaching Eme members. He said that he would straighten things out when he was released from prison. In the summer of 1994, the encroaching Eme members tightened the screws. They sent Carlos Alberto "Truco" Lopez into the territory to collect taxes directly on their behalf. This was part of a power move against Martinez. By then, both he and his main shot caller, Greedy Valerio, had been green-lighted by Eme leaders. Puppet's offenses were putatively "politicking" against other Eme members and promoting an associate to membership without the requisite vote of three members. Greedy, Frank's right-hand man, was judged by Eme to have falsely represented himself as an Eme member while collecting drug taxes on behalf of Frank. In reality, Puppet Martinez's Mexican Mafia *carnales* (brothers) simply thought he was vulnerable and wanted to wrest his lucrative business away from him.

In August 1994, Martinez was released from prison. He immediately set about "straightening things out." He green-lighted Truco Lopez, the interloping collector. Coco Zaragoza—the tattooed tough guy who told the LAPD that he knew nothing about any murder—was instructed to organize the hit. On the night of September 5, 1994, Coco and Juan Manuel "Termite" Lopez stood waiting on opposite sides of Burlington Street with AK-47 rifles. When the Chevrolet Suburban sport-utility in which Truco Lopez and Donatilla Contreras were riding came by, Coco and Termite hosed it down with bullets. Greedy Valerio was at the scene but did no shooting. Nonetheless, he soon found himself in custody. Coco and Termite were released. Greedy was detained and began singing his song for the LAPD tape recorder.

The murder of Truco Lopez was a transforming event for the Columbia Lil' Cycos. The clique had successfully beaten back Frank "Puppet" Martinez's rivals in the Mexican Mafia and established its exclusive writ within the territory it controlled. Little changed when Martinez was again arrested in 1994—this time on a federal felony charge of illegally reentering the country after deportation. Puppet was eventually convicted. During all of the time covered by the remainder of this story, he was incarcerated in various federal prisons. However, he continued to control the CLCS and its system of drug extortion through his trusted alter ego, Janie Garcia, whom he married in a prison ceremony. This jailhouse nuptial did not stop her from enjoying serial liaisons with others while Puppet whiled away his time in prison. "Mom" collected "Dad's" share of the take and held the proceeds in trust—except for hundreds of thousands of dollars she spent to maintain herself in the style to which she became accustomed.

As a reward for his role in the Truco murder, Termite—Juan Manuel Lopez Romero—was promoted to chief shot caller in charge of running the extortion scheme, replacing Greedy Valerio. Termite proved to be an effective manager. He reorganized the extortion scheme and greatly increased the gang's take. When Lopez Romero took over in 1994, the Lil' Cycos clique was collecting about $20,000 per week. By 1995, Termite had increased the haul to $50,000 per week. In 1999, the Lil' Cycos bagmen were moving a whopping $250,000 a month through their system. Termite tripled the gang's revenues in five years.

One of Termite's reforms was forcing regular shifts on the street dealers, in place of their prior practice of bunching up at peak times. The CLCS area was now open for business twenty-four hours a day, vastly increasing sales. Another Termite innovation was going after the wholesalers, mostly Honduran and known as *mayoristas*. Previously, the gang taxed only the *traqueteros,* the retail street dealers. In addition to a percentage, the gang enforced a flat fee on the drug dealers. "We didn't care about nothing, how much they sold or nothing," tough guy Coco Zaragoza testified in his inimitably self-incriminating manner. "Because if they didn't sell what they sell, they were going to pay regardless. You know what I mean? We had nothing to do with how much drugs they sold. We were just actually extorting them."

The Niagara of cash caused internal tensions within the Lil' Cycos, aggravated by the psychopathological gangster obsession with "respect" and violence. As FBI special agent Jim Wines observes, the gangsters' chief negotiating tool is the gun. They do not sit down to negotiate.

In 1995, shot caller Javier "Lefty" Cazales fell out of favor with Janie "Mom" Garcia on two counts. One, he was suspected of skimming from his crew's tax collections—holding back funds that were due Puppet Martinez. Two, he continually "disrespected" Janie by delivering his collections in small denominations, an obvious inconvenience for a person handling as much cash as was Janie Garcia. The irascible Coco Zaragoza was also annoyed with Lefty for slacking on neighborhood "work" and for questioning the propriety of killing a woman, Donatilla Contreras, in the course of the Truco murder. Coco appears to have actually regarded Garcia and Martinez—"Mom" and "Dad"—as surrogate parents. He was incensed by Lefty's disrespect to Janie and began "politicking" against his homey. On instructions from Martinez, Termite, now the chief shot caller, called Lefty in for a counseling session. Lefty agreed to make up the several thousand dollars he was accused of embezzling. But he delivered the money to Janie Garcia in a huge bundle of one-dollar bills.

Lefty Cazales might as well have attached to the bundle a note reading, "Kill me, please." By that affront to Janie, he signed his own death warrant. Martinez issued a green light on Cazales. Coco, the gang's enforcer, was again charged with setting up a murder. He assigned the task to a fellow gangster known as "Snoopy." Janie, Termite, and Snoopy met to discuss the best way to do the job. "The guy Snoopy asked me what would be my advice," Termite later testified. "I just told him, you know the guy has been carrying a gun . . . and he's going to try to shoot you first. . . . And Janie said, yes, of course, you're going to have to do it first, right, and they said yeah, okay."

In accordance with the plan, Lefty Cazales was lured to a meeting with Coco at Thu Do Billiards, a pool hall at 1811 West Sixth Street. Snoopy was waiting with a four-inch, forty-caliber Smith and Wesson Model 411 semiautomatic pistol, serial number TVW0472. Immediately after Lefty entered the hall, Snoopy shot him several times. Then, as the mortally wounded Lefty lay on his back on the floor, Snoopy stood over him, shoved the gun in Lefty's mouth, and shot him again. The assassin stood over his fallen victim and emptied the gun's magazine into his torso. Altogether, Snoopy shot Lefty seven times.

The murder of Lefty Cazales cast a long shadow. LAPD detectives found the Smith and Wesson forty-caliber pistol in one of Coco's residences. In the course of defending Coco on the resulting gun possession charge, Coco's lawyer demanded "discovery" documents from the LAPD files. "The homeboys know the legal system better than most lawyers," says FBI agent Sandford. "They use the rules of discovery and evidence in criminal cases to get 'paperwork' confirming who the rats are."

The Lil' Cycos hit pay dirt. Nestled among the materials the LAPD served up willy-nilly to Coco's mouthpiece was the "Greedy Tape"— Valerio's ramblings with homicide detectives during the investigation of the Truco murder in 1994. Coco now had all the "paperwork" he needed to nail Greedy. The only inconvenience was that he would now have to do his deadly machinations from a prison cell. He was charged with being a felon in possession of a firearm and spent the rest of the time period covered in this story in state prison.

Despite the internal violence and the imprisonment of two of their key leaders—Frank "Puppet" Martinez and Anthony "Coco" Zaragoza—the Lil' Cycos and their extortion scheme seemed to be doing quite well. Notwithstanding Greedy's candid chat with Detective Bub, the scheme of taxing drug sales had not come up on the radar screen of any law enforcement agency willing to pursue it. The enterprise was just so much wallpaper. Random arrests continued from time to time. But no agency was pursuing the big picture. Life was good for

"Mom," "Dad," and the boys. That was a comfortable illusion. Federal prosecutor Bruce Riordan and FBI special agent Carl Sandford were about to start circling in on the Lil' Cycos.

The theoretical potential of the power to bring gangsters like Mexican Mafia thug Frank "Puppet" Martinez and his underlings among the Columbia Lil' Cycos before the bar of federal justice is enormous. The individual prosecutions for murder, assault, and drug dealing typical of state cases are like a running series of infantry firefights. Some of the gang's soldiers may be knocked out of action. Fewer of its leaders will be hit, because they leave the dirty work to underlings. The criminal enterprise adjusts to its losses, recruits new cannon fodder for the streets, and continues its business. In contrast, prosecuting under the federal "enterprise theory" is like flying in a stealth bomber and dropping a blockbuster bomb straight down the chimney of the gang's headquarters. Federal criminal statutes offer a wider and more sophisticated web of offenses with which to charge equivalent criminal conduct. Federal penalties are draconian compared to most state penalties. The federal system offers no parole. Convicted gang leaders can be dispersed among different federal prisons. The principal federal investigative agencies and some of the lesser agencies have greater resources—funds, personnel, technical expertise, and equipment—than most local law enforcement agencies.

But actualizing this awesome potential and turning it into the successful prosecution of a complex organization is not an easy thing to do—except in the fevered imaginations of Hollywood writers and think-tanked civil libertarians. The chemistry required to ignite and sustain a major federal case is not intricate, but it is elusive. A few critical elements must come together at just the right time in just the right way to spark the reaction.

Principal among these critical elements is the joining together on a specific case of federal prosecutors and federal investigators who are equally interested, committed, and competent. The power to make a federal case work well is not something that is "shared" between federal prosecutors and investigators. It is "interactive." To say that a power is shared implies that it is held in a state of relative equality and that authority over and responsibility for the several elements of the process are parceled out in a more or less static equilibrium. That looks good on organization charts. But in the real world, the influence and control of each player waxes and wanes depending on the nature of the case at hand and on each player's commitment and willingness to cooperate with the other, or push an agenda, to achieve a particular goal. In some cases, the dominant force is the investigative agency; in others, the prosecutors. Random factors also come into play, including the individual preferences of prosecutors, agents, U.S. attorneys, attorneys general, agency directors, presidents, and the Congress. But two basic facts are consistently at play in this dynamic. No criminal case gets into federal court unless a federal prosecutor brings it there, and few cases land on the desk of a federal prosecutor unless a federal investigative agency puts them there.

A federal stealth strike on the Columbia Lil' Cycos gangster empire was destined the moment Bruce Riordan and Carl Sandford shook hands for the first time in Riordan's office. Each found in the other the critical missing elements he had been seeking after poking around Los Angeles's Latino gangs. "Bruce was fighting his demons and I was fighting mine," Sandford recalls of their respective agencies' attitudes at the time. "And we were both fighting the bad guys."

A print depicting the battle of Rorke's Drift hung on the wall of assistant U.S. attorney Bruce Riordan's office on the fifteenth floor of the U.S. Courthouse at 312 North Spring Street in Los Angeles. In the late afternoon of January 22, 1879, Zulu warriors numbering between four thousand and five thousand men attacked a detachment of about 140 British soldiers, including several dozen sick and wounded, bivouacked in a small missionary station at Rorke's Drift in Natal, South Africa. (A "drift" is a ford or river crossing—in this case, across the Buffalo River.) The attack began the day after a Zulu army massacred a British force at the Battle of Isandlwana, a humiliating defeat for the empire. Overcoming the superior firepower of the British invaders, the Zulu warriors at Isandlwana killed 850 European soldiers and 450 native soldiers in British service. No more than fifty-five Europeans survived the slaughter. The jubilant Zulu then sent a column to crush the paltry detachment at Rorke's Drift, about ten miles distant. Incredibly, the rump detachment led by Royal Engineers lieutenant John Chard repulsed the vastly superior number of Zulus who attacked in waves throughout the night and into the next morning. Eleven of the defenders were awarded the Victoria Cross (roughly the equivalent of the U.S. Medal of Honor) for valor in the face of the enemy. The battle of Rorke's Drift is taught today as among the greatest examples in military history of small-unit defense against superior force. The 1964 movie *Zulu*, in which actor Michael Caine made his film debut, tells the story. It is acclaimed as a historically accurate and evenhanded drama, portraying courage on both sides of the fight.

A white pith helmet of the type worn by the British at Rorke's Drift lay on a nearby table in Riordan's work space, among the typical flotsam and jetsam of a prosecutor's office—fat briefs, bulging boxes of files, plaques from investigative agencies, and a typhoon of random pleadings and notes swirling around an overloaded desk. The symbolism no doubt reflects the infusion of character into a man whose father flew as a bombardier-navigator on B-29 missions in the Pacific theater of World War II. "We watched all the old flying movies, and we knew every line," says Riordan. "The same with *Zulu*." If the battle at Rorke's Drift stands for anything greater than excellent unit tactics, it must be the honor of valor or the value of honor—the worth of self-discipline, the courage to stand fast, and the grit to stick by comrades in the face of withering odds. In the circumstances that handful of redcoated men faced in 1879, the instinct to flee must have been nearly irresistible. Bruce Riordan's supervision of the federal case against Frank Martinez and the Columbia Lil' Cycos demanded some portion of these qualities at several crucial junctures. At one point, he showed *Zulu* to his team of prosecutors and investigators to buck them up against the demoralizing indifference of higher-ups to their case.

It was not as if Riordan had not asked for the fight he was about to get into. He had finished his tour on Rookie Row and was now hitting full stride as a prosecutor. In the meantime, he had seen the whiz kid who was going to show the federal prosecutors in Los Angeles how to do big RICO cases against gangs, William Hogan, recalled to Chicago under an embarrassing cloud. A federal judge threw out the El Rukn convictions that made Hogan's name. The prosecutor was forced to defend himself against charges that he had condoned misconduct by some of his cooperating witnesses, including their using drugs and having sex in federal offices. Hogan's personal case dragged on for years—he was fired twice by the Justice Department—until a federal administrative law judge finally ruled in his favor and ordered him reinstated with back pay. Riordan wanted his own big case. "If you're going to climb up the ladder," he says, "you have got to make a big case."

"What's a big case?" he asks, then answers his own question. "It's like pornography. You'll know it when you see it. And I was starting to think I would never get a big one."

Bruce Riordan was born in Worcester, Massachusetts, in 1960. "My family was all Irish Catholic as far back as you can take it," he says. "All four of my grandparents came directly from Ireland, from Cork on my father's side and Galway on my mother's side." If there is such a thing as stereotypical as "Gaelic manhood," Riordan inherited his share of it. Though well-mannered and articulate, he is not a man one would be wise to take lightly in any competitive situation. His father was in real estate, his mother a public schoolteacher. Riordan admired an older brother and was deeply affected by his untimely death in an airplane crash when Bruce was eleven years old. "If anyone in the neighborhood had anything to fix, he would fix it," recalls Riordan. "Brian was the most mechanically capable person I have ever known."

Riordan attended the University of Massachusetts at Amherst, from which he graduated with honors in 1982. This was by way of a detour of three semesters in a special program of studies at Yale University, the result of a thesis he had written on jazz. He found the academic stimulation of his semesters at Yale "fantastic" and a boost to his self-confidence. "I realized that if I could succeed here," he recalls, "I am not going to fail." He went on to graduate with honors from Boston College Law School in 1986. He worked as a summer associate at O'Melveny and Myers during law school. After graduating, he won a clerkship with U.S. district judge William P. Gray. Described as "affable and influential" by the *Los Angeles Times* in his obituary, Gray presided over a number of difficult cases. During the year of Riordan's clerkship, Gray presided over lawsuits challenging jail overcrowding in Los Angeles and Orange counties, portents of a chronic problem that plagues California today.[18] "Judge Gray was both a mentor and a kind of grandfather figure to me," says Riordan. The judge also helped Riordan eventually land a job in the Los Angeles U.S. attorney's office.

After his clerkship, Riordan spent four years at O'Melveny and Myers working for a series of "brilliant" lawyers. "I thought being around them would make me brilliant," he says. One of them was "superlawyer" Charles P. "Chuck" Diamond, now the firm's litigation chief. Among other noted cases, Diamond guided Paramount Pictures to a strategic settlement after writer Art Buchwald won a breach-of-contract suit over the Eddie Murphy movie *Coming to America*. He also commanded the legal team that successfully defended the 2003 California recall that brought down Governor Gray Davis and led to the installation of Governor Arnold Schwarzenegger. "It was a pleasure to be beaten up by him," recalls Riordan of the relationship between a high-flying partner and a groundling associate.

However much he enjoyed getting intellectually battered, Riordan's heart was not in the pursuit of the dollar that drives the nation's law factories. Like Carl Sandford, also a lawyer, Riordan heard a call to public service. He had already applied twice to the U.S. attorney's office, once during his clerkship and again two years later. But U.S. attorneys rarely hire freshmen lawyers, and there was a hiring freeze at the time of his second application. The Los Angeles U.S. attorney's office was then considered one of the most prestigious in the nation, second only to the office of the Southern District of New York. Appointments were competitive. Twenty times as many lawyers applied as there were openings—when any were available at all.[19] More recently, the offices of all ninety-eight U.S. attorneys have been buffeted by hiring freezes, budget problems, and turmoil over policy and management at the highest levels of the Department of Justice. The number of unfilled full-time positions nationwide jumped from 198 in 2004 to 765 in May 2006. In the Los Angeles office, 40 out of 190 positions were vacant in July 2006, in the midst of a long-term hiring freeze.[20]

When Riordan told Diamond of his intent to try again to become a federal prosecutor, the superlawyer replied, "That's the one thing I've never done that I wish I had done." "Judge Gray went to the mat for me," says Riordan. "The third time was a charm." U.S. attorney Lourdes Baird hired Riordan, who reported for duty in September 1991. The real power in the office, however, was the senior career lawyer, Robert L. Brosio. Riordan would not have made it through the door without Brosio's nod. "Brosio looked for hard-chargers, someone who had a chip on his shoulder, looking to prove himself," Riordan says, implicitly describing himself.

By 1993, Riordan had earned his spurs and was seasoned enough to become the office's designated representative to the new federal multi-agency gang task force. He prosecuted a variety of gangsters on federal charges but was convinced that the office was missing the boat by not pursuing RICO charges against at least some of the more organized gangs. However, any such suggestion had to go through the office's Organized Crime Strike Force. The old bulls in organized crime dismissed the idea that a mere street gang merited the lofty attention of a RICO case. Stuck in the comfortably familiar old world of LCN gang busting, the old boys mocked Latino gang activities as "just street crime." The section summarily rejected a proposed RICO case against the Mexican Mafia when the FBI's investigators first brought it to the office. The determined FBI investigators then took the investigation to Lisa Lench, an assistant U.S. attorney prosecuting drug crimes. She grasped the possibilities and accepted the case. In May 1995, Lench won an indictment against twenty-two Mexican Mafia members and associates on RICO charges. It was the first RICO prosecution against a Latino gang in Southern California. In 1997, ten Eme bosses were sentenced to terms in federal prison of life without parole. Other members were given stiff sentences.

Having been pestered by Riordan for a "big case," Riordan's supervisor Dave Scheper claimed the 18th Street beat and assigned it to the young prosecutor in early 1993. There was a big catch, however. No one had started an in-depth investigation of the 18th Street gang, much less one aimed at a RICO indictment. The single-page "assignment sheet" handed to Riordan was essentially blank. "18th Street gang" were the only words written on it. "From that single piece of paper, the entire structure of the investigation was built," says Riordan. "I was truly working with a blank slate. That meant it was much harder than picking up an existing investigation. But it also meant that I could make of it whatever I wanted to. So long as I could find a team."

Wanting a team was one thing. Finding it was another. "You can only go so far as your investigator will take you," Riordan recalls being told early in his career. "Find one or two good agents and cultivate them." His early investigators on the 18th Street case were not even interested in leaving the barn. "Two FBI agents were assigned to the case," he recalls. "Both were inadequate for this particular job. One was a good guy who only wanted to serve out his time until his next transfer. The other was a really blustering guy who hated lawyers. Not a good team. Neither knew anything about the gang and neither was very curious." Riordan had to "beg, borrow, and steal information" from sources in the LAPD and INS. He "complained and whined enough" that the two agents were reassigned—the blusterer to "dark-side terrorism," which Riordan says "was then used as a dumping grounds for agents who could not work within the system." Their replacement was Carl Sandford.

"That began a great partnership," says Riordan. "I could see right away that Carl was smart, had a good sense of humor, and was a real FBI agent, a real detective, not a cowboy or a wannabe cop. His work was careful and organized." Sandford also proved to be a man to whom Riordan could trust his back. Another agent was frustrated by Riordan's refusal to accept for federal prosecution what the prosecutor concluded was nothing more than a "glorified state case." The angry agent went back and stirred up his supervisors at the FBI field office. They set about interviewing all the agents working with Riordan, in an apparent attempt to discredit him. "Only two agents bucked their superiors and stood up for me," Riordan explains. "One was Carl. I still work with the other. In fact, these two were the cornerstone of nearly everything I accomplished between 1997 and 2006."

One more thing impressed Riordan about the "mild-mannered and quiet" Sandford. The agent had only one nonfamily item hanging on the wall of his office cubicle. It was a picture of actor Clint Eastwood in his original "Dirty Harry" movie role, wielding a huge Model 29 .44 Magnum revolver, "the most powerful handgun in the world." "That confirmed it for me," says Riordan. "Here is a guy I can work with."

Gang squads were the shiny new toy within the Bureau," Carl Sandford says of the assignment he was given when he arrived in Los Angeles in July 1993. "I didn't know what a gang was. I didn't have a clue. But a lot of priority was being given to them." Sandford was part of a surge of FBI agents who were assigned to the Los Angeles Metropolitan Task Force on Violent Crime formed in the wake of the Rodney King Riots. There were ten FBI gang squads in the Los Angeles program. Eight of them were assigned to investigate black gangs. Brian Truchon was on one of them, investigating the Grape Street Crips set. Of the two remaining squads, one was devoted to investigating the Mexican Mafia.

When Sandford arrived in July 1993, he was assigned to a squad investigating black gangs. In November, he was reassigned to the tenth squad, which was further divided into two teams. "One group worked the Crips," Sandford says. "The other was assigned to investigate the 18th Street gang. It was really just me and two LAPD cops." Their task was formidable. The 18th Street gang was estimated to have twenty thousand members in Southern California at the time.[21] "We were not a priority," Sandford says of the disparities between the attention given the black and Latino gangs and the paucity of resources assigned to investigating the Latino gangs. "You can yell and scream," he adds, "but until something happens on the outside, nothing is going to change."

Sandford is broad-shouldered, fit, well over six feet tall, and speaks with relaxed confidence. His task force colleagues dubbed him "the Big Homey" after a defense lawyer badgered him on the witness stand to name the nonexistent "Big Homey" behind his client's criminal acts. When Sandford returned to the office the next day, he found a banner with the words "The Big Homey" streaming as a screen saver across his computer screen. Sandford approached his daunting task head-on but methodically, like a running back looking for a hole in the defensive line. "I told the cops that I didn't know my butt from a hole in the ground when it came to gangs," he says. "But I wanted to get educated. So they took me out to all the neighborhoods and I started to learn the lay of the land."

It was a whole new world for Sandford, who was born in Columbus, Ohio, in 1962. When he was eight years old, his family moved to Plantation, Florida (just west of Fort Lauderdale), where his father was a policeman. Sandford, who thinks of himself as a Floridian, graduated from Florida State University in 1984 with a bachelor's degree in criminology. He knew that he had no interest in being a "street cop" and "floated around" for a year trying to figure out his life's path. In 1985, he entered the Shepard Broad Law Center at Nova University (now Nova Southeastern University) in Davie, Florida. While he was in law school, he applied to the FBI, but he forewent the opportunity to become an agent in 1988 in favor of an offer from a civil law firm to do medical malpractice litigation. In less than a year, Sandford decided he wanted to do something more for his country than chase ambulances. He contacted the FBI and asked if his old test scores were still good and if the bureau was still interested in him. They were, and it was. In May 1989, Sandford was hired. He graduated from the FBI Academy in August 1989 and spent four years in Mobile, Alabama, on the white-collar crime squad. He was then ordered to Los Angeles.

Everything about Los Angeles was different from the slower pace and steady focus of work in Mobile. "There was all sorts of violent crime, and the murder rate was going through the roof," Sandford recalls. The pressure was on to hit the Los Angeles street gangs with RICO cases quickly, but the resources available were considerably less than the expectations of the higher-ups. "We were expected to produce results without any support, meaning enough manpower," Sandford recalls. "We were supposed to go after the gangs the way we went after the LCN, but the situation was entirely different. We had a lot of experience with the LCN. We had been working them since the 1960s. We knew who their players were, we had informants within their organizations, and we knew how they operated. But investigating the Los Angeles gangs was a whole new venture for us. We did what we could with what we had."

Sandford was a quick study. Shortly after his accelerated street orientation with the LAPD officers, he met Riordan. The team knew they could not take on the entire 18th Street gang. They decided to focus on a neighborhood in West Los Angeles known as Smiley Drive, not overly far from Beverly Hills. The Smiley Hauser clique of the 18th Street gang and a neighboring Crips set were engaged in constant violent skirmishes. "There was a lot of shooting back and forth," says Sandford, "and an LAPD officer was shot at." It seemed a good place to start digging around, but the immediate problem was finding a way to peer into the gang's criminal operations.

Many hours, days, nights, weeks, and months of basic shoe-leather investigation followed. The fantasy Feds of screen and television sit before omniscient computers, tap on a few keys, and call up glitzy screenloads of real-time surveillance. They find out within seconds who is doing what and where they are doing it, complete with three-dimensional details of interior building layouts in infrared, ultraviolet, X-ray renditions and high-definition sound. According to a seasoned senior prosecutor in the Justice Department's headquarters, even some federal judges without extensive law enforcement experience buy into such popular media myths. He says that frustrated prosecutors sometimes hear such ill-informed judges say, "The federal government, with all its resources, ought to be able to do such and such," when they pontificate from the bench about what they imagine the government's omnipotence to be.[22]

In the real world, an FBI agent opening a new investigation into a criminal organization, as Carl Sandford was, often spends long, mindnumbing hours observing what appear at first to be random—even chaotic—interactions among "persons of interest," some of whose names are not known and whose roles are at best murky. The agent often starts with old-fashioned visual observation of suspects—watching who does what on the street. "We spent a lot of time sitting in a van, watching people coming and going," says Sandford.

Observation is aided by a variety of ingenious means. They include specially constructed vehicles (e.g., one-way glass that looks like metal from the outside), hidden cameras (sometimes called "pole cameras") that can be left in strategic locations and observed remotely, disguises (e.g., as utility crews), and the use of observation posts inside nearby buildings. None of this basic investigation requires judicial warrant, as it is directed at public activity. Once the players and their roles are sorted out, other investigative means may be used, such as searches of motor vehicle and real estate records and the investigative files of local police agencies. In Sandford's case, this was all coordinated with the LAPD's very active "buy-bust" operations in the Smiley Drive area.

"We started by focusing on what we knew they were doing, which was selling drugs," Sandford explains. "None of them were going to talk to us unless we put them into a jam, because that's all they know, the only way they respond. So we started with small undercover drug buys, trying to develop the intelligence to support bigger cases."

It was during the Smiley Drive investigation that Sandford's team first started to hear vague references to another, bigger operation. "We started hearing about people named Frank, Janie, Termite, and Greedy," says Sandford. "But we really didn't know a lot about them." This was about the time that the Lil' Cycos were violently consolidating their organization while fending off the Mexican Mafia poachers. According to Sandford, the typical complaint from a Smiley gangster caught in a drug "buy-bust" sting went something like, "Why are you picking on us? All the money is being made down in Columbia. You should be going after 'Mom' and 'Dad.'"

The leaders of the Smiley clique were eventually brought up on charges of illegal distribution of crack cocaine. But it was no intelligence bonanza. All pleaded guilty, but none chose to take a plea bargain and become an informant. "They all took their lumps and went to prison," says Sandford. "So we decided next to go up and take a look at the Hollywood Gangsters."

Investigating the HGs brought the team a giant step closer to Frank Martinez's operation—by then, Puppet was collecting "rent" from the HGs as well as the Lil' Cycos. The whole scheme and its players may seem transparent in retrospect. At the time, however, they were opaque. Only glimmers of intelligence emerged from the murk. A key piece of intelligence came from a companion FBI investigation.

The task force squad assigned to the Mexican Mafia was industriously building a RICO case against Eme and a number of its leaders. That case got a generous start in 1993, when the Los Angeles County Sheriff's Department "flipped" a senior Eme leader, Ernest "Chuco" Castro, who was a major force in the Mafia's drive to harness the Latino street gangs in Southern California. Having recently been released from prison and still on parole, Chuco Castro was arrested on a charge of weapons possession. LASD gang sergeant Richard Valdemar's astute management of Castro's case was the lever that turned Castro's world upside down. Valdemar knew that Chuco was crazy about his infant daughter. The shot-calling gangster was settled down into the equivalent of upper-middle-class life. He dreaded going back to prison for what could in effect be a life sentence of up to seventy years. Valdemar and other deputies played Chuco Castro like a cello. When he agreed to cooperate, Valdemar scrambled to bring the U.S. attorney and the FBI on board. He knew that only the Feds had the necessary resources—money and a witness protection program—to fully exploit Castro's defection. Chuco set up a series of meetings with Eme leaders in motel rooms that the FBI wired for sound and video. Eventually, a massive RICO case—the one the old bulls turned down and the first of a series against the Mexican Mafia—was successfully prosecuted.

In early 1994, the FBI learned from the videotaped meetings of the Eme's "green lights" on Frank Martinez and Greedy Valerio. Martinez was arrested on the immigration charge of reentry after deportation, and Greedy—who would soon be questioned by the LAPD in connection with the Truco murder—was now on the FBI's radar screen. Riordan selected Greedy as the first member of what he came to call the "Green Light Club."

Readers of the *Los Angeles Times* opened their Sunday morning newspaper to the first installment of a three-part series on the 18th Street gang on November 17, 1996.[23] The news was disturbing, even to blasé Angelenos. "On average, someone in Los Angeles County is assaulted or robbed by 18th Streeters every day," the newspaper intoned. "The gang has left a bloody trail of more than 100 homicides in the city of Los Angeles since 1990—a pace three times that of many of the city's most active gangs."[24]

The first part of the series chronicled the gang's rise; the second, its devastating impact on the communities it infested; and the third, the failure of law enforcement agencies to bring the gang to heel. "Citing limited resources, law enforcement agencies have primarily focused on intermittent street-level crackdowns, bringing only fleeting relief to residents and merchants," the paper complained. "Authorities have had difficulty penetrating the gang's hierarchy and its suspected international drug connections."[25] That critical observation was salt in the wound for Carl Sandford and Bruce Riordan, who were precisely trying to penetrate the gang's hierarchy and make a RICO case against it. Both had been hampered by stingy resources and indifferent—at times hostile—managers. "I got little support from my front office," Riordan recalls. "They had convinced themselves that street gangs were disorganized hoodlums. They were unable to comprehend that 18th Street and Eme were running a protection racket—simple, old-fashioned organized crime."

The *Los Angeles Times* series had little impact on Riordan's situation. "I was forced to carry a full case calendar and pursue 18th Street as a hobby," he recalls. But the series stung the FBI, ever conscious of its crime-fighting image and local standing. The agency opened its pantry for Sandford's gang squad. "The Bureau in all of its wisdom now decides that maybe we should go after 18th Street, after all," says Sandford. "I suddenly get the manpower and support I need." At its height, Sandford's squad would grow from two agents and two LAPD officers to ten agents and fifteen LAPD officers. Among newly assigned agents who played major roles in the 18th Street investigations were James "Jim" Wines and Tiburcio "Tibs" Aguilar.

By early 1997, a rough sketch of the criminal enterprise that Eme boss Puppet Martinez and the Columbia Lil' Cycos were running had emerged. But "knowing" what was going on was hardly enough to bring an indictment, much less convict the sprawling pack of gangsters. The challenge was to methodically obtain hard, admissible evidence that tied the whole enterprise into a comprehensible package. Riordan wanted every jot and tittle nailed down tightly. He and Sandford put their heads together, took a page out of the FBI's long history of investigating LCN, and devised an investigative strategy that would leverage everything into a polished case. The fulcrum they selected was Greedy Valerio.

"No informant, no case" is an axiom of conspiracy cases in general and RICO cases in particular. ("No case, no problems" is another, more cynical aphorism.) The team set out to flip Greedy and make him their prime informant. From him, they would branch out to bring others into Riordan's exclusive "Green Light Club"—gang members who had been unfairly green-lighted by their shot-calling homies. "Carl and I would never use cheap jailhouse snitches," Riordan explains. "We sought command staff people who had been loyal *soldados* but who had fallen out of favor and were trapped by a rotten system that began to eat its own. Once these soldiers realize they have been betrayed by their paranoid and ruthless bosses, they no longer feel a sense of loyalty to those against whom they are going to testify."

Gang squad members Tibs Aguilar and John Neveda—FBI agents fluent in Spanish—set out to track Greedy down. Aguilar is taciturn and unnervingly wraithlike. He has an uncanny ability to blend into the background. If you turn your back for a moment during a conversation, he seems to disappear into thin air. This trait serves him well on the streets, where he is able to move about without attracting attention. He declines to talk much about himself for the very reason that he might be out on the street chatting up an unknowing Latino gangster at any given moment of day or night .

"We decided just to hit Greedy up cold," Sandford says. "Neveda and Aguilar found him, went to see him, and threw our pitch on him." The "pitch" was to lay out the stark truth to a man the FBI concluded was intelligent, rational, and not inherently violent. Riordan describes the script presented to Greedy: "You have already been branded as a snitch, even though you are not. So you may as well cooperate. You have no other choice. You can walk alone. Or you can work with us— on our terms. It is not personal; it is the correct business decision. You would be a fool to do anything else. Don't be a fool."

Greedy chose not to be a fool. "He'll talk to us," Neveda reported to Sandford. But that was only the first step in the long, careful process of interrogation and vetting that the best agents put into developing an informant into a useful and reliable asset. "We set up a meeting in a hotel room, sit down, and let him start talking," says Sandford. "He opened up the floodgates, and he was a guy who had firsthand knowledge of the entire operation. Then we had a series of meetings with him, because there are a lot of issues and details to work out. We needed to know exactly what he himself had done. For example, what precisely was his role in the Truco murder?"

It was a delicate dance, because the agents could not guarantee that Greedy would not end up in prison until they knew the whole story, and to get the whole story, Greedy had to talk. His truthfulness and the reliability of his evidence needed to be independently confirmed as well. Aguilar was responsible for managing Greedy and other informants in the case, a job that is something like being a surrogate parent to an emotional child. Informants tend to share every personal crisis with their handlers. "The individual is vetted thoroughly and painstakingly through debriefings that can last for hours and allow for a thorough cross-check of facts," says Riordan. In August 1997, for example, Sandford directed Greedy to call Janie Garcia and tell her he wanted to get right with the gang. His conversation with Janie established that he really had been a major player. It also set in motion internal maneuvering within the gang that ultimately helped the investigation. Greedy passed every such test given him.

"The next step is to create a comprehensive 302 [an FBI document] documenting the debriefing in detail," Riordan explains. "That serves as the master document for the next phase of the investigation, which is obtaining warrants and wiretaps." Although Greedy could not safely appear in his old neighborhood, he still had contacts with the *mayoristas*, or drug wholesalers. He started making drug buys while wearing a "wire," which, in today's high-tech world, is often as small as and disguised as a shirt button. Greedy helped the investigators steadily build up a treasure chest of evidence about the overall enterprise and its participants. At one point, Greedy helped move an undercover agent far enough into the web that a plan was devised for the agent to "buy" a street from shot caller Termite and become a *traquetero*, a street dealer paying taxes to the Lil' Cycos. The Department of Justice nixed the idea. It was okay to buy drugs in sting operations, but selling drugs was off the table.

Based on what Greedy told them and other evidence it developed, the FBI focused its attention on "Mom," Janie Garcia. "Trash pulls"—LAPD officers volunteered to get up early, ride the garbage trucks, and dig through Janie's trash—yielded tantalizing documentary evidence, such as discarded papers that appeared to be records of tax payments from shot callers. Techniques to track the numbers of incoming and outgoing telephone calls, called "pen registers" and "traps and traces," were used to map who was talking to whom—a technique called "pattern analysis." Pen registers show all numbers a given telephone calls. Trap-and-trace devices show the numbers of incoming calls. These investigative techniques require judicial approval. But since they do not make it possible to listen to conversations, a lower standard is applied than for an actual wiretap in which conversations are recorded. The evidence obtained from these devices documented Termite's key role. Recordings of phone calls that Frank and Coco made from their respective prisons were also obtained. No warrants were needed, since all prisoners are informed that their calls will be recorded and can be reviewed by authorities. "We established from these prison calls that Janie was basically running the show," Sandford says.

When the undercover plan was shelved, the team decided that it would have to "go up" with a wiretap. "Mom" Garcia was the logical choice. She seemed to be the most stable person in the group in terms of staying in one place, and she was at the center of the conspiracy. The process of getting and maintaining a Title III wiretap (acceptable under the Federal Wiretap Act) is vastly more difficult and time-consuming than is popularly imagined. Application for a warrant must be made to a federal judge, supported by a statement of "probable cause" and an affidavit detailing the investigation to date and why less intrusive means will not work. Theoretically, any federal law enforcement officer can make such an application. In practice, virtually all applications must be cleared through a special unit in the Department of Justice, the Office of Enforcement Operations (OEO). If a federal judge agrees and approves the warrant, it is good for only thirty days and must be renewed thereafter with a further statement to the judge justifying the renewal. Detailed records must be kept, and care must be taken to "minimize" the intrusion by listening only to conversations related to the probable crime. It is a difficult and time-consuming process.

Riordan was determined to get the wiretap application right. He knew that the defense lawyers would furiously attack it and the process by which the warrant was issued, if and when the case went to trial. If the wiretap were thrown out, all of the evidence flowing from it would fall as well. The case would be gutted. Sandford drafted the application and supporting affidavit. Riordan scoured every word. But defense lawyers were not their only problem. "Sometimes we fight ourselves more than the bad guys," reflects Sandford.

"Word came down from the U.S. attorney's front office that they did not want to pursue the wire," Riordan says. "They did not believe in the RICO theory of our case. This prompted a showdown." The OEO will not even look at a proposed application if the local U.S. attorney has not signed off on it. The front office could kill the application before its first breath. Riordan played his hole card in an all-or-nothing gamble at a sit-down with his bosses. His career was riding on the bet. "I said that there was no reason for me to proceed with the 18th Street investigation if we did not go forward with the Garcia wire," he recalls, "and that Carl felt the same."

There was a tense moment of silence as all present reflected on the stakes. If the investigation were abandoned, embarrassing questions might be asked from both inside and outside the Justice Department. Who knew what that could lead to? A bad decision would wreck more than one career. Riordan's bold call of the front office's obstructive move caused the old bulls to throw in their cards. "Fine," they apparently thought, "let this hotshot kid screw it up." After some editing to save front-office face, the application and affidavit were approved by the U.S. attorney in Los Angeles and sent on to the Justice Department in Washington. Overcoming its own doubt about using RICO against the Latino street gang, the OEO approved the application. A federal judge soon issued an order allowing the phone tap. In a move of careful foresight, Riordan attached a sealed statement identifying Greedy as the informant whose information was at the heart of the application and laying out Greedy's criminal history. He correctly foresaw that the defense lawyers would claim later that the judge would never have allowed the wiretap if he had known what a disreputable person the informant, Greedy, was. But the judge knew all about Greedy before he issued the wiretap warrant. The defense attack on the warrant never got off the beach. The Ninth Circuit Court of Appeals rejected the defense criticism.

The wiretap on Janie's phone went up in October 1998. The conspirators routinely tried to conduct business using amateurish code, as protection against just such an eventuality. But like most gangsters they were not disciplined enough to stick to their own plan. Moreover, agent Tib Aguilar's Spanish fluency and cultural familiarity helped break down Spanish idioms, colloquialisms, elliptical references—the gangsters often referred to themselves in the third person—and code names. Lil' Cycos enforcer Coco Zaragoza, in particular, could not resist hanging out the gang's dirty laundry, laying out a road map of players and their misdeeds. He growled, whined, complained, schemed, bragged, and politicked serially against one or another of his homies, all the while professing love and respect for "Mom" and "Dad." He supplemented his verbal grousing with a stream of jailhouse letters intercepted by the team. He encouraged Janie to string Greedy along after the latter called at Sandford's direction, then he set up a hit on Greedy to be carried out by a newly paroled convict. The investigators, of course, knew of the planned hit. They foiled it by arranging for the would-be hit man to be arrested on a parole violation.

For five months, the team used the wire to confirm, coordinate, cross-check, correlate, and capture evidence. "Anyone who says a wire is boring has never led a proper investigation," says Riordan. "You are right in the criminal's ear. Right in their head." But the wire is demanding. "A proper wire requires the agent who is supervising the phone to be in contact with an agent in the field who can cover the activity so you can corroborate the calls and build an ironclad case," Riordan explains. "The wire can get hot on a Friday afternoon while you are driving home in traffic and you have to pull off the road to consult with agents. It can get hot on a Sunday or a holiday and everybody scrambles."

The gangsters were becoming increasingly paranoid inside their bubble. They were by now aware of the Mexican Mafia investigation. They had also "made" a couple of surveillances. Once, they spotted a glint from a camera lens. A special vehicle within which agents were observing drew their attention another time, and children were sent out to inspect the truck closely. A constant suspicion was that a snitch was active within their midst. But who could it be? The beauty of the matter for the investigators was that greed is a relentless coachman. The gangsters could not stop what they were doing. They could not stop collecting taxes, could not stop talking about deliveries of tax collections, could not stop bringing bundles of cash to Janie, and could not stop jealous machinations against each other.

By early 1999, heavy pressures to make arrests and end the investigation were brought to bear on the team from above. Sandford's and Riordan's supervisors made it clear that the string was played out and that it was time to produce results. "We had only enough goodwill left in both of our offices to finish the Garcia wiretap," says Riordan, whose bet was now being called in turn. "Basically, we were at the point where we were either going to be successful or fall flat on our face," Sandford recalls.

The team needed one final piece of evidence: a clearly provable instance of proceeds from drug taxes being delivered to Janie. This would provide both physical evidence—cash—and acts tying the entire conspiracy together into a criminal enterprise. In March 1999, through a combination of surveillance and wire chatter, the agents established that Termite had delivered about nine thousand dollars in taxes to Janie. The team scrambled. "It was a round-the-clock fire drill," recalls Riordan.

The task of drafting an affidavit and application for a search warrant for Janie's house, her mother's, and Coco's wife's, fell to special agent Jim Wines—a former policeman from Connecticut whom Riordan calls "Velcro" because of his phenomenal ability to remember facts. Wines became Sandford's right-hand man on the Lil' Cycos case shortly after he arrived in Los Angeles in 1998, straight from the FBI Academy. When Sandford was transferred back to Mobile in October 2003, Wines stepped up as the lead agent in the continuing investigation of 18th Street cliques. In the meantime, Riordan tasked Wines with drafting an exhaustive internal evidentiary document that became the point of reference for the case through its trial. Riordan explains, "It was something that we all could refer back to when building the indictment, the factual basis for guilty pleas, and eventually the order of proof at trial."

On the day of the raid, Sandford and Wines hit Janie Garcia's home. It was a nerve-racking experience. Janie was out, but her mother, Olga Hamilton, was at the house. After thoroughly searching Janie's room, Wines found her copy of the "Greedy Tape," lots of expensive jewelry, and several incriminating documents that appeared to be crude accounting records. But the crucial nine thousand dollars that they were sure Termite had delivered only days before was nowhere to be found.

Another agent called from the team that raided Hamilton's house and announced, "We just solved the national debt." The raiders found a sealed cardboard moving box stuffed with cash. Riordan directed that someone go out and get money-counting machines. The machines racked up a total of $480,000. But even that half a million in cash was not proof of a direct link to the drug-taxing operation. They needed to find the nine thousand dollars.

"We were pulling our hair out," Sandford recalls. The two agents paced around, knocking on walls and looking under rugs, searching for a trapdoor or hidden safe. "Then Jim Wines took another look in Janie's big walk-in closet," remembers Sandford. " 'Hey, Carl,' he said. 'Let's look inside that vacuum cleaner.'" Wines found a bundle wrapped in black plastic inside the bag of the upright Oreck vacuum cleaner. The bundle was the cash they were looking for. Sandford took the package out to Olga Hamilton, who was sitting in the living room. "Hey, Olga," he said teasingly. "What's this we found in the vacuum cleaner?" "Oh," she replied innocently, without missing a beat. "I wondered what was wrong with that vacuum cleaner. I been trying to clean the house." Olga would later be taped over the wiretap giving Frank "Puppet" Martinez advice to stay calm and trust in God. She also waxed enthusiastically about how nice the FBI agents had been and how handsome Jim Wines was. These spontaneous effusions completely shut down any potential defense attack on the manner in which the raid was conducted.

Sandford knew that the case was now basically locked up. He called Riordan, and the two had an emotional telephone conversation, thanking each other for hanging tough. It had been a Rorke's Drift fight. Had either one broken and run away—a constant option—the other would have been hung out to dry. Instead, they proved their doubters wrong. The case was a slam dunk at trial. Bruce Riordan successfully prosecuted the first RICO case against a Latino street gang, blazing a trial that others now eagerly follow. The investigative material that Carl Riordan collected on the 18th Street gang established a solid base that continues to support active cases today.

The March 1999 raid on Janie Garcia's house set off a paroxysm of finger-pointing within the gang. It was clear that the federal agents knew exactly what they were looking for. The suspicion that there was a rat in the house hardened into a certainty. The prime candidate became shot caller Juan Manuel "Termite" Lopez Romero. Notwithstanding the fact that Termite had tripled the gang's income and was actually exceedingly loyal, Coco and Janie got it into their gangster-addled heads that he was a snitch. When the loyal Termite learned that Coco and Janie had Frank's ear and were politicking against him, he broke off with Frank, Coco, and Janie. He stopped handing over his tax collections. He also lobbied another shot caller, Carlos Wilfredo "Tiny" Carcamo, to break with "Mom" and "Dad." Tiny Carcamo played both ends against the middle. He pretended to go along with Termite but kept a finger in the wind. In the end, Tiny acted on a letter from Frank Martinez instructing him to "fumigate" the Termite. He cast his lot in with "Mom" and "Dad" and sent his crew to assassinate Termite in November 1999.

Tiny's crew bungled the murder. Although Termite and his driver were seriously wounded, both survived. Termite knew the shooters and set out to get his revenge by killing Tiny. To that end, he made a move that puzzled FBI agents monitoring his phone. He and his crew started talking about someone with an unfamiliar nickname—"Coma"—that the agents had never heard of before. It sounded at first as if this "unsub" (or "unknown subject") was being called "the commander." In fact, they would learn, Termite had contacted Nelson Comandari, the shot caller for the Coronado MS-13 clique, based on the other side of MacArthur Park from Lil' Cycos territory. Even though Mara Salvatrucha and the 18th Street gangs were blood enemies, money proved thicker than blood. Comandari agreed to cooperate with Termite and help kill Tiny. He brought several hit men up from Mexico to help. A powerful figure within MS-13, Comandari would later become the focus of a separate investigation and intensive manhunt. Even so, members of the team—Riordan, Sandford, Wines, and others—would all claim years later that they had no specific knowledge of Nelson Comandari's extended family, only that he came from an influential clan.

After preventing several planned hits on Tiny Carcamo by flooding the area around him with law enforcement officers and agents, the FBI decided that things were in serious danger of getting out of control. Tiny airily dismissed a warning from FBI agents that Termite was trying to whack him. "I'm shocked," he told Wines in a falsetto voice that the agent loves to mimic. "I'm so nice to everybody." The team decided to wrap up the investigation before there was more gunplay. Warrants were obtained, and a final series of raids were conducted. Arrests of the entire enterprise were made.

"Termite was a beaten man," says agent Tibs Aguilar, who arrested the loyal soldier unfairly labeled a rat. After consulting with his family, Termite "flipped." He was the government's star witness at trial. Frank "Puppet" Martinez and Anthony "Coco" Zaragoza were convicted on RICO charges and sentenced to terms of life imprisonment without parole, plus a few additional years on top for good measure. Janie Maria "Mom" Garcia was sentenced to twenty years in federal prison.

Only days before the final raids, Tiny Carcamo slipped off to El Salvador, which has no extradition treaty with the United States. He then made the mistake of going to Honduras to be with his girlfriend—as opposed to his wife, who was still in Los Angeles—and their new baby. His freedom was brief. An informant walked into the Los Angeles field office and told the FBI where he was. Jim Wines flew to Honduras. The Hondurans obligingly deported Tiny and stuck him on a flight to Miami. Wines was on the same flight. He arrested Tiny on the Miami airport tarmac, U.S. soil, and brought him back to face trial. Nelson Comandari—the enigmatic scion of two of El Salvador's most powerful families—eluded the net and disappeared for a while. But his day before the federal bar of justice was also coming.

Where is Ramiro "Greedy" Valerio? "Somewhere," a federal agent smiles enigmatically. "He's somewhere safe." Although no one will say so in so many words, Greedy is no doubt tucked safely away in the federal witness security program.

In the U.S., the police is always smarter than us.
In El Salvador if you kill someone, it's like killing
a dog.
—"GREÑAS," SIXTEEN-YEAR-OLD GANG MEMBER

6

BLOWBACK AND THE CARDINAL

A hand-lettered sign was one of the first things Chris Swecker saw as he made his way off the plane and into the Charlotte, North Carolina, terminal on November 13, 2003. It read, "You are my hero, Dad!" The exuberant message was held aloft by one of the forty-seven-year-old FBI agent's three teenaged daughters, welcoming him home from two months of dangerous duty in Baghdad.

Swecker, then special agent in charge of the Charlotte field office, had supervised the work of fifty FBI agents sent to Iraq on counterterrorism duty. He and his agents pored through files and interrogated suspects, searching for useful intelligence about the terrorist threat to the United States and its interests at home and abroad. A more gruesome part of the assignment was responding to the scenes of horrific car bombings. The agents meticulously worked through the smoking rubble of the bomb sites, littered with human body parts. They sought not only clues to determine who had done the bombing but information about the materials and techniques used in the bombings, for reference in investigation of future cases. Swecker's office in Baghdad was the most luxurious he had enjoyed since he began his FBI career in 1982—a suite in the palace compound of Saddam Hussein. The former dictator was on the run, and Swecker's agents were also helping track him down.

Born on a U.S. naval base in Spain and fluent in Spanish, Swecker looks every bit the scholarship football player he was at Appalachian State University. After graduating from Wake Forest University School of Law, he spent a while as an assistant district attorney, prosecuting criminals in eight eastern North Carolina counties. He actually wanted to be an FBI agent, but a hiring freeze was on. He thus was pleasantly surprised when the call from the bureau came in early 1982. After graduating from the FBI Academy, he reported on June 13, 1982, to his first duty station—Charlotte, North Carolina.

Twenty years later, his career had come full circle, but the circle was hardly closed. As the special agent in charge of the Charlotte office, Swecker supervised the work of about 240 FBI agents, support staff, and members of task forces. In two decades, he had run many of the most important bases of the FBI career track. Among other things, he had supervised the investigation of a Hezbollah terrorism cell in Charlotte, the search for 1996 Atlanta Olympics bomber Eric Rudolph, and security for the 2002 Winter Olympics in Salt Lake City. Swecker had also run major drug and public corruption investigations, served on an FBI SWAT team putting down a prison riot, and done a tour in the general counsel's office at headquarters. In 2003, he was young, well rounded, and ready for another assignment. In December, President George Bush awarded Swecker the prestigious Presidential Rank of Meritorious Executive. The award, handed to him by Attorney General John Ashcroft in January 2004, was a herald of his next assignment, to one of the hottest seats in the bureau, which was then under enormous pressures to transform itself—though there was no universal agreement about the form it would take.

In July 2004, Swecker became assistant director for the Criminal Investigation Division. From an office nowhere near as luxurious as a suite in Saddam Hussein's palace, Swecker was now responsible for the entirety of the FBI's criminal investigation program. It was a job that would be demanding at any time, but in the wake of the terrorist attacks of September 2001, the bureau was still reshaping itself. The reorganization was accompanied by a chorus of carping critics. It was clear to Swecker that the agency's program of criminal investigation would have to be restructured, not least because scores of agents had been drawn off to counterterrorism duties. He had to figure out how to do more with less. Focus and priority now became critical.

One of the most troubling results of the comprehensive review that Swecker ordered was news from field offices all over the country about the rising threat from street gangs, especially the transnational Latino gangs. Swecker decided that going after these gangs should become the top priority in criminal investigations. But deciding that something was a priority and implementing it were two different things. To do the job, Swecker would have to cut through the fog, the scores of suggestions and demands—from within and outside the bureau—on the Criminal Investigation Division's time and resources. In a city where everyone is an expert, static was in the air all around the FBI. Help, Swecker would learn, was coming over a very big hill.

On a warm night in the summer of 2002, Frank Wolf and his wife enjoyed a pleasant meal at a restaurant in the Northern Virginia suburbs of Washington, D.C. As Wolf started his car after dinner, he noticed a group of young men hanging around the margin of the parking lot. His antennae went up. Something about them did not feel right. "My father was a cop," says Wolf, who grew up in Southwest Philadelphia. "I got from him a kind of sixth sense, the ability to just 'feel' things. These guys got my attention. They were wearing a certain kind of clothing, acting in a vaguely threatening manner, had the paraphernalia. They looked and acted like gangsters. 'That's just not normal,' I thought. 'That's not normal for around here.'"[1]

Frank Wolf is not just anybody. He is a U.S. congressman who represents the Tenth Congressional District of Virginia, the most northerly of the Virginia districts. The Tenth District abuts both Maryland and West Virginia. It extends from the exclusive enclave of McLean, just across the Potomac River from Washington, over the Blue Ridge Mountains to the Shenandoah Valley. It includes CIA headquarters, a high-tech corridor, bedroom suburbs, farm country, hamlets, battlefields of the Revolutionary War and Civil War, Washington Dulles International Airport, and acres of land in transition from country barns to suburban bedrooms. Wolf, the most senior Virginia congressman, prides himself on keeping in touch with every corner of his diversified district. "I drive home every night," he says. "And I make it a point to talk face-to-face with people all over Northern Virginia."

Wolf was not just any congressman either. He was a "cardinal," the chairman of one of the appropriations subcommittees of the U.S. House of Representatives. The cardinals—an even dozen currently—may not be as well known as the Speaker of the House or other congressional media stars. But they are elite power brokers in Washington. Their hands firmly grip the federal money tap. Every penny the federal government spends flows through one of their subcommittees. The president can propose programs, and other committees can pass laws "authorizing" them, but unless and until it is "funded," any federal program is dead in the water. The money only flows when an appropriations bill opens the tap, and the cardinals control the money bills. The cardinals are invaluable as friends and one's worst nightmare as enemies.

The appropriations committee divides jurisdiction over the executive branch among the several appropriations subcommittees. When a cardinal calls the head of a federal agency under his writ, he gets an answer. In 2002, Wolf, a Republican, was chairman of the Subcommittee on Commerce, Justice, and State, the Judiciary and Related Agencies (renamed by the Democrats in 2007 as the Subcommittee on Commerce, Justice, Science, and Related Agencies). Among other things, the subcommittee holds the purse strings of the U.S. Department of Justice and the FBI.

The morning after his dinner, Wolf called the FBI and described his observations in the parking lot the night before. He also said that he had been hearing a number of disturbing things about gang activity in Northern Virginia. A few cases of brutal Latino gang violence had made it into the newspapers. The FBI was happy to send an agent right over to brief the congressman.

From that moment, Frank Wolf was on the case of the Latino gangs. There is nothing flashy about Wolf. He is a reserved man with a friendly but sober manner. He is also determined and has a record of being in the vanguard on humanitarian issues. From the plight of Jews in Soviet Russia to genocide in Darfur, Wolf has been among the first to go to the scene and then quietly use his office to make change. He does not give up easily, either. A graduate of Pennsylvania State University and the Georgetown University Law Center, he lost two consecutive elections before he was finally elected to Congress in 1980.

"A lot of public officials were saying that Northern Virginia did not have a gang problem," Wolf recalls. The cardinal thought otherwise. Over the next three years, Chairman Wolf became a bulldog on the gang issue. He would wake up state and federal officials to what was going on under the very noses of the Washington establishment. He would get them to work together. Almost single-handedly, he would push Northern Virginia's police, the Justice Department, and the FBI to focus on Latino gangs and create new structures to go after the worst of the gangsters.

While the cardinal was busy stoking up interest in Washington, the most violent Latino gangs of Los Angeles were mutating, spreading out across the United States, Mexico, Central America, and Canada. As of April 2007, the FBI had identified MS-13 cliques in forty-two states and 18th Street cliques in thirty-seven states. The cliques of these two mega-gangs are growing by leaps and bounds. They are bringing to the cities, suburbs, and rural areas of America a virulent new strain of remorseless violence that was born in the prisons of El Salvador, Guatemala, and Honduras. The transformation of these two local street gangs into transnational supergangs within two decades was sparked in large part by LAPD lieutenant Robert Ruchhoft's excellent idea—deporting illegal aliens involved in gang violence.[2]

M"S-13 has a huge presence in Central America, and we are to blame for that," says Hector J. Alfonso, a gang analyst with the Miami-Dade County Police Department and a nationally recognized expert on Latino gangs.[3] Alfonso is among many law enforcement officials who lay blame for the growth of transnational gangs directly on the federal Illegal Immigration Reform and Immigrant Responsibility Act, part of a putative omnibus "terrorism" law passed by the U.S. Congress in 1996.

The law was the culmination of a national deportation movement arguably ignited by Lieutenant Ruchhoft's plan to get alien gang members off the streets of Los Angeles by shipping them back to wherever they came from. The law allows "expedited removal" of noncitizens who have committed serious crimes. Moreover, one need not be in the country illegally to be eligible for deportation. If an alien has committed one of the predicate crimes—even served out a full sentence for it and resumed a productive, law-abiding life—he or she is a candidate for roundup and summary deportation.[4]

With passage of the law, thousands of MS-13 and 18th Street gangsters became instantly eligible to be frog-marched out of the country, without any of the procedural delays that had slowed things down in the previous decade. The Immigration and Naturalization Service and its successor, the U.S. Immigration and Customs Enforcement (ICE) branch of the Department of Homeland Security, formed squads to round up and summarily deport these so-called criminal aliens. "That was like throwing gasoline on a fire," says Alfonso. Many of the gangsters came to the United States as children, knew nothing of their birth country's culture, and had no family ties and no prospects for employment in the barely surviving economies of Central America. Many of them did not even speak Spanish. "I'm not really American or Central American," one twenty-two-year-old told the *New York Times* in 1997. "If anything, I'm a gang American."[5]

"These guys had no jobs and no money," says FBI agent Leo Navarette, the bureau's legal attaché in San Salvador. "They looked around and realized that there was one thing they knew how to do and there was no competition. So they formed gangs."[6] Recruiting among the poor and marginalized youth of Central America was easy. "And we kept shipping more experienced gang members down to them," Alfonso says.

The explosion of the violent Los Angeles gang culture immediately overloaded the fragile economies, social structures, and law enforcement resources of poor countries barely climbing out of decades of civil war and brutal internal conflict.[7] Moreover, the Latino gang problem that the United States sought to get rid of by exporting gangsters to the south has now "blown back." MS-13 and the 18th Street gang continue to consolidate their power throughout Central America and increasingly in Mexico.[8] They have become transnational—the gangsters move back and forth across international frontiers with relative ease and control many of the migration and smuggling routes. "The effect," one reporter notes, "is to churn gangs through the region."[9] A collateral effect is that international criminal organizations have found in the transnational street gangs "a chain or network to hook into."[10]

Many prisons both north and south of the border are effectively controlled behind the walls by gangs. They serve as institutions of higher learning for hardening gangsters and refining their knowledge of criminality. "Every time they go through the prison cycle, they get more vicious," observes Navarette.

At first, the bulk of the deported gangsters were dumped on El Salvador. U.S. immigration authorities failed to tell the receiving governments that the deportees were gangsters. In fact, to this day, the United States only informs the destination country of the deportee's latest conviction, which is often a vanilla immigration violation that masks more violent criminal behavior. "You could have spent the last five years in jail on a murder charge, then get deported as a criminal alien," says Navarette. "But the papers on you will only list the last charge, which is just being an alien in the country illegally." A personal status as vaguely defined as "gang membership" is shared only in special cases. This is partly out of concern for protecting U.S. law enforcement intelligence sources and partly out of concern for the rough justice that receiving countries might inflict on persons identified as gangsters. Latin American diplomats grin and bear it in public but seethe privately over what some see as the arrogance and destructive behavior of the United States, especially since the country has failed to rationalize its basic immigration laws to take account of economic realities.

The Salvadoran versions of MS-13 and the 18th Street gang erupted like volcanoes of criminal violence. Entire neighborhoods fell under their control, and small wars raged between the two rival gangs. The government reacted harshly, enacting draconian laws known as the Mano Dura (roughly, "iron hand") and Super Mano Dura. Gangsters and suspected gangsters were rounded up, often on the basis of a tattoo alone, and stuffed into the country's abysmal prisons. There they organized, took control, and established ties with their homies in the United States, from Los Angeles to New York. Meanwhile, a dark and hidden war broke out between the gangs and shadowy death squads of uncertain provenance.

The gang virus spread to Guatemala and Honduras, where similarly harsh measures led to tit-for-tat violence between the gangs and the governments. In Honduras in early 2003, gangs attacked several public transit buses, leaving half a dozen or so passengers dead and wounded. The Honduran gangs liked to leave their decapitated victims lying in public ways or to string their disemboweled intestines along fences.[11] But worse, much worse, was to come.

There was standing room only in the old yellow Ford bus on the evening of December 23, 2004. Most of the passengers dozed or stared straight ahead as Guillermo Salgado Pineda, the driver, steered the ancient vehicle through the night. The vehicle's dim headlights marked a torturous path through ruts and potholes. Pedestrians loomed out of the darkness as the bus crawled along the dirt road. The gear-grinding patch was the worst and darkest stretch of the route between the San Isidro and Ebenezer neighborhoods in the gritty suburb of Chamelecon, south of the industrial city of San Pedro Sula, Honduras. About half of the sixty or so passengers were women and children returning from last-minute Christmas shopping. Little ones nestled against their mothers, oblivious to the bus's bouncing progress, dreaming of the small gifts poor families give on glorious seasons. Other passengers were factory workers, headed home after a long day at one or another of the city's maquiladoras, factories devoted mostly to the textile trade. All were looking forward to the next day, Christmas Eve, a time for especially festive parties with family and friends in Honduras.[12]

Two other vehicles in the bus's wake appeared to be waiting for a place to pass. Suddenly, as the bus crawled past an empty soccer field, a blue Toyota pickup truck swerved around and cut the bus off, forcing the driver to stop. The white car behind also stopped. Its headlights cast eerie shadows through the emergency door in the rear of the bus. A few of the children stirred. An anxious murmur arose from the passengers. Two armed men emerged from the pickup truck. They held military assault rifles—one an AK-47, the other an M-16. Time stopped as the bus driver and Victor Ramirez, the fare collector, considered the possibilities. None of them were good. The two men could only hope for the best, a simple act of "tax collection" in which the armed men, almost certainly *mareros,* would collect a fee from the driver, rob the passengers, and leave.

There was to be no such merciful end at the foot of this season of peace on earth and goodwill among men. Without word or warning, the two men from the pickup truck and five others opened fire on the bus, raking it with eight hundred rounds from their assault rifles. The bullets sliced easily through metal, blew out every window in the bus, and ripped grievous wounds in the flesh of men, women, children, and the unborn. "People were screaming, and the more they screamed, the more they shot," a survivor recounted. The few passengers who bolted through the escape door in the back of the bus were gunned down in the road.

One of the armed men, twenty-six-year-old Ever Anibal Rivera Paz, boarded the bus. He pushed past the lifeless bodies of Ramirez, sprawled on the stairs, and Salgado, slumped over the steering wheel. Rivera Paz—or "El Culiche" (the Tapeworm), also known as "El Little Baby"—allegedly walked calmly down the gory aisle, poking the wounded with the muzzle of his M-16 rifle. "Are you still alive?" he asked. He shot those who showed any sign of life.

At length, the killing stopped. Only the moans of the wounded survivors, the cries of orphaned children, and pleas to a God who seemed to have turned his face away from these simple poor rose to the shocked and grieving stars above Chamelecon. Recollections differ among the survivors about how long the attack lasted. But at the end of a lifetime of hell, twenty-eight people were dead, twenty-eight more wounded. One of the wounded, a sixteen-year-old factory worker, was shot sixteen times. Of the dead, sixteen were women—one was three months pregnant—and six were children. The oldest among the slain was sixty-eight years old; the youngest, fourteen months.

A short video of the carnage at the scene and at a temporary morgue is circulated among law enforcement agencies. It is impossible to watch without averting one's eyes from horror words cannot express. The video is sometimes shown at antigang conferences and training classes.

There is invariably an awkward silence after the clip, as hardened gang detectives and police recover their composure. More than a few furtively brush tears away from their eyes, perhaps thinking of their own wives and children.

The attackers attached a missive—a long red scroll—to the hood of the bus. "Feliz Navidad" (Merry Christmas), it mocked. The rambling screed claimed the slaughter as the work of the Cinchonero Popular Liberation Movement, a defunct Honduran revolutionary group. The ruse confused some observers. But from shortly after they arrived at the scene, Honduran police knew better. According to an American law enforcement official, one of the attackers inadvertently dropped his cell phone on the side of the road. Within hours, police linked numbers in the phone to members of Mara Salvatrucha in Honduras. The roundup began immediately. On the next day, Christmas Eve, authorities announced the first arrest, a Mara Salvatrucha gang member. The bed of his pickup truck was still full of empty shell casings. By Christmas Day, police arrested six more gang members. By New Year's Eve, authorities confidently described the contours of the massacre and its planning. They had by then arrested thirteen of twenty-four gang members they said were involved. Seven were the actual shooters. The other seventeen were involved in planning and carrying out the attack.

Ever Anibal Rivera Paz, the man who survivors said walked methodically down the aisle shooting the living, was identified as the leader of Mara Salvatrucha in Honduras. He and another gang member, twenty-nine-year-old Juan Carlos Miralda Bueso, or "La Pantera" (the Panther), were named as the attack's principal masterminds. Rivera Paz had broken out of a Honduran prison—beating a guard senseless—in August 2004, after having been arrested in 2003, allegedly for possession of drugs and an AK-47 assault rifle. According to the Honduran government, the conspirators met at a gang member's house in the old colonial city of Comayagua to plot the attack. They bought their assault rifles from a corrupt Honduran army officer.

The Tapeworm and the Panther were among those rounded up after the attack and sent to prison to await trial. Another gang member, Juan Bautista Jimenez Mejia—or "El Pajaro" (the Bird)—was also arrested, and on January 18, 2005, he was sent to prison. He fared badly. According to Honduran officials, the Bird declined to be placed in a protective wing, preferring to go into general confinement to be with other MS-13 members, his "homies." The next morning—less than twelve hours later—he was found dead, hanging from a showerhead. His demise, however, was clearly shown not to be a suicide by hanging. He suffered multiple broken bones and contusions that could only have come from a severe beating. The motive for Jimenez Mejia's murder has never been conclusively determined. Several reasons have been suggested. He might have been murdered by fellow Mara Salvatrucha gang members, either to shut him up or because he had "failed" in his assigned mission by getting caught. Or he may have been killed by other inmates who were outraged by the massacre. The latter possibility gains some weight if Honduran press reports are accurate. According to those reports, when the Bird's body was being carried out of prison, other prisoners shouted in chorus, "Take that dog out and throw him in the trash." The prisoners also implored the prison guards to give them "just one or two minutes alone" with the Panther, whom they excoriated as a "killer of children." Miralda Bueso, El Pantera, was eventually convicted for his role. But Rivera Paz was destined for yet another audacious criminal adventure with a bizarre ending.

On February 10, 2005, scarcely two months after the bus attack, three cars were spotted moving fast along U.S. Highway 281, breaking the speed limit and sticking together in a convoy. To a Texas Highway Patrol officer and a Brooks County deputy sheriff patrolling the road nearly one hundred miles north of the Mexican border, it was a virtual certainty that a covey of illegal aliens would be flushed out of the speeding cars. The lawmen hit their warning lights and pulled the caravan over along a desolate stretch of the highway that lances straight through hardscrabble Texas scrub country.[13]

Falfurrias, the Brooks County seat, lies some eighty-four miles north of the crossing between Reynosa, Mexico, and Hidalgo, Texas (just south of McAllen). Brooks County was in contested territory until the Mexican-American War fixed it firmly within the United States. The land and its people are pure South Texas—mesquite and scrub oak, windblown sand, stingy soil, and an unforgiving sun. Ninety-two percent of the county's 2006 population of 7,731 souls were Latinos. The sheriff is named Balde Lozano, and most of the county's public officials have sturdily Latino names like *Molina, Garza, Garcia, Martinez,* and *Villarreal.* More than three-quarters of the population speak Spanish at home. The rest of the county's residents are a mélange: descendants of old-line Anglo ranchers who moved in after the Mexican cession, a smattering of blacks and Indians, retirees soaking up the sun, and just plain folk scraping by. The mean household income in 2004 was $21,717. About 29 percent of the population live below the poverty line. Dairy ranching dominates the economy. Brooks County butter is renowned among those who know dairy products. There is also some farming and gas production within the county's 943 square miles. People live in clusters; there are 8.5 persons per square mile in Brooks County, compared to 401.9 in the state of New York and 79.6 in Texas and the United States as a whole. Wealthy hunters hire guides to pursue deer, turkey, quail, and wild pigs. Air Force One has been seen parked like a rich and fat uncle on the tarmac at the Brooks County Airport just outside Falfurrias, the county seat. Both Presidents Bush enjoy the South Texas patrician ritual of stalking and killing animals.

The failed U.S. immigration policy has landed on Brooks County like a blockbuster bomb. The U.S. Border Patrol's checkpoint at Falfurrias is the last one along the belt that enforces the southern border. Illegal immigrants who get past it are likely home free. Residents complain that things have changed dramatically for the worse. In the old days—say, a decade ago—the migrants were polite men who slipped by alone or in pairs, headed north in the hiring seasons and south when the work was gone. Now they come through Brooks County in desperate packs, herded by "coyotes," human smugglers who charge three thousand dollars per head to smuggle emigrants from Mexico. A few local people subcontract with the coyotes. Tensions are high in Brooks County. The local Latinos favor immigration, but they want it safe and legal. Fearful people have armed up to protect themselves from scavengers, drug traffickers, and the gangsters who are increasingly mixed into the migrant flow. A resident vigilante force patrols actively, surrounding and holding illegal immigrants it finds until the border patrol arrives to take them into custody. Officially, the border patrol discourages vigilantism. But it takes the catch anyway.

Most of the migrants who make it past Falfurrias head for Houston. Many who do not make it die of thirst and exposure. They are often stragglers cut loose by the coyotes when they fall behind the pace. The cost of processing their bodies—bloated, blackened, desiccated, or torn to shreds by wild animals—has busted the Brooks County budget. The remains are cataloged by the Mexican consul resident in Falfurrias. Those who can be identified are claimed and escorted home by family or friends. The rest are buried anonymously by Brooks County.

The two lawmen who stopped the speeding convoy were not surprised by what they found in the three cars. Nine people were layered into the passenger compartment of one four-door Dodge Intrepid. This particular model of the all-American family sedan is favored by smugglers of drugs and human beings. Chrysler's designers placed the wheels at the far corners of the chassis to increase the size of the passenger cabin. Four more migrants were packed into the trunk. Among them was a man whose array of tattoos immediately raised the officers' suspicions. Taken to the border patrol checkpoint along with the others, he gave a false name. His real name emerged after his fingerprints were run through an FBI database. He was Ever Anibal Rivera Paz.

On January 23, four days after the Bird's murder in prison, the Tapeworm had escaped. On February 6, he slipped into the United States near Hidalgo. It had taken him just two weeks to make the transit from Honduras to the Rio Grande crossing, a journey that usually takes at least a month. As it happened, U.S. Border Patrol agents were in Honduras training Honduran agents on the day he escaped. They notified their counterparts in the United States to be on the lookout.

One would be hard pressed to find a better poster boy for the transnational face of MS-13 than Rivera Paz. Before his apprehension in Texas, he had been deported from the United States four times and charged with an increasingly violent series of crimes in the United States and Honduras. He epitomizes the revolving door through which the most dangerous—the smartest and most ruthless—gang members pass between Mexico, Central America, and the United States. His capture was trumpeted by politicians and senior law enforcement officials in Washington and Tegucigalpa. Honduran president Ricardo Maduro held a press conference to announce the Tapeworm's capture. Even though Rivera Paz had actually been snagged by two local law enforcement officers who turned him over to the border patrol, the Department of Homeland Security took credit for the capture. Assistant secretary Michael J. Garcia told a U.S. House of Representatives subcommittee on April 13, 2005, that "Rivera Paz was apprehended by Customs and Border Protection Border Patrol agents and placed into ICE custody."

According to Interpol, the Tapeworm was born in Honduras on October 8, 1975, at San Pedro Sula. Sometime before 1993, he illegally entered the United States. The details of Rivera Paz's early criminal adventures are sealed in the tomb of California's juvenile court records. According to the Honduran government, he was arrested in San Francisco on November 30, 1993, and charged as a minor with an offense in drug trafficking. On January 13, 1994, he was again arrested in San Francisco on charges of firearms and drug possession, but apparently he was never convicted. El Little Baby became a member of the extremely violent Normandie Locos Salvatrucha clique, one of the earliest MS-13 cliques in Los Angeles. According to the FBI, deported members of the Normandie Locos operating in Central America give directions and guidance to MS-13 cliques in Northern Virginia, Baltimore, Texas, and the West Coast.

Rivera Paz was first deported from Los Angeles on January 27, 1996. Within months, he popped up again in San Francisco, whence he was deported again on September 6, 1996. Scarcely six months later, on March 11, 1997, the Tapeworm was deported for a third time, again from Los Angeles. On June 25, 2001, four years later, he was convicted in Los Angeles for the relatively minor offense of presenting false identification to police and sentenced to thirteen days in jail. He had by then been charged but never convicted of other offenses, including drug trafficking, car theft, domestic violence, robbery, assault, and criminal conspiracy. An armed robbery charge, for example, was dropped when police could not find the victim. In short, Rivera Paz became a hardcore Los Angeles gangster. On August 15, 2001, he was deported for the fourth time, once more from Los Angeles.

When he sneaked into the United States once again in 2005, Rivera Paz committed the felony of "reentry after deportation" (*U.S. Code* 8 [2006], § 1326). News reports suggested that the notorious gangster would get at least two years in a federal prison. But El Little Baby would not serve any serious time for his offense. On March 2, 2005, the federal grand jury for the Southern District of Texas in Houston duly indicted him under the name Lester Rivera Paz, one of some thirty-five aliases he has apparently used, along with a variety of cell phones and a sense of humor that even federal agents acknowledge is intriguing, if not charming. On April 13, 2005, he pleaded guilty, and on July 8, he was sentenced to seven months in prison and one year of "supervised release." Because he had never been convicted of a serious violent crime in the United States, federal sentencing guidelines then in effect dictated the wrist slapping that federal judge David Hittner handed down. In essence, the notorious MS-13 gang leader was sentenced to serve little more than the time he had already spent in custody. Curiously, federal prosecutor Glenn Cook asked Judge Hittner to seal all the documents regarding the Tapeworm's sentence—including the presentence investigation report, the government's "confidential sentencing memorandum," the judge's statement of reasons for sentencing, and the prosecutor's motion itself. The judge agreed, and the record remains sealed. At his sentencing, Rivera Paz reportedly asked the judge, "Please send me back to my own country to pay for the crimes I caused there." That bizarre request was not granted. The government announced that Rivera Paz would be deported to Honduras for the fifth time, but only after he finished his seven months.

Nothing more was heard of El Culiche until February 11, 2007, when the *Houston Chronicle* dropped a journalistic bombshell. River Paz, the newspaper reported, had apparently escaped again. This time, fingers were pointed across international borders. ICE insisted that he was placed on a deportation flight to Honduras on November 17, 2005, and that the Hondurans were given plenty of notice that he was coming. ICE's standard routine is to obtain travel documents from the receiving country in such cases. So if ICE is telling the truth about what happened, someone in the Honduran government likely would have given ICE a travel document, such as a passport or identity card, for Rivera Paz. But Honduran authorities claimed that they had no notice that the man who had the lead role in the bus atrocity was coming. On the face of it, someone either dropped the ball or is lying. There were no bombastic press conferences this time. The *Houston Chronicle* found out about the puzzling escape more than a year after the fact, when one of its reporters obtained an FBI intelligence report warning that Rivera Paz may have returned to the United States and "has threatened to assassinate any officer that attempts to apprehend him." Interpol duly issued a wanted bulletin on Rivera Paz.

How can such a notorious gangster's disappearance be explained? Given the secrecy surrounding the case, it is impossible to know for certain. But several plausible alternatives come to mind. Rivera Paz could indeed have simply walked away from the airport in Tegucigalpa thanks to a bureaucratic snafu. After all, thousands of Hondurans deported from the United States return home to Honduras every year. Their offenses are garden-variety violations of U.S. immigration law. The formalities for these returning citizens are simple at the Honduran end. Unless one is clearly flagged, there is no reason for Honduran officials to detain them. It is conceivable that if Rivera Paz really were deported, he could have walked out in the crowd. Alternatively, he might have arrived in Honduras, gotten off the plane, and then suffered rough justice at the hands of a rogue death squad. It would not have been the first time a Honduran gangster or suspected gangster was summarily executed in some deserted corner of the land. His own gang brothers could also have whacked him. They might have decided that he was radioactive or had made too many errors of judgment and got caught.

The sealed documents suggest another set of possibilities. Rivera Paz may have "flipped" and become an informant, not necessarily to secure a lighter sentence in the United States but to avoid being sent back to Honduras. (A law enforcement official in Miami recounted to me the story of a tough-guy Honduran MS-13 member arrested there who broke into tears and bawling pleas when he spotted visiting Honduran police officers and mistakenly thought he was being turned over to them for questioning and return in their custody.) Perhaps the Tapeworm is now leading a new life in the federal witness security program. Or perhaps he is feeding information to the authorities from a gang hideout somewhere. Or it just may be that he made an agreement with the United States to inform, reneged on it, and is kicking back somewhere, enjoying his freedom and laughing up his sleeve. Whatever the truth of his whereabouts, Rivera Paz's story is a segue into the activities of MS-13 in Texas. From there, it is a short hop in the world of MS-13 to Congressman Frank Wolf's backyard.

On December 27, 2001—a crisp, clear Thursday—two men searching for a good fishing hole stumbled on a gruesome scene near Grand Prairie, Texas. Their discovery became a link in a ghastly chain of evidence connecting the Normandie Locos, El Culiche's old Los Angeles MS-13 clique, to horrific violence ranging across the United States from California, through Texas, to Virginia and many points in between.[14] The fishermen were exploring a wooded area in the northeast corner of Grand Prairie, near where the West Fork of the Trinity River meanders eastward between Fort Worth and Dallas.

An odd collection of sodden marsh and fingerlike pools—officially called the Bluebonnet Lakes—lies within these woods, a rare corner of wilderness amid the monotony of the Texas plain and the earnest growth of the city of Grand Prairie. The trees and brush extend in a rough quadrangle from the bank of the river on the north and west to the right-angle intersection of South MacArthur Boulevard and Interstate 30, the Tom Landry Highway, at exit 36. A wide margin of bare soil bounds the woods along both roads. In 2001, a crude dirt lane—now overgrown—cut through the woods from MacArthur Boulevard. Hanson Pipe and Products, one of Grand Prairie's major employers, operates an industrial facility on the far side of the boulevard. The sprawling plant makes concrete pipe (as tall as a man) and related connectors, used in large-scale civil engineering projects. A landfill lies beyond that.

On December 27, the ground in the woods was soggy from a string of cold, rainy storms that had soaked the area during the preceding weeks. The sight the two men came upon was enough to make the most hardened retch. The body of a young man lay in the soppy brush. A T-shirt was pulled up around the neck of the corpse, pants pulled down around its ankles. The victim was unrecognizable. He had been shot in the back of the head. His body was despoiled by scavenging animals, which authorities believe had dragged it from the dirt lane into the woods. No wallet or other identification was found. Grand Prairie police thought that the deceased had been a college student. His T-shirt bore the image of a galloping mustang, the mascot of Southern Methodist University in Dallas. The Greek letters of a sorority, Alpha Chi Omega, and a fraternity, Kappa Sigma, were printed on the shirt. Dallas police, however, soon responded to a bulletin describing the remains. The description matched that of Javier Calzada, a young man reported missing by his parents on December 17. Dental records confirmed the identification.

Calzada was not a college student. He worked in a Dallas auto detailing shop. By all accounts, he was a hardworking, likable young man. Like many young people in the Dallas area, Calzada enjoyed hanging out at Bachman Lake, a recreational area around which a complex of upscale shopping and fine lakeside dining has developed. A 3.3-mile trail surrounds the lake, which is used for boating and regularly stocked with catfish. It was at Bachman Lake that Javier Calzada had the fatal misfortune of crossing paths with evil incarnate in the form of members of the MS-13 gang.

A less pleasant side bounds the north of the Bachman Lake complex. This area, roughly defined by U.S. postal zip code 75220, is young, poor, and 80 percent Latino, predominantly Mexican, with a sprinkling of Salvadorans. More than a third of the households in the area earn less than twenty-five thousand dollars a year. Forty percent of the mostly rented homes are considered to be overcrowded. Seventy-three percent of the residents speak Spanish at home. Less than half were born in the United States. Latino gangs have spawned in the community, and with them have come a variety of violent crimes. A rash of carjackings and auto thefts plagued the area at the time. On Christmas Day 2001, for example, three young men were arrested for a carjacking at Bachman Lake. Among them was twenty-seven-year-old Juan Ramon Flores Parada. The letters "MS" were tattooed on Flores Parada's forehead in three-inch Gothic script. In 2001, only a few detectives in the Dallas area grasped the full significance of such a tattoo. A year or two later, however, it would be clear that gang violence in the Dallas area had been boosted by the infiltration of MS-13 gangsters from Virginia, North Carolina, and elsewhere on the east coast.

One of the attractions to all socioeconomic classes in the Bachman Lake complex is a shopping mall where young men and women enact the modern equivalent of ritual flirting in an old-fashioned town square. In the twenty-first-century version, cars make the promenade mobile, and Javier Calzada was especially proud of his green customized 2000 Chevrolet Malibu. The car featured large, distinctive, chromed alloy wheels. On December 16, 2001, Javier was happy to give a ride home to a group of cute young Latina women he met at the mall and knew casually. The next day, Calzada's parents reported him missing. The young man's wallet was soon found, discarded alongside a ramp at the Interstate 30 and Loop 12 interchange, roughly midway between Bachman Lake and Grand Prairie. His green Malibu was found covered with mud in North Dallas. Nothing more was seen or heard of Javier Calzada, however, until the two fishermen found his body in the woods around the Bluebonnet Lakes.

The Grand Prairie and Dallas police departments worked together on the Calzada murder investigation. There was little to go on. The physical evidence made clear what had happened. Who had done it remained a mystery. Leads turned into dead ends until sometime in January 2002, when a Dallas police detective called the Grand Prairie police.

"Dallas police gang detectives had been asked by Virginia authorities to help them find a fugitive gang member who was believed to have fled to Texas," according to Detective Sergeant Alan Patton, supervisor of the Grand Prairie Police Department Major Crimes Unit. "While they were conducting the search of a Dallas gang member's home they came across a shoe box. In the shoe box were some cassette tapes and a Blockbuster receipt in Javier Calzada's name." Under the circumstances, the Dallas gang detectives thought Calzada was just another Dallas gang member. But when they checked at his parent's home, they made the connection to the ongoing homicide investigation. A Dallas detective called Grand Prairie and gave Sergeant Patton the name of the shoe box's owner. She was a fifteen year old named Brenda Paz.

"We went to talk to Brenda Paz," says Patton. "We interviewed her twice and even had her taken into custody as a juvenile." But Patton's hope for a quick break in the case hit a dead end. "She was a tough one," he says. "She said she wasn't there and she didn't know anything about it. The district attorney didn't think we had enough evidence and would not take the case. So, based on that, we basically dropped the case."

Despite their strong suspicions, the police had no more evidence to link the Latina teenager or anyone else to the murder of Javier Calzada. Brenda Paz was not waiting around for more evidence to develop. She promptly left Dallas and headed to Northern Virginia—Congressman Frank Wolf's bailiwick—where she would become instrumental in resolving a case involving a murder on Daingerfield Island.

Daingerfield Island is really not an island at all. It is a bluntly shaped, wooded peninsula that thrusts out from the eastern bank of the Potomac River, a few hundred yards south of the runways at Ronald Reagan Washington National Airport and a few miles north of historic Alexandria, Virginia. On an ordinary day, passenger jets thunder closely overhead, swooping down to land or thrusting their way into the sky, depending on the wind's direction. The sky, however, was quiet on Monday, September 17, 2001.

Less than a week before, al Qaeda terrorists had crashed jet airliners into the World Trade Center in New York and the Pentagon, which lies just north of the airport and mere yards from the flight path. Washington National was closed to air traffic. It would stay closed until October 4, when it was the last major airport in the United States to reopen after the terror attacks. The politicians and other important people of Washington covet the close-in airport's convenience, preferring a fifteen-minute hop over a Potomac River bridge to forty-five minutes or more out to the Dulles International or Washington-Baltimore airports. Business interests were also heavily invested in the airport. Nabobs fought a pitched battle with the newly invigorated minions of national security, who favored closing the airport for good. The security experts worried about flight patterns that funnel fuel-laden aircraft to within seconds of a cornucopia of juicy targets, including the Pentagon, the White House, the Capitol, the State Department, and the Central Intelligence Agency—not to mention virtually all of monumental Washington. Thus the only sounds on Daingerfield Island the morning of September 17 were the slapping of sail lines against masts at the Washington Sailing Marina at the north end and the muted rumble of commuter traffic on the George Washington Memorial Parkway, a four-lane highway that runs close by the western edge of the peninsula.

The tight little universe of official Washington had bigger things on its mind at 10:30 a.m. that day, when a fisherman found a horribly mutilated body lying near the bank of the Potomac on Daingerfield Island.[15] Perhaps understandably, the news media took no notice of the barbaric murder of nineteen-year-old Joaquin Diaz, who had been chased through the woods the night before and brutally stabbed to death. His hands and arms bore the lacerations of a futile defense against a pack of knife-wielding assailants. His throat had been cut from ear to ear. In a final act of savagery, a chunk of his larynx and esophagus had been carved out of his throat and left on the ground next to his body. The medical examiner opined that Diaz might have survived the attack but for the excision of his throat. It was a nightmarish crime scene for a person bent on a quiet day of fishing to come across, and it was an eerie precursor to the way in which Javier Calzada's body was found in Texas.

Daingerfield Island is federal land, part of a long federal park system encompassing about 7,700 acres along more than thirty-two miles of the G. W. Parkway. Every offense from speeding on the parkway to murder is a federal crime within that system and falls under the investigative jurisdiction of the U.S. Park Police, a unit of the Department of the Interior. Joaquin Diaz's murder was thus a federal case. Some progress was made in the investigation through old-fashioned shoe-leather work by park police detective Scott Powers. But the case was blown wide open shortly after Brenda Paz rolled into town from Dallas in 2002. Paz, who was known as "Smiley" because of her bubbly personality and easy grin, became the girlfriend of a gangster named Denis Rivera. Known as "Conejo" (the Rabbit), Rivera was the leader of the Big Gangster Locos Salvatrucha, an MS-13 clique he founded in and around Alexandria, Virginia.

Paz had no trouble fitting into the Virginia MS-13 gangster scene. She had family credentials and a personal history that afforded her instant acceptance. Born in Honduras, Brenda Paz emigrated to Los Angeles with her parents. Her father, about whom little is known, became a member of the newly formed Mara Salvatrucha gang. A true father's daughter, Brenda took to the gangster life with enthusiasm and a distinctive flair. She started hanging around the gang when she was eleven, dropped out of school in the eighth grade, and became a full-fledged member of the Normandie Locos clique at age thirteen. Most young women—dare one call a child of thirteen a "girl"?—are "sexed in" to gang membership, meaning their rite of passage consists of serial sexual intercourse with the requisite number of gangsters. Brenda chose instead to be "jumped in." She subjected herself to an all-out beating by male gangsters for thirteen seconds. Joining Mara Salvatrucha was not an act lightly taken. "Once you're MS, you're MS for life," Brenda would declare several years later. "When you get jumped into MS, you have to go out and recruit. You have to go out and kill, bring money in for the gang."

When Brenda's parents broke up, she moved to Texas and then to Virginia, always finding shelter and companionship with fellow gangsters, her "homies." She was fully immersed in a murderous group in which extreme violence is accepted as normal, a highly adaptive gang that sustains itself by seizing upon every criminal opportunity it comes across, including, among other things, extortion of legitimate and criminal enterprises alike; mugging, robbery, burglary, and carjacking; fencing of stolen goods and transnational smuggling; cold-blooded murder in "defense" of territory and honor; and trafficking in drugs, guns, and human beings.

Brenda Paz was not your run-of-the-mill, dim-bulbed, superficial gang girl. She was intelligent, clever, possessed of an incredible memory, and kept afloat in her wretched life by the natural buoyancy and humor of her personality. People liked Brenda Paz. Wherever she went, she connected warmly and directly with her homies—the only real family and friends she ever knew. "First is God, then your mother, then your gang" is how Brenda once described the bizarre hierarchy of values in MS-13. "You live for your God. You live for your mother. You die for your gang."

The outlaw gang life was a perfect fit for the defiant wild child within her. Brenda Paz rebelled against society's rules, and MS-13 prides itself on audaciously breaking all of them. MS-13 has its own ruthlessly enforced rules, including the death penalty for cooperating with law enforcement. Even the gang's rules chafed on Brenda. For a good while, she was able to swim freely among them, obeying their spirit, if not their letter. Eventually, she would defy even the gang's rules. This would become a problem for her.

The feral side of Brenda's personality showed itself in another dimension, the opportunistic manipulation of others that one often sees in very clever criminals. The male gangsters that Paz hooked up with were usually gang leaders, not foot soldiers. She traveled through much of the country with such men. As a result, she witnessed their brutal crimes, saw how interstate gang business was done, and heard firsthand the thoughts, aspirations, and plans of MS-13's leaders.

Somewhere along the line, a fatal tension developed in Brenda Paz's inner life. She had an insightful—one might even say intellectual—bent of mind. Brenda liked to read, to think about things, and, most important, to preserve her life and observations in writing. She kept a series of date books and diaries. Eventually, a schism opened deep within her. She came to hate the sins but love the sinners. She abhorred the violence of the gang life but loved her homies—who were, after all, the only real human connection she had ever known. This fateful tension would drive her into a series of self-destructive actions worthy of a Greek tragedy.

For a time, Brenda Paz walked a tightrope stretched between the poles of her cognitive dissonance. But she lost her balance in June 2002, after Arlington, Virginia, police stopped a stolen car driven by her boyfriend, Denis "the Rabbit" Rivera, and found her a passenger in it. Because she was a minor and had no relatives in the area, Paz was taken into custody as a runaway. A local lawyer, Gregory T. Hunter, was appointed to be her guardian. At that point, some switch, lever, or spring within Brenda Paz's complex mind inexplicably tripped. She told her guardian and then police that she was ready, willing, and exceedingly able to rat out her beloved homies. "Your conscience starts working," she explained to her interrogators. "You start feeling bad about stuff. That's when you become a rat."

Astounded police quickly established that the engaging teenager was, in Hunter's words, not only an informant but "the Rain Man of witnesses." Paz could reel off names, dates, and details (as fine as license plate numbers) related to a string of MS-13 crimes across America. She knew about guns and drugs and where they were stashed. She explained the language of gang hand signs and what code words meant. Cops from half a dozen states and agents of the FBI were soon sitting down to listen to the diminutive, slightly pudgy girl with the engaging smile talk matter-of-factly, in an almost tutorial tone, about horrific crimes. As a minor, Paz could not be enrolled in the federal witness protection program. But working with Hunter, police trumped up a phony additional charge to keep her safely in custody and dispel suspicion among her homies that she had flipped. Her debriefing continued from June well into September 2002.

Brenda Paz was a genuinely invaluable informant. But she also fell into a category that experts consider to be dangerously volatile. At the time she began to cooperate, she had no motive other than a somewhat confused internal ethic and—it has been suggested—a grateful response to the humane manner in which she was treated by the Virginia cops. Authorities were not holding the hammer of a major crime with an intolerable prison term over her head. She had no revenge motive against her gang or anyone in it. Whatever impelled her conversion, she appeared to brush aside, like so many cobwebs, the very essence of her being, the vital connection between her gang and her personal identity. "All this stuff I've done through my life for this stupid gang," she said. "It's just two letters and it doesn't mean anything."

It is difficult to establish effective control over such a volunteer informant, and keeping control of the informant is rule number one in the game of snitches, the underbelly of law enforcement. The conscience is a fickle thing among people who, like Brenda Paz, have persuaded themselves to live a life in which what society declares to be good is bad and vice versa. Such a volunteer reformed do-gooder can easily change his or her mind at any time and clam up or decide to take a walk. The best thing in such circumstances is to vacuum as much as possible out of the informant as quickly as possible. The law enforcement hornets buzzing around Brenda Paz quite logically did just that.

Among the first people Brenda Paz fingered were her gang leader boyfriends in Dallas and Northern Virginia. On September 26, 2002, Hunter called Detective Sergeant Patton in Grand Prairie and told him that Paz was willing to talk about the murder of Javier Calzada. The very next day, Patton and Detective Rick Oseguera flew to Virginia and sat down again with Brenda.

"She just opened up," Patton recalls. "We left there with a statement that was four single-spaced typewritten pages long." Like some other law enforcement officials who interacted with Paz, Patton's experienced instincts told him that the intelligent young woman sitting across from him was playing both sides—running with the hare and playing with the hound. "While she was talking it was like she was looking at herself at the same time she was looking at us," Patton says. "I felt that she was doing counterintelligence, trying to find out how we do things and what we knew at the same time she was telling us about Javier Calzada's murder."

As Patton and Oseguera left their interview with Paz, each had exactly the same reaction. Brenda Paz, they agreed on the spot, did not appreciate the gravity of the situation in which she had put herself. "She was just plain unafraid," Patton says. "She had no concept of the danger she was in from MS-13. We looked at each other and said, 'They are going to kill her.'" Patton also felt that Paz was to some degree inflating her role, perhaps exaggerating about how much she knew. But so far as Patton, a detective trying to solve a specific murder, was concerned, what mattered in the end was that Brenda Paz's story was consistent with every important detail of the physical evidence.

When, on the last cold, rainy day of his life, Calzada dropped off the cute young girls with whom he had become friendly, some of Paz's gangster homies decided they wanted the shiny chromed alloy wheels from his 2000 Chevy Malibu. The gangsters instructed the girls to call Calzada and ask him to come back and take them for a ride. When the youth drove up, Paz and her boyfriend, gang leader Juan Ramon "Junior" Flores Parada, got into the car. Flores Parada pulled out a gun and forced Calzada to drive to a deserted dirt road through the woods around the Bluebonnet Lakes. Another carload of gangsters followed behind. Paz claimed that she stayed in the car while the men marched Calzada some distance though the rain. There he was brutally sodomized and then shot in the head. When Flores Parada returned to Calzada's car, he made a mocking sign of the cross; said, "God forgive me for my sins"; and burst into manic laughter. The gangsters were able only to rifle their victim's wallet and scavenge a paltry few of his possessions. One took his shoes. Brenda stole the cassette tapes and Blockbuster receipt out of the glove box. But the rain thwarted the gangsters' main plan. They could not figure out how to get the wet lug nuts off of the wheels. So they wiped the car clean of fingerprints and abandoned it in Dallas.

On his return to Texas, Patton discovered that Flores Parada and two other alleged participants in the Calzada murder were already in a Dallas jail, awaiting trial on another serious charge. They were the gangsters who had been arrested on Christmas Day 2001 for the unrelated carjacking at Bachman Lake. Flores Parada, the thug with the three-inch "MS" tattoo on his forehead, eventually pleaded guilty to Calzada's murder.

Meanwhile, Brenda Paz served up another murderous fish in Virginia. He was her latest lover, Denis Rivera. The Rabbit told her all about the murder of Joaquin Diaz on Daingerfield Island in September 2001. Rivera was the mastermind behind the murder. He told Paz that cutting out Diaz's larynx was no big deal. It was, he bragged, no more difficult than preparing chicken for cooking.

Denis Rivera was born in El Salvador on September 20, 1983. He was seventy-five hours shy of his eighteenth birthday when he coldly sliced out Diaz's throat. For the first eight years of his life, he was raised by his maternal grandmother in "a loving environment" in El Salvador, according to the federal judge who granted the government's motion to try him as an adult for the murder. Rivera then came to the United States to join his parents, but he left their home at age sixteen. The Rabbit had a long history of criminal charges in Northern Virginia, all related to his involvement with MS-13. They included several incidents of brandishing or shooting firearms and various attempts to "maim, disfigure, disable, kill, or maliciously wound" others. A Fairfax County, Virginia, probation officer testified that "probably more than average" was spent by local authorities in fruitless attempts to wean Rivera from MS-13 through rehabilitation services. He was described by experts as intelligent and "charismatic" in his relations with his fellow gangsters on the street.

Brenda's information gave a whole new impetus to the investigation of Diaz's murder. Within days after the body was found, Detective Scott Powers had identified the victim. He had even tracked down a surveillance video from a MacDonald's hamburger restaurant in Alexandria,

Virginia, recorded the night Diaz was killed. The victim was seen in the video, eating with two young Latino males shortly before he was slain. An Alexandria gang detective identified one of the men as MS-13 gang member Andy Salinas, known as "Lucifer." Brenda's information now identified a high-level target as the other man. Federal investigators and prosecutors conducted a classic conspiracy investigation—working inward from the margins—to snare the Rabbit and attack the MS-13 structure in Northern Virginia. One by one, they arrested and charged Salinas and two other lower-level members: Angel Barrera, or "Maldito" (Cursed); and Fredie Baires, whose nickname is given in court documents as "Travesio," a nonsense word, but probably was "Travieso" (Mischievous). Subjected to a potential federal death sentence on a charge of first-degree murder, each of the three eventually flipped and agreed to testify against Rivera and two others who had driven out to Daingerfield Island with Diaz the night of his murder. Ostensibly, the four were going to buy marijuana in the District of Columbia. But the trip was a ruse. By the time Joaquin Diaz got into the car, his fate had already been sealed. The man who was to become Brenda Paz's lover, Denis Rivera, had decided Diaz was a member of a rival gang and had to be killed.

Rivera was indicted for the murder on April 3, 2003, and trial was set for October. Brenda Paz was secretly slated to be a dynamite witness, not only against Rivera, but against much of the power structure of MS-13 in Northern Virginia. It was a date she was destined to break.

As a juvenile, Brenda was not eligible to be put into the federal witness security program run by the U.S. Marshals Service, an arm of the Department of Justice. According to the service, more than seventy-five hundred witnesses and ninety-five hundred family members have been protected, relocated, and given new identities since the program was started in 1970. The marshals boast that no participant who followed its rules for security has ever been harmed. The service also complains, however, that its resources have fallen behind the mushrooming number of persons it is charged with protecting.

In an effort to protect Paz while she continued to inform on her homies, the FBI moved her into a "safe house" in Silver Spring, Maryland, in late November 2002. But the collision of Paz's internal worlds had already spun out of control by then. Rather than going to ground, Paz turned the FBI safe house into an MS-13 party house. She told her fellow gangsters that the money for the apartment—and the drugs and booze—was coming from her father. On February 8, 2003, Montgomery County police arrived to investigate a rape reported at Brenda's apartment. On the next day, police returned and broke up a raucous party and arrested ten people. On the following day, February 10, Brenda disappeared.

As part of a frantic effort to find the key witness, police in Virginia turned to an unlikely source of help—Denis Rivera. The Rabbit had not yet been indicted for Diaz's murder but was being held on other charges. Rivera was not of much help in finding Brenda, but he confirmed that she was widely suspected within MS-13 of having become an informant. Being careful not to explicitly implicate himself, Rivera warned that some people might put a "green light" on her, meaning a gang order to kill her. Brenda's erstwhile boyfriend in Dallas, "Junior" Flores Parada, was naturally among them. He warned Rivera and others that he was sure Brenda had ratted him out. Other gang leaders in California, Texas, and El Salvador were also concerned that Brenda Paz was an informant whose life needed to be snuffed out.

Brenda eventually was tracked down by her guardian, Greg Hunter. He persuaded a Virginia judge to declare Paz to be legally an adult. The ruling opened the federal witness security program to the young gangster songbird. She was enrolled in March 2003, given a new identity, and moved to Philadelphia. Brenda's new law enforcement friends did their best to impress on her the danger she was in, even letting her listen to portions of recorded conversations in which her potential murder was discussed by her homies. But the headstrong teenager once again reached out to her gang. She was addicted to the human contact. The parties resumed in Philadelphia, and Brenda got pregnant in the process. An insane series of self-destructive acts ensued, as Paz willfully blew every cover the exasperated marshals gave her. She was moved to Kansas City, Missouri, and St. Paul, Minnesota. From each refuge, she promptly reconnected with her gangster friends. Sometimes she called them. Sometimes they called her. Several times, she simply took off on her own and headed east to resume the gang life in Virginia or Philadelphia. Hunter persuaded her several times to return to her havens, but it was no use. Brenda invited a group of gangsters to visit her in St. Paul in June 2003. When they packed up to return to Virginia, she went with them.

Paz had persuaded herself that she could get the camel of her betrayal through the eye of the gang's needle—its suspicions of her having violated its most sacred rule, the code of silence. In fact, her penchant for documenting her life in writing had by then already doomed Smiley. In February 2003, while she was in the FBI safe house, Brenda loaned a purse to Maria Gomez, another MS-13 gang girl. Gomez found in the purse the business cards of several detectives and agents. Suspecting the obvious, Gomez told Ismael Cisneros, known as "Arana" (the Spider), what she had found.

An illegal immigrant from Mexico, Cisneros was a member of the Centrales Locos Salvatrucha (CLS)—one of a half-dozen MS-13 cliques in the Washington metropolitan area—and a veteran of the revolving door. In 1999, he pleaded guilty to stabbing a high school student from Fairfax, Virginia. He was deported to Mexico in 2000 (where he stayed all of four days before heading north again) and was back in Virginia within a month. Cisneros was close to Paz and refused to believe that she was a snitch.

In any case, the Spider was busy doing what gangsters do. He was selling guns and drugs to an undercover agent of the federal Bureau of Alcohol, Tobacco, Firearms, and Explosives. Cisneros bragged to the agent that he could also supply hand grenades on demand, offered to set up a home invasion in which the occupants might have to be killed to eliminate witnesses, and suggested getting into the business of prostitution. So, for a time, suspicions about Brenda merely simmered without a definitive conclusion. But the game was finally up in June 2003, when Maria Gomez's brother searched the luggage Brenda brought back from St. Paul and found a diary and two date books. There, in Brenda Paz's own words and handwriting, was damnation itself.

On July 12, 2003, the CLS threw one of the gang's interminable parties in room 318 of the Holiday Inn near Fair Oaks Mall in Fairfax, Virginia. Before the fun started, the male members held a business meeting. As is customary, Brenda, other female gangsters, and men who were not members of the CLS clique waited outside until the meeting was over. She had no particular reason to believe that anything unusual had happened, joined in the party, and ended up sleeping in the arms of Ismael Cisneros, the man who had defended her several months earlier and later told investigators, "I loved her with all my heart."

In fact, the hinge of fate had closed. Brenda was "green-lighted" at the meeting. The next morning, Cisneros and two other gangsters invited her to take a ride with them to the Shenandoah Valley. They were ostensibly going to drop off one of the partygoers at his trailer park residence. On the way back, it was suggested that the group stop and go fishing at a scenic spot near a covered bridge that spans the idyllic Shenandoah River. After wending their way along the riverbank for some distance, Cisneros and another gangster, Oscar Antonio Grande, pulled out knives and struck Brenda "Smiley" Paz with more than a dozen slashing blows. "Why?" she asked in a last futile act of denial. "Because you're a rat," they answered. "Just leave me here," she finally begged as life ebbed from her body and that of the fetus within her.

Four days later, a fisherman and his son found Brenda Paz's grotesquely mutilated body wedged among rocks along the placid river's bank—an incredible third time that a brutal MS-13 murder linked to Brenda Paz in one way or another had been so discovered. She was nearly decapitated. Local authorities were nonplussed. Until then, they had little reason to believe the scourge of Latino gangs had crept in among their barns and byways. Paz was eventually identified when a gang detective in Northern Virginia recognized the tattoos sent out in a bulletin.

Denis Rivera was convicted on November 20, 2003, of first-degree murder in the slaying of Joaquin Diaz. A key witness was Gregory T. Hunter, Paz's guardian, who, in a hotly contested ruling (affirmed on appeal), was allowed to tell the jury what his ward told him about Rivera's involvement in the murder. In a nod to the legal niceties, the jury was not told of Paz's brutal murder, only that she was not available. On May 17, 2005, a jury found Ismael Cisneros and Oscar Antonio Grande guilty of having murdered Paz. Persuaded by a phalanx of psychiatric experts, the jury declined to impose the death penalty. Denis Rivera was acquitted in the same trial, at least in part because of an incredible blunder by federal prosecutors, who mistakenly identified the other party taped in a key telephone conversation with Rivera from his jail cell. The error was not discovered until midtrial, at which time it became a bludgeon in the hands of Rivera's lawyers.

The murder of Brenda Paz was not the only thing on Congressman Frank Wolf's mind when he called FBI director Robert S. Mueller in July 2004. But it was high on a list of gang murders, machete mutilations, and miscellaneous mayhem that he ticked through in his conversation with the director. Just weeks before the phone call, MS-13 gangsters had attacked a young man in a busy shopping mall with machetes and hacked off three of his fingers.

Mara Salvatrucha members were reported to have appeared in the Washington metropolitan area as early as 1995. By 2000, local police estimated that the gang had six hundred members in Fairfax County alone—just across the river from the District of Columbia. Cliques had formed in Latino neighborhoods of the capitol itself, notably Mount Pleasant and Columbia Heights. Many of these gangsters were older members from Los Angeles who headed for the relative safety of the Washington region after having been released from California jails or when the heat was turned up by the LAPD. These *veteranos* were said to be shuttling guns and drugs between the two coasts and working to better organize the local cliques along the lines of the brutal California gang model. The gangsters began recruiting young members from middle schools. Random violence began to alarm previously tranquil bedroom communities. In August 2000, a twenty-one-year-old man was stabbed to death by a fifteen-year-old Mexican gangster in the parking lot of a shopping center in Northern Virginia. The gangster's sister had been "sexed in" to the gang when she was ten years old. The victim had nothing to do with gangs. He was selected at random in a bid by the young hoodlum to elevate his status within his clique. The cold-blooded murder was only the tip of an alarming iceberg. MS-13 had by then been responsible for "dozens and dozens" of nonfatal stabbings—the kind of day-to-day, fear-inspiring, intimidating, community-wrecking violence that makes the news reports only on the slowest of slow days.

The problem was only getting worse by the time Wolf made his after-dinner observations in the summer of 2000. The congressman's first attempt to bring local, state, and federal law enforcement officials together to address the issue was thwarted by the outbreak of the Washington Beltway sniper murders. In November 2002—two weeks after the two snipers were arrested—Wolf finally held the first of what would become a series of hortatory meetings. In the first weeks of 2003, Wolf organized another meeting of federal officials and prodded them to set up a gang task force in his congressional district. The cardinal helped the effort by salting a federal spending bill with a bit more than half a million dollars for the combined effort of the FBI, the DEA, ATF, and the U.S. Marshals Service. In April 2003, Wolf "pulled together" yet another meeting, this time bringing in local law enforcement officials from Alexandria, Arlington, and the Shenandoah Valley. More than a few of the local cops—especially those from the rural areas—were not yet persuaded that they had a local "gang problem." Many of them were oblivious to the whole phenomenon of Latino migration into their fields and factory farms. Wolf nonetheless made sure that the Northern Virginia Regional Gang Task Force got another $1.4 million for 2004 operations. He also arranged another half-million dollars to set up a statewide Virginia gang task force and three hundred thousand dollars for gang intervention and prevention programs in the state. And so it went. With one hand, Wolf kept "pulling people together" to talk about the Virginia gang problem. With the other, he kept writing funds into the federal budget to do something about it. In March 2004, he called the entire Virginia congressional delegation together so they could hear directly from federal and local law enforcement officials just what was going on in the Old Dominion.

By July 2004, it had become obvious to Wolf that the problem was much bigger than Virginia. So he called Director Mueller with a direct question. What, he asked, was the FBI doing on a national level about these gangs that were plaguing Virginia? Mueller had his hands full redirecting the FBI—he took office one week before the terror attacks of September 11, 2001—but said he would find out in detail and get a report up to the cardinal right away. Then he told his secretary to summon Chris Swecker to his office.

The professional life of Robert Swan Mueller III (his last name is pronounced "Muller") has been the antithesis of the self-serving opportunism that has come to characterize many of Washington's most influential law firms—conglomerations of law and lobbying devoted to peddling influence and caddying white-collar miscreants around the playing fields of power. On paper, Mueller might likely have spent a comfortable career carting lucre from such a factory on K Street or Wall Street. Born on August 7, 1944, to a family of means in New York, he was raised on Philadelphia's Main Line and attended the best schools. He was a sports captain—an honor he shared with John Kerry—at St. Paul's School in Concord, New Hampshire. (Among other notable alumni was Efrem Zimbalist Jr., the actor—son of a concert violinist—who played Inspector Lewis Erskine, television's archetypical G-man, in the 1960s ABC series *The F.B.I.*) He graduated from Princeton in 1966 and earned a master's degree from New York University in 1967. He then took a commission in the U.S. Marine Corps. His three years of service included a year in Vietnam as a rifle platoon leader. He was wounded in action and decorated for "fearlessly . . . with complete disregard for his own safety . . . and skillfully" leading his platoon through a horrific firefight and recovering the body of a mortally wounded Marine.

After graduating from the University of Virginia School of Law in 1973, Mueller tried his hand as a litigator with the prestigious San Francisco law firm of Pillsbury, Madison, and Sutro. But he was a prosecutor at heart, and within three years, he became an assistant U.S. attorney in San Francisco. From there, he rose to a distinguished career as a crime-fighting bulldog in the Department of Justice, including the unusual record of serving as the U.S. attorney in two separate postings, first in San Francisco and later in Boston. He dipped back into the pool of private practice twice more, as a partner at Boston's now dissolved Hill and Barlow (other former partners included Michael Dukakis, Deval Patrick, and William Weld) in 1988–89 and as a partner in the Washington office of another Boston firm, Hale and Dorr (now absorbed into megafirm WilmerHale), from 1993 to 1995. But Mueller was always drawn back to his love of busting bad guys. It was from his latter position that Mueller made a decision that captures his measure. Earning an annual salary estimated at four hundred thousand dollars, Mueller simply was not happy. He picked up the phone and called Eric Holder Jr.,

U.S. attorney for the District of Columbia, whom Mueller had supervised from his last post as assistant attorney general in charge of the Criminal Division of the District U.S. attorney's office. Would Holder hire him, he asked, as a line prosecutor in the Superior Court Division's Homicide Section? It was a "no-brainer." Holder quickly agreed, and within weeks, Mueller was working out of a cubbyhole.

Within a year, Mueller was supervising the Homicide Section and is widely credited with dramatically reducing backlogs and boosting the conviction rate. The period of his tenure was an institutional golden era, as Mueller's staff of ambitious prosecutors challenged each other to be the best there was. Besides Mueller, other alumni of the mid-1990s Homicide Section who rose to prominence include Kenneth L. Wainstein, who later served as U.S. attorney for the District of Columbia; the FBI's general counsel; and, since 2006, the first assistant attorney general for the National Security Section. Another, J. Patrick Rowan, became Wainstein's deputy for counterterrorism and counterespionage. A third was Kevin Carwile, an intense young man who rose to become one of the Justice Department's expert busters of organized crime. Carwile was destined to become the department's point man on criminal street gangs.

Mueller has a reputation for a direct intensity. "There is no warm and fuzzy Bob Mueller at the office," one of Mueller's mentors, William F. Weld, said of him. "He has only one gear, and that's straight ahead."[16] So when Chris Swecker gave Mueller a briefing on the FBI's antigang effort—based largely on the Safe Streets Initiative—his boss's reaction was vintage Mueller. "That," the director said, "is bullshit. I want you to put together a national task force. Something along the line of the Enron task force."

Swecker was delighted. His project now had the interest of a powerful congressional ally, and he had the direct approval—indeed, the orders—of the FBI director to take aim directly at street gangs in general and at the Latino gangs in particular. He left Mueller's office with no doubt about his mission. But he soon ran into a patch of bureaucratic mud. The effort bogged down for a few months. Then he turned to one man whose past accomplishments indicated that he could do the job right and do it quickly.

7

"HI, WE'RE FROM WASHINGTON, AND WE'RE HERE TO HELP YOU!"

Special agent Robert "Bob" Clifford happened to be in Washington in September 2004, shortly after FBI director Robert Mueller and assistant director Chris Swecker agreed to create a task force to investigate MS-13. Clifford had flown back from Greece to receive an award from the Washington-based Partnership for Public Service (PPS). The nonprofit group dedicated to improving federal public service gave Clifford its highest honor, naming him the "2004 Federal Employee of the Year." The agent was feted at a gala dinner, where he was handed a medal and an honorarium of ten thousand dollars.

"Robert Clifford is an extraordinary public servant," said PPS's president, Max Stier. "He has been essential in wrapping up a terrorist network." Clifford called the experience "humbling" and credited others for his achievement.[1] Had Stier addressed the whole of Bob Clifford's career, however, he would have used the plural and credited the ebullient, dark-haired agent with bringing down "terrorist networks." Clifford was honored specifically for helping Greek authorities crack the infamous November 17 (N-17) terrorist group. But N-17 was not the first terrorist network the FBI agent had cracked. Nor is it likely to be the last.

A basic problem that the FBI and other agencies have faced since the end of the relative stability of the cold war era is the acceleration of the pace at which new transnational threats emerge and old ones change. How can the bureau nimbly deploy its resources in an era in which threats evolve at lightning speed? How can it avoid lurching from one new priority to another—from conspiracies in drug trafficking to international terrorism to transnational street gangs to mortgage fraud—and risking the loss of its core mission in the process? What is the FBI's core mission, anyway? Can the organization be everything it is expected to be, from domestic intelligence agency to premier federal criminal investigative agency to international partner with the police and security services of other countries? Congressman Frank Wolf devoted much of his tenure as appropriations subcommittee chairman to exploring these issues with FBI director Robert Mueller and independent experts. Wolf is offended by the exploitation of this problem at sensational news conferences by some of his colleagues.

Criminals and terrorists—and the technology and global systems of commerce and communication that they exploit—are changing, adapting, and coalescing into fluid networks. Unlike the traditional vertical bureaucracies of law enforcement (and governments generally), criminals and terrorists increasingly operate in horizontal, shifting alliances. These groups and individuals come together opportunistically, when their different interests, expertise, and goals coincide. Leadership of these dark, flexible, and highly adaptive networks is amorphous. It changes depending on the specific purpose at hand. As quickly as technology mutates, criminals and terrorists adopt it to their ends. Conversely, they adapt their operations to counter the use of technology by law enforcement.[2]

Within the last two decades Latino criminal street gangs that once operated only provincially, confined largely to street crime in local barrios, have been drawn into bigger and more sophisticated criminal networks. In Southern California alone, there have been busts and prosecutions or active federal investigations of at least half a dozen criminal enterprises similar to the extortion racket that Mexican Mafia boss Frank Martinez and the Columbia Lil' Cycos clique of the 18th Street gang built around MacArthur Park in Los Angeles. MS-13 and 18th Street gang members are used as "muscle" and "mules" by Mexican drug-trafficking organizations both within the United States and in Latin America.

MS-13 is "spearheading alien, weapons, and narcotics smuggling operations," according to U.S. Immigration and Customs Enforcement, the law enforcement arm of the Department of Homeland Security. ICE agents claim to operate the best intelligence system in the Western Hemisphere concerning criminal aliens—those who are in the United States illegally and have committed crimes. It aggressively debriefs gangsters who fall into its hands. Its "hammer" is the fact that many deportable criminals would rather go to prison in the United States than face brutal treatment in their own countries. ICE accommodates those who cooperate and give up useful information. The agency says that MS-13 "controls stash houses on both U.S. and Mexico sides of the border" and is "in control of border smuggling corridors." ICE believes that MS-13 may even control "all passenger traffic in freight lines running from South Mexico to South Texas," as well as smuggling routes through Guatemala that "could be used to smuggle drugs and weapons." The gang imposes "taxes" on others who use these routes. It is also "working jointly with Colombian and Mexican Drug Trafficking Organizations . . . possibly trading guns for drugs with Colombian cartels" and is "providing security and enforcement services for narcotics traffickers."[3]

The law enforcement community debates the extent to which street gangs are involved with larger criminal networks and organizations, as well as their precise roles. Some observers think that the extent to which gangs have been integrated into such entities is exaggerated. But virtually all agree that the potential danger is formidable. The harm that could arise from extensive integration of street gangs into more sophisticated criminal and terror global networks extends beyond the problem of violent crime to questions of national security and even of the viability of democratic government in some Latin American countries.[4]

Quick reaction to these changing threats is difficult. The FBI may be the finest investigative agency in the world. But it is constrained by constitutional limits and bounded by its legislative authority. It must compete annually for limited resources within an executive branch budget cycle that is cumbersome and often driven by transient political goals and ephemeral law enforcement fads. It is locked into the glacial pace, political grandstanding, and sometimes backbiting nature of the congressional legislative process. Congress often creates new federal crimes and heaps law enforcement record-keeping requirements—from tracking car thefts to making background checks for gun sales—onto the FBI's plate without providing equivalent resources to do the new jobs.[5] (This is partly because many congressional committees initiate new laws, but only budget committees provide funds, and coordination among them is haphazard.) Under these conditions, how does the bureau anticipate, much less quickly react to, the agility of its opponents? This is a hard question. It is not adequately answered by the Washington political sport of second-guessing and dragging senior officials to the pillory. This sport has driven some of the bureau's finest and most talented senior agents into early retirement.

Bob Clifford was born on March 12, 1959, in Oxnard, California. His family soon moved to Ojai, some sixty-five miles northwest of Los Angeles. The third of eight children, Clifford considered a career in the Catholic missionary priesthood but ended up as an intelligence officer assigned to the U.S. Navy's elite SEAL (sea, air, land) teams. His job was planning how to get in, get out, and exploit local help on highly classified missions—during a period of violent turmoil and rampant terrorism in the Middle East. Released from the navy in 1985, Clifford was a special agent with the Naval Investigative Service until 1988, when he joined the FBI.

In 1991, the bureau sent Clifford to Bolivia, where he took down his first terrorist organization, a radical fringe group that assassinated a pair of American missionaries. He was next posted to the bureau's

Washington field office in 1992, where he led an international manhunt to find Omar Mohammed Rezaq, an Abu Nidal Organization hijacker who murdered several Americans. Clifford learned that Rezaq was in Ghana, flew to Africa in an executive jet to arrest him, and brought him to the United States, where he was successfully prosecuted.

Clifford was next put in charge of the Iran/Hezbollah Unit of the International Terrorism Section at FBI Headquarters. The unit was a sort of Sleepy Hollow when Clifford arrived in 1994. It was documenting what it learned, filing it away without taking direct action. Clifford shook things up and made the unit proactive. He was one of the early boat-rocking advocates of changing how the FBI handled terrorism investigations. After September 11, 2001, many of the reforms that Clifford and others advocated were finally implemented. High on the list was breaking down an artificial "Chinese wall" that prohibited sharing of information between intelligence units and criminal investigators.

In 1997, Clifford was sent to Charlotte, North Carolina, where he used what he had learned about Hezbollah and bagged another terrorist organization. Chris Swecker was the special agent in charge of the Charlotte field office and supervised the entire operation. Working with Rick Schwein, another young agent with a background in special operations and an aggressive nature, Clifford busted a Hezbollah cell operating in the unlikely venue of this "new South" city. A group of Lebanese radical Shiite Muslims, most of whom were in the country illegally, were running a multimillion-dollar criminal operation to raise funds and export war-fighting technology to Hezbollah's terror organization in Lebanon.

After wrapping up the Hezbollah cell, Clifford was asked in June 2000 to go to Athens as the bureau's legal attaché and chief of its operations in the Balkan area. Two items were at the top of his priority list. The first was helping repair the antagonistic relationship between the United States and Greece on counterterrorism. Because the Olympic Games were set for Greece in 2004, it was critical to overcome what the Greek security minister candidly described as a "climate of mistrust" between the two countries on fighting terror.[6] His second task was more specific. Clifford was charged with helping the Greeks crack the mysterious N-17 terrorist organization. Since its first action, the assassination of CIA station chief Richard Welch in December 1975, the group had killed more than twenty people (including four Americans) in more than one hundred attacks.

The group was still very much alive. On June 8, 2000—only six days after Clifford was told of his new assignment—N-17 assassinated the British defense attaché in Athens, Brigadier Stephen Saunders. Breaking N-17 was a tall order. Not a single member had been identified in its twenty-five-year history.[7] But the Greek government was revamping its counterterror program. It brought in fresh talent with an aggressive outlook.[8] Scotland Yard also sent help. Clifford thrives in such joint operations. He helped establish a counterterrorism training program, improved case management, encouraged better use of forensics, and advised on legislative reform targeted at terrorism. An opening came in June 2002, when an N-17 operative accidentally detonated a bomb he was trying to activate. A defective Chinese timer set the infernal device off prematurely. A ballistic trace on the thirty-eight-caliber revolver he was carrying and other evidence gathered at the scene led to additional clues. This time, the Greek system, largely revamped because of Clifford's efforts, was ready to capitalize on the break. Within months, nineteen members of N-17 had been identified and arrested, and by the end of 2003, Greek courts had convicted fifteen of them.

Meanwhile, Assistant Director Swecker was in a bind. Congressman Wolf was pressuring Director Mueller, and Director Mueller was "putting a lot of heat on Swecker" for results on the new MS-13 project. But the plan was stalling. The agent originally assigned to the project was nearing retirement. In the view of an insider close to the events, the agent saw the task force as an opportunity to create an elaborate "off-campus" farm on which to leisurely serve out his tenure. Swecker was not buying that. He needed someone who could take charge, jumpstart the stalled program, and kick it into high gear. In October 2004, he picked up the phone and called Athens. Swecker asked Clifford if he would come back to Washington a year earlier than scheduled, to get the new MS-13 task force moving, and how soon he could get on an airplane. "Sure," Clifford replied to his old friend and boss. "But what's MS-13?"[9]

Like many in law enforcement, Clifford had never heard of MS-13.

For weeks after he reported for duty on December 17, 2004, he occasionally misspoke and referred to MS-13 as "MS-17" or "NC-13." But he soon got his gyroscope in order and zeroed in on his target. Clifford knows his way around the federal law enforcement and intelligence establishments. There were a number of agencies he wanted to go to and people he wanted to see right away. Among the people were two very bright federal prosecutors. One was Kevin Carwile, a career lawyer who was a deputy chief of the Justice Department's Organized Crime and Racketeering Section, located right across Pennsylvania Avenue from FBI Headquarters. Carwile would soon be tapped to head the department's new Gang Squad. He was already seeing an increasing amount of work involving gangs on his desk. The other person was Bruce Riordan. Clifford walked across the street to talk to Carwile, then flew out to meet Riordan in Los Angeles.

Riordan and Clifford hit it off famously. "Bob had the drive," recalls Riordan. "All he needed was information and a point in the right direction. Then he went out with all guns blazing." Among other things, Riordan briefed Clifford on Nelson Comandari, the MS-13 shot caller who had put aside intergang animosity and imported gunmen from Mexico to help 18th Street shot caller Termite try to knock off his rival Tiny. The prosecutor was peeved because he felt that the FBI had dropped the ball after two agents, Carl Sandford and Jim Wines, handed off what they learned about Comandari to the MS-13 gang squad in the Los Angeles field office. Leads frittered away, and Comandari, by then known to be an important figure in MS-13, had disappeared. Clifford went into action. He put out a BOLO (be on the lookout) notice on Comandari and arranged for a more aggressive special agent, John Bauman, to take over as lead agent on the case. Those actions would lead shortly to an unusual series of events regarding a man whom one law enforcement investigator describes as a potential John Gotti, the "Teflon Don" of New York's LCN.

Jason Hess was half of a two-person detective squad in Stayton, Oregon (population about seven thousand). On June 17, 2003, a young Latino named Erick Morales showed up at the police station—next door to the town's sole movie theater—and asked to speak to a detective. Hess was the half of the squad on duty. Stayton had been spared any serious gang problems, even though Latino gangsters from California had been migrating to Oregon for years. They settled in cities like the state capitol, Salem, about fourteen miles distant, and Portland. From the cities, a few, the rootless sons of families following jobs, seeped out into rural communities like Stayton. A few local Latino kids went into Salem from time to time and got mixed up in gang trouble.[10]

Stayton is located at the mouth of the Willamette Valley, which flares down from the Cascade Range. It once hummed with lumber mills and cabinet factories. As the timber industry faded over the last several decades, jobs became fewer, lower-paying, and insecure. At the same time, the area diversified into other enterprises, including agricultural packing plants. This transitional economy attracted Latinos from California and south of the border. Some came for seasonal agricultural work and stayed for jobs in the timber industry—insecure jobs from which the local population increasingly shied. A few Latinos set up local businesses, including a Mexican bakery, aimed at the Latino trade.

Morales, the twenty-five-year-old man who sat down on the other side of Hess's desk, was clearly anguished. He told the detective that he had recently returned to his Catholic faith and had a criminal confession to make. Hess turned on a tape recorder, asked Morales to acknowledge that he had come in on his own accord, and let him talk. "I killed two men in Los Angeles," Morales said. "I killed them for my gang, for Mara Salvatrucha. I need to confess this for my faith, for my church."

By the time he finished talking, Morales provided the details of two cold cases, unsolved murders in Los Angeles. One of the victims was shot once in the face and three times in the back, then dumped beside a freeway. The other was stabbed several times, chased down when he tried to flee, and shot to death. Morales fled to Oregon after the murders. For a while, MS-13 paid him a subsidy, but that stopped.

If he had quit talking there, Erick Morales would have done nothing more than close the LAPD's books on a routine pair of unsolved murder cases. But while the tape rolled, he rambled. He talked about a man identified in the California appellate description of Morales's subsequent appeal only as "N.C." He described N.C. as a sort of godfather of MS-13 in Los Angeles, the man behind the scenes who provided the guns and gave the orders for the murders Morales committed. N.C. was involved in drug trafficking with the Mexican Mafia.

Detective Hess called the LAPD and described Morales's confession. A homicide detective flew up from Los Angeles the next day. Morales repeated his story in another tape-recorded interview. He was taken back to Los Angeles, convicted of both murders and sentenced to two consecutive terms of life in prison without the possibility of parole. However sincere his religious experience may have been at the time of his confession to Detective Hess, it did not stop him from later trying to escape from the Los Angeles County Sheriff's Department Jail. Nor did it keep him from smuggling a razor into the courtroom during his trial and slashing his court-appointed lawyer's arm. LAPD investigators believe Morales was a hit man for Mara Salvatrucha, who may have committed other murders in Los Angeles and at least one in El Salvador.

Erick Morales's story provides a few pieces of the puzzle that is the gangster N.C., Nelson Agustin Varela Comandari. As of this writing, only two sentences have been written about him in the U.S. news media, so far as exhaustive searches of the Internet and Nexis reveal. Yet according to some law enforcement officials, Nelson Comandari came as close to being a Don Corleone—a *cappo di tutti cappi*, the boss of all bosses, the ultimate "Big Homey"—as Mara Salvatrucha has seen in its brief, violent history. He is a man that law enforcement agencies prefer not to talk about publicly. This is perhaps because of sensitive negotiations, rather than an unwillingness to embarrass his prominent family. In either case, mention of his name causes senior FBI and Justice Department officials in Washington to blanch. "You can write about that if you want," warned one Justice Department lawyer. "But no one around here will ever talk to you again if you do." A number of others in the law enforcement establishment have made it clear, however, that they would not mind at all if Comandari's story became public.

Nelson Comandari confounds the typical gangster model. He was born not into poverty but into the union of two prominent families. At this writing, he is being held on a federal drug-trafficking charge brought on an indictment in the Southern District of New York. But his case may never go to public trial. Although Comandari's counsel insist that he is not an informant or "cooperator," it is clear that law enforcement authorities would very much like to "flip" him as part of an omnibus deal that would close several ongoing investigations in which he is a central figure.[11]

One of the more intriguing things about Comandari is the Middle Eastern origin of his maternal lineage. The Comandari family is Palestinian, part of the Tarajmeh clan of Bethlehem. The name is sometimes spelled with two *m*'s (i.e., "Commandari") and with other slight variations (e.g., "Comandarie"), even for the same person. (The federal documents regarding Comandari spell his name "Commandari," but he and his family in El Salvador use only one *m*. The second *m* is superfluous in Spanish.) The name itself likely descends from Arabs who served as translators for the Crusaders. They took or were given the European name, which is probably Italian in origin. Comandaris, or Commandaris, are not uncommon in Latin America, but they are hardly numerous. Like many other Middle Eastern Arabs—conceptually lumped together in much of Latin America with Jews from the Middle East as "Syrians"—they sought economic opportunity and political freedom when the Ottoman Empire collapsed in the early twentieth century. "One common thread that the descendants of Palestinian immigrants who settled in El Salvador and Honduras shared was that, unlike in the United States, if we shared the same last name, we are all connected to the one patriarch that migrated to Central America in the late 1920s," says a native Latin American of Middle Eastern descent who is familiar with the history of the extended family.

Nelson Comandari's maternal great-grandfather, Emilio Comandari, was the patriarch who came to El Salvador from Palestine in the 1920s. Members of the Comandari family are prominent in commerce, including coffee plantations and coffee export. Some are described by a U.S. law enforcement official knowledgeable about the family as major "crime figures," possibly involved in drug and firearms smuggling. According to that source, one of Nelson's great-uncles—Alfredo "Fredi" Comandari—was incarcerated during the 1980s at the Peninsula Penitentiary in San Miguel. Prisoners in El Salvador depend largely on outside help for adequate food and necessities. Fredi Comandari had no problem. He lived in a luxury room with a television and other amenities and was always accompanied by hired bodyguards. The source estimates that it cost Fredi "approximately $125,000 a year to live in this manner while in custody."

Nelson was born in El Salvador sometime around 1977 and came to the United States after the attempted assassination of his paternal grandfather. Since then, he appears to have traveled widely in the United States, Mexico, and Central America as an important figure in Mara Salvatrucha. His paternal grandfather was Col. Agustin Martinez Varela, a prominent and powerful right-wing figure in Salvadoran political life. Agustin Martinez Varela served for many years in top government posts, including a term as the minister of the interior. His brother, Col. Juan Antonio Martinez Varela, also served as minister of the interior and as chief of staff to former Salvadoran president Alfredo Felix Cristiani Burkard, a scion of one of the original "Fourteen Families" of El Salvador. Cristiani appointed Col. Juan Antonio Martinez Varela to be one of the two government officials who negotiated the peace accords with the Farabundo Martí National Liberation Front in 1989. His son, also named Juan Antonio Martinez Varela, is the air force major general who met with Secretary Rumsfeld in 2001, and he is now El Salvador's ambassador to Guatemala. Nelson's maternal grandfather, Antonio Comandari, made minor medical history in 2004 when a new heart-monitoring device was implanted in his chest at a hospital in Miami, where he is reported to be a resident.[12] Little is known about Nelson's father, Nelson Agustin Varela, except that he is separated from Nelson's mother, "Jenny," Antonio Comandari's daughter. Jenny, Nelson's father, and his two uncles all live quietly in Texas.

In 1996, the Salvadoran national civil police arrested one "Nelson Comandari" on charges of possessing an AK-47 rifle and marijuana. According to a knowledgeable U.S. law enforcement official, this is the person in whom we are interested here. A photograph of the man arrested in El Salvador is identical to a photograph of Nelson Comandari that appears in a PowerPoint presentation regularly given in law enforcement classes by a U.S. gang expert on MS-13. If these two are indeed the same man, as appears likely, the 1996 arrest is the first publicly reported encounter of Nelson Comandari with the law. The Salvadoran police described Comandari in 1996 as the head of a gang engaged in auto theft, drug and firearms trafficking, armed assault, and counterfeiting, according to news reports in El Salvador. Comandari was set free within a few months and apparently left El Salvador for Los Angeles. In 1998, a Salvadoran law enforcement official was accused of having planted the gun and drugs to frame Comandari. The matter became a minor cause célèbre among human rights activists. The official was later cleared and returned to duty in the police force.

Comandari "first surfaced to federal attention" when his name came up in the FBI wiretap on 18th Street shot caller Juan Manuel "Termite" Lopez Romero sometime in the fall or winter of 1999, after the abortive assassination attempt on Termite by minions of Carlos Wilfredo "Tiny" Carcamo. Although he was himself a shot caller for 18th Street's mortal enemies, MS-13, "Comandari agreed to help Termite kill Tiny for a price—likely to be a piece of drug money when Tiny was out of the way," says a law enforcement official close to the case. "The conspiracy to kill was in place," the official explains, but because of preventive steps taken by the FBI and local law enforcement, "the hit never materialized."

Bruce Riordan complains that when his team handed Comandari off to the FBI MS-13 squad, "they squandered the effort and did nothing from January 2000 until January 2005, when Bob Clifford and I took over." A senior FBI agent agrees that "the MS-13 unit in Los Angeles was a mess." It had fallen behind and had a "big backlog" of Title III wiretap tapes, meaning it could not effectively do real-time coordination with other investigative means. Meanwhile, the murders that Erick Morales said he committed at Comandari's order happened on July 21, 1999, and November 1, 2000. According to Los Angeles Superior Court records, Nelson Comandari was convicted of "carrying a dirk or dagger" on May 30, 2001. Comandari was reported to have been spotted as far north as Alaska, in Texas, and in Colorado, among other places. He is said to have been carrying a Colorado driver's license when he was once stopped by police in Los Angeles. A Colorado law enforcement official explains that the Colorado licenses are notoriously easy to obtain.

Comandari was not an ordinary gangster. An LAPD officer who testified as an MS-13 gang expert in Erick Morales's trial told the *Washington Post* in August 2004 that Comandari was the "CEO" of Mara

Salvatrucha. (This short reference appears to be the only mention of Comandari in the English-language news media and uses a variant—probably phonetic—spelling.) Other law enforcement sources say that Comandari has a charismatic personality, a cold-blooded willingness to use violence, and a vision that goes beyond the ordinary street level, perhaps the result of the background in organized crime reputed for some members of his family and the sophisticated political skills of others. These sources say that Comandari wanted to pull Mara Salvatrucha together with a well-organized transnational structure, like the LCN. He has many attributes that would be useful to such an effort. Because he was either loved or greatly feared by other leaders in MS, he moved easily among the gang's cliques, not only in California, but all over the United States. When Mara Salvatrucha originally refused to knuckle under, pay "taxes," and recognize the Mexican Mafia's suzerainty, Comandari reportedly brokered a deal that ended the deadlock. After Eme whacked several Mara Salvatrucha members, Comandari negotiated a more or less peaceful resolution. MS thereafter added "13" to its name, for the letter *m*, the thirteenth letter of the alphabet, signifying La Eme. Before his latest arrest, Comdari was reportedly in line to be "made" as a member of the Mexican Mafia and slated for an Eme leadership position.

In sum, Nelson Comandari had the brains, the ambition, and the cold blood to start a large-scale integration of a transnational street gang and organized crime. This potential for a Latino gang like MS-13 to coalesce into something rivaling the old LCN is the precise threat that most worries FBI and Justice Department officials. "Our mandate includes not letting any other criminal groups take root and grow into organized crime the way the Mafia did," says Kevin Carwile, chief of the U.S. Justice Department's Gang Squad.

Something spooked Comandari in mid-2001. He disappeared for a while. According to Erick Morales's story, Comandari was laying low in El Salvador during the summer of that year. He appeared to be suffering from a bout of gangster's paranoia. When Morales called Comandari to ask that his subsidy be resumed, Comandari invited him to come to El Salvador. When Morales demurred, Comandari accused him of working for the police. Morales's decision not to go to El Salvador was a wise one according to an informed official, who says, "A meeting like that with Nelson Comandari is one you don't come back from." After Morale's confessions in 2003, the LAPD built a substantial dossier on Comandari. According to LAPD and federal officials, Los Angeles authorities believe that Comandari is "good for" between six to ten murders, allegedly having either committed them himself or ordered them to be committed by others.

Comandari eventually resumed travel (if he ever actually suspended it) between El Salvador and the United States. On April 22, 2004—while Bob Clifford was still in Greece and nothing much was happening in the Los Angeles MS-13 gang squad—a grand jury in New York returned a secret indictment charging Comandari with being part of a conspiracy to distribute cocaine. The sealed indictment was based at least in part on a wiretapped conversation between Comandari and another conspirator in New York or New Jersey in October 2003.

The wiretap may well have been the work of the mysterious Special Operations Division (SOD) of the Department of Justice. The SOD is administratively located within the Drug Enforcement Administration's Operations Division. It is physically located in a "secret" location in Chantilly, Virginia, near Dulles International Airport. Few visitors driving into the massive parking lot of the Smithsonian Institution's Steven F. Udvar-Hazy Center—which houses full-sized aircraft from aviation history—realize that they are passing only a few dozen yards from this high-technology nerve center of the war against drugs. The SOD is a joint task force aimed at dismantling the leadership of international drug-trafficking organizations. It is staffed by lawyers from the Narcotics and Dangerous Drug Section of the Justice Department's Criminal Division and federal agents from the DEA, the FBI, the Internal Revenue Service, ICE, and other agencies.

Federal officials and documents refer only cryptically to the SOD, but the skeleton can be fleshed out with bits and pieces of more detailed information found in budget documents, job descriptions, and official biographies. Its mission, as formally stated, is "to coordinate multi-agency, multi-jurisdiction, and multi-national Title III investigations against the command and control elements of major drug trafficking organizations, operating domestically and abroad."[13] In plain English, the

SOD has two prime functions. One is to coordinate major international investigations. The other is to provide one of the principal means by which such investigations are conducted: international wiretaps.

The need for such a specialized organization devoted to communication intercepts grows out of the tightly closed and highly secretive nature of drug-trafficking organizations. Their leaders typically come from common ethnic roots, neighborhoods, and families. Penetrating their core is extremely difficult. But all organizations require a communications system, through which flow orders, operational details, and financial data. Attacking drug organizations from these margins is an important law enforcement strategy. It is a fair inference that the code-breaking and international listening capabilities of the National Security Agency, as well as specialized capabilities of other intelligence agencies, are central to the mission of the SOD.

Comandari eluded arrest until Clifford and Riordan turned up the heat in early 2005. As a result of Clifford's BOLO and agent John Bauman's "beating the bushes," Nelson Comandari was finally arrested by DEA agents in Houston, Texas, on March 16, 2005. The case has stalled ever since. It features several odd indicia that something is going on behind the scenes. The customary self-congratulatory press release boasting of a big catch was never issued by the DEA, the FBI, or the Justice Department. This is all the more curious because, at the time, law enforcement agencies, particularly the FBI, were touting MS-13 as an international menace and the "most dangerous gang in America." Only a month before, much had been made of the apprehension in Texas of Ever Anibal Rivera Paz, the Honduran MS-13 leader known as "the Tapeworm." One would have thought that the capture of Comandari, MS-13's alleged "CEO," would have merited some public notice.

Although Comandari has been held in a federal facility near metropolitan New York for something approaching three years at this writing, his case has never moved beyond a preliminary hearing. His trial has been repeatedly postponed by a series of terse motions and succinct court orders jointly agreed to by defense and prosecution lawyers. (The judge's orders are clearly boilerplate, as Comandari's name is misspelled in each of them as "Comadari.") Moreover, Comandari has two counsel of record, both from the same law firm specializing in high-profile cases, one retained and one court-appointed. The presence of two defense lawyers in a federal case in which one is an appointed defender—paid by public funds—is unusual. It is often a hallmark of a potential death penalty, according to a former federal prosecutor. If a defendant in a noncapital case can afford to retain counsel, the court will usually terminate the appointed lawyer to save public funds. However, the Federal Death Penalty Act specifically requires that a defendant have two counsel competent in death penalty cases when the ultimate punishment is on the table. No public charge carrying the death penalty has been made against Comandari, but it may be a possibility and would be an excellent bargaining "hammer" if it were lurking in the mix. Comandari's lawyers have not responded to several requests for an explanation of his dual representation.

The continuing series of postponements in such a case is often an indicator that a defendant either is cooperating or is, at a minimum, in serious negotiations with the government, according to experienced defense lawyers and prosecutors. "You can do the math," said one former prosecutor. "Criminal cases are like fish, not like wine. They don't get better with age." In other words, a prosecutor better have a good reason to let a case get old, as Comandari's has. The defendant's potential for cooperation would be such a good reason. A federal law enforcement official intimate with the case said, "Nelson Commandari could be the next Sammy 'the Bull' Gravano." Gravano, also known as "King Rat," was a Gambino family hit man and underboss who flipped and testified against the notorious John Gotti, thus helping the FBI finally bring down the elusive "Teflon Don." However, one of Comandari's lawyers insisted in November 2007 that Comandari is not a cooperator and claimed that the delay is "attributable to Mr. Comandari's exposure to other ongoing investigations."

The presence of "other ongoing investigations"—likely including, at a minimum, the interests of Los Angeles authorities—makes negotiating any omnibus deal with Nelson Comandari extremely complex. Any concessions given Comandari in exchange for his "flipping" would have to not only meet federal expectations but also satisfy police, prosecutors, and politicians in Los Angeles, who want him held accountable for the half-dozen or more murders for which they think he was responsible. Federal authorities would want to use his intimate knowledge of the gang to help cripple MS-13's transnational structure and its operations. The knot appears to be Gordian. According to informed sources, a number of meetings were held well into 2007 among federal prosecutors from New York and Los Angeles and senior officials at the Justice Department and between the Justice Department and Los Angeles city officials. "Part of what's going on is internal politics in the Justice Department," said one source. "Prosecutors from the Southern District of New York are jostling with their peers in the Central District of California over who gets this juicy defendant."

As of June 2008, however, nothing was being said publicly about Nelson Comandari. His case was in a deep freeze. Senior FBI and Justice Department officials refused to talk about Comandari. Many whom one would think should have known—from case agents to unit supervisors—all claimed that they knew nothing about his family background. Even if Comandari had already agreed to cooperate—which his lawyers insist he has not—prosecutors would want to test the quality and veracity of his information before making an agreement final. If Comandari were to become a cooperator, the public may never know the whole story. Everything about the final disposition could be sealed from the public eye, just as in the case of the notorious Honduran "Tapeworm," who supposedly disappeared on a flight to Tegucigalpa.

"MS-13 is truly a gang without borders," Bob Clifford says earnestly. "That's why we have to stop them here and now." When he reported to Washington in December 2004, Clifford was ushered into an empty office space and handed the equivalent of a prepaid credit card. Assistant Director Swecker told him he could have whatever he needed— so long as it did not require any new money. Congressman Wolf had seen to it that ten million dollars were added to the FBI's funding to start up another project he favored, the National Gang Intelligence Center. But no new funds were provided for the MS-13 task force. This was in part because the project was hatched internally by the FBI between budget cycles. But the Justice Department, nominally the FBI's superior agency and through whom the bureau's budget must pass on its way to Congress, was lukewarm to the idea and thwarted separate funding for the project.

Housed in Stalinesque office blocks that square off at each other across eight lanes of Pennsylvania Avenue, the two agencies are engaged in a perpetual power struggle, often waged by separate public relations and lobbying staffs. The temperature of that conflict has ranged from the deep freeze of Director Louis Freeh's open contempt for President Bill Clinton and his attorney general, Janet Reno, to Director Robert Mueller's determination to work out a warmer civil relationship with the dysfunctional reign of Alberto Gonzales, despite the fact that many of Mueller's senior career staff were shocked by the rank politics they thought were wrecking the parent department. Moreover, when the MS-13 task force was being organized, in December 2004 and January 2005, the White House and the Justice Department were intensely focused on the so-called War on Terror, a black hole into which law enforcement resources and intellectual energy continue to be sucked. Attorney General John Ashcroft, who oversaw the war's legal architecture, was leaving office. Gonzales's nomination was in heavy weather on Capitol Hill. No one was prepared to spend political capital on a new war against a gang they never heard of—just as, years before, the establishment had dismissed the warnings of legendary FBI counterterrorism warrior John O'Neill about another gang they had never heard of, al Qaeda.

None of this deterred Clifford, who had a free hand from Swecker to build the task force from the ground up. "We didn't even have a name yet," Clifford says. "I knew it had to have 'MS-13' in it somewhere. That was Congressman Wolf's singular focus. It had to be a task force. That was what director Mueller ordered. And I wanted it to sound like a national program, not something limited to Northern Virginia or Los Angeles." Thus was born the name of the MS-13 National Gang Task Force.

Substantively, Clifford was strongly influenced by his counterterrorism experiences in Charlotte and Athens. He had seen the importance of integrating intelligence and investigation. "It couldn't be just intelligence," Clifford says. "It had to integrate operational units with the intelligence effort." He had also seen how effective multiagency task forces could be in proactively combining the unique capabilities of diverse agencies. In Charlotte, he had worked with ATF, the Internal Revenue Service, the Department of State's Diplomatic Security Service, and several state and local police agencies to dismantle the Hezbollah cell. In Greece, he had worked with Scotland Yard, the Greek security services, and other U.S. agencies to crack N-17. Looking at MS-13, Clifford saw that "all the federal agencies were out doing their own thing" and that "there needed to be a single coordinating entity." The FBI has a long history of creating and coordinating multiagency task forces, and Clifford saw this as an opportunity for "everyone to check their badges at the door and work together on a common problem."

Finally, Clifford thought it was important to reach out and work closely with the governments of Central America. Regardless of who was responsible or why, MS-13 was now transnational. It was deeply rooted north and south of the border. The gang's leaders were operating and cooperating, however crudely, without regard to national boundaries. Law enforcement agencies in Central America also needed help revamping a whole range of techniques and laws to effectively confront the gangs.

By spring 2005, the task force had taken shape. Assistant Director Swecker told Congress that its goal was "to disrupt and dismantle this gang, now, before it has the opportunity to become more organized and sophisticated and more difficult to attack." Swecker described the mission in more detail.

> The goals of the MS-13 National Gang Task Force are to enable local, state, and federal, as well as international law enforcement agencies, to easily exchange information on MS-13; to enable local and state law enforcement agencies to identify the presence of MS-13 in their territories; to identify related investigations; and to coordinate regional and/or nationwide, multijurisdictional law enforcement action, including federal Racketeering (RICO) and Violent Crimes in Aid of Racketeering (VICAR) prosecutions.[14]

Clifford set out to recruit other federal and national security agencies to become part of the new task force. Neither he nor Swecker envisioned it as an exclusively FBI operation. Kevin Carwile at the Justice Department was a "key ally," says Clifford. The FBI agent approached the other agencies in the federal law enforcement alphabet: ATF, Customs and Border Protection (CBP), the DEA, ICE, and the U.S. Marshals Service. He talked to the National Security Agency (which breaks codes and collects foreign "signals intelligence"), the CIA, and the State Department. He briefed the U.S. Southern Command in Miami, a joint defense command responsible for security in Central and South America and the Caribbean. "I was trying to sell the idea that we can all work together. I met varying degrees of enthusiasm and resistance," Clifford says diplomatically. Of the law enforcement agencies, only the CBP and U.S. Marshals Service seemed enthusiastic. The others gave lip service to the idea and attended some meetings, apparently mostly to gather intelligence on what the FBI was up to.

A senior official in the Criminal Division of the Justice Department puts it more bluntly. "Bob got stiff-armed by the other law enforcement agencies," he says. In the treacherous atmosphere of interagency politics in Washington, Clifford could not re-create the cooperative relationships he had enjoyed with other agencies in the more sophisticated world of international relations or during the case-specific hunt for terrorists at the local level. There are some interagency crime-fighting task forces that seem to work well at the national level—among them the Organized Crime Drug Enforcement Task Force and the secretive SOD. But the MS-13 task force was not destined to be one of them. At the parochial level of the law enforcement "suits" in Washington, nobody from other agencies wanted to give up an inch of turf to what they perceived to be an FBI show.

ATF sent representatives to task force meetings while the officials at its headquarters openly trashed the idea that MS-13 was a more organized or more dangerous gang than any other. "The most dangerous gang in America is the gang that's in your neighborhood," they liked to say. "The best way to fight gangs is to take them off the streets one at a time, the way we do it." Clifford watched with bemused irritation during one task force meeting as a senior ATF agent surreptitiously slipped into his briefcase a background paper that Clifford had specifically asked not leave the room. Clifford let it go. It was not worth blowing things up over an amateurish and penny-ante act of interagency cloak and dagger. "Look, you've got to understand this," a former senior ATF executive told the author in explaining the dynamic between the two agencies. "We're like the carpenters and plumbers of federal law enforcement. Most of our guys are former street cops. The FBI guys are like the doctors and lawyers. Since the days of J. Edgar Hoover they get drilled into their heads at the FBI Academy that they are the best, that nothing can stop them, and they believe it. So our guys are always a bit resentful of their air of superiority. And maybe we have a little inferiority complex of our own."

More treacherous and potentially damaging were the actions of the Department of Homeland Security's ICE, which had its own antigang program called Operation Community Shield on the drawing board. There is nothing wrong with the concept of ICE's program. In theory, it consists of periodically conducting highly publicized "sweeps" rounding up gangsters who are "criminal aliens"—persons in the country illegally who have committed serious crimes—and shipping them out. In October 2007, for example, ICE claimed to have swept up more than thirteen hundred violent gang members over a three-month sweep in twenty-three cities. At a press conference touting the sweep's success, Julie L. Myers, assistant secretary for ICE, intoned, "Violent foreign-born gang members and their associates have more than worn out their welcome, and to them I have one message: Good riddance."[15]

But some local officials and journalistic postmortems call ICE's gang-busting numbers into question. In November 2007, for example, the *New York Times* reported that of eleven persons arrested in a September Long Island ICE sweep, only one was in fact a putative gang member. The other ten were run-of-the-mill aliens—persons with neither gang affiliations nor criminal arrest records—who had the misfortune to be at the wrong place at the wrong time. These ten were nonetheless thrown into ICE's statistical hopper as "gang members and their associates."[16] The Long Island raids also generated a miniature political firestorm. Nassau County executive Thomas Suozzi assailed ICE agents for being disorganized, having a "cowboy mentality," failing to make use of up-to-date local gang databases, and even aiming their guns at local police.[17]

Local cops give ICE's sweeps mixed reviews. Some police agencies enthusiastically welcome the raids as a quick and easy means to get "bad guys" off the streets. "When it comes to local law enforcement, we use anything within the toolbox to make our cities safer," Fort Worth's police chief said in October 2007, commenting on the ICE sweep.[18] A Los Angeles deputy chief was equally sanguine. "We welcome ICE's direct and targeted intervention in identifying criminal gang members, criminal offenders and habitual offenders that are here unlawfully," he said.[19] Others are less enthusiastic. On balance, the latter believe, ICE sweeps do more harm than good because they exacerbate the already difficult problem of policy-community relations in Latino neighborhoods.

"To some extent, it seems like it's a publicity campaign," the director of a national pro-immigration umbrella group said. "But to us it's worrisome when there are issues of racial profiling, constitutional rights, not to mention the fear that they generate in the community when they see ICE is picking up people."[20] Under such conditions, the argument goes, residents are even more reluctant to come forward as witnesses, report crime, or act as informants after they have seen their neighbors swept up and deported. "The ICE guys swoop in, they leave and then we still got to police the streets on a regular basis," said Nassau County's Suozzi. "We can't do that effectively if we don't have the support of the community."[21]

For federal law enforcement and specifically the FBI, a major problem with ICE's sweeps is its refusal to cooperate meaningfully in what is called "deconfliction," or sharing plans among law enforcement agencies to make sure that one operation, such as an ICE raid, is not going to disrupt another ongoing operation. "They are just kicking the ant heap," complains now retired Chris Swecker. "And their refusal to cooperate with us created real problems in March 2005." Despite the fact that ICE representatives came to several task force meetings, none of them bothered to inform Clifford or the FBI that ICE was rolling out its new program with a massive national sweep that month.[22] In the event, ICE wrecked a couple of ongoing FBI operations by rolling up assets, including informants, that the bureau had spent considerable time developing. According to one report at the time, ICE "nabbed" a gang member that the FBI was "intensely interested in" but was not ready to "scoop up."[23]

Swecker and Clifford learned of the sweep in the news media. They ended up sorting things out in several urgent meetings at the level of the attorney general. When Clifford raised the issue of deconfliction at a subsequent meeting, a senior ICE official in charge of Los Angeles operations stood up and shouted, "ICE is not part of the task force, we stand alone!" In response to FBI grumbling to the news media at the time of the sweep, an ICE official replied that "the bureau thinks it has jurisdiction over everything."[24] One observer in Washington argues that ICE is just doing what it must in the vacuum left by Congress's failure to forge an effective national immigration policy: "Deconfliction sounds nice in theory but ICE really has no choice. It has 535 bosses. If ICE lets just one really bad felon go and he commits some notorious or obnoxious crime, they're going to hear about it from a member of Congress or senator in whose state or district the crime occurred. What's in it for them?"

Ironically, the MS-13 National Gang Task Force's own long-planned and carefully coordinated international arrest sweep got almost no notice the following September. Even though police officials from Central America came to Washington to be on hand, the public rollout of the task force's first operation was swallowed up by Hurricane Katrina—and the Department of Homeland Security's disastrous handling of the storm's aftermath. Clifford got a much better and, in the long run, more important reception from the National Security Agency and the CIA. Both of these agencies would prove invaluable in dealing with international intelligence and communications monitoring in relation to the transnational gang-busting effort, through the SOD and other means. Clifford also built the framework for more effective relations between the FBI and law enforcement agencies in Central America.

At the end of the year he had committed to stay, however, Clifford wanted another assignment. Swecker agreed, and Clifford returned to Charlotte, North Carolina. (Like Swecker, he was later assigned to lead a team of FBI agents in Iraq, which is where he is at this writing.) When he and Chris Swecker looked around for a replacement to head the task force, they found an ideal candidate, a man whose career had many similarities to Clifford's—Brian Truchon.

Truchon had a high and rising reputation within the FBI and several specific qualities that Swecker, Clifford, and others thought were needed for the job. He had proven grit from elite military service, management experience, about seven years of conducting or supervising gang investigations, and a headquarters tour under his belt. There was one problem, though, that they would have to overcome.

Truchon left Los Angeles in 1996 for a two-year tour in the FBI's Safe Streets Initiative headquarters unit, where he managed gang investigations in field offices all over the country. He quickly found that every coin has two sides. "I went from 'those jerks in headquarters' to 'those guys in the field trying to screw us over,'" he jokes, addressing the different perspectives of agents on the street and managers in headquarters. "Now I had to be the guy calling and asking for information to send upstairs." The headquarters unit coordinated investigations, managed deconfliction, and set national priorities. Above all, it controlled allocation of the funds that fuel local Safe Street task forces, money for such things as overtime for local police officers, equipment, and informants. Even so, the allocation of power between headquarters and field is a constant negotiation. "We're salesmen at headquarters," Truchon says. "We see the connectivity that perhaps those in the field don't, so we try to sell them on it. We're selling the 'real deal' aluminum siding, the 'ultimate desert protection' package. We tell them in the field, 'Three years from now you're going to thank us.'"[25]

"The good thing about working in headquarters is that you see how it all connects," he continues in a more serious tone. "It opens up your perceptions. Supervisors in the field who have spent time at headquarters 'get it.'" Truchon credits his military experience—particularly the U.S. Army Ranger School—with giving him a solid base of managerial skills. He joined the Reserve Officers Training Corps and went to parachute jump school while he was in college. He was commissioned when he graduated in 1984 and went on to the army's Pathfinder School and Ranger School.

Army pathfinder units were created during World War II after a disastrous airborne operation in the Allied invasion of Sicily in July 1943. Half of the paratroopers missed their landing target. There were several causes, but the net result was that although the airborne troops fought valiantly, they did not fight as the intended organized units. Adopting the motto "First in, last out," the pathfinders were specially trained paratroopers whose mission was to find the drop zone and jump into it well ahead of the main force. They used a variety of means—lamps, radio beacons, smoke, and colored panels—to guide the main airborne force to the zone. Pathfinders today have a similar mission, but the technology of the battlefield has changed. They use more sophisticated equipment and techniques to guide and coordinate not only airborne operations but the variety of aircraft involved in today's combat operations.

The black and gold shoulder tab of a ranger is an essential credential for any ambitious U.S. Army Infantry officer. Getting into the Ranger School is hard, and staying in until the end is harder. It is not uncommon for half of a class to wash out. Each student must win a passing grade as the leader of at least one patrol in every phase. There were four phases when Truchon graduated—city, low-level mountaineering, desert, and jungle. "Ranger School is physical," Truchon says. "The Pathfinder School is more intellectual. It requires some book smarts. You don't get a 'do over.'" Like every other holder of the coveted ranger badge, Truchon calls Ranger School a "life-changing" experience. "It is the best small-unit leadership school in the world," he says. "The rest of the world teaches management. The Ranger School teaches leadership. You don't learn that in seminars or from in-box exercises."

In 1998, Truchon was assigned to Phoenix, Arizona, as a supervisory field agent. He spent the last five of eight years there supervising the Safe Streets gang task force. In that capacity, he supervised an investigation that demonstrates just how close to the heart of the American system of justice the ruthless violence of Latino gangs can get. The case involved a prison gang called the New Mexican Mafia and a criminal enterprise known as the Cisneros Organization, which operated in Arizona and New Mexico.[26]

The name "New Mexican Mafia" derives not from the state of New Mexico but from the intention of its founders to break away and distinguish themselves from La Eme, the original Mexican Mafia. Its origins go back to the early 1970s, when inmates at the Arizona State Prison formed a group they called the "Mexican Mafia," patterned after the California gang. In 1978, the Arizona prison gang broke into two factions, one of which eventually called itself the "New Mexican

Mafia" and the "New Eme." This faction declared its independence from the original California Eme and its followers in Arizona's prison system, who call themselves the "Original Mexican Mafia" and the "Califas Faction." Like the California Mafia, both of these factions readily use lethal violence to exert control, and both seek to extend their reach outside of the prison system into street gangs.

The Cisneros Organization became entwined with the New Mexican Mafia in an interstate criminal enterprise sometime in the early 1990s. The combine's activity included trafficking in methamphetamine, cocaine, and marijuana; laundering money; car theft; and murder, most particularly the flagrant assassination of potential witnesses. Several state investigations, including the planned murder of the director of the Arizona Department of Corrections, were derailed when more than a dozen witnesses ended up dead before trials could commence. One potential witness in Arizona survived several bullet wounds in an attack. He was then put into protective custody and moved out of state, where he was eventually shot to death in a second attack.

Federal authorities in New Mexico and Arizona—including the Safe Streets task force Truchon supervised—investigated the group. The first of a series of federal indictments in New Mexico was brought in December 2001. As the investigation broadened, later indictments in New Mexico superseded the original, adding RICO charges and more defendants. As the case moved toward trial, the federal judge to whom the case was assigned ordered tightened courthouse security in light of the gang's record of making witnesses go away. Prosecutors beefed up their security steps, too—those working on the case were provided security at home and allowed to carry firearms. Special secure parking was provided for their cars. Then, in June 2003, investigators discovered shocking news. The defense team had conducted an inquiry on its own and questioned courthouse personnel about security measures. Moreover, Truchon's task force learned of a plot to assassinate its lead investigator, a Phoenix detective. The two U.S. attorneys involved agreed that the trial could not be safely conducted at the courthouse in Albuquerque, since it was not clear who was leaking security information. An extraordinary request was approved by Attorney General John Ashcroft. A new and broader indictment was brought in Arizona, and the case was dropped in New Mexico. The ringleaders pleaded guilty in December 2005 to RICO counts that netted them life terms in prison.

Truchon had a problem of career management when Assistant Director Swecker called and asked if he would take over the MS-13 National Gang Task Force. He had already been vetted for a tour as assistant special agent in charge of the field office in Portland, Oregon. The assignment as an "ASAC" would give him the credit for holding a management position that he needed in order to move up in the FBI system. When Swecker came back with an offer to count the tour on the task force as a management position on Truchon's record, the deal was made.

In the meantime, the gang problem had bubbled up across the street in the Department of Justice. The White House and senior Justice Department officials were pressing for a special antigang effort, largely independent of Congressman Wolf's pressures on the FBI. One motivation may have been a long memorandum that the U.S. attorney in Northern Virginia, Paul McNulty, wrote in the wake of the MS-13 cases linked to Brenda Paz. (McNulty would later come to grief as deputy attorney general when scandal swamped Alberto Gonzales's tenure.) The department turned to career prosecutor Kevin Carwile to take the lead.

If you don't become a lawyer," a family friend advised fourteen-year-old Kevin Carwile around 1974, "I don't know what your mother is going to do."[27] That contingent disaster never had to be faced. Kevin Carwile fulfilled his mother's dream to a fare-thee-well. He became a lawyer's lawyer, one of the top career executives in the Criminal Division of the U.S. Department of Justice. He is an expert's expert on the text, meaning, and application of the federal laws against racketeering and racketeering violence.

Although by no means stuffy, Carwile speaks with the air of measured seriousness that is characteristic of the Justice Department's career lawyers. If the United States is a nation of laws, these lawyers are the guardians of its ultimate arsenal. The weight of that responsibility never seems to be far from their minds. They consider every word about their charge with care. This responsibility goes far toward explaining the demoralizing effect of the tenure of Alberto Gonzales. "It's embarrassing for a professional to work for the Department of Justice today," Senator Arlen Specter—a former district attorney—said at a 2007 hearing of the Senate Judiciary Committee.[28] Gonzales and his retinue were perceived by many as a children's army of ideologues. They never seemed to have grasped the principle that enforcement of the law must rise above partisanship, or as the Supreme Court once put it, that the Justice Department's lawyers represent "a sovereignty whose obligation to govern impartially is as compelling as its obligation to govern at all; and whose interest, therefore, in a criminal prosecution is not that it shall win a case, but that justice shall be done."[29] Carwile has devoted most of his professional life to seeing that "justice shall be done" by bringing the worst of the worst—murderers, racketeers, and drug lords—to unrelenting judgment. His way was guided by the coordinates of his father's hardworking blue-collar example and his mother's book-driven inspiration.

He was born in 1960 and raised in Colonial Heights, Virginia, an independent city. The town is one of many that were founded along the fall line, a topographic edge that slices down the North American seaboard from Maryland to Georgia. The fall line marks the point at which waterfalls and rapids prevented seagoing colonial vessels from sailing further up the New World's rivers. As settlement progressed westward from the fall line, towns and villages devoted to transshipment sprang up at this natural boundary. European goods were offloaded and trundled westward by cart and beast of burden. Colonial products, largely tobacco in Virginia, were hauled in and taken aboard for ocean transport to the European market. Later, mills and factories were constructed to take advantage of water power.

Colonial Heights is at the fall line of the Appomattox River. It lies just north and across the river from the modern city of Petersburg, where Kevin's father was born and worked all of his life. The earliest settlers arrived about 1620. The town's current name derives from an incident during the Revolutionary War when the French general Marquis de Lafayette's troops, known as "Colonials," occupied the high ground and shelled the British, who were hunkered down in Petersburg. Confederate general Robert E. Lee headquartered on the heights for a while in 1864 during the Civil War. Colonial Heights became a sort of factory town in the early twentieth century. Many of its residents, like Kevin's father, worked at the Brown and Williamson Tobacco Corporation factory and warehouses in Petersburg. The plant was an economic mainstay of the area for half a century. Life progressed at a measured pace, a blend of rural farming and blue-collar factory labor. "My life revolved around salt-of-the-earth people," Carwile recalls from his office in the headquarters building of the U.S. Department of Justice. "People who get up in the morning, put on their pants, go to the coffee shop, and go to work."

Kevin was an only child. His parents, Paul and Jan Carwile, "were not people of means" but "put everything they had into that one child." "My dad was a blue-collar worker," Carwile says. "He worked his entire life in the Brown and Williamson tobacco factory. He was a shop foreman, probably one of their best employees. His whole life was his job. The only thing I recall that he ever had as a hobby was bowling. He was pretty good at it, too. He was a competitive bowler and was always on the 'house team.'" In the 1980s, after Kevin had gone on to college, Brown and Williamson consolidated. It shut down the Petersburg plant, which once employed five thousand workers, and moved its manufacturing operations to a more modern plant in Macon, Georgia. Paul Carwile retired.

Carwile's mother worked for the federal government as a budget analyst at the army's nearby Fort Lee. "My mother was the motivator," he says. "She was a big reader, and that's still her primary pastime. She pushed me. 'You've got to get the education.'" Not only that, Jan Carwile was "taken with lawyers" in her reading. "She liked the high-profile stories," Carwile remembers, "murders, legal dramas, F. Lee Bailey kind of things." Kevin Carwile found himself drawn to the same kind of books and thus, early in life, saw a path to the American dream of advancing beyond one's parents' station. He is the only person in his extended family to have won an advanced degree.

If Carwile's early life was not idyllic, it was something close. Kevin lived the traditional rhythms of small-town America. He played high school football—offensive end—and ran track in the off-season to stay in condition. Over the summers between high school years, he worked in construction. He was elected class president in his senior year at

Colonial Heights High School. It is somehow a measure of the man's gravitas and abiding love of his roots that he takes seriously the responsibility to organize his class reunion every ten years. In 1982, he graduated from Virginia Tech (a name authorized by the institution as a shorter version of its formal name, Virginia Polytechnic Institute and State University) and went on to Wake Forest University School of Law.

"I never had any interest in the big law firm track," Carwile says. "I always thought I would come back to Virginia." He eschewed the pursuit of a place on the school's law review, often perceived as a useful credential for employment in the big firms. "Law review didn't interest me very much," he explains. "It seemed just a place to write something with a bunch of footnotes." Rather, Carwile was drawn to the arena, to the contest of advocates in the courtroom. He won a string of first-place awards for oral argument and brief writing in regional and national moot court competitions. During his last year of law school, he got hands-on experience in the Winston-Salem district attorney's office. Certified under the state's "third-year practice" rule, he helped write motions and briefs under the supervision of senior assistant district attorneys. Several of the cases on which he worked involved the death penalty. The gravity of the decisions to be made by prosecutors in such cases deeply impressed him.

Working in a prosecutor's office seemed a natural fit for Carwile. "I would have been happy to go to work for the district attorney when I graduated," he says, but for one thing. "The problem was financial, the economic straits of law school," he explains. "And I had married while I was in law school. I tried to 'split the baby'—find a private firm that would let me get into the courtroom and litigate." He found a fit at the Charlotte, North Carolina, firm of James, McElroy, and Diehl, which focuses a substantial part of its practice on civil and criminal litigation. For five years, Carwile honed his lawyerly craft, devoting about equal amounts of time to civil and criminal litigation. On the civil side, the firm took advantage of Carwile's experience in the construction trades while he was in high school. He found himself doing "a lot" of civil litigation involving construction work. He also pursued appointments under the Criminal Justice Act of 1964, a federal law that provides for court-appointed lawyers to represent indigent defendants in criminal cases. Carwile cut a name for himself. When the local chief judge called the firm to ask former prosecutor Edward T. Hinson to represent the defendant in a particularly demanding case, Hinson agreed on condition that Carwile be appointed cocounsel. By 1990, however, the firm's interest in getting more heavily into civil work was chafing against Carwile's interest in criminal trials. Hinson counseled Carwile that the best place to get the kind of trial work he wanted would be as a prosecutor in the office of a U.S. attorney.

Carwile "shopped around" for a position as an assistant U.S. attorney. Within months, he reported for duty in the office of the U.S. attorney for the District of Columbia. That office, the largest among the ninety-four U.S. attorneys' offices, is unique. Because the District is a federal enclave, the office prosecutes not only the usual federal crimes but also all serious local criminal offenses committed by adults. Murders, assaults, and thefts that would be the province of a local prosecutor elsewhere in the country are handled by assistant U.S. attorneys in the Superior Court of the District of Columbia. Federal crimes are prosecuted in the federal district court.

Carwile's tenure in the District office was blessed by two serendipities. The first was that shortly after he had arrived and completed mandatory rotations handling appeals and run-of-the-mill cases, such as solicitation of prostitution, the entire office was locked down in a hiring freeze. "Everything came to a standstill," Carwile recalls. "Wherever you were, that's where you stayed. My good fortune was that at the time I was in federal court doing multiple defendant drug cases." The next four or five years were an intense tutorial on the intricacies and practical application of the federal laws aimed at conspiracies and violent crimes associated with them. He also found that having been a defense attorney gave him an edge as a prosecutor. He anticipated defense strategies and took advantage of his ability to understand and develop rapport with the defendants themselves.

The second fortunate turn was that he was next assigned to the Homicide Section. That posting coincided with the section's "golden era" under future FBI director Robert Mueller, who had returned from a lucrative private practice to his love of service. Carwile was given discretion to develop "targeted cases," using a federal grand jury as part of the investigative work. The District of Columbia was in the midst of a tidal wave of violence by primarily black youth gangs—called "crews" in Washington—that had begun in the late 1980s. The median age for homicide victims in the District had fallen from thirty-four in 1976 to twenty-four in 1995, and the age of suspects had dropped from thirty to twenty-one.[30] Like many in image-conscious cities, District officials denied that the gang problem existed, until, in 1991, police chief Isaac Fulwood Jr. declared war on what had become the obvious.[31] Carwile was assigned to prosecute cases from the city's Seventh Police District, which was teeming with gang crime and had the city's highest crime rate. While investigating targeted homicide cases, Carwile used the grand jury to probe deeply into the gang's overall criminal activity.

It was an exciting period for the prosecutor, working in an office in which excellence challenged excellence. "I never lost a homicide case," he declares. "I even won some that the defense attorneys were certain they would win. At the same time, I was trying to keep a foot in federal cases. I was trying to simultaneously prosecute straight homicides in Superior Court and spin off RICO cases to federal court." Over these years, Carwile developed a strong belief that "by the time you indict a case, 95 percent of the time you have either lost or won. You better do your spadework while you have the grand jury, bring in witnesses and lock them into their stories, and make sure you get no surprises at trial."

Carwile's energy and thoroughness in pursuit of local racketeering cases caught the attention of the Justice Department's Organized Crime and Racketeering Section. In 1997, he was recruited to join the elite section. Among the homicide cases of which Carwile is most proud are two that he "wrapped up" just before moving up to "Main Justice" and handed off to other prosecutors to finish. One was the case involving the deaths of the Littles brothers, a double homicide that was the spawn of a running feud between the Fairfax Village Crew in southeast Washington, D.C., and the Rush Town Crew across the line in Prince George's County, Maryland.

On August 20, 1996, the two Littles brothers—Larell, twelve, and Larnell, nineteen—were tossing a football around in the front yard of their home in the Fairfax Village section of Washington. A car full of Rush Town Crew gangsters drove by, took the boys for rival gang members, and opened fire. Both brothers died in a hail of bullets. Neither had any gang affiliation. The victims were "tragically killed as the result of being in the wrong place at the wrong time," Carwile said at the time. "The outrage . . . results from the fact that the wrong place was the victims' own front yard."[32] Carwile succeeded in "flipping" one of the gangsters, who agreed to testify against the others. The boys' mother sponsored a thank-you party for police and prosecutors a year after the government won life sentences for three principals and lengthy prison terms on the guilty pleas of two others. Carwile was reported to have "teared up recalling how he cried as he looked at his own sleeping children while reading details of the killing at home."[33]

"I am in control, but not robotically so," Carwile says when asked about the emotions a prosecutor experiences in such a case. He explains,

> Can I see a set of facts like that and not have it affect me? Absolutely not. It's one of the reasons I don't change to another career. What we do every day makes a difference. Wearing the "white hat" is part of the emotional appeal of my job. But to be an effective prosecutor, you also have to exercise good judgment and know when to overrule those motivating emotions. Sometimes that means taking a plea or not pressing a case as far as it might theoretically go. Those decisions in a good prosecutor are informed by experience over time in investigations, the courtroom, and life in general.

In the Littles case, that meant making the difficult decision not to pursue a death penalty charge under VICAR.

Carwile also saw to a successful conclusion the notorious case of Georgian diplomat Gueorgui Makharadze, who was driving drunk at eighty-five miles per hour when he crashed into the rear end of a car stopped at a red light on Connecticut Avenue near Dupont Circle in Downtown Washington. The car he struck was thrown into the air and landed on another car, killing a sixteen-year-old girl, Joviane Waltrick, and injuring four others. Makharadze, second in command at the embassy, claimed diplomatic immunity. But Georgian president Eduard Shevardnadze waived Makharadze's immunity in response to public outrage, led by the girl's mother. Carwile was determined to lock the case down tight, especially given the fact that Makharadze hired a crew of top guns in the Washington defense bar. "I knew the defense team would leave no stone unturned," he says. "I basically used my experience as a defense attorney to anticipate everything they would do and head them off." The diplomat was so boxed in by Carwile's thorough preparation that he pleaded guilty rather than go to trial.

As odd as it may seem today, up until the 1960s, there was no such thing as organized crime—at least in the eyes of J. Edgar Hoover and his FBI. That would change after Robert F. Kennedy was appointed attorney general in 1961 by his brother, President John F. Kennedy. The provenance of the Justice Department's Organized Crime and Racketeering Section winds back to those days.[34] Robert Kennedy had become intimately acquainted with what was then known as "the mob" or "the Mafia" when he was chief counsel to the Senate Select Committee on Improper Activities in the Labor or Management Field, usually known as the McClellan Committee. The panel conducted a series of widely publicized investigative hearings into the structure and activities of the Mafia. The aggressive young lawyer is said to have been shocked by what he learned of the Mafia's national reach and ruthless power. As attorney general, Kennedy was determined that the full power of the federal government's law enforcement establishment be brought to bear against what would eventually become known as the LCN.

Attorney General Kennedy was, however, "appalled to discover that America's highest law enforcement officials not only had no strategy for combating mobsters but, even more disturbing, refused to recognize the existence of powerful Italian-American groups."[35] The FBI had little intelligence on the mob, and what it had was all but useless, reportedly consisting mainly of newspaper clippings. The Justice Department's organized crime section of seventeen lawyers was an apathetic slough. With characteristic Kennedy vigor, Robert Kennedy, wielding the clout of his being the president's brother, shook things up. He quadrupled the organized crime section's staff, brought in aggressive new blood, and forced federal law enforcement agencies to cooperate in a coordinated assault on the mob. Hoover got the message. Overnight he created the Special Division for Organized Crime. The FBI suddenly found dozens of mob members worthy of its investigation.

President Kennedy's assassination in November 1963 effectively cut off Robert Kennedy's legs as attorney general. President Lyndon B. Johnson personally disliked the younger Kennedy, who, as his brother's campaign manager, had lobbied against including Johnson on the 1960 election ticket. Kennedy resigned in September 1964. The FBI's interest in organized crime waned. One issue left hanging was the politically charged question of the relationship between the Justice Department headquarters and local U.S. attorneys on mob cases. This was a particularly sensitive variant of the tension between Washington's long-term, national priorities and the local interests of a dispersed cadre for whom appointment to the office of U.S. attorney is usually a product of political connection and a short-term stepping-stone to other ambitions. Some U.S. attorneys were more interested in making a splash with quickly developed prosecutions than in devoting their time and resources to lengthy organized crime investigations that might become public only after they had moved on. Someone else would get the credit. This stew of personal ambition and local politics, seasoned by the occasional dash of corrupt influence, resulted often enough in organized crime cases being moved further down local prosecutors' priorities than Washington desired.

The Johnson administration is sometimes criticized for taking the wind out of the Kennedy attack on organized crime. But Attorney General Ramsey Clark, whom Johnson appointed in 1967, formalized a system of "organized crime strike forces" that effectively cut local U.S. attorneys out of the organized crime loop. Career prosecutors in Washington had informally created the system, originally disguised as an interagency "study group," to make an "end run" around the FBI. These teams of specialized Justice Department prosecutors were deployed to major mob cities. They reported directly to the department's organized crime section. Their work was coordinated and supervised from Washington, bypassing local U.S. attorneys. The early mob prosecutions under this system most often came from the Internal Revenue Service as tax evasion cases. The FBI again got the message and eventually began working closely with the strike forces.

The strike forces' independence annoyed some U.S. attorneys. They resented the infringement on their turf and the implication that they could not be trusted to do the job as well as some hotshot from Washington. Some senior officials in the Justice Department also disliked what they perceived to be an independent "fiefdom" within the department. An early critic was onetime Pennsylvania governor Richard Thornburgh, who, among other accomplishments, served as U.S. attorney for Western Pennsylvania from 1965 to 1977 and as assistant attorney general in charge of the Criminal Division under President Gerald Ford.

Thornburgh was appointed attorney general by President Ronald Reagan in 1988 and immediately floated a plan to dismantle the strike forces. He criticized the system of strike forces as a redundant source of "turf wars." In addition, Thornburgh argued, the strike forces had not responded quickly enough to the emergence of criminal street gangs and drug-trafficking organizations, such as the Colombian cartels and the Jamaican drug gangs. Most of the 140 or so prosecutors on the strike forces would be moved over to local U.S. attorneys offices. About twenty would be posted to Washington to consolidate their expertise within the Organized Crime and Racketeering Section. Thornburgh's plan was questioned in Congress and on the editorial pages of influential newspapers, including the *New York Times* and the *Washington Post*. A number of prosecutors quit the strike forces in protest, complaining that the plan would be the death knell of the government's war on organized crime. Kept on the job by President George H. W. Bush, Thornburgh implemented the plan in 1990, without apparent ill effect.

Thus was established the current system. Federal prosecutors are still organized in strike forces against organized crime in about twenty-one districts. But they are now located in the office of the local U.S. attorney. They report both to the U.S. attorney and to the Organized Crime and Racketeering Section in Washington. The section helps set national priorities, coordinates action among federal agencies, supervises all organized crime prosecutions, and has a cadre of experienced prosecutors who travel when needed to help local prosecutors, especially in complicated RICO cases.

After he reported for duty in 1997, Kevin Carwile moved quickly up the ranks of the Organized Crime and Racketeering Section. Within two years, he was promoted to assistant chief in charge of the RICO unit. There he became one of the department's experts on RICO and VICAR prosecutions, the federal government's core means to attack organized crime. The attorneys he supervised in the Washington RICO unit reviewed all prosecutions brought under these two laws anywhere in the country. The attorneys scour local racketeering cases. They carefully review key documents, such as indictments and warrant applications, to ensure that they not only meet the department's guidelines but put forth the most effective case for prosecution. Carwile traveled in this capacity to cities all over the United States, teaching courses and advising federal prosecutors on the intricacies of successfully investigating and prosecuting complex, multidefendant cases. Many of the cases he worked on involved gangs.

He was promoted again in 2000 to become one of three deputy chiefs of the Organized Crime and Racketeering Section. The deputies' responsibilities were divided up geographically. Carwile was responsible for overseeing all federal racketeering cases brought west of the Mississippi River. He also coordinated the entire department's program on Asian organized crime. Gangs and organized crime are related more often in the western part of the country—especially in cities like Los Angeles, San Francisco, and Las Vegas—than in the east. Accordingly, Carwile saw an increasing number of racketeering cases aimed at gangs, as such federal prosecutors as Bruce Riordan started reshaping old tools—created with the LCN in mind—to new uses against motorcycle gangs, prison gangs, and street gangs.

In early 2005—about the same time that Bob Clifford was pulling together the FBI's MS-13 task force—the Bush White House and newly confirmed attorney general Alberto Gonzales began to focus on the problem of criminal street gangs. Although pressure from Congressman Wolf was clearly a major influence on the FBI's approach, the Justice Department was more broadly motivated by a combination of anecdotal and statistical information, including an increase in violent crime in some cities and public concern about the type and level of violence related to street gangs. Gonzales directed that an antigang coordinating committee be set up to review what the various components of the Justice Department were doing and to organize a coordinated antigang effort.[36] He also asked each of the ninety-four U.S. attorneys to designate an antigang coordinator for their districts.

The strategy that emerged from the coordinating committee had two prongs, a prevention and intervention side aimed at discouraging people from joining gangs in the first place and a law enforcement side to suppress, disrupt, and dismantle criminal gangs. The prevention program consisted principally of pumping a modest surge of additional funding through the existing ATF antiviolence program called Project Safe Neighborhoods. Six metropolitan areas determined to have acute gang problems—Los Angeles, Tampa, Cleveland, Dallas–Fort Worth, Milwaukee, and the so-called 222 Corridor along Pennsylvania Route 222 in six southeastern and central Pennsylvania counties—were each given a onetime grant of $2.5 million for prevention of gang violence and for law enforcement antigang initiatives.

Kevin Carwile was the natural choice to direct the law enforcement component of the Justice Department's antigang program. He was an expert in RICO and VICAR, had already overseen a number of major gang prosecutions, and had more than seven years of management experience, during which he had developed contacts all over the country. The department was feeling its way to a new program, and for a while, it simply piled new responsibilities on Carwile's plate without a clear new organizational structure. At one point, Carwile found himself operating out of three separate offices, two in the Justice Department building and one across the street in FBI Headquarters. Eventually, however, the department settled on two new components, each of which reports directly to the assistant attorney general in charge of the Criminal Division.

Carwile was appointed chief of one of the new units, the Gang Squad. This is a cadre of expert prosecutors devoted to working closely with the other new unit in a coordinated national attack on the worst gangs. The second unit, called GangTECC, is the National Gang Targeting, Enforcement, and Coordination Center. GangTECC, says Carwile, is a "true multiagency task force," in contrast to the MS-13 National Gang Task Force, which he describes as having "winnowed down to pretty much just an FBI operation now." The difference may be that GangTECC enjoyed the benefit of direct orders from the deputy attorney general to constituent agencies of the Justice Department—the DEA, FBI, ATF, Bureau of Prisons, and U.S. Marshals Service—to assign agents to this national investigative arm. "At some point," Carwile observes, "It would make sense to fold the FBI's national gang task force into GangTECC." At this writing, no such merger has occurred, nor does the FBI seem enthused with the idea.

Carwile tried to enlist Bruce Riordan to come to Washington and take over the GangTECC unit. But Riordan declined. He had just married, and his bride was not enthusiastic about leaving Los Angeles. Riordan was also not sure he would pass muster under the political litmus tests that Gonzales's staff were applying to all senior appointments in the department. Riordan prided himself on being a nonpartisan career prosecutor, but he had heard enough from other lawyers who had been subjected to the departmental inquisition to know he wanted no part of it. Through this writing, Carwile continues to wear two hats—as director of the gang unit and acting director of GangTECC.

By the end of 2007, it was clear that the more or less coordinated federal initiative against MS-13 was yielding fruit. Major RICO cases had been brought against factions in Maryland, New York, Tennessee, and the motherland of Los Angeles. Former FBI assistant director Chris Swecker expects more to come. "It takes about five years for a major national effort like this to mature," he says. "That's about what it took when we mounted our last major initiative against the LCN."[37]

Looked at from a distance, the architecture is inelegant, but the system seems to be working. The FBI has its own entities—the National Gang Intelligence Center, the basic Safe Streets Initiative, and the MS-13 National Gang Task Force, to which was added responsibility for the 18th Street gang in 2007. (Brian Truchon has since moved on to head the FBI's undercover operations.) Across the street, the Justice Department's GangTECC replicates some of the same functions. Meanwhile, other federal law enforcement agencies continue to pursue their own ideas. Even so, those at the center of the effort, such as Kevin Carwile, seem to be shaking things down into a working system, taking pages from the government's long war against the LCN and inserting them into the new textbook on fighting street gangs. Major cases using the antiracketeering laws have been brought in cities as diverse as Los Angeles and Charlotte, North Carolina. More are in the system.

It may seem pretty cool to be a Supreme Inca
when you're the leader on the street of a gang
until the title "Supreme Inca" becomes "lead
defendant."

—U.S. ATTORNEY PATRICK FITZGERALD

8

A THIRST AFTER JUSTICE:
MEDICAL EXAMINER CASE NO. 338

"This is all wrong," thought Gustavo "Gino" Colon as a detail of prison guards roused him from sleep at 4:15 a.m. on Thursday, September 18, 1997. "No, man, there's some mistake here," he tried to explain as the guards marched him out of his comfortable private room in the "honor dormitory" at the Menard Correctional Center and through a blur of accelerated paperwork. "I'm supposed to get out of here for good tomorrow," he protested. Before he knew it, Colon was indeed outside the walls of the Illinois state prison and firmly in the custody of grim-faced federal agents holding a warrant for his arrest. "Get comfortable," the agents advised their befuddled charge in the brightening light of dawn. It is a six-hour ride from the town of Chester, almost as far south as you can get in Illinois, to the federal Bureau of Prisons Metropolitan Correctional Center in Downtown Chicago. You can watch the corn grow along the way.[1]

Colon was right about one thing. This was not the way his twenty-five-year stretch in state prison was supposed to end. During those decades, while serving time for a brutal gang murder he committed in 1971, "Lord Gino" Colon ruthlessly fought his way to the top of the North Side faction of the Almighty Latin King Nation in Chicago. Latin King power in the Windy City is divided uneasily between the predominantly Puerto Rican North Side faction and the predominantly Mexican South Side faction. Colon ran the northern faction from his room in the honor dormitory, technically called the Interperimeter Office. Unlike ordinary convicts, Gino had a key to his comfortably appointed private room. He walked around the campus freely whenever he felt like it, even while others were confined to their cells during lockdowns. Colon eschewed prison garb. He dressed like a gangster, in sneakers and sweats accented with a glittering medallion on a gold chain. Life in prison is never good. But it was not bad for the man the Latin Kings called "El Jefe," "Lord Gino," and "El Magnate."

Gino's perks were all part of the Illinois prison system's accommodation to the reality of gang power inside the walls. If you made nice to the leaders, they would help keep the lid on. Colon used telephone privileges and personal visits to relay orders to his subordinates, deputizing his wife, Marisol, to speak for him on the outside. He married Marisol while incarcerated and somehow fathered two of three children during her visits, even though conjugal relations were technically forbidden. Illinois prison officials, stung by reports of the cozy life led by Colon and others and by videotapes of mass murderer Richard Speck getting high on gang-supplied drugs, would crack down on gangs and gang leaders' perquisites over the next five years. They shipped many of the top gangsters off to the supermaximum-security Tamms Correctional Center.[2]

After serving a dollop of extra time for dealing heroin while in prison, Colon was supposed to be released that Friday morning. His gangster underlings had arranged for a limousine to pick him up and bring him back to Chicago in a triumphal procession. Instead, at day's end on Thursday, Lord Gino Colon found himself locked up without a personal key in a real prison cell, waiting arraignment on a multiple-count federal indictment that included charges of drug conspiracy and continuing criminal enterprise. "He got his ride back to Chicago—but it wasn't in a limousine," said a federal law enforcement spokesman.[3]

According to the feds, Colon was running a criminal enterprise that was both selling drugs and taxing drug dealers in Chicago's Humboldt Park area. The operation was said to have netted at least six million dollars during the two years it was under investigation. The case, code-named "Los Cuatro Reyes" (The Four Kings), was to be a gratifying victory for three special agents of the federal Bureau of Alcohol, Tobacco, and Firearms—Terry Jackson, Elizabeth Ragusa, and Laurie Jolley. Working for an underdog agency that enjoys considerably fewer resources than the FBI, the three agents sometimes felt that they were holding things together with nothing but tape, paper clips, and pure grit.

The timing of the predawn arrest on the day before Lord Gino Colon's scheduled release was intentionally harsh. "The point was that he would never be free," interim U.S. attorney Scott R. Lassar said.[4] Worse would come for El Magnate. He would see gang loyalty crumble and key members of his royal court, including his wife, cooperate with the government, making statements and even testifying against him and his enterprise in the hope of leniency in sentencing. Gustavo Colon would end up about as badly ratted out as a supreme leader could be.

Street gangs have been a part of Chicago's history since the early twentieth century. The first great study of gangs was Frederick M. Thrasher's 1927 classic *The Gang: A Study of 1,313 Gangs in Chicago,* published by the University of Chicago Press. But the highly organized, bureaucratically structured, criminally efficient black and Latino mega-gangs for which the city is now known are products of the latter third of that century. According to the Chicago Crime Commission, the seven biggest gangs in Chicago account for 80 percent of the city's gang membership. The statement, however, is necessarily imprecise—as are virtually all such "authoritative" pronouncements about gang numbers. The commission states in the same report that estimates of gang membership in the Chicago area range from 25,000 (according to the Chicago Police

Department) to 125,000 (according to the National Drug Intelligence Center).[5] Whatever the actual numbers and proportions, most observers agree that these "supergangs" are large and violent. They include the Gangster Disciple Nation, Black Gangster/New Breeds, Latin Kings, Black P. Stone Nation, Vice Lords, Four Corner Hustlers, and Maniac Latin Disciples. The city also suffers the scourge of neighborhood microgangs that wax and wane over time.

The Latin Kings were originally organized in Chicago. Like some of the other Chicago supergangs, they have metastasized. Gangs calling themselves "Latin Kings"—affiliated, renegade, and hybrids—now exist in many areas of the Midwest and the eastern United States. Latin Kings have even popped up as organized entities as far away as Spain. The large eastern Latin Kings gangs in New York (known as "Almighty Latin King and Queen Nation") and Connecticut (known as "Almighty Latin Charter Nation") are also well known. They started out as unauthorized outliers, flirted with giving fealty to the mother gang, but grew into independent organizations. They are not affiliated in any meaningful way with the original Latin Kings of Chicago, known as the "Motherland."

The shores of Lake Michigan may not strike one as a likely Latino neighborhood, much less the motherland of a national Latino gang. But the 2000 census found that 26 percent of the residents of the city of Chicago were Latinos, as were slightly more than 22 percent of the residents of Cook County.[6] Of these 1.4 million Latinos, the two largest subgroups were of Mexican and Puerto Rican origin—an estimated 980,000 Mexicans and 113,000 Puerto Ricans.[7] Twenty-five percent of the children in Chicago's public schools were of Mexican origin in 2001, a proportion that has grown even larger since then. The histories and cultures of these two dominant Latino groups are significantly different.

Mexicans were drawn to the Midwest generally and to Chicago specifically by essentially the same forces that drew them to the Southwest and Los Angeles. Jobs—first in agribusiness, then on the railroads, and finally in heavy industry—were the original magnet. But the Midwest and West Coast Mexican communities developed differently. Because Mexicans in Chicago were farther away from the border than those in the Southwest, they were less likely to have frequent direct contact with Mexico. Even though the Chicago community celebrated its

Mexican origins, consciously sought to preserve its cultural traditions, and stayed in touch with family and friends in Mexico, its members assimilated more easily and quickly than those in the border areas—albeit at a slower pace than Chicago's white ethnics, who arrived earlier and were not stigmatized on racial grounds. Mexicans in Chicago had no sense of living with the "historic baggage" of their compatriots in California and the rest of the old Mexican northern territory. They were more urbanized than those in the Southwest, even in Los Angeles, still a sleepy village dreaming a booster's dream when Chicago was already a world-class metropolis.[8]

Mexicans first came to the Midwest around 1900 as migrant workers in the sugar beet fields. These workers, called *betabeleros,* were mostly solo males recruited by labor contractors called *enganchistas* ("the ones who hook you"). By 1910, growing demand for labor opened up other opportunities, which Mexicans were quick to seize. One was *el traque,* working on the railroads, which were both a source of jobs and a conduit to the north. By the late 1920s, more than 40 percent of the workers on the railroad tracks in Chicago were Mexican. As the demand for industrial production increased during World War I, Mexicans were actively recruited to alleviate an acute shortage of labor caused in part by the war's disruption of European labor streams. They came to work in steel mills, auto factories, and meatpacking plants. As women came, families and Mexican *colonias* grew. Mexican entrepreneurs established businesses catering to Mexican tastes—tortilla factories, restaurants, and grocery markets. Life centered around the Catholic Church. Social, labor, and mutual benefit groups formed. Some industrialists exploited Mexicans and blacks as strikebreakers from the late 1910s until as late as the 1940s, thus increasing Chicago's already notorious racial tensions.

Just as in the Southwest, Mexican migration in Chicago has reflected the cycles of the U.S. economy. When times are bad, migration slows and sometimes reverses itself. Many Mexicans left Chicago during the Great Depression. As in the Southwest, some citizens or legal residents and their American-born children were forcibly repatriated or pressured to leave because they "looked Mexican." But when labor was desperately needed, Mexicans were called back. Emergency measures during World War II and the Korean War—*bracero* programs—opened doors wide to Mexicans, whose strong backs and arms were urgently needed. Mexicans were not only welcomed but actively recruited.

The Puerto Rican migration to Chicago was completely different from the Mexican experience. Puerto Ricans are, of course, American citizens. But Chicago held little attraction for all but an elite few of them until the 1950s. Prior to that, a few wealthy families sent their children to be educated at prestigious institutions like the University of Chicago. Most of those children returned to live in Puerto Rico after graduation. Puerto Ricans who came to the United States preferred to live in New York City. The 1910 census reported only 15 Puerto Ricans in Chicago. By 1950, that number had crept up to 255. This contrasts with the nearly quarter million Puerto Ricans who lived in New York City in 1950.

Several forces combined to change these preferences in the 1950s. In the late 1940s and early 1950s, labor contractors went to the island and recruited about a thousand Puerto Ricans for jobs in foundries and as domestic workers. Puerto Rican perceptions also changed around this time, perhaps as a result of family communications networks. It came to appear to Puerto Ricans that jobs had dried up in New York but were plentiful in the great blue-collar city of Chicago. For the first time, large numbers of Puerto Ricans migrated to Chicago. By 1960, the number of Puerto Ricans had risen to 32,370.

The catch was that most of these new migrants were unskilled laborers who spoke little or no English. They were relying on the great ladder of industrial blue-collar work by means of which those without language or trade had traditionally pulled themselves up in pursuit of the American dream. But the perception that the ladder still existed in Chicago was a cruel illusion. Puerto Rican hopes, along with those of the black and Mexican communities that had been in Chicago for decades, were crushed by the shift in the economy from manufacturing to service jobs, well in progress by the 1960s. The city was hemorrhaging blue-collar work. It was losing jobs at an alarming rate, as factories shut down and shipped them off to management-friendly, nonunion suburban and rural locations or offshore to countries in the third world. Puerto Ricans found themselves in a scrum, competing for lower-paying, dead-end jobs. Those who could find work typically became janitors, hotel and restaurant workers, yardmen, domestics, and assembly-line drones in light industry. Like Mexicans and blacks, Puerto Ricans were racially classified and subjected to social and economic discrimination. The three groups were pushed around the map of Chicago as demanded by the forces of gentrification, development, and politically motivated racial "fire walls"—physical barriers skillfully erected by means of highway construction and urban development projects to wall off minority communities. It was in this turbulent atmosphere that what became the megagangs of Chicago were born.

Gang histories are elusive. It is not hard to find authoritative statements about the "real" history of most street gangs. They litter the Internet, the publications of gang investigators, government studies, and academic works. But these histories are often contradictory, usually the work of outsiders relying on the word of purported insiders, and frequently angled to grind the author's ax. Those who would ordinarily be best able to tell the stories—the original gangsters—are not the sort of persons interested in objective historiography. Even if they were, most of them are dead, befuddled, or interested only in manipulating opinion to perpetuate self-serving legends. Skeptical approximations are the best that can be hoped for in most cases. In one sense, it does not matter. Gangs are what they are today regardless of the allegedly noble motives of their founders.

Although Mexicans were firmly ensconced in various communities around Chicago by the 1920s, Thrasher makes only passing reference to Mexicans in his descriptive tour of Chicago's "gangland."[9] An example he gives of "moral contagion" from the gang life of Mexican boys comes from a survey done in El Paso, Texas.[10] Most of the early gangs in Chicago were white ethnics—Irish, Polish, Italian, German, Jewish— and black. It might be rash to conclude that there were no gangs or protogangs among Chicago's early Mexican population. But there seems to have been nothing like the long historical line of burgeoning Mexican gangs in Los Angeles and its environs.

By the 1950s, however, the first generation of Mexican American youth in Chicago were facing pressures similar to those that confronted Mexican youth in California a decade earlier—intergenerational conflict, ambiguous cultural identity, and institutionalized social and economic discrimination. Sometime in the late 1950s or early 1960s, marginalized youth formed one of the earliest Mexican gangs, the Latin Counts, in the Pilsen neighborhood. The area is named after the city of Pizen—the birthplace of the clear golden beer known as Pilsener (or Pilsner)—in what is now the Czech Republic. Chicago's Pilsen was populated in the late nineteenth century primarily by Czechs, along with various ethnic groups from the Austro-Hungarian Empire and a smattering of other European ethnics. By the time the Latin Counts were created, Pilsen was transitioning into one of the two major Mexican neighborhoods in Chicago. The other, just to the west, is called Little Village. Together they comprise the greatest Mexican barrio east of Los Angeles. Pilsen is today under pressure of gentrification, which some in the Latino community have organized to resist. According to the Chicago Crime Commission, the Latin Counts were formed "to protect themselves from gangs already in the neighborhood."[11] Be that as it may, the Latin Counts today are active in a number of locations in the Great Lakes region. They are heavily involved in drug trafficking—the street-level distribution of cocaine, marijuana, and heroin—as well as armed robbery, arson, assault, auto theft, and murder.

The Latin Kings are the largest Latino gang in Chicago. They were formed by Puerto Rican youth originally, sometime in the early to mid-1960s, likely in the Humboldt Park area on the North Side of Chicago. A 2004 regional law enforcement intelligence report maintains that the gang emerged in response to discrimination against Puerto Ricans. According to one intelligence report, "the gang was founded on the belief that they . . . could provide protection to those who were discriminated against." It originally took form as "informal social-type groups, that functioned to protect and preserve the identity of their culture and ease the integration of Puerto Rican immigrants into the United States." These early "club" members supposedly functioned in effect as voluntary social workers. "By the mid-1960s," continues the report, "the Latin Kings were recognized by law enforcement and the community as a street gang."[12]

Like other cities in the United States in the mid-1960s, Chicago was wracked by racial violence. One of the most notorious incidents involving Latinos was the Division Street riot (called an "uprising" by activists on the Left). The riot broke out on June 12, 1966, in the wake of the first large Puerto Rican parade. It was precipitated when a white policeman shot and wounded Arcelis Cruz, a twenty-year-old Puerto Rican man. The community perceived this as an egregious example of the continual police brutality to which it was subjected. The area erupted into a riot lasting several days, during which sixteen people were injured, fifty buildings were destroyed, and damages costing millions of dollars were suffered.

This was the threshold of an era during which governments at all levels were trying to cork the genie of racial conflict. The grievances of minority communities like Chicago's Puerto Ricans were violently brought to the governing establishment's attention. Just as money and services poured into Los Angeles after the Watts Riot, so social services and community outreach programs expanded in Chicago. Many of the most powerful gangs—in Chicago and elsewhere—got on board the government funding train. They held themselves out as agents of social change, "heralding either an optimistic or opportunistic approach to addressing social problems, depending on one's point of view."[13] The gravy train eventually went off the rails, and the backlash was enormous. Most (but not all) policymakers and legislators soured on the idea of recruiting or remolding gangs into responsible political and social institutions. According to the Chicago Crime Commission, the "most powerful Chicago gangs tried to mask their illegal gang activity in the 1970s and appear as legitimate organizations wanting to serve their communities." They were "quite effective" in getting "major dollar grants from private foundations and the federal government." This funding, however, in fact underwrote gang recruitment and criminal activity, "creating the foundation for their 'super gang' status."[14]

A 1996 report on the Latin Kings by the National Gang Crime Research Center points an accusing finger straight at a YMCA program for "detached gang workers" in the late 1960s as an example of what not to do. The report states that although "done with good intentions by probably sincere social workers," the YMCA program in effect rewarded bad behavior with "fun resources." The worst gangsters got the most attention. "Clearly," says the report, "the Latin Kings was one of these gangs our society inadvertently nourished as an organizational entity."[15] Today, the Latin Kings gang, in various manifestations, exists in at least thirty-three states. The gang has expanded beyond its Puerto Rican origins. It is more racially and ethnically diverse but remains primarily a Latino institution. Chicago's northern and southern factions are still primarily Puerto Rican and Mexican, respectively. But many of the distinctions and antagonisms between the factions mellowed as the gang morphed into essentially a street-level business of drug distribution.

The Latin Counts and Latin Kings are by no means the only Latino gangs in the Chicago area. Pilsen, Little Village, and other Latino neighborhoods teem with smaller gangs. "There are so many different gangs in such a small area," a state prosecutor said of Little Village in 2004. "They're so close that shooting becomes the only way you can mark your territory."[16] For the Latino gangs, marking territory is about more than business. "African American gangs are about making money," says Cook County assistant state's attorney Tom Mahoney, who supervises units of prosecutors of gang crime. "Their gang shootings typically have a financial motive, such as someone took someone else's drug spot. But with Hispanic gangs it's about history and turf. They have been shooting at each for 35 years and they don't even know why. Sometimes they'll do anniversary date shootings. 'Hey, Popeye got shot two years ago today. Let's go shoot somebody.'" Frequently enough, that violent way of remembering anniversaries, perpetuating rivalries, and marking turf has unintended consequences.

It was hot and humid in Chicago as the clock approached midnight on Wednesday, August 30, 2003. The thermometer hit 91.4 degrees during the day. On Thursday, it would rise to 98.6 degrees—the normal core body temperature of a human being. The residents of the 2300 block of Eighteenth Place in Pilsen sat out on their stoops, seeking relief in the cooler evening air from the heat that had built up inside their houses during the day. Among them was Maria Felix Mateo and her children.[17]

Maria's husband, Federico Mateo, came to the United States from Mexico in 1987 seeking work. He found it in Chicago. While Federico worked in a factory as a metal polisher, Maria stayed home and cared for their children. The oldest, Edgar, was fourteen years old. The youngest, Ana, was seven. In between were three girls—Mayra, ten; Evelyn, eleven; and Aurora, twelve. In his spare time, Federico was renovating their row house, into which they had moved two years before. Day by day, rung by rung, the Mateos were making it in America, working hard and living by the rules.

Two blocks east of the Mateo house, Eighteenth Place is blocked off. A small paved plaza with a few shade trees in front of St. Ann Catholic Church and St. Ann Catholic School, at the intersection with Leavitt Street, makes it a cul-de-sac. Residents often heard the sound of gunfire coming from other streets nearby. But the Eighteenth Place cul-de-sac was a comparatively quiet enclave. That is not to say that it had escaped the influence of gangs. Two Mexican gangs, the Satan Disciples and the Party People, had been engaged for some time in one of the small wars that sweep like thunderstorms over America's gang-infested urban battlefields.

Maria was particularly worried about Edgar. At fourteen years of age, he had already become a target of Satan Disciples recruiters, who urged him to quit being a "neutron"—gangster lingo for the unaffiliated—and sign up with their gang. They not only approached him on the street but brazenly walked up to his front door and pestered him to join. In July, they had spray-painted a taunting message on the door. But Edgar wanted nothing to do with gangs. "All they do is cause trouble," he said.[18]

It had been a long day for Maria, who had just returned with Ana from visiting a sick friend. She wanted to go inside at midnight, as was the family's usual practice. Federico had to go to work the next day and was already sleeping. But little Ana, the youngest child, pleaded for more time. She and her six-year-old friend Jasmine Tapia were having fun racing the remote-controlled monster truck and station wagon that Ana got at a flea market on Sunday. It was hard to say no to Ana. She was a bubbly, happy child at a magic age. She loved to play with water balloons with her siblings and run around in the backyard. Ana was taking catechism classes in preparation for her First Communion at St. Pius V Catholic Church. The day before, Maria had taken Ana for a conference at the nearby Cooper Elementary Dual Language Academy, getting ready for the new school year.

Shortly after midnight, a Chicago Police Department car routinely patrolling beat 1223 turned off of South Western Avenue and on to Eighteenth Place, adding a sense of security. Just after the car rolled past the Mateo residence, Maria heard what she thought were three bottle rockets. Pop. Pop-pop. When she turned around, she saw Ana lying on her back on the sidewalk. For a moment, she thought her daughter was pretending to have fainted. It was a little game Ana enjoyed. Then Maria saw that Ana's eyes had rolled back. She was still holding the remote control in her hand. Her little hand was trembling.

Maria Mateo scooped her daughter up. When she did, she saw two large bloodstains on the sidewalk. "Help!" she shouted, still not comprehending what had happened. "Help me! My little girl is not moving!" She ran across the street to get help from a neighbor who was a nurse. The nurse tried to stanch the bleeding. Ana lifted a small hand and touched her mother's face. But there was little help to be had for seven-year-old Ana Mateo.

The bottle rockets Maria thought she heard were gunshots—seven of them, it would be learned later. Pop. Pop-pop-pop-pop. Pop-pop. One of them, a single nine-millimeter bullet from a Walther P38 handgun, fired from two blocks away on the other side of the cul-de-sac, had struck the back of her head, entering the right rear of her skull and stopping inside the left front without exiting. Ana was rushed first to Mt. Sinai Hospital and then to Children's Memorial Hospital, where she died at 7:00 p.m. A beautiful and wholly innocent child thus was taken from life by a random missile no larger than the forward joint of an adult's little finger. Ana Mateo became Chicago Medical Examiner Case No. 338.

The murder of Ana Mateo enraged the neighborhood, the police, the mayor, the news media, and anyone who could find a voice to express outrage. The two officers in the passing patrol car heard the shots and saw a young black man, Randy Edmondson, running toward them, away from the other side of the cul-de-sac. Unscathed, he was the intended victim. Based on the initial story Edmondson gave police and on other evidence, including the ongoing gang feud, the conclusion seemed obvious. The death of Ana Mateo was collateral damage of the war between the Satan Disciples and the Party People. The police activated a new "zero-tolerance" program called Operation Just Cause and came down on the two gangs like the furies of hell.

"If they are caught drinking, urinating, or throwing a candy wrapper out the window, they are subject to arrest," a police spokesman explained.[19] For the next six months, the cops would harrow the Satan Disciples and the Party People with a vengeance. Detectives hauled in and sweated at least fifteen Satan Disciples. They would gather an immense amount of intelligence as they pounded away at the gangsters. They would learn, for example, that a splinter group called the Renegade Satan Disciples had broken off and was now in a running battle with the main gang as well as with the Party People. But there was just one problem in all of this. None of the three gangs had anything to do with Ana Mateo's murder.

One outstanding feature distinguishes the Latin Kings (and some other Midwest gangs) from the California-style gangs. Power in the California gangs is by and large shared horizontally among a core of relative equals—the shot callers. The Latin Kings, however, have a formal vertical leadership structure with specific offices. It is replicated at various levels within a structured hierarchy of regional and local units. The gang also has organic documents similar to an organizational charter or constitution, regular mandatory meetings, dues collections, and established procedures for raising funds to take care of imprisoned members. If one erased their criminality, the Latin Kings would look like one of the fraternal orders so popular in middle America during the last century.

On a cold February night in a dingy Chicago Police Department squad room, police officer Homero Ramirez patiently walked me through the basic organization of the Latin Kings' Motherland. Like LAPD detective Frank Flores and retired LASD sergeant Richard Valdemar, Ramirez is a walking refutation of the softly racist proposition—popular among gang "activists" and some politicians—that gangs are the only real choice for Latino youth raised under modest circumstances. Ramirez's father was born in Del Rio, Texas; his mother, in Mexico. Ramirez himself was born in Ciudad Acuna, Mexico, just across the Rio Grande (or Rio Bravo) River. For years, the city was the home of the "border-blaster" radio station XERF-AM, from which famed U.S. disc jockey "Wolfman Jack" blasted after-midnight rock and roll ("howling at a quarter million watts down here with the donkeys") to youthful listeners across the United States.

Ramirez came with his family to the predominantly Polish Bucktown neighborhood of Chicago in 1970. "We were probably the first Mexican boys for blocks around in that area," Ramirez recalls. Some Puerto Rican kids lived around the corner. Young Homero needed a special letter to enroll in Thomas Drummond Elementary School—he did not speak English. Now he works on a Chicago Police Department investigations unit, following in the footsteps of both of his grandfathers, who were policemen in Mexico. There are, however, some relatives in Mexico whom he avoids today. They and he are on opposite sides of the law.

At least nominally at the top of the Motherland hierarchy are two *coronas* (crowns)—Lord Gino Colon and Raul "Baby King" Gonzalez. Colon is in a federal "supermax" prison. Gonzalez was released from his latest confinement, nine years in federal prison for cocaine trafficking, in 2007 and is on parole. In addition to controlling the North Side faction, Colon was and might still be the nominal leader of the entire Motherland. According to some accounts, Colon and Martinez seized control of the Latin Kings in the early 1980s by arranging for the demise of the prime founder and original leader, a man known as "Papa King" or "Papa Santos." The relationship between the two has reportedly been tense. But according to ATF agent Terry Jackson, Gonzalez was always deferential to Colon in the telephone conversations that were monitored in the course of the Four Kings investigation.

"Underneath the two leaders are an assortment of positions and middle-management slots," according to the National Gang Crime Research Center.[20] A senior executive officer directly under the two coronas is called the "Supreme Regional" or "Supreme Inca." The current Supreme Inca is Fernando "Ace" King, whom federal authorities arrested in December 2006—along with nearly thirty others—on drug-trafficking and firearms charges. King's arrest was the result of a three-year investigation spearheaded by ATF, the biggest assault on the Latin Kings' Motherland since Colon's takedown in 1997.

"It may seem pretty cool to be a Supreme Inca when you're the leader on the street of a gang until the title 'Supreme Inca' becomes 'lead defendant,'" U.S. attorney Patrick Fitzgerald quipped at the time of King's arrest.[21] The incarceration or arrest of the top leaders of the Latin Kings in recent years raises a central question. Who, if anyone, is really running the Latin Kings' show? A regional law enforcement intelligence report states that "the Latin Kings are currently in a fragmented state" and that "there is a re-empowerment struggle taking place."[22] As has happened in the case of other criminal enterprises fractured under law enforcement pressure, younger leaders are apparently fighting veterans for control. It is a standard law enforcement strategy to watch (and listen to) the fallout from post-takedown shakeouts to identify emerging leaders as targets for the next round of investigations and indictments.

There is an elaborate infrastructure of committees, councils, and subdivisions below the coronas from which new leadership might emerge. The Motherland is divided into nine regions throughout the Midwest. Currently, the biggest and most powerful is the Little Village region, according to Officer Ramirez. The regions are further broken down into chapters and, below the bigger chapters, sections. Each chapter is governed by a uniform set of officers. They include an *Inca* (roughly, the equivalent of a president), *cacique* (i.e., vice president), *enforzador* (enforcer), *tesorero* (treasurer), *secretario* (secretary), and *investigador* (investigator). Incas and caciques are elected by chapter members to terms of indefinite office. They appoint the other officers. Chapters hold regular mandatory meetings at which roll is taken. Dues and special assessments (e.g., for survivors of members killed) are collected and sent up the chain of command. Rules are enforced by a system of punishments, called "violations," that range from beatings to death. Some observers, however, suggest that this old-line gang structure, its rituals, and its traditions are crumbling. In this view, the gang has become little more than a coalition of locality-based franchises that call themselves Latin Kings, a network of criminal enterprises that care less about gang solidarity than about making money by "moving weight" (selling drugs).

Whether intended or not, the elaborate corporate structure of the Latin Kings proved ideal for the illicit enterprise of the street-level distribution of drugs. That is the gang's principal business. In Chicago, the gang taxes nonmember drug dealers and also sells drugs through its own members. The Latin Kings' retail operation sells marijuana, cocaine, and various pills. For whatever reason, almost since its beginning, the Latin Kings gang has forbidden members from using or directly selling heroin. This has apparently not stopped some Latin Kings chapters from making cooperative agreements with other gangs that do sell heroin.[23]

Mexican drug-trafficking organizations are the main wholesale suppliers of drugs to Chicago's street gangs. Gino Colon's operation was getting its cocaine from one of them, the notorious Herrera organization, which has vexed law enforcement agencies in Chicago since the 1950s. It has the nine lives of a cat.

The Chicago metropolitan area is one of the largest illegal drug markets in the United States.[24] It is a large retail market in its own right. It is also a hub of drug transportation, linked to the rest of the country by rail, air, and highway. Chicago is the nation's largest trucking center and has the second busiest airport and the busiest rail and postal facilities. The highly integrated, experienced, and professional Mexican drug-trafficking organizations have exploited these resources to turn Chicago into a vast transshipment center. Cocaine, heroin, marijuana, and other drugs are shipped up from Mexico through Chicago, then moved out to other midwestern and eastern retail markets. Wholesalers in Chicago have invested in scores of legitimate businesses. They often set up households in affluent suburbs, where they can elude surveillance while storing and distributing drugs and laundering money.

The Herrera organization is one of the oldest and most thoroughly entrenched of the Mexican drug-trafficking organizations. Its sprawling family connections link Chicago at one end and Durango, Mexico, at the other, with offshoots across the United States and Latin America. Infiltrating the tightly held family enterprise has been next to impossible for law enforcement agencies, who have had to rely on communications intercepts and informants to make cases against the organization.

Family patriarch Jaime Herrera-Nevares established the drug dynasty in the mountain village of Los Herreras in the 1940s. As early as 1957, the organization was highly integrated, running what the DEA has called a "farm-to-the-arm" operation in heroin trafficking. The Herreras were pioneers in developing smuggling techniques—such as a false driveshaft sleeve packed with dope—for their network, known as the "Heroin Highway" and the "Durango Pipeline." When U.S. drug enforcers smashed the "French Connection" heroin conduit from Turkey to New York via Marseilles in the early 1970s, the Herrera organization stepped in to fill the gap with Mexican heroin made from poppies grown in its own fields high in the Sierra Madre mountains. By 1978, the family controlled 90 percent of the Chicago heroin market. It grossed at least sixty million dollars a year. In the 1980s, when drug enforcement went after the transportation nets of the Colombian cartel, the Herrera organization was ready with a well-established distribution system. It diversified and put its network to use moving cocaine.

At various times since the 1970s, federal law enforcement and Chicago police agencies have pronounced the Herrera organization to be broken, crippled, and wiped out. Yet it has proven big enough and resilient enough to shrug off attacks and keep on trucking drugs north. It is estimated to employ at least two thousand blood relatives and another three thousand associates. Those who work in the organization have proven exceedingly loyal. It has been characterized by some as being able to use less violence than other organizations to discipline its internal operation, though its willingness to kill when necessary is not doubted. Family members have reportedly held virtually every law enforcement post in the Mexican state of Durango at one time or another. U.S. officials complain that the organization is well protected in Mexico. As recently as 2001, law enforcement officials estimated that the Herrera organization was operating at least twelve "cells" in Chicago. There was bound to be a Herrera somewhere in the mix when federal organizations started investigating Lord Gino Colon's Humboldt Park cocaine business.

Mayor Richard Daley was not happy. "These are 15- and 16-year-old punks," he said two days after seven-year-old Ana Mateo was killed by a stray bullet in August 2003. "The community better stand up. The police can only do so much."[25] Daley was expressing more than anger about Ana Mateo's murder. He was angry about innocent children dying. By the end of 2003, Chicago would suffer 598 murders for the year, the most in the nation. Among these, thirty victims were under the age of sixteen, eleven under the age of eight.[26] The mayor was also venting frustration about the Latino community's singular reluctance to step forward and name murderers.

Murder investigations involving Latinos are solved—or, more accurately, "cleared"—at the lowest rate among ethnic groups in Chicago. A case is considered "cleared" when a suspect is arrested, charged with the offense, and turned over for prosecution. A case might also be cleared in exceptional circumstances, as when a suspect who meets the other conditions is killed before prosecution. Clearing a case does not mean solving it, nor does it mean that a prosecution will end in a conviction. In April 2004, the rate of murder cases cleared by Chicago police was reported to have been 64 percent for whites, 53 percent for blacks, and 51 percent for Latinos.[27] But the problem extended beyond the rate for Latinos. The overall clearance rate in Chicago hit a historic low in 2000 at 40 percent and had only limped back up to hover in the neighborhood of 50 percent.[28] That meant that at least half of Chicago's killers were literally getting away with murder.

The silver lining in this cloud for Chicago is that it is not alone in facing a clearance problem. The national rate for murder clearance has fallen from 95 percent in 1961 to 60.7 percent in 2006.[29] There are many reasons for this decline. Prime among them is the rise of stranger-to-stranger homicides, as opposed to acquaintance homicides in which the victim somehow knew the killer. Gangs, guns, and drugs have fueled the rise of stranger homicides. A murder investigation is one thing when a husband shoots his wife. It is another thing entirely when a teenager is shot down from a speeding car. "The big secret of detective work is that you've got to get somebody else to tell you what happened," a lieutenant from the New York Police Department observed in 2006.[30] That "somebody" is often missing in stranger killings, especially in gang murders, where witnesses know their lives may be imperiled if they talk to police. The situation is compounded by the general difficulty of police work in Latino communities and mistrust caused by immigration raids, so that "law enforcement must now work with a type of homicide that has a high likelihood of never being solved."[31]

In the case of Ana Mateo, the situation was even worse. Investigators were misled from the beginning. When Chicago police officers Orozco and Nielson drove into the shooting that night, they heard gunfire coming from in front of them and observed three things in rapid order. The first was Randy Edmondson running toward them. The second was another man with a gun in his hand, headed east, away from Edmonson and them and toward the cul-de-sac. The third was yet another person getting into a dark blue sedan on the far side of the plaza, at the corner of Leavitt and Eighteenth Place. They chased the man with the gun, but he ran between two buildings and disappeared. The plaza across Eighteenth Place prevented their pursuing the sedan.

It was reasonable to conclude that the man with the gun was the shooter. In fact, he was not. Sergio "Smoke" Rojas had merely come out with gun in hand when he heard the shooting. Rojas was, however, a member of the Satan Disciples gang. He and intended victim Edmondson knew each other and talked briefly as the cops approached. Then Rojas took off. Edmondson was not a member of the Satan Disciples. He was a wannabe, a hanger-on. If the police had not been right on the spot, Edmondson, by his own account, would have run off as well. But now that he had to talk to the police, he wanted to do two things: protect Rojas's identity and get involved in the investigation as little as he possibly could. The shooter was in fact the third man, Edmondson explained, the one the officers saw getting into the car. But he led police to believe—as he himself thought—that the shooter was likely a member of the Party People gang, the rivals with whom the Satan Disciples were at war. This was consistent with what police knew about the ongoing feud in the area. But it was not what had happened.

So the investigation of Ana Mateo's murder spun its wheels for six months. Then two young men popped up independently in unrelated investigations. Each had his own reasons to tell police what had really happened that night. When they did, three young assistant state's attorneys working for Tom Mahoney—Michael Golden, Brian Holmes, and Mary Jo Murtaugh—were waiting and anxious to bring the shooter to justice. There would, however, be the matter of a criminal trial before judgment could be finally pronounced. A jury would have to be persuaded beyond a reasonable doubt that the man accused of the murder had done it. The Ana Mateo murder investigation was cleared. But would justice be done?

Interviewed as a group, the three prosecutors project a sort of film noir toughness, as if they have already seen too much evil for their age. The image is lightened with a streak of internal shtick, jokes made at one another's expense. This is not a movie or a television "reality" show, however. This is the real deal. Murtaugh, Holmes, and Golden are daily combatants in one of the thousands of local trial courts where most of America's criminal justice is administered. This is where sullen gangbangers come in, all shiny and cleaned up by their mouthpieces, and sit impassively while their violent deeds and the bloody consequences are methodically laid down for twelve ordinary citizens in the jury box. There are no federal stealth planes flying over to drop a RICO bomb down the pipe in these courtrooms. This is trench warfare, fought at close quarters with evidentiary shotguns and rhetorical bayonets. Jurors learn about the path of bullets, the patterns of spattered blood, the meaning of splintered bone, and the spray of brain matter. They need to be persuaded. The lawyerly contest is not always genteel. This is grappling. Prosecutors press hard. Some defense lawyers are not above reaching for a handful of sand to toss ever so subtly in the direction of the jury's eyes. There would be sand in the air at the trial of Ana Mateo's accused killer.

The break came in February 2004, when two members of the Latin Counts were arrested in different cities at different times for different crimes. Both flipped like acrobats. The first, Jason Chapman, was arrested for burglary in suburban Stickney, home of the largest plant for wastewater treatment in the world. Looking for a break, Jason volunteered to tell Stickney police what he knew about "the little girl who got shot in Chicago." When detectives from the Chicago Police Department came out and interviewed him, Jason Chapman named three gangsters who he said had been in the car that night. One of them was his brother, Justin, from whom he had heard the story when they were out drinking one night. The other two were people he knew only as "Drac" and "Adrian." But the detectives were skeptical. Some parts of Jason's story did not jibe with the evidence. His account was thin and secondhand. A week later, however, they got a call from an FBI agent in Toledo, Ohio. Another Latin Counts gangster named Jorge Cervantes had been arrested in connection with a kidnapping and attempted murder. Cervantes also offered to trade information about the shooting. This time, detectives were persuaded. Cervantes not only named three Latin Counts—"Vamp," "Adrian," and Jason's brother, Justin Chapman—he had firsthand knowledge of enough solid details to lay out the whole sordid train of events. The story fit together, because the Latin Counts had their own little war going on with the Satan Disciples. Police arrested the alleged shooter on March 5, 2004, as he left school in his mother's SUV (which he crashed into a tree in the process).

The tragedy of Ana Mateo's death is made all the more poignant by the banality of what happened. "Drac" and "Vamp" were the same person, a sixteen-year-old member of the Latin Counts named Juan Garcia, also known as "Lil' Vamp," "Dracula," "Lil' Juanie," and "Shorty." The other two players were twenty-three-year-old Justin Chapman and twenty-five-year-old Adrian Covarrubias. The story is uncomplicated. The three were at a Latin Counts party some distance away at a gathering place behind an apartment building. The gangsters called the place "the Pit" because it lay at the bottom of a sloping yard. Sometime around 10:30 p.m., Garcia, Chapman, and Covarrubias went cruising in a dark blue, four-door 1986 Buick LeSabre that one of them had borrowed. The precise reason for their mission was never determined. Chapman drove. Garcia sat in the front passenger seat. A nine-millimeter semiautomatic pistol was stuck in his waistband. Covarrubias sat in the back. The three were drinking beer and smoking marijuana.

About half an hour later, over on Eighteenth Place, Maria and Ana Mateo got home from their visit to their sick friend. Ana saw her friend Jasmine, whom she had not seen in three days, and begged to stay outside and play. Up the street, on the other side of the plaza, across from St. Ann Catholic Church, Randy Edmondson was on the sidewalk at the corner of Eighteenth Place and Leavitt, talking to his friend Lori Rincon. She was standing on the steps of her house, an iron picket fence between them. Their long conversation was interrupted shortly after midnight when the Buick LeSabre pulled up under the streetlight, just a few feet from Edmondson. There is no evidence that this was anything other than a random encounter. The occupants did not know Edmondson. They were just a carload of gangsters in enemy territory, looking for adventure, high and ready for whatever came their way.

The window was down on the passenger side. Garcia "threw" a gang sign, not that of the Latin Counts (fingers shaped into the letters *L* and *C*), but that of the Satan Disciples (a pitchfork made by extending the thumb and two other digits while folding down those in between). Gangsters call this "false flagging." The term originated in naval warfare in the days of the great sailing fleets, when it was considered ethical to fly an enemy's flag to lure him into position, as long as one's true flag were hoisted before actual hostilities opened up. "False flagging" is also practiced in the worlds of covert operations and terrorism, where one actor plants evidence implicating another. Adrian Covarrubias, who flipped and testified for the state, told the jury that Garcia threw the false flag to lure Edmondson closer.

"Are you Satan Disciples?" Garcia challenged Edmondson. "No man, I don't know what you're talking about," Edmondson replied, initially moving closer to get a look at the men in the car. Garcia pressed: "You sure? You sure you're not Satan Disciples?" At this point, Justin Chapman, the driver, urged Garcia to shoot the other man, saying, "Buck him! Buck him!" Garcia opened the car door, pulling the gun from his waist as he stepped out. Edmondson saw what was coming and took off, zigzagging as he ran west across the plaza in the direction of the Mateo front stoop, 980 feet away. Pop! At least one round hit a parked panel truck a block away. Pop-pop-pop-pop! Garcia blasted away, missiles flying into the night. Pop-pop!

That was it. Ana Mateo fell, mortally stricken. An innocent little girl at play was killed for the sake of ten seconds of false gangster machismo. Garcia had no idea what he had done and got back into the car laughing. The three Latin Counts drove back to the Pit, where they boasted that they had "bucked" a black Satan Disciple. In a while, however, the party quickly broke up. The Latin Counts at the Pit had a police scanner. Word came over the scanner that the tough guys had not bucked a black gangster after all. They had killed a seven-year-old girl. "Oh, shit, man," someone muttered. "We got to lose that gun."

Shell casings, bullet fragments, and the bullet in Ana Mateo's skull would be found. But the gun never was. That was the first handful of sand Garcia's lawyers picked up when his case came to trial in November 2006, more than three years after the murder. Another handful was what is called the "*CSI* defense." A third was a defensive argument along the lines of "Maybe a little green gangster from Mars did it."

The state's case was straightforward, and Mary Jo Murtagh laid it out in an equally straightforward opening statement. For the remainder of the trial, she and her colleagues, Michael Golden and Brian Holmes, took turns hammering away at Garcia, who never, in their opinion, betrayed a flicker of emotion. Justin Chapman had pleaded out, and Adrian Covarrubias was a witness for the prosecution. Covarrubias claimed that his father had died as a gangster when he was a toddler and that he had left the gang because he did not want the same thing for his son.

Garcia had his own story. He claimed that he was really sorry about Ana Mateo but that he was never near her neighborhood that night. His formal defense was the alibi that he spent that night at his mother's home, which his mom swore was true. But Garcia's lawyer tossed the first handful of sand, the "*CSI* defense" in the opening argument. The term comes from the warped impact that the popular CBS television series *CSI: Crime Scene Investigation* has had on juries all over the country. In the fictional vignettes, lab technicians doubling as street cops and detectives (or street cops and detectives doubling as lab technicians—it is never clear which) seamlessly nail down crimes of every stripe by astounding feats of forensic science. No trace of body fluids, DNA, dandruff, or miniscule fragment of torn clothing escapes the gimlet eye of these television sleuths, no matter how old or degraded the crime scene, improbable the find, or extreme the science. Knowing that many jurors have come to expect to be entertained by the same kind of evidentiary wizardry, even in cases where forensic science simply is not relevant or probative, defense lawyers toss the sand. Prosecutors have to anticipate the inane and elicit testimony explaining the lack of a scientific sound-and-light show.

"You will not hear about DNA," thundered Garcia's lawyer. "You will not hear about fingerprints located on cartridges." He argued that with no gun, no DNA, an alleged perpetrator who was home sleeping at mommy's house, no hair fibers in the car (tracked down two years later after two changes of ownership), and no confession, how could the jurors not have a reasonable doubt? Playing bass ground under all of this, slipped in from time to time to the irritation of both judge and prosecutors, was the clever insinuation that this trial was really the sinister result of a vast conspiracy, an intragang plot to protect the real shooter (the aforementioned shadowy little green gangbanger from Mars).

Every trial, even a slam dunk, is a gamble. All it takes is one determined vote of "not guilty," one oddball, one holdout, one juror who—for whatever reason—gets his or her fur up, or one skeptic who just is not persuaded and has the steel to stand firm against eleven who are. When it was all over and the jury retired to deliberate, the question hung in the air: would Juan Garcia—Ana Mateo's alleged killer—be convicted?

Gino Colon also tried the "home with mom" alibi defense. In his trial for murder in 1972, he claimed that he had been nowhere near the corner of North Leavitt Street and West Potomac Avenue, the location at which Colon was accused of shooting to death a man named Glen Burr—3.7 miles and fifteen minutes straight north of Leavitt and Eighteenth Place, where Randy Edmondson was shot at thirty-one years later. (Colon was also egged on by a companion, Florentine Menendez, who urged young Gino to "shoot that black motherfucker.") Colon claimed to have been at his mother's house, enjoying a party celebrating his brother Jose's return from the army. The alibi defense went south, however, when Jose testified that there had been no party and that on the evening in question, he was actually at his father's house in Brooklyn, hiding out because he had just gone AWOL from Fort Dix, New Jersey.

Colon made good use of his twenty-five years in prison, earning a place in the "honor dorm" by clawing his way to the top of the Latin Kings' Motherland, not incidentally eliminating inconvenient rivals on the way up. He was still in his prime as his quarter century of penal rehabilitation drew to a close, looking forward to living out a prosperous life as "Supreme Corona," "Sun King," "El Magnate," and father to two of his three children. It may be small consolation to a "Sun King," but the ATF agents who brought him down—Terry Jackson, Elizabeth

Ragusa, and Laurie Jolley—had nothing so grandiose in their sights when they started out. They still have a sense of wonder that they did it. "The most amazing part of this case is that we were able to overcome all the hurdles, the obstacles, and the difficulties that were in our way," Jackson says.[32]

ATF agents pride themselves on doing one of the most dangerous jobs in law enforcement—going after guns and the people who traffic in them. The nature of ATF's mission puts its agents out on the streets a lot, typically working in a short-term undercover capacity and sometimes going "deep" undercover for long-term investigations. The agents build federal criminal cases by buying guns and drugs from very bad people, such as convicted felons and illicit gun traffickers. They occasionally come across people willing to sell more lethal firepower, like ground-to-air missiles. The arm of the agency that investigates criminal activity is tiny, however, compared to the FBI. When Gino Colon was toppled in 1997, for example, ATF employed 1,775 full-time investigative agents out of a total full-time staff of 3,988. (The rest were inspectors and administrative personnel.) In the same year, the FBI employed 11,233 special agents (and 920 intelligence officers) out of a total staff of 27,140.[33] "The FBI has more agents in New York than we have in the entire country," says a senior ATF agent in Chicago. Over the years, however, ATF has built deep networks and intelligence files and is often at the lead of major investigations targeting Chicago's supergangs.

Terry Jackson got the idea of working in law enforcement from his brother, who is a police officer in Houston, Texas. He graduated from ATF Academy in Glynco, Georgia, in August 1988 and was assigned to Chicago. "There was a big push on then to work gangs," he says. "Our main focus was to work on 'felon-in-possession' cases, the worst of the worst." Federal law prohibits firearms possession by convicted felons and carries stiff penalties for violators. At about the same time, the Chicago field office made a decision to concentrate a substantial part of its resources on gangs on the North Side, in the Humboldt Park area, working closely with the Chicago Police Department. "The Latin Kings were the biggest gang, had the most guns, and were the most violent, " Jackson says. "Originally, we were making gun buys. But we were always hearing talk about 'Lord Gino' in the background."

Elizabeth Ragusa joined the agency in 1990 and ended up out on the streets of the North Side, making drug and gun buys. She also managed to have three children during the investigation. "Our cases just kept getting bigger and bigger," she recalls. "We were getting really good informants. Eventually, we were hearing that Lord Gino was still in control and that he was enforcing his control through a lot of personal violence."

Ragusa and agent Laurie Jolley were having a lot of success making federal firearms law cases through their illicit gun buys. But the U.S. attorney was pushing the agency for bigger, conspiracy-type cases. The idea of taking down an entire section of the Latin Kings was kicked around, and the decision was made to target Colon's operation. This was done, says Jackson, who became the lead agent, the old-fashioned way—by flipping little fish to work their way up the feeding chain to the big fish. "You always need a flipper to make a case like this work," he says. "You also have to have dope on the table and a gun on the table. You have to get right in there."

By July 1996, ATF had an informant who was able to get an undercover agent close enough to make cocaine buys from Colon's retail outlet at 2420 North Kedzie. This operation, they learned, was being supervised by gangster Wilfred Escobar. By means of a court-authorized electronic surveillance device placed on Escobar's car and visual surveillance, the agents linked Escobar to Jorge "Chico" Martinez, aka "Danny," who was then Colon's "Supreme Regional" and was supervising the operation's taxation of drug dealers.

Martinez had been in office only a few months. He had been nominated by Gino's wife, Marisol Colon, to replace the former Regional, Jose "Bam Bam" Souffront. Souffront fell out of favor after a Chicago police raid—unrelated to the ATF investigation—uncovered a substantial quantity of drugs and a firearm in his apartment. Colon deposed Souffront, and he was invited to come in for a "violation"—a punishment for sloppy security in getting caught with drugs and a gun in his home. He was told the violation would consist of being shot in the leg. In fact, from transcriptions of tapes of prison phone calls, agents learned that Lord Gino had ordered a contract taken out on Bam Bam's life. Souffront declined the invitation to get shot in the leg and left town. He was later apprehended by ATF, willingly gave a statement, and surrendered a diary that lay out the enterprise's drug operations.

In early 1996, the agents got a grand jury subpoena for Illinois state prison tapes of Colon's phone calls. Access to the calls was not all that easy, however. The prison did not separate calls out by inmate. They were all simply recorded on one tape in the order they went out. The tapes were big, old-fashioned reel-to-reel tapes, and the prison system recycled the tapes every thirty days, taping over old conversations with new ones. Given ATF's paucity of resources, the fact that the agents were able to find Colon's calls in the welter, penetrate the codes and the Spanish language, and make effective use of the conversations was nothing short of miraculous, a monument to sheer dedication.

By early 1997, the team had enough evidence to get a warrant authorizing pen registers and trap-and-trace devices installed on the phones of Wilfredo Escobar and Marisol Colon. Getting a Title III wiretap, as the FBI often does, was out of the question, because the three agents simply did not have backup staff or time to handle the burdensome administrative procedures associated with a tap, much less to do the substantive listening and minimization. What they did get was enough. In February 1997, Wilfredo Escobar was arrested. He immediately gave a statement and agreed to be an active cooperating witness, meaning he flipped and helped set up the rest of the enterprise.

Seven months later, the grand jury returned indictments, and Lord Gino Colon got his ride back to Chicago in the backseat of a government car. Marisol was arrested and also gave a helpful statement. By the time the case went to trial, she had decided that she was a helpless victim of Gino's Svengali-like powers. A psychiatrist testified that this was true, but the jury did not buy it. She and Gino, along with their principal associates, were convicted. Gino was sentenced to life in prison, a term he is now serving in the federal supermaximum-security prison at Florence, Colorado. Marisol was sentenced to ten years. There is no parole in the federal system, but with time off for good behavior, Marisol is out of prison. She reportedly says Gino is isolated and "doesn't want anything to do" with the Latin Kings.[34]

When the jury filed in after deliberating over Juan Garcia's case, Maria and Federico Mateo were in the courtroom. "Guilty" was the verdict. Juan Garcia was sentenced to fifty-five years in prison. "It's a victory," Federico Mateo said later about the case. "But with no one really winning anything. Because no matter what, nothing brings back my daughter."[35] There is a small shrine on the sidewalk in front of the Mateo home, a poignant memorial to Ana. In it are a few faded photographs, a collection of sentimental objects, and a biblical inscription:

> Blessed are the poor in spirit: for theirs is the kingdom of heaven.
> Blessed are the meek: for they shall posses the land.
> Blessed are they who mourn: for they shall be comforted.
> Blessed are they that hunger and thirst after justice: for they shall
> have their fill.
> Blessed are the merciful: for they shall obtain mercy.

I realized that I was capable of having feelings, and that much of what had happened to me in my life was my fault, and maybe I could change that.

—DANIEL OCHOA, FORMER GUATEMALAN GANG MEMBER

9

THE BAKER'S TALE

Early on a beautifully cool and sunny spring morning in May 2007, an eclectic group of people made their individual ways to the residence of Guillermo Castillo, the Guatemalan ambassador in Washington, D.C. The house is tucked away on a steep hillside lane in a lovely upscale neighborhood just north and west of Rock Creek Park. Azaleas, daffodils, flowering dogwood trees, and the rich green of the grass marked the arrival of spring. Inside the residence, conversation in Spanish and English buzzed around a buffet breakfast. Diplomats, congressional staff, news media, scholars, institutional experts and other interested persons exchanged air kisses, *abrazos* (hugs traditionally exchanged by men in Latino culture), and handshakes. Egos collided here and there. It was a long way culturally and geographically from the wretchedly poor barrios of Guatemala, within which there are estimated—with the usual imprecision—to be no less than 14,000 and perhaps as many as 165,000 members of criminal street gangs.[1]

The program started shortly after 8:00 a.m. The subject seemed the stuff of an only moderately interesting seminar—the social responsibility of business in addressing the problem of gangs in Guatemala. The customary litany of wise remarks made its way down the requisite chain of dignitaries. A promotional video was shown, followed by more wise remarks. One began to look for an appropriate point at which to make a moderately gracious exit.

Then Daniel Ochoa, twenty-five years old, rose to speak. The restless room stilled. Guests leaned into the story of this modest, prepossessing young man. A former gangster, his nickname in his new, aboveground world was "Panadero" (the Baker). The business suit he wore covered up an atlas of tattoos inked onto his body. They mapped what he now regarded as a shameful descent into the hell of life as a member of Barrio 18, the Guatemalan variant of the 18th Street gang. They once covered his face as well. But he had had those on his face removed and was looking forward to erasing the rest. "When I got the tattoos off my face, I felt liberated," he said. "Now I want to get rid of the ones on my body. They link me to my past and to the crazy things I have done."[2]

Ochoa was nervous as he began to speak, perhaps a bit intimidated by where he was and among whom he was speaking. Dr. Eduardo Stein, Guatemala's vice president, sat only feet away on the dais. Yet Daniel's voice gained resonance as he told his story simply and without embellishment. The bitter life and redemption of Daniel Ochoa emerged with an eloquence and depth rare in a city whose wheels are driven by sound bites and greased with vacuity. "I quit school and went out on the streets trying to support my family when I was ten years old. I joined the gang when I was twelve years old," he said. "My father died of alcoholism when I was two years old. I never met him."

The Baker is not a tall man. He stood with the stoic stance of a boxer. It was as if each fact he bluntly recounted from his past was a fresh blow against his own humanity. He pushed on and did not flinch from describing the violence he had done for his gang. "I found in the gang feelings that I could not get at home—support, acceptance, people who would even die for me," he recounted. "I felt very good being a gang member. I had prestige, I felt accepted."

When Daniel Ochoa was born, Guatemala was in the midst of a

merciless internal war. For thirty-six years, from 1960 to 1996, the Guatemalan state scathed its people, waging war on those it regarded as its enemies—"communists" and "insurgents." These categories were like balloons. Pumped up by infusions of paranoia, they grew to include virtually anyone who dared disagree in the slightest degree with the country's grim military rulers. The war was more than just local. Its roots went back to 1954, when the United States, in the grip of panic about the rise of Soviet Russia and Communist China, unleashed the CIA to orchestrate a violent coup against President Jacobo Arbenz Guzman. Arbenz wanted to implement land reform, unionization, and other social and political reforms. Cuba's hand was involved as well. Fidel Castro sent aid and advisers to the insurgency when it broke out in the 1960s.

Restraints fell aside as the national security apparatus—the military, a brutal counterinsurgency force called the Kaibiles, and the civilian police, who were subordinated to the military and became raw agents of terror—conducted a ruthless, racist war. "The human rights records of the Guatemalan security services," concluded the U.S. Intelligence Oversight Board in 1996, "were generally known to have been reprehensible by all who were familiar with Guatemala."[3] At the conflict's end, at least two hundred thousand Guatemalans were dead. Eighty-three percent of the identified victims were indigenous Mayan people.[4]

Deserters from the Kaibiles have since joined with deserters from U.S.-trained units of Mexican special forces known as "Zetas," who use their elite skills to act as paramilitary muscle for Mexican drug-trafficking organizations.[5] The Kaibiles help train new members of the Zetas, who have "established alliances with prison and street gangs operating in the United States."[6] Ironically, the Zetas emerged from a special anti-drug unit trained in part by the U.S. Army.

The effects of the long and agonizing war on Guatemalan society have been profound. They include widespread "psychosocial trauma" (PTSD), the normalization of violence as a legitimate way of settling disputes, and the distrust of law enforcement mechanisms that had become blunt instruments of repression. Education was also stunted, as classrooms closed under pressure of fighting, scarce resources, and targeting of teachers as "subversives." As a result, combat and firearms skills "easily applied in gangsterism, acquisitive crime, and cross-border trafficking" may be the only talents possessed by "a generation of young people without alternative identities or employment."[7] In the mid-1990s, when Ochoa joined Barrio 18, the war was winding down. But the exhausted country was already being hit by the Los Angeles gang culture exported by the United States. Between 1998 and 2005, the United States deported about forty-six thousand convicts to Central America, a number that does not include ordinary deportations for lack of papers.[8]

From the moment he joined the gang and throughout his entire teenage life, Daniel Ochoa served Barrio 18 willingly and enthusiastically. He was imprisoned. He suffered through gunshot wounds that brought him to death's door. He swaggered with the worst of his peers. But at bottom, he was little more than a human cork in a toxic sea of violence.

At some point after his brush with death, something important changed inside him. "I began analyzing my life," he said. "Slowly, I started realizing that my heart wasn't in it anymore. I looked around and saw other people's lives, having families, raising children. Maybe I want that, too, I thought." Ochoa arrived at a conclusion that he phrased in words remarkably like those that MS-13 informant Brenda Paz used to describe her feelings. "As I matured, I started realizing that the comfort I got from my gang was a false comfort," he said. "I realized it was foolish to maybe sacrifice my life for two numbers—my gang. I decided to change."

But breaking free was difficult. One does not simply turn in one's resignation to a violent street gang. "Blood in, blood out" is the common phrase to describe the lifelong bond to which one commits when joining such a gang. You bleed to get in, you bleed to get out, and the latter means death at the hands of one's fellow gangsters. Aside from that, Ochoa wore the blatant indicia of his gang membership—the tattoos on his body and his face. Worst of all, he was a drug addict. "I was completely addicted," he recalled. Even if he could find work, no one would hire an unskilled, addicted gangster. His dilemma grew within him. "I didn't know how to change," he said. "I didn't have the means to change. Even though I wanted to change, I didn't know how to get out. I didn't even know how to act around other people. And what would I tell my fellow gang members?"

Ochoa got a break one day while he was still struggling with his predicament. He met a man on the street who took an unusual approach to the gangster. Daniel was used to being treated as an object of fear and revulsion. This man simply asked if he could stop by and talk. Daniel said yes. Eventually, the man invited Ochoa to visit a church. Again, the young man said yes, and step-by-step, he was led to a religious conversion. "I asked God to help me defeat my drug addiction," he said. "I was able to overcome it. And then I vowed never to touch weapons again."

Not knowing where to turn or what to do next, Ochoa holed up at his aunt's house, trying to break away from his gangster friends. Gang members hunted him down and shot up the house. So he moved. "Basically," he explained, "I spent a year hiding out in my mother's house." Every step outside his sanctuary was perilous. But on one outing, Daniel Ochoa caught another break. He ran into an ex–gang member who had been helped in his own ascent by a nongovernmental organization working with gangs. The man offered to teach Ochoa how to bake bread. Thus Daniel became "Panadero."

Only in fairy tales would that be end of it. Barrio 18 tracked him down again. "Two boys, aged thirteen and fourteen, came to kill me," he recalled. "It was their initiation rite. They beat me up so badly that I spent twenty days in the hospital." Still Ochoa stuck to his conversion and his determination to leave the gang life. Then came an odd invitation that would change his life completely and bring him to that spring morning at an ambassador's house in Washington. He was invited to appear as a contestant on an odd—some might say bizarre—reality game show.

Desafío 10—Paz par los Ex, whose title translates "Challenge 10—Peace for Ex," was the idea of Harold Sibaja, Latin American regional director for Creative Associates International, an international consulting firm based in Washington, D.C. Sibaja's inspiration was to use the popular format of reality competition to do three things at once—help ex–gang members become self-reliant by starting their own small businesses, involve the Guatemalan business community as stakeholders in solving the gang problem, and sensitize the public to the need for the entire civil community's involvement. The idea was to divide ten gang members into two teams, have them live together in one house, provide intensive guidance from mentors in small business, and give the teams fourteen days within which each would try to make a go of a small business—a car wash for one team and a shoeshine stand for the other.

"The solutions to the gang problem are not something that are written down somewhere," Sibaja said as he introduced Daniel Ochoa at the breakfast meeting. "We are still trying to find solutions. But we know that the solution is not only the responsibility of the government and the police." Sibaja directs the USAID-supported Youth Alliance Program in Guatemala, aimed at providing a second chance for the tens of thousands of marginalized youth like Daniel Ochoa in that country. "We don't work with active gang members," he said. "But we know that there are many who wish to leave the gang but cannot because they have no other opportunity. No one would hire anyone with a tattoo, no matter what their original intention in getting it was. If you have a kid who is hungry and who doesn't have a job, that kid will go back to doing what he has to do to survive." Sibaja hastened to affirm that law enforcement is important. But what, he asked, about the gangsters who want out? He found that the key to unlocking the conundrum was to look at gangsters in a different way—as human beings. "Once you start seeing the human behind the youth," explained Sibaja, "you start seeing the options."

There were risks involved in participating in the reality show. "The kids could face retaliation from their gangs," said Sibaja. Finding businesspersons willing to help was not easy either. "Who wants a gang member in your business? It's like inviting a criminal into your home," Sibaja explained. But USAID bought the idea and provided seed funding, and other support from the Guatemalan community came in.

The ten contestants for the show were recruited and screened with the help of nongovernmental organizations and churches, where many former gang members seek refuge in Guatemala. "Many in the faith-based community are trying to help these youth," Sibaja said. "But they don't have jobs." Daniel Ochoa was one of twenty-five original candidates and made the cut to the final ten. He and the others wore masks to disguise their identity during taping for the televised show.

As improbable as it may seem in the United States—whose television media is often soaked in cynical hypersensationalism—the program was a success. More important, both businesses created during the show succeeded and were thriving. The Guatemalan business community rallied to help, and a bigger program was born—Challenge 100. Not a television show, Challenge 100 pairs a hundred former gang members with local businesses, which provide real employment and on-the-job training. One ex–gang member broke down in tears the first time he was handed a paycheck. He had never before earned his way in his life. "Some former gang members have left the program for various reasons," Sibaja said. But at the time he spoke, "no one left because they stole from their employers or because they went back to their gang."

After the program, Daniel Ochoa's life was suddenly full of opportunity. He wanted to get an education, expand his business, and raise a family. The most important thing about the program he said, was that it did not treat him like a gangster. "They treated me with dignity," he said, choking up. "They treated me like a human being."

Many left the ambassadorial residence feeling uplifted. Daniel Ochoa's story was inspiring evidence that approaches other than law enforcement—in his case, intervention—might work even under the most difficult circumstances, like those in Guatemala. His race, however, was not yet fully run.

The best prevention is good enforcement," quips Hector Alfonso, a colorful, fast-talking, wise-cracking gang analyst in the Miami-Dade County Police Department. Alfonso thinks he knows why national gangs stay out of Miami. "Our gang problem is in check because of the way we enforce it," he claims.[9]

Alfonso is a member of a growing cadre in law enforcement ranks—the specialized gang analyst who supports the work of detectives and patrol officers with databases, detailed analysis, and in-depth studies of gangs and gangsters. The purpose of crime analysis, according to a standard text, is to "find meaningful information in vast amounts of data and disseminate this information to officers and investigators in the field."[10] "We're not 'the guy,'" Alfonso explains. "We're the guy that the guy comes to. I provide an extra set of analytical eyes to the officers on the street." In addition to his analytical work, Alfonso coordinates an aggressive regional task force for gang suppression—the Metropolitan Area Gang Task Force (MAGTF)—whose mission is to root up and crush gang sprouts. "We put our foot right on their necks," he smiles benignly. "MAGTF has a reputation. 'Watch out,' they say when we're on the streets, 'Those guys lock *everybody* up.'"

The result, Alfonso argues, is that Miami is a big city with only a small-town Latino gang scene. Although the big national Latino gangs will always have some presence, he says, most of the gangs in Miami-Dade are "wannabes" and small-bore neighborhood groups. He appears to be right, at least through mid-2007. Although MS-13 appears to be making a bid for a stronger presence and although national gangs like the Latin Kings have stepped up recruiting efforts, Miami-Dade County has no significant national Latino gang presence, at least according to officials in the Miami-Dade County Police Department and on the Gang Strike Force in the Miami-Dade County State's Attorney's Office. The FBI field office agrees. It declined two requests in 2007 for interviews about Latino gangs in Miami on the grounds that there would be nothing to talk about. Alfonso says the national Latino gangs treat Miami as a safe haven in which to blend into the Latino community and hide when the heat is on elsewhere. It is also a "neutral zone" within which they are free to encounter each other without the violent armed conflict that often occurs when rival gangsters meet in other cities.

The situation with other ethnicities is very different, it should be noted. The South Florida area, including at least Miami-Dade and Broward counties, is plagued by extremely violent Haitian criminal gangs—heavily armed with AK-47 assault rifles. But Alfonso says that even the Haitian gangs are not street gangs in the strictest sense. "The Haitian gangs are criminal enterprises," he explains. "They are not like conventional street gangs. They are called 'gangs' only because they happen to have names. But their thing is not about colors or turf. They are very nationalistic and strictly in it for the crime."

Putting aside the Haitian gangs, what accounts for Miami's relative placidity in the national Latino gang world? If Alfonso and others interviewed are right, Miami-Dade is an example of the law enforcement approach to gang suppression working effectively. Alfonso makes wry reference to the popular "weed and seed" concept for fighting crime in marginalized areas. "Weed and seed" programs take a two-pronged approach: law enforcement "weeds out" violent criminals, and social service agencies "seed" prevention, intervention, treatment, and neighborhood restoration programs. "Everybody wants to seed," he says. "But nobody wants to weed. We do our weeding."

Another element may underlay the success of Miami-Dade's suppression program. Differences between the dominant Miami Latino community and the Latino communities of Los Angeles and Chicago include its overall attitude toward law enforcement. That may be one reason why the Miami-Dade County Police Department is able to patrol a much larger area, with a smaller force, than the Los Angeles Police Department. "We are the gateway to the Americas, so Miami has always been attractive to criminal organizations," Alfonso explains. "The Latin Kings have tried to form here for years, but it's never happened. The city is not conducive to the kinds of gangs you see in Los Angeles and Chicago. We don't have the 'hood' or the 'barrio' mentality. It's not like those communities where the gang is actually the norm. Here you have a community that is more likely to call law enforcement when they see a problem. Things like graffiti and gang colors are going to draw the attention of someone in the community, and the community is then going to draw it to the attention of law enforcement." The aggressive metropolitan regional antigang program is another check on gangs. Alfonso says confidently, "If they get big enough to be a problem, they are going to run right into law enforcement."

Prosecutor Frank Ledee—chief of the Gang Prosecution Unit in the Miami-Dade County State's Attorney's Office—takes a slightly more tempered view. He sees a growing risk of national Latino gang infiltration. But he agrees that the dominant Latino community and aggressive law enforcement have so far worked together to suppress any major Latino gang problems. "There has been no influx of gangs in Miami because there is no history of colonization here, " he says, contrasting Miami with Los Angeles. "It was a cultural thing. When the Cubans came, they worked hard and did very well." Although the Cuban émigrés clashed with the dominant culture on many fronts, they shared the general respect of the established Anglo and Jewish communities for law and order.

Ironically, if the material, social, and political success of Miami's Cuban population has indeed suppressed the emergence of national Latino gangs, it also has had a singular effect on the debate about immigration in the United States. The violence of Latino street gangs is often put forth as one of the more serious negative consequences of immigration by its opponents. But if one takes out the element of gang crime in a Latino community that has done well materially and participates enthusiastically—albeit on its own terms—in the political system, what remains as objectionable is almost purely a cultural aversion.

Florida, like California, was originally part of the great Spanish conquest of the New World. In 1513, Ponce de Leon sailed into Biscayne Bay. Another explorer, Pedro Menendez de Aviles, is credited with properly colonizing Florida in 1565, when he founded St. Augustine (which claims to be the oldest continuously occupied European city in the continental United States). Thereafter, Florida was administered for centuries by the Spanish captain general in Cuba. Spain's possession was regularly contested by the British and freebooters who had their own territorial designs on the peninsula and, latterly, by the United States. Spanish contact with the native inhabitants of the Miami area, the Tequesta Indians, was episodic. There were a few short-lived missions, sufficient to ensure the eradication of the Indians primarily through their infection with European diseases. Spain ceded Florida to the United States by treaty in 1819.

Not much population growth happened in the Miami area until the last decade of the nineteenth century. Then, like Los Angeles, Miami was born of the union of the railroad and agribusiness. It thrived with infusions of "snow birds," tourists and Anglo migrants fleeing the northern climate. After the "Great Freeze" of the winter of 1894–95 wiped out Florida's citrus groves—except for those in the Miami area—railroad magnate Henry Morrison Flagler was persuaded to extend his Florida East Coast Railroad south from Palm Beach to Miami. The railroad opened up South Florida. Crops went north. Tourists and those drawn to a balmier clime came south.

The region went through several cycles of boom and bust between the two world wars. It was an ideal military training ground during both wars. Miami Beach was practically taken over by the armed services during World War II. One consequence was that GIs from the north "got sand in their shoes" during their training and came back after the war. Miami became a big city with few native-born residents, a place where everybody was from somewhere else.

Among the newcomers were thousands of Jewish veterans, and Miami's Jewish population exploded. There were an estimated 8,000 Jews in the Miami area before the war. By 1950, this population grew to 55,000, a much greater rate of growth than that of the area generally. By 1960, about 140,000 Jews lived in Miami, making up 15 percent of its population.[11] Jewish entrepreneurs—investors, developers, and hoteliers—were largely responsible for turning Miami Beach into "a national icon of popular culture in the 1950s."[12]

A parallel force was the establishment of an elite white business and political class. Through the 1950s and into the 1960s, "Miami was essentially a southern city, albeit one with a large Jewish presence and an eye to the Caribbean."[13] The world of southern white civic power was embodied in an informal cadre of corporate elites—called the "Non-Group"—organized by an executive of the Knight Ridder newspaper combine to chart a more progressive future for the city. The *Miami Herald*, Knight Ridder's flagship paper, was accustomed to being the voice of the city's rulers.

The success of Fidel Castro's Cuban revolution in 1959 would rock this world in a way that the white ruling class in Miami could not foresee, even years after the bearded dictator rolled triumphantly into Havana. The city's boosters were mapping out ways for Miami to move beyond its dependency on fading tourism, diversify, and become a world-class city. They envisioned it connected with the markets of the Southern Hemisphere—but connected from the perspective of traditional Anglo-American power. Over the next two decades, Cubans fleeing Castro's Communist regime washed over those plans as if they were written in sand. The Cubans reshaped the city's economic and political profile in their own image.

Although there have been significant migrations of other Latino nationalities since—Venezuelans, Colombians, Nicaraguans, and other Central Americans, each group fleeing its own political disorder or seizing profitable opportunity—Cubans are today by far the largest segment of the Latino population in South Florida. Of an estimated 2,376,014 residents in Miami-Dade County in 2005, slightly more than 60 percent were Latinos.[14] In the city of Miami itself, almost 66 percent of the population were Latino,[15] and in the city of Hialeah, just over 90 percent were.[16] More than half of these Latinos are estimated to be Cuban in origin.

From the beginning, Miami's establishment and its voice, the *Miami Herald,* failed to grasp—or refused to accept—that the Cubans who came to Miami in the crucial early waves were not unlettered fruit pickers coming with hat in hand. They were in large measure the island's elite, educated, skilled, and, in many cases, well capitalized. Reduced only in condition, they had the vision and abilities to make a new life. Moreover, they were, for the most part, determined to make Fidel Castro's tenure as short as possible and to return to their homeland in triumph. Joan Didion reports, "They shared not just Cuba as a birthplace but Cuba as a construct, the idea of birthright lost."[17] Although helped by generous immigration rules and other federal accommodations, the Cubans had no intention of melting themselves down into generic hyphenated Americans. The exile in Florida was "at the deepest level construed by Cubans as a temporary condition, an accepted political option shaped by the continuing dream, if no longer the immediate expectation, of a vindicatory return."[18]

The Cubans' obstinate gestalt was a recipe for cultural conflict. It clashed directly with the establishment's perfervid expectations and strong desire that the Cubans assimilate along traditional lines, including adopting the language of their new country as soon as possible. At best, Anglos tended to treat the Cubans condescendingly, as democracy's trophies in its global war against Communism. The Cubans preferred to re-create their new world on their own terms. Since they did so well so quickly economically and politically, there was no particular benefit in learning English. Over the next several decades, the Cubans transformed Miami, in Samuel P. Huntington's turn of phrase, "from a normal American city into a Cuban-led Hispanic city." This "enclave city" is seen by some as an example of an existential threat to American identity, since within its boundaries, "assimilation and Americanization were unnecessary and in some measure undesired."[19] Reaction to this culturally and linguistically distinct enclave "spawned the contemporary English-only, immigrant backlash movement that reverberated throughout the United States."[20]

In an interesting way, the reaction to what Huntington calls the "Hispanization" of Miami is a reiteration of a pattern of Jeffersonian hope and disappointment described in Patricia Nelson Limerick's study of the conquest of the American frontier. Caught between their Enlightenment beliefs in the common dignity of all humanity and the obstacle the Indians presented to the Anglo destiny of westward expansion, the Jeffersonian idealists entertained the unreasonable hope that "Indians could change rapidly from savages to citizens" if they were only properly exposed to the new civilizing environment of white Anglo-Saxon Christianity. "White people would repeatedly try to rush change, fail, and then embrace an easy resignation and disillusionment," writes Limerick. The conclusion the whites drew—that the Indians were "persisting in their ways like a patient willfully remaining ill to frustrate the doctor who tried to save him"—became a conscience-salving rationale to support the brutal process of Indian removal.[21]

Just so, the refusal of Miami's Cuban community to assimilate on traditional terms infuriated many in the Anglo community, who came to see the Cubans as ungrateful invaders. "The truculence a millionaire who spoke only two words of English might provoke among the less resourceful native citizens of a nominally American city," writes Didion, "was predictable and manifested itself rather directly."[22] Uncomfortable in their new status as the cultural and linguistic minority, Anglos first tried the blunt instrument of "English-only" regulation. When that failed to stem the tide, they fled in droves. The fleeing Anglos displayed their angry wound in the form of a popular bumper sticker that lamented, "Will the last American to leave Miami please bring the flag."[23] The Cuban subversion of a "normal" American city and their putatively perverse reverse assimilation became object example and searing justification for a national English-only campaign and anti-immigrant measures intended to ensure that future newcomers swallow the doctor's prescription and get well.

Cuban youth gangs formed in Miami in the early 1960s but had disappeared by 1978.[24] The gangs appeared in the two major neighborhoods in which Cuban exiles took up residence in Miami—Hialeah and an area just north of Coral Gables now known as Little Havana. These groups called themselves "fraternities," probably because of the proximity of Little Havana to the University of Miami campus, where Greek-letter fraternities were quite active in the 1960s. What appears to be the only published study of these gangs, by J. Bryan Page, suggests that they were formed at least partly in response to the stress of cultural conflict—"the non-Hispanic boys picked on Cuban boys mercilessly if they did not have gang affiliation."[25] The gangs' names were etymologically related to fighting qualities or toughness: Vulcans, Jutes (possibly Utes or Yutes), Aztecs, and Hawks. Gang members wore distinctive clothing and colors. Gang activities included partying, aggressive brawling, drug use (marijuana and inhalants), and criminal violence. One alleged gang leader was sentenced to sixty years in prison for attempted murder of two police officers at whom he shot during a car chase.

The disappearance of the Cuban gangs in the late 1970s may indicate how a community's growth out of widespread marginality and the existence of economic opportunity can eliminate the utilitarian function of gangs. The gangs became "irrelevant and unnecessary" as the Cuban community grew to economic, cultural, and political dominance. "The development of a strong Cuban community did not completely erase the social problems associated with exile," writes Page, "but they reduced the numbers of people facing them so that there was no longer a critical mass of youth between 13 and 27 who needed gang membership to adapt to difficult or oppressive situations."[26]

By 1984, other problems related to street gangs were emerging in South Florida. The appearance of the gangs raised the issue of "denial," a phenomenon that continues to be a problem for law enforcement in communities throughout the country. "Denying the presence of gangs significantly hampers effective enforcement and intelligence gathering, both of which are vital during the early stages when violence is limited and active measures can effectively impact the problem," analyst Hector Alfonso wrote in an analytical paper. "By the time communities and institutions acknowledge that they have a gang problem, the situation may be out of control."[27]

Kevin Carwile, chief of the U.S. Justice Department's Gang Squad, and other law enforcement officials agree that denial is often a problem. Denial occurs when the political or law enforcement leadership of a given community insists that the community does not have a "gang problem," in the face of evidence to the contrary. The evidence of gang activity runs through a spectrum from outbreaks of identifiable gang graffiti, law enforcement intelligence gathered in the course of arrests or field interviews, crimes traced to verified gang members, and intergang violence. Motivations for denial are usually political or economic but may be perceptual ("that can't happen here"). Political motivations include reluctance to concede that a problem has emerged during one's tenure and avoidance of the need to raise or reallocate scarce law enforcement and community social service resources to deal with the problem. Economic motivations include the desire not to discourage business investment in the community or to lower real estate values. The problem of denial may be particularly acute in areas where tourism is an important industry. Politicians and local business leaders have a common motive in downplaying public notice of any crime issue that might frighten tourists and discourage them from coming into the area.

According to several long-term law enforcement observers, what to do about the emerging "gang problem" was a political hot potato in the Miami area during the mid-1980s. Few police or political leaders wanted to be the first to speak out publicly about what many knew was happening. To solve the dilemma, community and law enforcement leaders quietly turned to a relatively unusual use of the grand jury sitting in the local state judicial district. The principal function of most grand juries is to return specific charges (indictments) in the case of serious crimes (felonies). Florida's grand juries—local and statewide— have also been asked from time to time to explore and report on broad problems related to law enforcement. Using the grand jury in this manner has allowed the public ventilation of serious issues without putting any single elected leader or law enforcement official on the spot.

In its fall 1984 term, the grand jury for Miami-Dade County studied the question of whether the area did indeed have a gang problem. The grand jury's report, issued in May 1985, acknowledged the difficulty of addressing the questions—including problems in defining gangs, gathering reliable information beyond anecdotal accounts, and even whether publicizing gang crime contributed to the growth and formation of gangs.[28] But the jury concluded that there was enough evidence for measured concern. It estimated that there were between twenty and thirty relatively disorganized gangs "composed nearly exclusively of Black and Hispanic youths." The report did not further discriminate among the ethnicity of the Latino gangs, although among them was a group known as the Little Aztecs, which one might speculate was a vestige of the Aztecs, one of the old Cuban fraternities. The grand jury reported that Dade County's gangs had not yet been recruited into adult criminal activity, but it warned that "given the high level of narcotics trafficking in Dade County," such recruitment "may well be imminent."[29]

The report stressed that the emergent gangs were "less a police or law enforcement problem than a community problem touching our schools and after-school recreational options for teenagers."[30] Accordingly, the grand jury devoted most of its discussion to what would today be called "prevention" and "intervention" programs, ticking off a catalog of educational, recreational, and vocational "seed" activities. Almost as an aside, the report suggested "the formation of specialized units in the Metro-Dade and City of Miami Police Departments, as well as in the State Attorney's office, which gather and distill information regarding youth gangs and their activities."[31]

The tone of this first report was anything but stentorian. Following its publication, several local police departments—in the cities of Hialeah, Miami, and Miami Beach—established specialized gang units. There was, however, no area-wide coordinating group. Three years later, however, another grand jury returned to the gang question, and its report was filled with urgency.

The report of the grand jury for the fall term of 1987 was clearly intended to sound an alarm. The jurors found that there were now more than seventy gangs in the Miami-Dade area, with more than thirty-five hundred members. "If this issue is not effectively addressed by the private and government sectors," warned the report, "it may escalate to the unmanageable levels experienced today in such cities as Los Angeles and Chicago."[32] In contrast to the first report's observation that gangs were loosely organized, the latter report concluded that "the structure of Dade's gangs has become surprisingly well organized" and that "local gangs are increasingly being influenced and organized by established gangs from such cities as Chicago, where there is a long history of organized, structured gang activity."[33] Many gangs had evolved from basically neighborhood groups into "sophisticated drug networks" with "healthy arsenals of high-powered weapons." The result was that "gang related violence and criminal activity is far greater today than it was three years ago."[34]

The 1987 grand jury also reported that gangs had become "highly mobile, and for the most part, have broken the tradition of being neighborhood or 'turf' gangs."[35] Such mobility had serious implications for an area with as many communities and law enforcement agencies as South Florida. The grand jury approvingly noted the creation during its term of a multiagency task force, the MAGTF, for which Hector Alfonso now serves as lead analyst and coordinator. This task force has aggressively pursued gangs ever since. It has had its ups and downs, at times being cut back because of its very success. But at this writing, it is again on the resurgence, using high-profile saturation and patrol tactics (like those of the LAPD but with little of the hostile community reaction), including monthly sweeps in selected areas.

It would certainly go too far to say that MAGTF and related aggressive prosecutions have eliminated any Latino gang problems in the Miami area. Quite clearly, they have not. But they do seem to have suppressed—at least until now—the perverse grip of the major national Latino gangs, such as MS-13, the 18th Street gang, and Chicago's Latin Kings. These all have some presence in the Miami area, and persons claiming the gangs are arrested and prosecuted for typical crimes. But none seems to control entire neighborhoods or command major criminal enterprises in Miami as they do in Los Angeles, Chicago, and elsewhere.

On September 17, 2007, only a few months after his inspiring talk in Washington, Daniel Ochoa was on a shopping trip with his fiancée. He was looking for leather for his business. She was a few paces in front of him. There was a series of popping noises, and when she turned, Daniel lay on the ground. He had been shot in the back of the head, mortally wounded.

It is not known who killed Panadero. Was it a hit squad from his former gang? Or was it a hit squad of vigilantes who perhaps saw a tattoo, still visible on his neck, and assumed the worst? At this writing, it remains a mystery, sad evidence of the difficulty of extracting oneself from the violence of gang life.

Wherever we go, we recruit more people.

There's no way they can stop us. We're going

to keep on multiplying.

—LOS ANGELES MS-13 GANGSTER

CONCLUSION

There is little reason to believe that the Latino gangs described in preceding chapters will disappear anytime soon. On the contrary, there is every reason to believe that they will continue to grow in size, disperse with the larger migrant stream, become more sophisticated, and strengthen their ties to domestic and transnational organized criminal groups.

Increased law enforcement attention, federalization, and international cooperation may have slowed gang proliferation, constrained some of their criminality, and prevented the immediate emergence of a new "Mafia" similar to the Italian LCN. The evidence is mixed. But the fundamental social and economic problems out of which Latino gangs emerged and which supply their ranks continue largely unchanged. Moreover, the integration of Latino street gangs into transnational drug-trafficking networks has bred a hybrid gang strain, grafting the emotional ties of the old barrio gang to the cynical imperatives of criminal enterprise. That strain is not likely to be less resistant to law enforcement than other elements of the transnational drug-trafficking system, all of which have adapted and survived decades of the "war on drugs" with no end in sight.

This forecast is bad for any number of reasons:

- The very existence of gangs poisons and distorts public discourse about immigration and crime.
- Gangs prey first on their own communities. But they have a corrosive effect everywhere they touch. This effect ranges from the blight of graffiti, through a panoptic array of violent crimes, to widespread fear of violence in public places, such as parks, shopping malls, schools, and recreational facilities.
- There is no immunity for the majority population. Clients of the drug traffickers that gangs serve come from all levels of society, all communities, and all ethnicities.
- The potential—even likelihood—of a highly organized Latino megagang (along the lines of the LCN) continues to lurk just beneath the surface.

The transnational nature of gangs like MS-13 and 18th Street poses challenges to national security beyond that of criminality. The networks in which Latino street gangs serve as critical links and nodes not only move drugs and human beings north. They also are directly involved in the traffic of firearms south from the relatively unregulated civilian markets of the United States. These smuggled guns have become an important part of the arsenals of armed groups in Mexico, for example, where even fifty-caliber antiarmor sniper rifles made in America and sold in its civilian market have been used in assassinations and armed attacks on public authorities. Not a few regional experts believe that the violence of such armed groups—directly against governments as well as against public order in general—threatens to destabilize democratic governance in Mexico and Central America. Moreover, although there has been no publicly documented instance of a street gang directly aiding a terrorist group against the United States or its interests, there is no persuasive reason to believe that the criminal networks and smuggling routes in which the gangs are involved could not be put to evil use by terrorists, with or without the gangs' direct knowledge. (Some law enforcement officials believe that this has already happened.)

This unsettling future invites the question, what can be done about it? Any real examination of that question demands confrontation with deep questions about the culture and politics of the United States. Skeptics would say that the current addiction of politicians to media-driven sound-bite bromides and poll-driven policy formulations based on "triangulation" of voters' topical sentiments does not bode well for either the process of confrontation or its likely outcome.

The first confrontation needed is an honest dialogue about who the United States is as a nation and where it is going, without conflating the question of gangs and immigration. Noted critics of "Hispanization," such as Huntington, and fearmongers of the *reconquista*, such as Buchanan, have given up on the idea of the United States as a "melting pot," because it no longer produces the sterling ingots of Anglo-Saxon culture with which they are comfortable and that they believe made the United States what it is. The products cast from the stream of the southern migration are darker and more varied—the dreaded "multicultural" other—than the sterling variety imagined to be quintessentially and indispensably "American." Critics argue that this darker coinage threatens the very meaning of the United States as a nation. A patchwork and incoherent national debate has emerged out of these propositions. Is it true that the melting pot in fact no longer "works?" If the melting pot does not work, what are the implications? Should the United States stem the tide or celebrate diversity?

One need not have the answers to these questions to understand that the use of Latino gangs as a stalking horse is intellectually dishonest—because so removed from the facts of immigrant criminality—and is only slightly less offensive than the racist predicates of the American immigration policy that discriminated against "Southern Europeans" in the last century. (Ironically, some of the descendants of these erstwhile "threats" to the American soul—the grandchildren of Italians, Greeks, Spaniards, and other "Mediterranean types"—are busy minting new versions of the old arguments, as if their forebears stepped off of the *Mayflower* itself.) If anti-immigrant advocates do not like Latino social or political culture, let them be honest enough to say so and say why. But please let them not pretend that the "inherent" criminality or "violent nature" of Latin Americans, supposedly made tangible in Latino gangs, is the wellspring of their wish to slam shut the golden door.

The second confrontation needed—one more directly related to gangs and their criminality—is an honest look into what U.S. national polity has become with respect to crime and criminals in general and gangs in particular. One might fairly conclude that U.S. national policy differs from the often-criticized Mano Dura policies of Central American governments only in degree, not in character. We in the United States talk a lot about prevention and intervention, but in reality, we have off-loaded the problem of street gangs for all intents and purposes to our law enforcement agencies. These state instruments are infinitely better funded, more efficient, and more effective than those of our poor southern neighbors. Gangsters in the United States also enjoy the benefit of a criminal justice system—courts and prosecutors—that by and large respects the primacy of law over arbitrary action. Our prisons are somewhat less nightmarish. We do not have vigilante death squads. But, in essence, we as a nation act on the widely endorsed premise that crime is a question of personal morality and can and should be dealt with as a police matter, not by social engineering. Put another way, the way in which we deal with gangs would look very different if the basis of our national policy included the premises that every child should have a sound and efficient education, that every drug addict should have access to effective treatment, that every person willing to work should have a job, and that prisons should rehabilitate (not warehouse) offenders.

Whether the "police state" approach, the "welfare state" approach, or a more balanced blend of the two would ultimately result in a safer and more stable society is by no means an answered question. The current approach may be politically penny-wise but culturally pound-foolish. One can easily construct a notional future or thought exercise in which the arcs of street gangs and drug abuse and trafficking, prison warehousing and offender reentry, transnational criminal and perhaps terrorist organizations, and weakened democratic governments to the south converge in such a way as to result in extraordinary criminality, violence, and disorder within the United States.

Putting aside the idea of confronting ourselves and our national character, what "practical" steps might be suggested? If we continue to rely on law enforcement as our principal means of dealing with gangs, then we should be "in for a dime, in for a dollar." This means consistently allocating the resources necessary to do effective gang suppression at every level—local, state, and federal. Low-grade on-again, off-again antigang programs are like incomplete antibiotic regimens. Taking a lower dose than that prescribed or quitting before the infection is eradicated only strengthens the infecting organism and makes it more resistant to the next round. The gang organism likewise adapts. The single most frequent complaint that I heard from federal agents and local law enforcement officers alike is that commitment to fighting street gangs is episodic and subject to "reallocation" with the next "fad" crime.

Beyond law enforcement, it seems obvious that our national immigration policy needs to be rationalized. The economic and cultural stabilization of Latino immigrant populations is fundamental to the building of communities willing to come forward, cooperate with law enforcement, and confront the gangsters within their midst. Hounding ten million (more or less) undocumented immigrants into fearful hiding and breaking up their families cannot help construct such communities. The putatively "antigang" and "anticriminal" sweeps in which ICE specializes are the lowest grade of antibiotic being administered today, ensuring little in the long term but relocation of the infection and its resurgence elsewhere.

So where does the answer lie? Is it in community programs of prevention and intervention, like the challenge program that gave Daniel Ochoa a chance at a new life? Or is it in tough foot-on-the-neck gang suppression, like Miami-Dade's MAGTF, the FBI's National MS-13 Gang Task Force, and RICO prosecutions?

The fate of the early Cuban youth gangs lends a supporting model to advocates of prevention and intervention programs, demonstrating, on the face of it, that gangs can disappear if youth have real alternatives. The unique Cuban experience in the Miami area, however, has only limited applicability to the problem of entrenched street gangs in severely and chronically marginalized communities like those of Los Angeles, Chicago, and entire Central American nations. It is difficult to see how a local gang intervention or prevention program on a scale that might be funded in today's political climate could reverse such global phenomena as the decline of manufacturing, the rise of service industries, and the export of jobs. Even if Congress decided to fund prevention and intervention programs, unless they were created on a scale rivaling that of the Marshall Plan for reconstructing Europe after World War II, could such programs achieve results comparable to what happened to Miami's early Cuban gangs?

Even given such an unlikely commitment and real funds, what would be the specific elements of such plans? What viable enterprises could be created to ensure not just make-work jobs but real ladders of opportunity? What educational facilities would be needed to provide the skills and abilities needed to be successful in those jobs? At the same time, how would the multibillion-dollar illicit drug industry be shut down or, at a minimum, unhooked from its primary retail distribution network, the street gangs? What would be done about the constant influx of illegal aliens that perpetuates the marginality of entire communities and vast numbers of youth, as in East Los Angeles?

In sum, the problem of Latino street gangs is not something that stands apart from some of the deepest problems of American society generally. It is, rather, woven tightly into the most fundamental challenges that the nation faces in law, culture, and economics. The degree of economic foresight and social engineering required for such a happy end as the elimination of street gangs is staggering—even if one were persuaded that the nation would support such government engineering.

Nonetheless, *la esperanza nunca muere* (hope never dies). One may hope that out of the controlled collision of our national debate about the knot of these problems, some useful initiatives will emerge. If they do not, we are in for a long and violent ride.

NOTES

INTRODUCTION

1. The story of the Houston shootout is based on the following sources: interviews with FBI special agents Bob Clifford and Brian Ritchie (the latter by telephone); Houston Police Department, "Incident at 5709 Liberty Road," news release, November 4, 2005; Monica Guzman, "Federal SWAT Team Kills 2 Men in Anti-gang Initiative," *Houston Chronicle*, November 5, 2005; Kevin Johnson, "MS-13 Gang Growing Extremely Dangerous, FBI Says," *USA Today*, January 6, 2006.

2. Johnson, "MS-13 Gang Growing Extremely Dangerous."

3. Rubén G. Rumbaut et al., "Debunking the Myth of Immigrant Criminality: Imprisonment among First- and Second-Generation Young Men, " *Migration Information Source*, June 2006, http://www.migrationinformation.org/Feature/display.cfm?id=403.

4. Randall G. Shelden, Sharon K. Tracy, William B. Brown, *Youth Gangs in American Society*, 2nd ed. (Belmont, CA: Wadsworth, 2001), 26.

5. Finn-Aage Esbensen et al., "Youth Gangs and Definitional Issues: When Is a Gang a Gang, and Why Does It Matter?" in *American Youth Gangs at the Millennium*, ed. Finn-Aage Esbensen, Stephen G. Tibbetts, and Larry Gaines (Long Grove, IL: Waveland, 2004), 53.

6. U.S. Department of Justice, *Attorney General's Report to Congress on the Growth of Violent Street Gangs in Suburban Areas* (Washington, DC, 2008), 4.

7. Jordan Rau, "Democrats Stake Out Turf War on Gangs," *Los Angeles Times,* March 16, 2007.

8. Richard C. McCorkle and Terance D. Miethe, "The Political and Organizational Response to Gangs: An Examination of a 'Moral Panic' in Nevada," in Finn-Aage Esbensen, Tibbetts, and Gaines, *American Youth Gangs at the Millennium,* 302.

9. McCorkle and Miethe, "Political and Organizational Response to Gangs," 318.

CHAPTER I

The epigraph is from Associated Press, "Refugee Children Escape Bullets, but Not Memories," November 7, 1983.

1. U.S. Department of State, Bureau of Western Hemisphere Affairs, "Background Note: El Salvador," 2007, http://www.state.gov/r/pa/ei/bgn/2033.htm; U.S. Department of Defense, "DOD 101: An Introductory Overview of the Department of Defense," http://www.defenselink.mil/pubs/dod101/.

2. *Little brown brother* was a term Americans used to refer to Filipinos during colonial rule of the islands by the United States. The term was coined by Governor-General William Howard Taft, who later became president of the United States. Author O. Henry coined the phrase *banana republic* to refer specifically to Honduras but generally to small Latin American countries—poor, small, and ruled by military juntas.

3. *Merriam-Webster's Collegiate Dictionary,* 10th ed. (Springfield, MA: Merriam-Webster, 2000).

4. Andrew M. Grascia, "Hispanic Gangs: A Growing Trend," presentation at the National Summit on Gang Violence, Arlington, VA, June 1, 2006.

5. Charles M. Katz and Vincent J. Webb, *Policing Gangs in America* (New York: Cambridge University Press, 2006), 2.

6. Daryl F. Gates, *Chief: My Life in the LAPD,* with Diane K. Shah (New York: Bantam, 1992), 292.

7. Telephone interview with Spencer Eth (professor of psychiatry, New York Medical College, and medical director, Behavioral Health Services, St. Vincent Catholic Medical Centers), June 16, 2006.

8. Matthew J. Friedman, "Posttraumatic Stress Disorder: An Overview," U.S. Department of Veterans Affairs, National Center for Posttraumatic Stress Disorder, http://www.ncptsd.va.gov/ncmain/ncdocs/fact_shts/fsptsd_overview prof.html?opm=1&rr=rr14&srt=d&echorr=true.

9. Friedman, "Posttraumatic Stress Disorder."

10. "DSM-IV and DSM-IV-TR: Posttraumatic Stress Disorder (PTSD)," BehaveNet Clinical Capsule, http://www.behavenet.com/capsule/disorders/ptsd.htm.

11. Wikipedia identifies the *DSM* as "the handbook most often used in diagnosing mental disorders in the United States" ("Diagnostic and Statistical Manual of Mental Disorders." http://en.wikipedia.org/wiki/Diagnostic_and_Statistical_Manual_of_Mental_Disorders).

12. William Arroyo and Spencer Eth, "Children Traumatized by Central American Warfare," in *Post-Traumatic Stress Disorder in Children*, ed. Spencer Eth and Robert S. Pynoos (Washington: American Psychiatric Press, 1985), 103.

13. Telephone interview with Spencer Eth.

14. Jan Ziegler, "Shell Shock Has a Fancy Name," United Press International, October 17, 1983.

15. Elissa P. Benedek, "Children and Psychic Trauma: A Brief Review of Contemporary Thinking," in Eth and Pynoos, *Post-Traumatic Stress Disorder in Children*, 11.

16. Aric Press, Don Waitt, and Rick Wassner, "War Echoes in the Courts," *Newsweek*, November 23, 1981, 103.

17. Telephone interview with Spencer Eth.

18. Benedek, "Children and Psychic Trauma," 4.

19. Telephone interview with Spencer Eth.

20. Katz and Webb, *Policing Gangs in America*, 6.

21. Telephone interview with William Arroyo (director of children's mental health services, Los Angeles County Department of Mental Health, and clinical assistant professor of psychiatry, University of Southern California School of Medicine), June 21, 2006.

22. Peter H. King, "Medical Marvel; Care Amid the Chaos at County-USC," *Los Angeles Times*, January 27, 1985.

23. King, "Medical Marvel; Care Amid the Chaos."

24. Anne C. Roark, "A Science Honed on Violence," *Los Angeles Times*, February 15, 1990.

25. Roark, "A Science Honed on Violence." Later renamed Martin Luther King Jr.–Harbor Hospital, the hospital closed in August 2007, financially starved, tangled in racial politics, and scorned for its poor standards of medical care. A score of financially strapped private hospitals were left to pick up the forty-seven thousand patients who had used its public emergency room in 2006 (Daniel Costello, "Fiscal Woes Jeopardize Area Hospitals," *Los Angeles Times*, September 23, 2007).

26. Tony Perry, "Medical Move Cuts Combat Deaths in Iraq, Navy Reports," *Los Angeles Times*, October 1, 2003.

27. George Tita and Alan Abrahamse, "Gang Homicide in LA, 1981–2001," *At the Local Level: Perspectives on Violence Prevention* (California Attorney General's Office, Sacramento) 3 (February 2004): 2.

28. Tita and Abrahamse, "Gang Homicide in LA," 16.

29. Hector Becerra, "Taste of Combat at County-USC," *Los Angeles Times,* March 8, 2003.

30. Becerra, "Taste of Combat at County-USC."

31. Becerra, "Taste of Combat at County-USC."

32. Perry, "Medical Move Cuts Combat Deaths in Iraq."

33. Telephone interview with William Arroyo.

34. Patrice Gaines-Carter, "Salvadoran Pupils Here 'Still at War,'" *Washington Post,* October 15, 1985.

35. Telephone interview with Spencer Eth.

36. Eth and Pynoos, *Post-Traumatic Stress Disorder in Children.*

37. Telephone interview with Spencer Eth.

38. Dennis Anderson, "Nightmares and Culture Shock Torment Children Who Sought Refuge in U.S.," United Press International, March 17, 1984.

39. See the discussion of "primary agents of social control" in James Diego Vigil, *A Rainbow of Gangs: Street Cultures in the Mega-City* (Austin: University of Texas Press, 2002), 7–8.

40. *Washington Monthly* reports, "Over a period of about five years, [President Ronald Wilson] Reagan told the story of the 'Chicago welfare queen' who had 80 names, 30 addresses, 12 Social Security cards, and collected benefits for 'four nonexisting deceased husbands,' bilking the government out of 'over $150,000.' The real welfare recipient to whom Reagan referred was actually convicted for using two different aliases to collect $8,000. Reagan continued to use his version of the story even after the press pointed out the actual facts of the case to him" ("The Mendacity Index," 2003, http://www.washington monthly.com/features/2003/0309.mendacity-index.html).

41. Constance L. Rice, "L.A.'s Budding Mogadishus—Nearly Feral Areas Need Help," *Los Angeles Times,* December 23, 2004, op-ed.

42. Katz and Webb, *Policing Gangs in America,* 11.

43. Anderson, "Nightmares and Culture Shock Torment Children."

44. Associated Press, "Refugee Children Escape Bullets, but Not Memories."

45. Benjamin Schwartz, review of *Our Own Backyard: The United States in Central America, 1977–1992,* by William LeoGrande, *Atlantic Monthly,* December 1998.

46. See, e.g., "Maras, El Fruto Envenenado," *El Mercurio* (Ecuador), September 26, 2005.

47. *Oxford Spanish Dictionary,* 3rd ed. (New York: Oxford University Press, 2003).

48. *Diccionario Esencial Santillana de la Lengua Española* (Madrid: Santillana, S.A., 1991).

49. Vigil, *A Rainbow of Gangs,* 142.

50. A forum discussion on WordReference.com explains, "Este palabra existe en Guatemala desde los 70s, si bien tenia un connotación amistosa y jovial. Irse con la 'mara' era irse con los muchachos, los amigos; La mara era un grupo de chicos, alegres y bullangueros. Poco después, ser 'marero' era lo mismo que ser delincuente, degenerado, pervertido, antisocial, sociopata, etc." ("'Mara' or 'maras' (gang or gangs)," http://forum.wordreference.com/showthread.php?t=66613).

51. Wikipedia, "Killer Ant," http://en.wikipedia.org/wiki/Killer_ant (accessed July 1, 2006).

52. Bert Holldobler and Edward O. Wilson, *Journey to the Ants: A Story of Scientific Exploration* (Cambridge, MA: Belknap, 1994),163.

53. The modern history of El Salvador has been a contentious matter in the United States, primarily because of strongly divided opinion about the role and necessity of U.S. military support for the government during the civil war in the 1980s. Except where otherwise specifically noted, the brief summary of that history in this chapter is drawn from the following sources: Richard A. Haggerty, ed., *A Country Study: El Salvador,* 2nd ed. (Washington, DC: Library of Congress, Federal Research Division, 1990), http://lcweb2.loc.gov/frd/cs/svtoc.html; Benjamin Schwartz, review of *Our Own Backyard;* Thomas E. Skidmore and Peter H. Smith, *Modern Latin America,* 6th ed. (New York: Oxford University Press, 2005), 382–89; PBS, "El Salvador," *Enemies of War,* http://www.pbs.org/itvs/enemiesofwar/elsalvador.html; UN Security Council, Annex, *From Madness to Hope: The 12-Year War in El Salvador: Report of the Commission on the Truth for El Salvador,* S/25500, March 15, 1993; Robert Armstrong and Janet Shenk, *El Salvador: The Face of Revolution* (Boston: South End, 1982).

54. Stephen C. Johnson, "Latin America's Security Puzzle," statement before the House Committee on Armed Services, September 21, 2005, http://www.house.gov/hasc/CDR/Johnson21Sep05.pdf.

55. "Countries of the World by Highest Population Density," WorldAtlas.com, http://worldatlas.com/aatlas/populations/ctydensityl.htm.

56. PBS, "El Salvador."

57. PBS, "El Salvador."

58. U.S. Agency for International Development, *Central America and Mexico Gang Assessment* (Washington, DC, 2006), annex 1, "El Salvador Profile," 44.

59. UN Security Council, *From Madness to Hope,* 10.

60. Gaines-Carter, "Salvadoran Pupils Here 'Still at War.'"

61. Associated Press, "Refugee Children Escape Bullets, but Not Memories."

62. Arroyo and Eth, "Children Traumatized by Central American Warfare," 110–15.

63. Schwartz, review of *Our Own Backyard*.

64. Schwartz, review of *Our Own Backyard*.

65. Carey McWilliams, *Southern California: An Island of the Land* (Layton, UT: Gibbs Smith, 1973), 13.

66. President Ronald Reagan used both phrases to contrast the values of America against those of the Soviet Union: "I've thought a bit of the 'shining city upon a hill.' The phrase comes from John Winthrop, who wrote it to describe the America he imagined. What he imagined was important because he was an early Pilgrim, an early freedom man. He journeyed here on what today we'd call a little wooden boat; and like the other Pilgrims, he was looking for a home that would be free. I've spoken of the shining city all my political life" (farewell address, January 11, 1989, http://www.millercenter.virginia.edu/scripps/digitalarchive/speeches/detail/3418); "I urge you to beware the temptation of pride—the temptation of blithely declaring yourselves above it all and label both sides equally at fault, to ignore the facts of history and the aggressive impulses of an evil empire" (speech to the National Association of Evangelicals, March 8, 1983, http://www.millercenter.virginia.edu/scripps/digitalarchive/speeches/detail/3409).

67. For a survey of these waves, see Carlos B. Cordova, "Causes of Salvadoran and Central American Emigration and Waves of Migration," in *The Salvadoran Americans* (Westport, CT: Greenwood, 2005), 55–68.

68. Cordova, "Causes of Salvadoran and Central American Emigration," 64–66.

69. Vigil, *A Rainbow of Gangs*, 132.

70. Daniel J. Tichenor, *Dividing Lines: The Politics of Immigration Control in America* (Princeton: Princeton University Press, 2002), 266.

71. Norma Chinchilla and Nora Hamilton, "Changing Networks and Alliances in a Transnational Context: Salvadoran and Guatemalan Immigrants in Southern California," *Social Justice* 26, no. 3 (1999): 4.

72. David W. Haines, ed., *Refugees in America in the 1990s: A Reference Handbook* (Westport, CT: Greenwood, 1966), 345.

73. Ricardo Guevara, "'El faraón' del montículo," *El Diario de Hoy,* October 17, 2000, http://www.elsalvador.com/noticias/EDICIONESANTERIORES/2000/OCTUBRE/octubre17/VIDA/.

74. Ross Gelbspan, *Break-ins, Death Threats, and the FBI: The Covert War against the Central America Movement* (Boston: South End, 1991), 35–36; "El Salvador," *BBC Summary of World Broadcasts*, April 4, 1980.

75. Cordova, *Salvadoran Americans*, 75.

76. Judith Cummings, "The World of the Immigrant: Low-Paying Jobs and Overcrowded Housing," *New York Times*, April 13, 1987.

77. Chinchilla and Hamilton, "Changing Networks and Alliances in a Transnational Context."

78. Joan W. Moore, *Going Down to the Barrio: Homeboys and Homegirls in Change* (Philadelphia: Temple University Press, 1991), 19 n.13.

79. Greg Schneider and Renae Merle, "Reagan's Defense Buildup Bridges Military Eras," *Washington Post*, June 9, 2004. Stated in 2005 dollars, defense spending rose to $456.5 billion in 1987 from $325.1 billion in 1980.

80. Norma Chinchilla, Nora Hamilton, and James Loucky, "Central Americans in Los Angeles: An Immigrant Community in Transition," in *In The Barrios: Latinos and the Underclass Debate,* ed. Joan Moore and Raquel Pinderhughes (New York: Russell Sage Foundation, 1993), 61.

81. John Johnson, "War Refugees Form Deadly L.A. Gangs," *Los Angeles Times*, December 17, 1989.

CHAPTER 2

The epigraph is from Octavio Paz, *The Labyrinth of Solitude, The Other Mexico, and Other Essays* (New York: Grove, 1985), 11.

1. Paul Weyrich, "Border Security: Drawing 'a Line in the Sand,'" *Townhall,* October 26, 2006, http://www.townhall.com/Columnists/PaulWeyrich/2006/10/26/border_security_drawing_a_line_in_the_sand.

2. Rubén G. Rumbaut et al., "Debunking the Myth of Immigrant Criminality: Imprisonment among First- and Second-Generation Young Men," *Migration Information Source,* June 2006, http://www.migrationinformation.org/Feature/display.cfm?id=403.

3. Myron Magnet, "City Journal Writers Long Sympathetic to Immigration's Economic and Social Benefits Have Turned against Illegal Immigration with a Vengeance," *American Spectator,* December 2007.

4. Patrick J. Buchanan, "Can the GOP Be Saved? Perhaps," *Human Events,* September 5, 2006, http://www.humanevents.com/article.php?id=16852.

5. Terence Jeffrey, "Americans Want the Border Secured Now," *Human Events,* September 25, 2006, http://www.humanevents.com/article.php?id=17181.

6. William D. Carrigan, "The Lynching of Persons of Mexican Origin or Descent in the United States, 1848 to 1928," *Journal of Social History* 37, no. 2 (2003). For an in-depth examination of the theme, see Patricia Nelson Limerick, *The Legacy of Conquest: The Unbroken Past of the American West* (New York: W. W. Norton, 1987).

7. Tomas Almaguer, *Racial Fault Lines: The Historical Origins of White Supremacy in California* (Berkeley: University of California Press, 1994), 29, 71.

8. U.S. Bureau of the Census, "More than 300 Counties Now 'Majority-Mi-

nority,'" press release, August 9, 2007, http://www.census.gov/Press-Release/www/releases/archives/population/010482.html.

9. Hector Tobar, "Voices from the First Generation: The Ramirez and Hernandez Families," *Los Angeles Times,* November 5, 1989; John Johnson, "War Refugees Form Deadly L.A. Gangs," *Los Angeles Times,* December 17, 1989.

10. James Diego Vigil, *A Rainbow of Gangs: Street Cultures in the Mega-City* (Austin: University of Texas Press, 2002), 141.

11. James Diego Vigil, *Barrio Gangs: Street Life and Identity in Southern California* (Austin: University of Texas Press, 1988), 7.

12. Quotes of Detective Frank Flores and stories from his life are based on personal interviews, e-mail exchanges, and telephone conversations with him on several dates throughout 2007.

13. Ruben Martinez, "East Side Stories: Joseph Rodriguez's Images of East L.A.," in *East Side Stories: Gang Life in East L.A.,* by Joseph Rodriguez and Ruben Martinez (New York: powerHouse, 2000), 14.

14. Jerry Pacheco, "Juarez: Growing City with Many Issues," *Albuquerque Journal,* April 23, 2007.

15. Manuel Roig-Franzia, "Waning Hopes in Juarez; After Murders of Hundreds of Women, Statute of Limitations Takes Hold," *Washington Post,* May 14, 2007; Associated Press, "Inquiry on Juarez Slayings Closed; Federal Officials in Mexico Have Returned the Unsolved Cases to State Authorities," *Los Angeles Times,* July 26, 2006.

16. Scott Gold, "School Takeover Views Mixed," *Los Angeles Times,* April 23, 2006. In 2002, only 39 percent of Latino students in the Los Angeles Unified School District graduated high school (Erika Hayasaki and Erica Williams, "Staying the Course at L.A.'s Urban High Schools," *Los Angeles Times,* March 25, 2005).

17. Rodriguez and Martinez, *East Side Stories.*

18. Martinez, "East Side Stories," 19.

19. Vigil, *A Rainbow of Gangs,* 7.

20. Vigil, *A Rainbow of Gangs,* 8.

21. Martinez, "East Side Stories," 18.

22. Vigil, *A Rainbow of Gangs,* 8.

23. Vigil, *Barrio Gangs,* 39.

24. Rumbaut et al., "Debunking the Myth of Immigrant Criminality."

25. Rumbaut et al., "Debunking the Myth of Immigrant Criminality."

26. Vigil, *Barrio Gangs,* 25.

27. Vigil, *Barrio Gangs,* 39.

28. Vigil, *Barrio Gangs,* 2.

29. David J. Weber, ed., *Foreigners in Their Native Land: Historical Roots of the Mexican American* (Albuquerque: University of New Mexico Press, 1973), 96.

30. Douglas V. Meed, *The Mexican War, 1846–48* (New York: Routledge, 2003), 88.

31. Manuel G. Gonzales, *Mexicanos: A History of Mexicans in the United States* (Bloomington: Indiana University Press, 1999), 82.

32. The origin of the derogatory term *greaser* is obscure. Noted California chronicler Carey McWilliams thought it had to do with the stinking hides and tallow that Mexican laborers carried on their backs into the holds of sailing ships (*Southern California: An Island of the Land* [Layton, UT: Gibbs Smith, 1973], 57). Others thought that it originated in reference to the Indian practice of anointing their skin, the supposed similarity between grease and the skin tones of Mexicans, or the "dirty, greasy" appearance of darker-skinned Mexicans in the eyes of Anglos. See Arnoldo DeLéon, *They Called Them Greasers: Anglo Attitudes toward Mexicans in Texas, 1821–1900* (Austin: University of Texas Press, 1983), 16.

33. Limerick, *Legacy of Conquest*, 227.

34. Almaguer, *Racial Fault Lines*, 26.

35. McWilliams, *Southern California*, 52.

36. Almaguer, *Racial Fault Lines*, 212.

37. Gonzales, *Mexicanos*, 82.

38. Almaguer, *Racial Fault Lines*, 46.

39. Gustavo Arellano, "Brown Pride," *LA Weekly,* January 12–18, 2007, 20.

40. Robert F. Heizer and Alan J. Almquist, *The Other Californians: Prejudice and Discrimination under Spain, Mexico, and the United States to 1920* (Berkeley: University of California Press, 1971), 202.

41. Reginald Horsman, *Race and Manifest Destiny: The Origins of American Racial Anglo-Saxonism* (Cambridge, MA: Harvard University Press, 1981), 6.

42. Gonzales, *Mexicanos*, 83.

43. Limerick, *Legacy of Conquest*, 46 (Indian land), 231–32, 240–41 (Mexican land).

44. Horsman, *Race and Manifest Destiny*, 208.

45. Horsman, *Race and Manifest Destiny*, 4.

46. Almaguer, *Racial Fault Lines*, 55.

47. Limerick, *Legacy of Conquest*, 247.

48. See, generally, Clara E. Rodriguez, *Changing Race: Latinos, the Census, and the History of Ethnicity in the United States* (New York: New York University Press, 2000).

49. Limerick, *Legacy of Conquest*, 247.

50. Almaguer, *Racial Fault Lines*, 46.

51. Edward J. Escobar, *Race, Police, and the Making of a Political Identity: Mexican Americans and the Los Angeles Police Department, 1900–1945* (Berkeley: University of California Press, 1999), 8.

52. Limerick, *Legacy of Conquest*, 239.

53. McWilliams, *Southern California*, 65.

54. Heizer and Almquist, *Other Californians*, 141.

55. Limerick, *Legacy of Conquest*, 239.

56. Gonzales, *Mexicanos*, 85.

57. McWilliams, *Southern California*, 4.

58. Heizer and Almquist, *Other Californians*, 150.

59. Gonzales, *Mexicanos*, 88.

60. Heizer and Almquist, *Other Californians*, 144.

61. Gonzales, *Mexicanos*, 86.

62. Heizer and Almquist, *Other Californians*, 126.

63. Heizer and Almquist, *Other Californians*, 149.

64. Gonzales, *Mexicanos*, 86–87.

65. Heizer and Almquist, *Other Californians*, 147.

66. Carrigan, "Lynching of Persons of Mexican Origin."

67. *Oxford Spanish Dictionary*, 3rd ed. (New York: Oxford University Press, 2003).

68. "History of the LAPD," http://www.lapdonline.org/history_of_the_lapd.

69. Gonzales, *Mexicanos*, 85.

70. Carrigan, "Lynching of Persons of Mexican Origin."

71. McWilliams, *Southern California*, 60.

72. Heizer and Almquist, *Other Californians*, 128, 131.

73. Heizer and Almquist, *Other Californians*, 151.

74. Gonzales, *Mexicanos*, 88.

75. McWilliams, *Southern California*, 61.

76. Heizer and Almquist, *Other Californians*, 147.

77. Gonzales, *Mexicanos*, 89.

78. Limerick, *Legacy of Conquest*, 240.

79. McWilliams, *Southern California*, 69.

80. Limerick, *Legacy of Conquest*, 240.

81. Gonzales, *Mexicanos*, 114–21.

82. Gonzales, *Mexicanos*, 113.

83. McWilliams, *Southern California*, 317.

84. Limerick, *Legacy of Conquest*, 244; Escobar, *Race, Police, and the Making of a Political Identity*, 95–96; Gonzales, *Mexicanos*, 123–25.

85. Escobar, *Race, Police, and the Making of a Political Identity*, 9.

86. Joan W. Moore, *Homeboys: Gangs, Drugs, and Prison in the Barrios of Los Angeles* (Philadelphia: Temple University Press, 1978), 13–14.

CHAPTER 3

The epigraph is from Jeff Cooper, "Cooper's Corner," *Guns & Ammo*, April 1991, 104.

1. *People v. Leon,* 2006 Cal. App. Unpub. Lexis 10888 (Ct. App. 2006).

2. Notes on photographs in Joseph Rodriguez and Ruben Martinez, *East Side Stories: Gang Life in East L.A.* (New York: powerHouse, 2000), 122.

3. "New Injunction Targets One of Los Angeles' Oldest Street Gangs," City News Service (Southern California), August 25, 2004.

4. *People v. Holguin,* 213 Cal.App.3d 1308 (Ct. App. 1989); *People v. Nava,* 2007 Cal. App. Unpub. Lexis 3057 (Ct. App. 2007); *People v. Curiel,* 2006 Cal. App. Unpub. Lexis 232 (Ct. App. 2006); *People v. Medrano,* 2005 Cal. App. Unpub. Lexis 5388 (Ct. App. 2005); *People v. Villalobos,* 2003 Cal. App. Unpub. Lexis 5443 (Ct. App. 2003); *People v. Sosa,* 2002 Cal. App. Unpub. Lexis 7847 (Ct. App. 2002); *People v. Alvarez,* 2002 Cal. App. Unpub. Lexis 7382 (Ct. App. 2002); *People v. Castro,* 2002 Cal. App. Unpub. Lexis 6552 (Ct. App. 2002).

5. Art Marroquin, "Wanted Gang Member Caught," City News Service (Southern California), July 19, 2007.

6. "New Injunction Targets One of Los Angeles' Oldest Street Gangs," City News Service (Southern California), August 25, 2004.

7. William Dunn, *The Gangs of Los Angeles* (Lincoln, NE: iUniverse, 2007), 63–64.

8. *People v. Zammora,* 66 Cal.App.2d (Ct. App. 1944).

9. Dunn, *Gangs of Los Angeles,* 79.

10. Manuel G. Gonzales, *Mexicanos: A History of Mexicans in the United States* (Bloomington: Indiana University Press, 1999), 168.

11. Eduardo Obregon Pagan, *Murder at the Sleepy Lagoon: Zoot Suits, Race, and Riot in Wartime L.A.* (Chapel Hill: University of North Carolina Press, 2003), 55.

12. Gonzales, *Mexicanos,* 143.

13. Joe Domanick, *To Protect and to Serve: The LAPD's Century of War in the City of Dreams* (Los Angeles: Figueroa, 2003), 32.

14. Joan W. Moore, *Homeboys: Gangs, Drugs, and Prison in the Barrios of Los Angeles* (Philadelphia: Temple University Press, 1978), 17.

15. Joan W. Moore, *Going Down to the Barrio: Homeboys and Homegirls in Change* (Philadelphia: Temple University Press, 1991), 18.

16. Gonzales, *Mexicanos,* 137.

17. Gonzales, *Mexicanos,* 138.

18. Moore, *Going Down to the Barrio,* 18.

19. James Diego Vigil, *Barrio Gangs: Street Life and Identity in Southern California* (Austin: University of Texas Press, 1988) 5–6.

20. Patricia Nelson Limerick, *The Legacy of Conquest: The Unbroken Past of the American West* (New York: W. W. Norton, 1987), 245.

21. Moore, *Going Down to the Barrio,* 12.

22. Dunn, *Gangs of Los Angeles,* 31.

23. Ruben Martinez, "East Side Stories: Joseph Rodriguez's Images of East L.A.," in Rodriguez and Martinez, *East Side Stories*, 14.

24. Vigil, *Barrio Gangs*, 3, 5.

25. Dunn, *Gangs of Los Angeles*, 39.

26. Dunn, *Gangs of Los Angeles*, 39.

27. Moore, *Going Down to the Barrio*, 26.

28. Bob Baker, "Deeply Rooted in L.A.; Chicano Gangs: A History of Violence," *Los Angeles Times*, December 11, 1988.

29. Moore, *Going Down to the Barrio*, 25.

30. Dunn, *Gangs of Los Angeles*, 39.

31. Moore, *Homeboys*, 57.

32. Moore, *Going Down to the Barrio*, 31.

33. Moore, *Going Down to the Barrio*, 60.

34. Vigil, *Barrio Gangs*, 130.

35. Moore, *Homeboys*, 65–66.

36. Dunn, *Gangs of Los Angeles*, 57–58.

37. Edward J. Escobar, *Race, Police, and the Making of a Political Identity: Mexican Americans and the Los Angeles Police Department, 1900–1945* (Berkeley: University of California Press, 1999), 156.

38. Gonzales, *Mexicanos*, 166.

39. George J. Sanchez, *Becoming Mexican American: Ethnicity, Culture, and Identity in Chicano Los Angeles* (New York: Oxford University Press, 1995), 264.

40. Vigil, *Barrio Gangs*, 39–40.

41. Moore, *Homeboys*, 37.

42. Gonzales, *Mexicanos*, 166.

43. Moore, *Homeboys*, 37.

44. Gonzales, *Mexicanos*, 167.

45. Moore, *Homeboys*, 59.

46. Pagan, *Murder at the Sleepy Lagoon*, 37.

47. Moore, *Homeboys*, 62.

48. Sanchez, *Becoming Mexican American*, 265.

49. Pagan, *Murder at the Sleepy Lagoon*, 39.

50. Sanchez, *Becoming Mexican American*, 265.

51. Pagan, *Murder at the Sleepy Lagoon*, 100.

52. Domanick, *To Protect and to Serve: The LAPD's Century of War*, 137.

53. Moore, *Homeboys*, 64.

54. Vigil, *Barrio Gangs*, 40.

55. Dunn, *Gangs of Los Angeles*, 63.

56. Cecilia Rasmussen, "The City Then and Now: Where Latino March toward Justice Began," *Los Angeles Times*, April 24, 1995.

57. O'Melveny and Myers, "Company History," http://www.fundinguni
verse.com/company-histories/OMelveny-amp;-Myers-Company-History.html.

58. Pagan, *Murder at the Sleepy Lagoon*, 62.

59. "Zoot Suit Riots," *American Experience*, PBS, 2001, transcript, http://
www.pbs.org/wgbh/amex/zoot/eng_filmmore/pt.html.

60. Pagan, *Murder at the Sleepy Lagoon*, 224–26.

61. Pagan, *Murder at the Sleepy Lagoon*, 56.

62. Sanchez, *Becoming Mexican American*, 266.

63. William Triplett, "Gang Crisis," *CQ Researcher*, May 14, 2004, 424.

64. Richard C. McCorkle and Terance D. Miethe, "The Political and Organizational Response to Gangs: An Examination of a 'Moral Panic' in Nevada,"
in *American Youth Gangs at the Millennium*, ed. Finn-Aage Esbensen, Stephen
G. Tibbetts, and Larry Gaines (Long Grove, IL: Waveland, 2004).

65. Gebe Martinez, "Speaker Tries to Debunk Stereotypes of Latino Gangs,"
Los Angeles Times, November 8, 1992.

66. Escobar, *Race, Police, and the Making of a Political Identity*, 6.

67. Escobar, *Race, Police, and the Making of a Political Identity*, 32.

68. Escobar, *Race, Police, and the Making of a Political Identity*, 28.

69. Moore, *Homeboys*, 59.

70. Escobar, *Race, Police, and the Making of a Political Identity*, 157–60.

71. Robert M. Fogelson, *Big-City Police* (Cambridge, MA: Harvard University Press, 1977), 54.

72. Ed. Duran Ayres, "Statistics: The Nature of the Mexican American Criminal," Online Archive of California, http://content.cdlib.org/ark:/13030/
hb6m3nb79m/.

73. For a complete discussion of the history and development of this view, see
Escobar, *Race, Police, and the Making of a Political Identity*.

74. Gonzales, *Mexicanos*, 169.

75. Domanick, *To Protect and to Serve: The LAPD's Century of War*, 137.

76. Moore, *Homeboys*, 62.

77. Al Valdez, "A History of California's Hispanic Gangs," National Alliance of Gang Investigators' Associations, 1998, http://www.nagia.org/
Gang%20Articles/Hispanic%20Gangs.htm.

78. Dunn, *Gangs of Los Angeles*, 95.

79. Dunn, *Gangs of Los Angeles*, 97.

80. Moore, *Going Down to the Barrio*, 32.

81. Interview with LAPD detective Frank Flores, March 28, 2007.

82. Dunn, *Gangs of Los Angeles*, 151.

83. Dunn, *Gangs of Los Angeles*, 112–16.

84. "History of the LAPD," http:www.lapdonline.org/history_of_the_lapd.

85. Fogelson, *Big-City Police*, 187.

86. Robert C. Wadman and William Thomas Allison, *To Protect and to Serve: A History of Police in America* (Upper Saddle River, NJ: Pearson Prentice Hall, 2004), 143.

87. Daryl F. Gates, *Chief: My Life in the LAPD*, with Diane K. Shah (New York: Bantam, 1992), 34–35.

88. Domanick, *To Protect and To Serve: The LAPD's Century of War*, 111.

89. William J. Bratton, foreword to *Images of America: Los Angeles Police Department*, by Thomas G. Hays and Arthur W. Sjoquist (Charleston, SC: Arcadia), 6.

90. Matthew J. Hickman and Brian A. Reaves, *Local Police Departments, 2003* (Washington, DC: U.S. Department of Justice, Bureau of Justice Statistics, 2006), 2, exhibit 1.

91. "Los Angeles Almanac," http://www.laalmanac.com/geography/ge10.htm; "NYC Statistics," http://nycvisit.com/content/index.cfm?/pagePkey=57; Chicago Public Library, "Facts about Chicago," http://www.chipublib.org/cpl booksmovies/cplarchive/facts/index.php.

92. *Local Police Departments, 2003*; Miami-Dade Police, "MDPD Careers," http://www.miamidade.gov/mdpd/careers.asp.

93. Limerick, *Legacy of Conquest*, 221.

94. Bratton, foreword to *Images of America*, 6.

95. Lou Cannon, *Official Negligence: How Rodney King and the Riots Changed Los Angeles and the LAPD* (Boulder, CO: Westview, 1999), 64.

96. Wadman and Allison, *To Protect and to Serve: A History of Police in America*, 144.

97. Wadman and Allison, *To Protect and to Serve: A History of Police in America*, 144.

98. Fogelson, *Big-City Police*, 259.

99. Fogelson, *Big-City Police*, 260.

100. Domanick, *To Protect and to Serve: The LAPD's Century of War*, 111.

101. Cannon, *Official Negligence*, 18.

102. David Freed, "Policing Gangs: Case of Contrasting Styles," *Los Angeles Times*, January 19, 1986.

103. "Daryl Gates: L.A.P.D. History," *Frontline*, PBS, February 27, 2001, interview, http://www.pbs.org/wgbh/pages/frontline/shows/lapd/interviews/gates.html.

104. George Tita and Alan Abrahamse, "Gang Homicide in LA, 1981–2001," *At the Local Level: Perspectives on Violence Prevention* (California Attorney General's Office, Sacramento) 3 (February 2004).

105. H. Range Hutson et al., "The Epidemic of Gang-Related Homicides in Los Angeles County from 1979 through 1994," *Journal of the American Medical Association* 274, no. 13 (1995): 1031.

106. Moore, *Homeboys*, 40.

107. Moore, *Going Down to the Barrio,* 59.

108. Hutson et al., "Epidemic of Gang-Related Homicides."

109. Baker, "Deeply Rooted in L.A.; Chicano Gangs."

110. Hutson et al., "Epidemic of Gang-Related Homicides."

CHAPTER 4

The epigraph is from "Rodney King's Statement" in Richard A. Serrano, "Kings Case Aftermath: A City in Crisis," *Los Angeles Times,* May 2, 1992.

1. Lou Cannon, *Official Negligence: How Rodney King and the Riots Changed Los Angeles and the LAPD* (Boulder, CO: Westview, 1999), xx.

2. Tim Schreiner, "Simi Valley, South-Central L.A.—Sharp Contrasts," *San Francisco Chronicle,* May 1, 1992.

3. Jim Newton, "ACLU Says 83% of Police Live Outside L.A.," *Los Angeles Times,* March 29, 1994.

4. Schreiner, "Simi Valley, South-Central L.A."

5. "Rodney King," *Time,* April 25, 2007, http://www.time.com/time/specials/2007/la_riot/article/0,28804,1614117_1614084_1614831,00.html.

6. The quotes from Brian Truchon are based on interviews on June 20, 2006; September 28, 2006; and November 8, 2006, supplemented by several e-mail exchanges to clarify various specific points.

7. Aaron Betsky, "A Marriage of Convenience from the 'Systems Thinking' Generation," *Los Angeles Times,* August 12, 1993.

8. Hugo Martin, "Many Antelope Valley Drivers Still Going Solo," *Los Angeles Times,* June 22, 1992.

9. U.S. Department of Justice, Federal Bureau of Investigation, "FBI-Los Angeles," http://losangeles.fbi.gov/.

10. Sharon LaFraniere, "FBI to Seek More Funds to Fight Gang Violence," *Washington Post,* January 10, 1992.

11. Grant D. Ashley, assistant director, Criminal Investigative Division, Federal Bureau of Investigation, "The Safe Streets Violent Crimes Initiative," statement before the Senate Judiciary Committee, September 17, 2003, http://www.fbi.gov/congress/congress03/ashley091703.htm.

12. David Johnston, "F.B.I. to Shift from Cold War to Crime War," *New York Times,* January 9, 1992.

13. Johnston, "F.B.I. to Shift from Cold War to Crime War."

14. Andrea Ford, "FBI Reassigns 22 Agents to Gang Task Force," *Los Angeles Times,* February 6, 1992.

15. Jim Doyle, "FBI Counterspy Agents to Tackle Bay Crime," *San Francisco Chronicle,* January 10, 1992.

16. Cannon, *Official Negligence,* 21.

17. There remain many different points of view about every fact, the motivations of each player, and the fairness of every outcome in the Rodney King case. "It was a very, very extreme use of force—extreme for any police department in America," Chief Daryl Gates wrote in his autobiography. "But for the LAPD, considered by many to be perhaps the finest, most professional police department in the world, it was more than extreme. It was impossible." Criticizing his own men, Gates said at the time and later wrote that King "should never have been hit fifty-six times" (Daryl F. Gates, *Chief: My Life in the LAPD*, with Diane K. Shah [New York: Bantam, 1992], 4). Sgt. Koon has a very different view. He wrote in his memoir that King was a very big man, out of control, certainly drunk, and possibly under the influence of the drug PCP. He had proven impossible to subdue either by Taser or hands-on force. The "power strokes" were a controlled application of "minimum necessary force," the sergeant argued. "The only other alternative was to shoot him." To Koon, Gates's condemnation of his own officers' actions "can be explained only as an effort to appease minority leaders and thus, hopefully, to avoid confrontation" (Stacey C. Koon, *Presumed Guilty: The Tragedy of the Rodney King Affair*, with Robert Deitz [Washington, DC: Regnery Gateway, 1992], 18, 58). Journalist Lou Cannon offers a neutral perspective, arguing that the beating resulted because the LAPD and the politicians of Los Angeles had for years neglected to provide street cops with the proper equipment and training to handle a situation like the one King presented. "The King beating was a systems failure," he writes, "the result of a breakdown in which political leaders, the police chief, and senior officers ignored what was happening in the field" (Cannon, *Official Negligence*, 107).

18. *Powell v. Superior Court of Los Angeles Cty.*, 232 Cal.App.3d 785, 789, 791 (Cal. App. 2nd Dist. 1991).

19. Cannon, *Official Negligence*, 195.

20. Cannon, *Official Negligence*, 217.

21. "Los Angeles Riot Still Echoes a Decade Later," *CNN.com*, April 29, 2002, http://archives.cnn.com/2002/US/04/28/la.riot.anniversary/index.html.

22. Cannon, *Official Negligence*, xx.

23. "Reginald Denny," *Time*, April 25, 2007, http://www.time.com/time/specials/2007/la_riot/article/0,28804,1614117_1614084_1614511,00.html.

24. Koon, *Presumed Guilty*, 191.

25. Compare, e.g., Koon, *Presumed Guilty*; "Los Angeles Riot Still Echoes a Decade Later"; "Rodney King."

26. Seth Mydans, "After the Riots: 4 held in Attack at Riot's Outset," *New York Times*, May 13, 1992.

27. Seth Mydans, "F.B.I. Setting Sights on Street Gangs," *New York Times*, May 24, 1992.

28. David Freed, "Under Fire: Guns in Los Angeles County; Proliferation of Guns May Be Bloody Legacy of Riots," *Los Angeles Times*, May 17, 1992.

29. See, e.g., Eric Malnic, "Area's First Indictments Filed under Federal Carjacking Law," *Los Angeles Times*, February 13, 1993.

30. U.S. General Accounting Office, *Violent Crime: Federal Law Enforcement Assistance in Fighting Los Angeles Gang Violence*, Report to the Attorney General, GAO/GGD-96-150 (Washington, DC, 1996), 5.

31. Jim Newton, "U.S. Mounts Sweeping Crackdown on L.A. Gangs," *Los Angeles Times*, July 4, 1992.

32. U.S. General Accounting Office, *Violent Crime*, 5.

33. Newton, "U.S. Mounts Sweeping Crackdown on L.A. Gangs."

34. Somini Sengupta, "$3-Million Grant to Help Authorities in Gang Crackdown," *Los Angeles Times*, October 10, 1992.

35. Marc Agnifilo, Kathleen Bliss, and Bruce Riordan, "Investigating and Prosecuting Gangs Using the Enterprise Theory," *United States Attorneys' Bulletin* (Executive Office for United States Attorneys, Columbia, SC) 54, no. 3 (May 2006): 15.

36. Agnifilo, Bliss, and Riordan, "Investigating and Prosecuting Gangs," 16.

37. Agnifilo, Bliss, and Riordan, "Investigating and Prosecuting Gangs," 16.

38. Mydans, "F.B.I. Setting Sights on Street Gangs."

39. The quote is from an experienced federal prosecutor who prefers not to be further identified and is from author's notes of an extensive interview.

40. The quotes from Bruce Rordan in this chapter are from interviews on July 10, 2006, and January 19, 2007, supplemented by a number of telephone conversations and e-mail exchanges.

41. Cannon, *Official Negligence*, 282.

42. Paul Lieberman and Richard O'Reilly, "Most Looters Endured Lives of Crime, Poverty," *Los Angeles Times*, May 2, 1993.

43. Steven R. Belenko, *Crack and the Evolution of Anti-Drug Policy* (Westport, CT: Greenwood, 1993), 3–5.

44. U.S. Drug Enforcement Administration, *DEA History, 1985–1990*, http://www.usdoj.gov/dea/pubs/history/1985-1990.html.

45. Belenko, *Crack and the Evolution of Anti-Drug Policy*, 5.

46. U.S. Drug Enforcement Administration, *DEA History, 1985–1990*.

47. Belenko, *Crack and the Evolution of Anti-Drug Policy*, 5, 23.

48. See, e.g., Belenko, *Crack and the Evolution of Anti-Drug Policy*, generally; Maia Szalavitz, "Cracked Up," *Salon*, May 11, 1999, http://www.salon.com/news/feature/1999/05/11/crack_media.

49. See, e.g., John Leo, "The New Scarlet Letter: Herpes, an Incurable Virus, Threatens to Undo the Sexual Revolution," *Time*, August 2, 1982, 62; Jean Seligmann, "The AIDS Epidemic: The Search for a Cure," *Newsweek*, April 18, 1983, 74.

50. Susan Chira, "Children of Crack: Are the Schools Ready?" *New York Times*, May 25, 1990.

51. See, generally, Andrew Lang Golub and Bruce D. Johnson, *Crack's Decline: Some Surprises across U.S. Cities* (Washington, DC: U.S. Department of Justice, National Institute of Justice, 1997).

52. See David Stout, "Retroactively, Panel Reduces Drug Sentences," *New York Times,* December 12, 2007; Solomon Moore, "Rules Lower Prison Terms in Sentences for Crack," *New York Times,* November 2, 2007.

53. Peter Kerr, "Morgenthau Calls U.S. Bid to Fight Cocaine 'Minimal,'" *New York Times,* July 11, 1986.

54. Quoted in Michael Isikoff, "Justice Dept. Opposes Using Agents," *Washington Post,* March 22, 1989.

55. Gates, *Chief,* 295–96.

56. Summary of "How Bad Was Crack Cocaine? The Economics of an Illicit Drug Market," by Steven D. Levitt and Kevin M. Murphy, *Capital Ideas: Selected Papers on Price Theory* (University of Chicago Graduate School of Business), April 2006, http://www.chicagogsb.edu/capideas/apr06/5.aspx.

57. Michael J. Ybarra and Paul Lieberman, "U.S. Labels L.A. a Center of Drug Trade, Violence," *Los Angeles Times,* August 4, 1989.

58. Comment posted by Sergeant Richard Valdemar, http://www.veterans forsecureborders.us/feedback/feedback13.html.

59. E-mail message from Brian Truchon, September 11, 2007.

60. This and subsequent quotes from Wes McBride in this chapter are from an e-mail message from McBride, September 10, 2007.

61. See, e.g., William Branigin, "INS Pursuing Aliens in Urban Gangs," *Washington Post,* May 2, 1997.

62. E-mail message from Jim Wines, September 10, 2007.

63. E-mail message from Kevin Carwile, September 10, 2007.

64. Sara A. Carter, "Minuteman Head Out for Border Detail; Vocal Opposition Monitors Their Moves," in "Beyond Borders: Special Report on Immigration," *Inland Valley Daily Bulletin* and *San Bernardino Sun,* April 3, 2005, http://lang.dailybulletin.com/socal/beyondborders/latest_news/040305_min uteman_border.asp.

65. Associated Press, "Border Patrol Considering Use of Volunteers, Official Says," *New York Times,* July 21, 2005.

66. Robert Hilburn, "Rage with a Brand Name: Compton," *Los Angeles Times,* December 3, 2006.

67. Luke Burbank, "Terror, Hope on the Streets of Compton," part 2, *National Public Radio,* March 7, 2006, http://www.npr.org/templates/story/ story.php?storyid=5248673.

68. Megan Garvey, "Deadly Straits for Compton Residents; Killings Rise, but Officials Can't Afford to Hire More Sheriff's Deputies," *Los Angeles Times,* April 4, 2005.

69. Kazuyo Tsuchiya, "Race, Class, and Gender in America's 'War on

Poverty': The Case of Opal C. Jones in Los Angeles, 1964–1968," *Japanese Journal of American Studies* 15 (2004): 222–23.

70. *Understanding the Riots: Los Angeles before and after the Rodney King Case* (Los Angeles: Los Angeles Times, 1992), 10.

71. Stuart Pfeifer and Robin Fields, "In Jail and in Danger; Violence Has Left 14 Dead and Hundreds Hurt since 2000 in L.A. County Lockups," *Los Angeles Times*, December 17, 2006.

72. David Freed, "Policing Gangs: Case of Contrasting Styles; Strides Made by Sheriff's Dept. Cast a Pall on Methods Used by the L.A. Police Dept.," *Los Angeles Times*, January 19, 1986.

73. Gates, *Chief*, 294.

74. Sebastian Rotella, "Longtime Rivals, Immigrants Blur Gang Battle Lines," *Los Angeles Times*, June 9, 1991.

75. Gates, *Chief*, 294.

76. Jerry Belcher, "Police Target Aliens in Gangs for Deportation," *Los Angeles Times*, September 5, 1986.

77. Belcher, "Police Target Aliens in Gangs."

78. Stephen Braun, "U.S.-L.A. Task Force Deports 175 with Ties to Drug, Gang Activity," *Los Angeles Times*, April 12, 1989.

79. Belcher, "Police Target Aliens in Gangs."

CHAPTER 5

The epigraph is from Government Exhibit 1119, letter from Anthony Zaragoza to Janie Garcia, *United States v. Francisco Ruiz Martinez et al.*, U.S. District Court for the Central District of California (2002).

1. This chapter is largely based on multiple interviews, e-mails, and telephone conversations with former assistant U.S. attorney and deputy chief of the Los Angeles organized crime and terrorism section Bruce Riordan (now senior supervising attorney for antigang activities for the city of Los Angeles), three FBI special agents (Carl Sandford, James Wines, and Tiburcio Aguilar), and retired Los Angeles County deputy sheriff Sgt. Richard Valdemar; trial transcripts, memoranda, affidavits for warrants, and other materials in *United States v. Francisco Ruiz Martinez et al.*, U.S. District Court for the Central District of California (2002); and various federal appellate decisions, most particularly *United States v. Frank Fernandez*, 388 F.3d 1199 (9th Cir. 2004), concerning the Mexican Mafia. Other sources are cited as appropriate. All quotes from gang members are from trial transcripts or appellate records.

2. "Man, Woman Slain Near Downtown," *Los Angeles Times*, September 5, 1994.

3. Debra Cano, Rich Connell, and Robert J. Lopez, "An Inside Look at 18th St.'s Menace," *Los Angeles Times,* November 17, 1996.

4. Sheryl Stolberg, "Some Crime Witnesses Pay High Price for Civic Duty," *Los Angeles Times,* August 30, 1992.

5. Robert J. Lopez and Rich Connell, "Gang Turns Hope to Fear, Lives to Ashes," *Los Angeles Times,* November 18, 1996.

6. See, e.g., Bob Sipchen and Darrell Dawsey, "Neighborhood Has Learned Coexistence Secret," *Los Angeles Times,* October 20, 1989; Maria Newman and Louis Sahagun, "1 Killed, 7 Wounded in Major Turf Battle," *Los Angeles Times,* November 25, 1989.

7. U.S. Department of Justice, *Attorney General's Report to Congress on the Growth of Violent Street Gangs in Suburban Areas* (Washington, DC, 2008), 7–8.

8. U.S. Government Accountability Office, *Drug Control: U.S. Assistance Has Helped Mexican Counternarcotics Efforts but Tons of Illicit Drugs Continue to Flow into the United States,* Report to Congressional Requesters, GAO-07-1018 (Washington, DC, 2007), 10.

9. U.S. Government Accountability Office, *Drug Control,* 10.

10. U.S. Department of Justice, National Drug Intelligence Center, *National Drug Threat Assessment 2007* (Johnstown, PA, 2006), 54.

11. U.S. Department of Justice, *Attorney General's Report to Congress on the Growth of Violent Street Gangs,* 8.

12. U.S. Department of Justice, National Drug Intelligence Center, *Los Angeles High Intensity Drug Trafficking Area Drug Market Analysis* (Johnstown, PA, 2007), 2.

13. See, e.g., Anthony Millican, "For Pico-Union Vendors, It's Marked Turf," *Los Angeles Times,* December 20, 1992; Marc Lacey, "Extortion Patrols Hit Streets on Foot, Bikes," *Los Angeles Times,* December 28, 1992.

14. State of California, Office of the Inspector General, press release, March 14, 2006.

15. Robert J. Lopez and Jesse Katz, "Mexican Mafia Tells Gangs to Halt Drive-Bys," *Los Angeles Times,* September 26, 1993.

16. Lopez and Katz, "Mexican Mafia Tells Gangs to Halt Drive-Bys."

17. Lopez and Katz, "Mexican Mafia Tells Gangs to Halt Drive-Bys."

18. Jim Newton, "William P. Gray; U.S. Judge Ruled on Jail Overcrowding," *Los Angeles Times,* February 12, 1992.

19. See William Overend, "U.S. Atty.'s Office Gets 'Cream of the Crop,'" *Los Angeles Times,* November 30, 1986.

20. Joe Mozingo, "Attorney's Offices' Staffing is Decried," *Los Angeles Times,* July 25, 2006.

21. United Press International, "Alien Gang Member Given 8 Years for Reentering U.S.," January 7, 1993.

22. The person who described this problem has extensive federal criminal trial experience but does not wish to be further identified. The quote is from the author's notes of an interview in Washington.

23. Cano, Connell, and Lopez, "An Inside Look at 18th St.'s Menace"; Lopez and Connell, "Gang Turns Hope to Fear"; Robert J. Lopez and Rich Connell, "Police Shortcomings Stymie Efforts to Contain Gang," *Los Angeles Times*, November 19, 1996.

24. Cano, Connell, and Lopez, "An Inside Look at 18th St.'s Menace."

25. Lopez and Connell, "Police Shortcomings Stymie Efforts to Contain Gang."

CHAPTER 6

The epigraph is from Eyder Peralta, "Gang Members Seem Conflicted as Witnesses," *Houston Cronicle*, July 1, 2007.

1. The story of Congressman Frank Wolf's influence on the FBI's MS-13 National Gang Task Force is based primarily on interviews with Representative Wolf (June 27, 2007), former FBI assistant director Chris Swecker (by telephone, June 8, 2007), FBI agent Bob Clifford (on several occasions), and Kevin Carwile, chief of the Justice Department's Gang Squad (on several occasions), as well as biographical material and press releases from Representative Wolf's Internet Web site (http://wolf.house.gov) and news accounts of his activity regarding funding for antigang programs.

2. This summary description of the growth of MS-13 encapsulates extensive information gathered in interviews with knowledgeable law enforcement officials—including former FBI assistant director Chris Swecker; FBI agents Bob Clifford and Brian Truchon, each of whom led the FBI's MS-13 National Gang Task Force; Kevin Carwile, chief of the Justice Department's Gang Squad; Detective Frank Flores of the Los Angeles Police Department, a nationally recognized MS-13 expert; and Frank Ledee, chief of the Gang Prosecution Unit of the Miami-Dade County State's Attorneys Office—as well as from presentations about MS-13 made by other experts at law enforcement gang seminars in Virginia and El Salvador. Literally hundreds of news media reports from throughout the United States—many of which are in the author's files and are far too numerous to list here—anecdotally document and confirm the law enforcement experts' descriptions of the spread and violent nature of this gang. For a current FBI summary description, see "The MS-13 Threat: A National Assessment," January 14, 2008, http:/www.fbi.gov/page2/jan08/MS13_011408.html. There is also a growing number of reported cases involving MS-13 from courts throughout the country. For one example of a journalistic overview and summary relevant to this chapter, see Mike Ward, "Gang's Violent Grip: Group with Central

American Roots Leaves Bloody Trail across U.S.," *Austin (TX) American-Statesman,* January 22, 2006.

3. Hector J. Alfonso, presentation at the National Summit on Gang Violence, a gang training seminar, in Arlington, Virginia, June 2, 2006.

4. For a view of the law's genesis and its effects, see David Johnston, "Government Is Quickly Using Power of New Immigration Law," *New York Times,* October 22, 1996; Jonathan S. Landay, "Legal Immigrants Deported If They Have a Criminal Past," *Christian Science Monitor,* September 5, 1996; S. L. Bachman, "Legal Immigrants Face Terror in Terrorism Law: Deportation," *San Jose Mercury News,* June 3, 1996; "U.S. Efforts to Expand and Strengthen the Fight against Illegal Immigration," remarks of President William J. Clinton, *Dispatch* (U.S. Department of State) 6, no. 7 (February 7, 1995): 88.

5. Deborah Sontag, "U.S. Deports Felons but Can't Keep Them Out," *New York Times,* August 11, 1997.

6. This and subsequent quotes of FBI agent Leo Navarette are from an interview in Washington, DC, September 29, 2006.

7. See Mary Helen Johnson, "National Policies and the Rise of Transnational Gangs," *Migration Information Source,* April 2006, http://www.migra tioninformation.org/Feature/display.cfm?id=394; Ana Arana, "How the Street Gangs Took Central America," *Foreign Affairs* 84, no. 3 (May/June 2005): 98–110; S. Lynne Walker, "Gang Members Deported from U.S. Take Deadly Culture to Their Home Countries," Copley News Service, January 18, 2005; Scott Wallace, "You Must Go Home Again: Deported Los Angeles Gang Members Are Crime Problem in El Salvador," *Harper's Magazine,* August 1, 2001, 47; Margaret H. Taylor and T. Alexander Aleinikoff, "Deportation of Criminal Aliens: A Geopolitical Perspective" (working paper, Inter-American Dialogue, Carnegie Endowment for International Peace, Washington, DC, 1998), www.igloo.org/libraryservices/download-nocache/Library/subjects/peacesec/ domestic/deportat.

8. See, e.g., Kevin Sullivan, "Mexico Battles Influx of Violent Gangs," *Washington Post,* January 21, 2005.

9. Ginger Thompson, "Shuttling between Nations, Latino Gangs Confound the Law," *New York Times,* September 26, 2004. For summaries of the problem in addition to the cases described in this chapter, see, e.g., Ron Sylvester, "Border a Revolving Doorway for Authorities, Illegal Immigrants," *Wichita Eagle,* October 29, 2006; Pauline Arrillaga, "AP Investigation: 'Catch and Release' Policy Frees Illegal Immigrants to Move about U.S.," Associated Press, July 5, 2005; Sontag, "U.S. Deports Felons but Can't Keep Them Out."

10. Randall Richard, "An AP Investigation: Deportees from the U.S. Bring Gang Warfare to Central America," Associated Press, November 1, 2003 (quoting Dr. Louise Shelley, director of the Transnational Crime and Corruption Center at American University in Washington, DC).

11. Thompson, "Shuttling between Nations"; Richard, "Deportees from the U.S."; "Honduras: Brutal Murders as Street Gangs Show Strength," *Latin News Daily*, September 1, 2003.

12. Sources for the story of the Christmas bus massacre and Ever Anibal Rivera Paz's odyssey include interviews with several senior FBI officials; the author's notes from the Third Annual International Anti-Gang Conference (sponsored by the FBI and the Salvadoran National Civil Police), Sonsonate, El Salvador, April 24, 2007; docket entries in the case of *United States v. Lester Rivera Paz*, United States District Court for the Southern District of Texas docket no. 4:05-cr-00091; and the following media reports: Elvis Guzmán, "Dos pagaran la masacre," *La Prensa* (Honduras), February 21, 2007; Freddy Cuevas, "Honduras: 2 Gang Members Convicted in 2004 Bus Attack That Killed 28," Associated Press Worldstream, February 21, 2007; Susan Carroll, "Blame Passed in Escape of Gang Leader," *Houston Chronicle*, February 11, 2007; Zeke Minaya and Harvey Rice, "Reputed Honduran MS-13 Leader to Be Deported," *Houston Chronicle*, July 9, 2005; Brian Chasnoff, "Ranchers Fear Violent Gang Moving across Region," *San Antonio Express-News*, June 7, 2005; Dave Montgomery, "Gang Leader in Custody, Officials Say," *Fort Worth Star-Telegram*, February 25, 2005; Hernan Rozemberg, "Hondurans Laud Arrest of Man in South Texas," *San Antonio Express-News*, February 25, 2005; Jeorge Zarazua and Macarena Hernandez, "Massacre Suspect Held in Texas," *San Antonio Express-News*, February 24, 2005; Suzanne Gamboa, "Suspect in Honduras Bus Massacre Arrested in Texas," Associated Press, February 24, 2005; "L 400 mil por Culiche y Snoopy," *La Prensa* (Honduras), May 1, 2005, (accessed online at http://www.laprensahn.com; "Capturan a 'cerebro' de matanza en Chamelecon," *El Heraldo* (Honduras), February 24, 2005 (accessed online at http://www.elheraldo.hn); AFP, "En el baño de la penitenciaria encuentran ahorcado el 'marero' acusado de matanza en Honduras," *Washington Hispanic*, January 21, 2005 (accessed online at http://www.washingtonhispanic.com); "Aparece muerto en prisión sospechoso de masacre de 28 personas," *El Nacional* (Honduras), January 20, 2005 (accessed online at http://www.elnacionalnews.com); "Ni 12 horas duro 'El Pájaro' en la PN," *El Heraldo* (Honduras), January 19, 2005 (accessed online at http://www.heraldohn.com); Freddy Cuevas, "One of the Alleged Masterminds of Honduran Bus Attack Found Dead in Prison," Associated Press Worldstream, January 19, 2005; "Testigo hunde a 'La Pantera,'" *El Heraldo* (Honduras), January 12, 2005 (accessed online at http://www.elheraldo.hn); Associated Press, "President: Honduran Police Arrest Presumed Leader of Gang Responsible for Massacre on Public Bus," January 3, 2005; Associated Press Worldstream, "Honduran Police Say Two Dozen Gang Members Linked to Attack," December 31, 2004; Michael A. W. Ottery, "Many Hondurans Say Guerrillas, Not Gangs, Were Behind Massacre," *Miami Herald*, December 30, 2004; Chris Kraul, "Hondurans See Massacre as a

Warning," *Los Angeles Times*, December 27, 2004; "Masacre en Honduras," *El Nuevo Diario* (Nicaragua), December 26, 2004 (accessed online at http://archivo.elnuevodiario.com.ni); Chris Kraul and Alex Renderos, "Tensions High in Honduras after Bus Massacre," *Los Angeles Times*, December 25, 2004; Ginger Thompson, "Gunmen Kill 28 on Bus in Honduras," *New York Times*, December 25, 2004; Freddy Cuevas, "Assailants Gun Down 28 People on Public Bus in Northern Honduras," Associated Press, December 24, 2004; Sergio de Leon, "Attack That Killed 28 on Honduran Bus Escalates Criminals' War with Government," Associated Press, December 24, 2004.

13. The description of the Brooks County and Falfurrias area is based on the news reports of Rivera Paz's capture cited in the preceding note and on the following sources: "Brooks County," *The Handbook of Texas Online*, http://www.tshaonline.org/handbook/online/articles/BB/hcb16.html; "Falfurrias, Texas," *The Handbook of Texas Online*, http://www.tshaonline.org/handbook/online/articles/FF/hff1.html; U.S. Bureau of the Census, "Brooks County, Texas," *State and County QuickFacts*, http://quickfacts.census.gov/qfd/states/48/48047.html; James Pinkerton, "Border's Eyes Focusing on Bloody Gang," *Houston Chronicle*, August 26, 2005; Mary Jo McConahay, "They Die in Brooks County," *Texas Observer*, June 1, 2007, http://www.texasobserver.org/article.php?aid=2509.

14. The story of Javier Calzada's murder is based primarily on the following sources: telephone interview with Detective Sergeant Alan Patton, Grand Prairie Police Department, September 28, 2007; David McLemore, "For Witness to MS-13 Crimes, Betrayal Was a Death Sentence," *Dallas Morning News*, October 29, 2006; Chris Kraul, Robert J. Lopez, and Rich Connell, "L.A. Violence Crosses the Line," *Los Angeles Times*, May 15, 2005; "Arlington Area Briefs," *Fort Worth Star-Telegram*, April 23, 2003; Robert Tharp, "Convict Pleads to Murder," *Dallas Morning News*, April 5, 2003; Tim Wyatt, "Salvadoran Gang Suspected in Spree," *Dallas Morning News*, December 2, 2002; Staishy Bostick Siem, "Suspected Gang Member Held in Dallas Man's Death," *Dallas Morning News*, October 5, 2002. Background on the Bachman Lake area is from the following sources: La Voz de la Familia, *2005 Bachman Area Community Assessment*, http://www.injurypreventioncenter.org/pdf/2005_bachman_assessment.pdf; Wikipedia, "Bachman Lake," http://en.wikipedia.org/wiki/Bachman_Lake; Holly Yan, "Robberies Worry Bachman Lake Visitors," *Dallas Morning News*, July 12, 2007; Drake Witham, "Teens Held in Woman's Death," *Dallas Morning News*, May 12, 2000.

15. The primary sources for the story of Joaquin Diaz's murder, Brenda Paz, Denis Rivera, Ismael Cisneros, and MS-13 in Northern Virginia include documents in several dockets in the U.S. District Court for the Eastern District of Virginia: "Notice of Intent to Seek a Sentence of Death," October 1, 2004, and indictment of June 24, 2004, in *United States v. Rivera*, criminal docket no.

1:04CR283; "Government's Rule 404(b) Notice," August 15, 2003, "Government's Motion in Limine to Admit Murdered Witness's Testimony," August 15, 2003, and superseding indictment of April 2, 2003, in *United States v. Rivera,* criminal docket no. 02-376-A; criminal complaint and affidavit in support of complaint in *United States v. Salinas,* criminal docket no. 02-567-M. Reported decisions serving as sources include *United States v. Cisneros,* 385 F.Supp.2d 567 (E.D. Va. 2005); *United States v. Rivera,* 412 F.3d 562 (4th Cir. 2005); *United States v. Cisneros,* 363 F.Supp.2d 827 (E.D. Va. 2005); *United States v. Grande,* 363 F.Supp.2d 623 (E.D. Va. 2005); *United States v. Rivera,* 405 F.Supp.2d 662 (E.D. Va. 2005); *United States v. Rivera,* 363 F.Supp.2d 814 (E.D. Va. 2005); *United States v. Rivera,* 292 F.Supp.2d 827, 828, 838 (E.D. Va. 2003); and *United States v. D. R.,* 225 F.Supp.2d 694 (2002). Media sources include U.S. Attorney for the Eastern District of Virginia, press releases, May 17, 2005, and November 30, 2003; excerpts of police interrogation of Brenda Paz in the National Geographic video *World's Most Dangerous Gang* (2006); Jamie Stockwell, "Convicted Gang Members Urged to Help Teens," *Washington Post,* September 10, 2005; Mark Sherman, "Witness Protection a World of Closely Held Secrets," Associated Press, July 18, 2006; Jerry Markon, "MS-13 Jury Hoped to Deter Others," *Washington Post,* June 16, 2005; Jamie Stockwell and Jerry Markon, "2 Get Life in Slaying of MS-13 Witness," *Washington Post,* June 15, 2005; Jerry Markon, "Protecting a Witness Who Doesn't Want Protection," *Washington Post,* June 12, 2005; Matthew Barakat, "Prosecutors Ask Jury for Death Sentence in Gang Slaying," Associated Press State and Local Wire, June 9, 2005; Jerry Markon, "MS-13 Members Should Die, Prosecutors Tell Jury," *Washington Post,* May 24, 2005; Paul Bradley, "Penalty Phase to Begin in Trial," *Richmond Times Dispatch,* May 22, 2005; Paul Bradley, "Arguments End in Gang Members Murder Trial," *Richmond Times Dispatch,* May 11, 2005; Jamie Stockwell, "For Girls in Gangs, a Risky 'Obsession,'" *Washington Post,* May 8, 2005; Jamie Stockwell and Jerry Markon, "Gang Member Says He Saw Va. Slaying," *Washington Post,* May 5, 2005; Paul Bradley, "Defense Rests in Gang Members' Trial, "*Richmond Times Dispatch,* May 6, 2005; Paul Bradley, " 'I Did Not Kill Miss Paz,'" *Richmond Times Dispatch,* May 5, 2005; Paul Bradley, "Defendants to Testify in Trial," *Richmond Times Dispatch,* May 4, 2005; Paul Bradley, "Prosecutors Rest Case against Gang Members," *Richmond Times Dispatch,* May 3, 2005; Jerry Markon, "Authorities Blamed in Killing of Va. Witness," *Washington Post,* May 3, 2005; Paul Bradley, "Witness Ties Boyfriend to Killing," *Richmond Times Dispatch,* April 28, 2005; Paul Bradley, " 'To Me, She Was A Snitch,'" *Richmond Times Dispatch,* April 22, 2005; "Calls from Jail Described," *Richmond Times Dispatch,* April 27, 2005; Paul Bradley, "Another Teardrop Has Been Earned," *Richmond Times Dispatch,* April 21, 2005; Paul Bradley, "It Was Like an Obsession," *Richmond Times Dispatch,* April 20, 2005; Paul Bradley, "Witness: Gang Members Who Snitch Die," *Richmond Times*

Dispatch, April 19, 2005; Paul Bradley, "Crime Scene Described in MS-13 Trial," *Richmond Times Dispatch*, April 14, 2005; Arlo Wagner, "Slain Girl Disliked Safe House," *Washington Times*, April 13, 2005; Paul Bradley, "Gang Member's Story Is Recounted," *Richmond Times Dispatch*, April 13, 2005; Jerry Markon and Jamie Stockwell, "Oversight of Slain Witness Faulted," *Washington Post*, April 13, 2005; Paul Bradley, "Driven Out, Only to Be Drawn Back," *Richmond Times Dispatch*, April 10, 2005; Mark Sherman, "Witness Protection Rolls Stretching, Number of Protectors Shrinking," Associated Press, March 14, 2005; Matthew Brzezinski, "Hillbangers," *New York Times*, August 15, 2004; Jerry Markon and Maria Glod, "Four N. Va. Gang Members Charged in Slaying of Witness," *Washington Post*, June 25, 2004; Paul Bradley, "Gang Members Charged in Woman's Death," *Richmond Times Dispatch*, June 25, 2004; Maria Glod, "Guardian of Slain Woman Replaces Her as Witness," *Washington Post*, November 7, 2003; Maria Glod, "Prosecutors Describe Gang-Style Execution as MS-13 Trial Opens," *Washington Post*, November 6, 2003; Jerry Markon and Maria Glod, "Slaying Trial Marks Gang Crackdown," *Washington Post*, November 3, 2003; Maria Glod, "Gang Trial Judge Allows Statements," *Washington Post*, October 7, 2003; Jerry Markon and Maria Glod, "Prosecutors Hope to Quote Dead Witness," *Washington Post*, August 16, 2003; Jerry Markon and Maria Glod, "Giving Up a New Life for a Gang Death," *Washington Post*, August 10, 2003; David C. Greene and Paul Adams, "Reagan National Sets to Reopen Tomorrow," *Baltimore Sun*, October 3, 2001; Craig Timberg and Spencer S. Hsu, "National Can't Reopen Soon, Officials Say," *Washington Post*, September 17, 2001.

16. Neil A. Lewis, "Man in the News; A Man Made for Law Enforcement—Robert Swan Mueller III," *New York Times*, July 6, 2001.

CHAPTER 7

The epigraph is a line spoken by actor Edward G. Robinson in the movie *Little Caesar* (1931).

1. Earnest Winston, "Real Prize: Catching Terrorists," *Charlotte Observer*, September 28, 2004.

2. On the subject of global criminal and terror networks, see John Arquila and David Ronfeldt, eds., *Networks and Netwars: The Future of Terror, Crime, and Militancy* (Santa Monica, CA: RAND, 2001); Moisés Naim, *Illicit: How Smugglers, Traffickers, and Copycats Are Hijacking the Global Economy* (New York: Doubleday, 2005); John Robb, *Brave New War: The Next Stage of Terrorism and the End of Globalization* (Hoboken, NJ: John Wiley and Sons, 2007).

3. U.S. Immigration and Customs Enforcement, "Operation Community

Shield," presentation at the Third Annual International Anti-Gang Conference (sponsored by the FBI and the Salvadoran National Civil Police), Sonsonate, El Salvador, April 24, 2007.

4. This paragraph is based on discussions with senior federal officials at various times from 2005 to 2007, statements made at a closed meeting of law enforcement representatives that the author was permitted to attend in 2007, and a 2005 FBI intelligence assessment to which the author has had access.

5. See, e.g., Jerry Markon, "Anti-Human Trafficking Bill Would Send FBI Agents on Trail of Pimps," *Washington Post,* November 29, 2007. Legislation proposed by "anti-trafficking activists and members of Congress" would extend federal law to cover prostitution, requiring the FBI to devote resources to what has historically been a local offense.

6. George Gedda, "US, Greece Attempt to End Mistrust," Associated Press Online, September 7, 2000.

7. Katherine McIntire Peters, "Success Begets Success: FBI Agent Robert Clifford Worked Meticulously to Help Dismantle a Greek Terrorist Organization," *Atlantic Monthly,* December 1, 2004.

8. See Nicholas Gage, "Race against Terror," *Vanity Fair,* January 2007, 64.

9. The story of Bob Clifford's assignment to the MS-13 National Gang Task Force is based primarily on interviews with Congressman Frank Wolf, former FBI assistant director Chris Swecker, Kevin Carwile, chief of the Justice Department's Gang Squad, former assistant United States Attorney Bruce Riordan, and Clifford himself.

10. The story of Erick Morales is based primarily on the following sources: *People v. Erik [sic] Isaac Morales,* 2007 Cal. App. Unpub. Lexis 528 (Ct. App. 2007); "Man Accused of Attacking Attorney in Court Is Sentenced for Double Murder," City News Service (Southern California), April 6, 2005; Caitlin Liu, "Inmates to Be Screened at Courts," *Los Angeles Times,* March 23, 2005; Michael Gougis, "Injunction Has Limited Use in Gang Control," *Daily News of Los Angeles,* November 16, 2003.

11. The information in this chapter relating to Nelson Comandari is based primarily on the following sources: interviews, telephone conversations, and exchanges of e-mails with law enforcement sources familiar with Nelson Comandari's history, including a gang detective with the LAPD, a retired deputy sheriff from the LASD, a deputy sheriff on active duty with another department in the western United States, four FBI special agents, and a former federal prosecutor; e-mail exchange with one of Comandari's defense attorneys, Nancy Lee Ennis; trial transcript, *United States v. Francisco Ruiz Martinez et al.,* U.S. District Court for the Central District of California (2002); documents filed in *United States v. Nelson Commandari [sic]*, U.S. District Court for the Southern District of New York, docket no. 1:04-cr-00384-PKC; Los Angeles Superior Court, *Index of Defendants in Criminal Cases,* www/lasuperiorcourt.org/On

lineServices/criminalindex/index.asp; Tom Jackman, "Gangs Pushed beyond Turf Battles," *Washington Post,* August 1, 2004; Edward Gutierrez, "Arriaza Chicas regresa a la policía," *El Diario de Hoy,* April 19, 2004 (accessed online at http:/www.elsalvador.com); David Marroquín, "El polémico caso de falsas pruebas," *La Prensa Grafica,* November 21, 2003 (accessed online at http://archive.laprensa.com.sv); Alberto López and Maria T. Pérez, "PNC suspende a Arriaza Chicas por seis meses," *El Diario de Hoy,* July 15, 2000 (accessed online at http://www.elsalvador.com).

12. John Pain, "Device Can Detect Heart Failure Symptoms," Associated Press Online, December 16, 2004.

13. U.S. Drug Enforcement Administration, *FY 2002 Budget Summary— Salaries and Expenses,* http://www.usdoj.gov/jmd/2002summary/html/dea_sal _and_exp.htm.

14. Chris Swecker, statement before the House Subcommittee on the Western Hemisphere, April 20, 2005.

15. Theo Milonopoulos, "Operation Targets Gang Members," *Los Angeles Times,* October 10, 2007.

16. Nina Bernstein, "Immigrant Workers Caught in Net Cast for Gangs," *New York Times,* November 25, 2007.

17. Michael Amon, "Immigration; The Political Debate: Gridlock in the Halls of Power," *Newsday,* October 14, 2007; "Ice Breakers; Raids by Immigration Agents Were Hamfisted Attempts at Law Enforcement," *Newsday,* October 5, 2007, editorial; Frank Eltman, "186 People Captured in Long Island Immigration Raids," Associated Press State and Local Wire, October 1, 2007.

18. Milonopoulos, "Operation Targets Gang Members."

19. Rachel Uranga, "Immigration Arrests Jump; Critics Contend Raids Target More than Criminals," *Daily News of Los Angeles,* November 3, 2007.

20. Uranga, "Immigration Arrests Jump."

21. Amon, "Immigration; The Political Debate."

22. See, e.g., Rich Connell and Robert J. Lopez, "Gang Sweeps Result in 103 Arrests," *Los Angeles Times,* March 15, 2005.

23. Arian Campo-Flores, "The Most Dangerous Gang in America," *Newsweek,* March 28, 2005, 22.

24. Campo-Flores, "Most Dangerous Gang in America."

25. The quotes from Brian Truchon are taken from interviews on June 20, 2006; September 20, 2006; conversations during a conference in El Salvador during the week of April 23, 2007; and several e-mail of various dates.

26. The discussion of the New Mexican Mafia and the Cisneros Organization is based on the following sources: interviews and e-mail exchanges with FBI special agent Brian Truchon; *United States v. Cisneros,* 328 F.3d 610 (10th Cir. 2003); Arizona Department of Correction, "Security Threat Groups: New Mex-

ican Mafia," http://www.azcorrections.gov/adc/divisions/support/stg/nmm.asp; Scott Sandlin, "8 Plead Guilty in Car Theft, Drug Case," *Albuquerque Journal,* December 17, 2005; Beth DeFalco, "8 Offer Pleas in Mexican Mafia Case," Associated Press State and Local Wire, December 16, 2005; Dennis Wagner, "Prison Gang Members to Plead Guilty in Murders," *Arizona Republic,* December 15, 2005; Dennis Wagner, "Murder Trial Shifting to Phoenix," *Arizona Republic,* September 29, 2003; Scott Sandlin, "Judge OKs Moving Trial in Guard's Killing to Arizona," *Albuquerque Journal,* September 17, 2003; Guillermo Contreras, "Alleged Double Life Ends," *Albuquerque Journal,* January 27, 2003; Guillermo Contreras, "Trail of Blood: Witnesses Linked to Mob Keep Dying," *Albuquerque Journal,* January 26, 2003.

27. The quotes from Kevin Carwile in this chapter are from interviews on December 11, 2006; January 22, 2007; and June 20, 2007.

28. Dana Milbank, "Ashcroft and the Night Visitors," *Washington Post,* May 16, 2007. For brief assessments of the impact of Gonzales's tenure on the department's professionalism, see Jamie S. Gorelick, "A New Agenda for Justice," *Washington Post,* August 28, 2007; Stuart Taylor Jr., "Another Gonzales Horror Story," *National Journal,* May 19, 2007.

29. Justice Sutherland in *Berger v. United States,* 295 U.S. 78, 88 (1935).

30. Justin Gillis and Bill Miller, "In D.C.'s Simple City, Complex Rules of Life and Death," *Washington Post,* April 20, 1997.

31. Robert E. Pierre, "D.C. Anti-Gang Efforts Marked by Frustration," *Washington Post,* March 9, 1997.

32. Avis Thomas-Lester and Philip P. Pan, "4 Arrested in Deaths of D.C. Brothers," *Washington Post,* September 10, 1996.

33. Avis Thomas-Lester, "Mother, in Sadness and Gratitude, Honors Those Who Caught Killers," *Washington Post,* October 9, 1998.

34. Principal sources for the history of the Organized Crime and Racketeering Section include interviews with P. Kevin Carwile, chief of the Gang Squad, Criminal Division, U.S. Department of Justice; Selwynn Raab, *Five Families: The Rise, Decline, and Resurgence of America's Most Powerful Mafia Empires* (New York: St. Martin's, 2005), 108–53; Thomas A. Reppetto, *Bringing Down The Mob: The War against the American Mafia* (New York: Henry Holt, 2006), 67–85; U.S. Department of Justice, Executive Office for United States Attorneys, "Interview with Deputy Assistant Attorney General John C. 'Jack' Keeney," *USA Bulletin* (Washington, DC), March 1999, 4, 6–7; Associated Press, "Mafia Prosecutors Quitting as Strike Forces Disband," *New York Times,* January 4, 1990; Bill McAllister, "Prosecutors Taking Over Strike Forces," *Washington Post,* December 28, 1989; Michael Wines, "Details Are Given on New Crime Plan," *New York Times,* June 20, 1989.

35. Raab, *Five Families,* 127.

36. For a brief overview of the history of the Justice Department's antigang effort and its current programs, see Federal News Service, "Justice Department Briefing, Efforts to Combat Gang Violence," January 16, 2007.

37. Telephone interview with Chris Swecker, June 8, 2007.

CHAPTER 8

The epigraph is from Jeff Coen and Rudolph Bush, "Top-Level Member of Gang Collared," *Chicago Tribune*, December 6, 2006.

1. The story of the investigation and trial of Gustavo "Gino" Colon is based in part on an interview with ATF special agents Terry Jackson and Elizabeth Ragusa and on filings in the case of *United States v. Gustavo Colon*, U.S. District Court for the Northern District of Illinois, docket no. 97-CR-659, including application for search warrant and accompanying affidavit of special agent Ralph Rider, February 19, 1997; ATF "Report of Investigation" submitted by special agent Laurie A. Jolley, October 24, 1997; ATF "Report of Investigation" and attached "Statement of Jose G. Souffront" submitted by special agent Terry S. Jackson, April 2, 1997; ATF memorandum titled "Collateral Request Reply" from special agent in charge, Boston Field Division, to special agent in charge, Chicago Field Division, October 20, 1997; plea agreement of Wilfredo Escobar, March 23, 1998; undated filing titled "Government's Version of the Offense"; and undated statement of Marisol Colon. Other court sources for the story are *People v. Colon*, 314 N.E.2d 664 (Il. Ct. App. 1974); *United States v. Gustavo Colon*, 1998 U.S. Dist. Lexis 6200 (1998); *United States v. Souffront*, 338 F.3d 809 (2003). Media sources include "Gang Leader's Wife Gets 10-Year Term," *Chicago Tribune*, September 16, 2000; Matt O'Connor, "Jailed Gang Leader Is Put Away for Life," *Chicago Tribune*, May 23, 2000; Joseph T. Hallinan, "Inmates Dial Up Dollars for Illinois," *Chicago Tribune*, August 25, 1999; Matt O'Connor, "U.S. to Beef Up Drug Fight in City," *Chicago Tribune*, July 24, 1998; Abdon M. Pallasch, "Man Guilty of Being Gang Boss from Prison," *Chicago Tribune*, July 23, 1998; Abdon M. Pallasch, "Witness Takes Jury on Visit to Gang Boss," *Chicago Tribune*, June 2, 1998; Abdon M. Pallasch, "Jury Is Told Tapes Reveal Inmate Ran Drug Deals," *Chicago Tribune*, May 19, 1998; Matt O'Connor, "Ex-Member Perils Gang's Alleged Drug Network," *Chicago Tribune*, March 20, 1998; Dirk Johnson, "A Jailed Chicago Gang Leader Is Charged as a Drug Criminal," *New York Times*, September 21, 1997; Gary Marx and Mark S. Warnick, "Latin King Leader and 13 Others Indicted," *Chicago Tribune*, September 19, 1997; Michael Gillis, "Gang Boss Given Round Trip to Jail," *Chicago Sun-Times*, September 19, 1997; Gary Marx, "Power Struggle behind Bars," *Chicago Tribune*, November 10, 1996.

2. Gary Marx and Jeff Coen, "Gang Kingpins Disappearing in Chicago,"

Chicago Tribune, December 10, 2007; Gary Marx, "State Tries to Turn Its Top Gang Inmates," *Chicago Tribune,* January 10, 2000.

3. Gillis, "Gang Boss Given Round Trip."

4. "Quotes of the Day," *Chicago Tribune,* September 19, 1997.

5. James W. Wagner and Kate Curran Kirby, eds., *The Chicago Crime Commission Gang Book* (Chicago: Chicago Crime Commission, 2006), 11.

6. U.S. Bureau of the Census, "Chicago (city), Illinois," *State and County QuickFacts,* http://quickfacts.census.gov/qfd/states/17/1714000.html; U.S. Bureau of the Census, "Cook County, Illinois," *State and County QuickFacts,* http://quickfacts.census.gov/qfd/states17/17031.html.

7. See Rita Arias Jirasek and Carlos Tortolero, *Mexican Chicago* (Chicago: Arcadia, 2001), 160; Wilfredo Cruz, *Puerto Rican Chicago* (Chicago: Arcadia, 2004), 7.

8. Principal sources for the discussion of Latino history in this section are Manuel G. Gonzales, *Mexicanos: A History of Mexicans in the United States* (Bloomington: Indiana University Press, 1999); Jirasek and Tortolero, *Mexican Chicago;* Cruz, *Puerto Rican Chicago;* Felix M. Padilla, *Puerto Rican Chicago* (Notre Dame, IN: University of Notre Dame Press, 1987); Chicago Historical Society, "Mexicans," in *The Electronic Encyclopedia of Chicago,* http://www.encyclopedia.chicagohistory.org/pages/824.html.

9. Frederick M. Thrasher, *The Gang: A Study of 1,313 Gangs in Chicago,* abridged ed. (Chicago: University of Chicago Press, 1963), 10.

10. Thrasher, *Gang,* 264.

11. Wagner and Kirby, *Chicago Crime Commission Gang Book,* 28.

12. Mid-Atlantic Great Lakes Organized Crime Law Enforcement Network (MAGLOCLEN), "Latin Kings Intelligence Report" (restricted document in author's files, 2004), 2.

13. William Triplett, "Gang Crisis," *CQ Researcher,* May 14, 2004.

14. Wagner and Kirby, *Chicago Crime Commission Gang Book,* 11.

15. George W. Knox, *Gang Profile: The Latin Kings* (Chicago: National Gang Crime Research Center, 2000), http://www.ngcrc.com/ngcrc/page15.htm.

16. Carlos Sadovi and Rex W. Huppke, "Gangs Cut Swath of Death, Payback in Little Village," *Chicago Tribune,* June 5, 2004.

17. The story of Maria's daughter Ana Mateo in this section is based primarily on the following sources: interview with Cook County assistant state's attorneys Thomas Mahoney, Brian Holmes, Michael Golden, and Mary Jo Murtaugh; trial transcript, *People v. Juan Garcia* (Circuit Court of Cook County, Illinois, 2006), criminal docket no. 04-CR-10613; Eric Herman, "'Barbarism' Blamed in Slaying of Girl, 7," *Chicago Sun-Times,* December 21, 2006; Carlos Sadovi, "Teen Gets 56 Years in '03 Slaying of Girl," *Chicago Tribune,* December 21, 2006; Josh Noel, "Guilty Plea in Drive-by Shooting That Killed Girl," *Chicago Tribune,* November 20, 2006; Eric Herman, "Alleged Gang Member

Guilty in Girl's Death," *Chicago Sun-Times*, November 16, 2006; Carlos Sadovi, "Alleged Gang Member Convicted in Girl's Death That Jolted Pilsen," *Chicago Tribune*, November 16, 2006; Carlos Sadovi, "Man Tells Court He Didn't Shoot Girl, 7," *Chicago Tribune*, November 15, 2006; Carlos Sadovi, "Mother Tells of Finding Girl Lying in Blood," *Chicago Tribune*, November 10, 2006; Stefano Esposito, "Accused Killer of Girl, 7, 'Wasn't There': Defense," *Chicago Sun-Times*, November 10, 2006; Hal Dardick, "2nd Suspect Held in Pilsen Girl's Slaying," *Chicago Tribune*, March 14, 2004; Maudlyne Ihejirika, "Berwyn Man Is 2nd Charged in Summer Murder of Girl, 7," *Chicago Sun-Times*, March 14, 2004; "Bond Is Denied in Girl's Slaying," *Chicago Tribune*, March 9, 2004; Stefano Esposito, "Dad Feels 'Sad' for Teenager Who Allegedly Killed Daughter," *Chicago Sun-Times*, March 9, 2004; H. Gregory Meyer and David Heinzmann, "Arrest in August Killing Fails to Comfort Family," *Chicago Tribune*, March 8, 2004; Glenn Jeffers, "Pilsen Mourns Another Gunfire Victim," *Chicago Tribune*, August 26, 2003; Stan Donaldson, "Vigil Held for Slain Pilsen Girl," *Chicago Tribune*, August 23, 2003; Brett McNeil, "Pilsen Gangbangers Being Put on Notice," *Chicago Tribune*, August 22, 2003; Cheryl L. Reed and Frank Main, "Three Gang Members Sought in Slaying," *Chicago Sun-Times*, August 22, 2003; Grace Aduroja, "Police Hunt 4 Gang Members after Pilsen Girl Fatally Shot," *Chicago Tribune*, August 21, 2003; Cheryl R. Reed and Ana Mendieta, "Girl, 7, Killed by Stray Gunfire," *Chicago Sun-Times*, August 21, 2003.

18. Reed and Main, "Three Gang Members Sought in Slaying."

19. Reed and Mendieta, "Girl, 7, Killed by Stray Gang Gunfire."

20. Knox, *Gang Profile.*

21. Coen and Bush, "Top-Level Member of Gang Collared."

22. MAGLOCLEN, "Latin Kings Intelligence Report," 1.

23. See Glenn Jeffers, "Chicago Police Take Bow after a Year of Less Crime," *Chicago Tribune*, December 29, 2004; "Cops Shut Down Heroin Operation," *Chicago Tribune*, October 26, 2004.

24. The remainder of this section is based primarily on the following sources: interviews with ATF special agent Terry Jackson and Chicago police officer Homero Ramirez; U.S. Department of Justice, National Drug Intelligence Center, *Chicago: High Intensity Drug Trafficking Area Drug Market Analysis* (Johnstown, PA, 2007); Library of Congress, Federal Research Division, *Organized Crime and Terrorist Activity in Mexico, 1999–2000* (Washington, DC, 2003); U.S. Department of Justice, National Drug Intelligence Center, *Illinois Drug Threat Assessment* (Johnstown, PA, 2001); U.S. Drug Enforcement Administration, "Jaime Herrera-Nevares," *DEA History, 1975–1980,* http://www.dea.gov/pubs/history/1975-1980.html; U.S. Drug Enforcement Administration, "French Connection," *DEA History, 1970–1975,* http://www.dea .gov/pubs/history/1970-1975.html; Charles Bowden, "Chuy Carrillo Is Dead and Living Somewhere Far, Far Away," *Esquire,* October 1997, 120; Mike Gallagher, "N.M.

Sees New Drug Traffickers," *Albuquerque Journal,* April 13, 1997; Matt O'Connor, "Drug Dealer Tied to Nationwide Narcotics Ring Gets 25 Years," *Chicago Tribune,* February 18, 1990; E. R. Shipp, "134 Indicted in Nationwide Drug Distribution Case," *New York Times,* July 24, 1985; F. N. D'Alessio, "Domestic News, Chicago," Associated Press, July 24, 1985; "The Arrest of Jaime Herrera," *Washington Post,* October 23, 1978; Dennis A. Williams and Sylvester Monroe, "Busting the Heroin Pipeline," *Newsweek,* May 22, 1978.

25. Brett McNeil, "Pilsen Gangbangers Being Put on Notice," *Chicago Tribune,* August 22, 2003.

26. Meyer and Heinzmann, "Arrest in August Killing Fails to Comfort Family."

27. Rick Jervis, "Latino Murder Cases Prove Most Elusive," *Chicago Tribune,* April 20, 2004.

28. Kathryn Masterson, "1 Year after Chicago Man's Murder, Family Still Hunting for Clues," *Chicago Tribune,* March 22, 2005.

29. U.S. Department of Justice, Federal Bureau of Investigation, "Clearances," *Crime in the United States, 2006,* http://www.fbi.gov/ucr/cius2006/offenses/clearances/index.html (2006 clearance rate); Deborah A. Richardson and Rachel Kosa, "An Examination of Homicide Clearance Rates: Foundation for the Development of a Homicide Clearance Model" (draft, Police Executive Research Forum, Washington, DC, 2001), 2, available under the rubric "homicide" at http://www.policeforum.org/library.asp (1961 clearance rate).

30. Jo Craven McGinty, "New York Killers, and Those Killed, by Numbers," *New York Times,* April 28, 2006.

31. Richardson and Kosa, "An Examination of Homicide Clearance Rates," 2.

32. Quotes from ATF agents are from interviews with ATF special agents Terry Jackson and Elizabeth Ragusa on July 12, 2007; additional background on ATF operations was obtained in interviews with special agents Tom Ahern and Rich Marianos on April 6, 2006, an ATF undercover agent (whose name must be withheld) on October 23, 2006, and deputy director Carson Carroll on May 16, 2006.

33. Syracuse University, Transactional Records Access Clearinghouse, "Bureau of Alcohol, Tobacco and Firearms Staff: 1992–2002," http://trac.syr.edu/tracatf/trends/v04/atfstaff.html; "FBI Staffing Trends: FY 1986–2006," http://trac.syr.edu/tracfbi/newfindings/current/include/20yearstaffingtable.html.

34. Marx and Coen, "Gang Kingpins Disappearing."

35. Noel, "Guilty Plea in Drive-by Shooting."

CHAPTER 9

The epigraph is from the author's notes of remarks made by Daniel Ochoa at a presentation titled "Business Social Responsibility: Addressing the Gang Challenge in Guatemala," held in Washington, DC, on May 23, 2007.

1. U.S. Agency for Internal Development, Bureau for Latin American and Caribbean Affairs, *Central America and Mexico Gang Assessment* (Washington, DC, 2006), 35.

2. Quotes from Daniel Ochoa and Harold Sibaja are from author's notes of remarks made by Ochoa and Sibaja at a presentation titled "Business Social Responsibility: Addressing the Gang Challenge in Guatamala," held in Washington, DC, on May 23, 2007, and e-mails from Harold Sibaja on January 15, 2008.

3. Intelligence Oversight Board, *Report on the Guatemala Review* (Washington, DC, 1996), available at http://www.ciponline.org/iob.htm.

4. Guatemalan Commission for Historical Clarification, *Guatemala: Memory of Silence* (1999), available at the Web site of the Science and Human Rights Program of the American Association for the Advancement of Science, http://shr.aaas.org/guatemala/ceh/report/english/toc.html.

5. See, e.g., Alex Sanchez, "Mexico's Drug War: A Society at Risk—Soldiers versus Narco-Soldiers," Council on Hemispheric Affairs, 2007, http://www.coha.org/2007/05/mexicos-drug-war-a-society-at-risk-soldiers-versus-narco-soldiers/.

6. Federal Bureau of Investigation, "Los Zetas: An Emerging Threat to the United States" (intelligence assessment, copy in author's files, 2005).

7. United Nations, Office on Drugs and Crime, *Caught in the Crossfire: Crime and Development in Central America* (Vienna, Austria, 2007), 14.

8. United Nations, *Caught in the Crossfire,* 40.

9. Quotes from Hector Alfonso are based on author's notes of Alfonso's presentation at the National Summit on Gang Violence, in Arlington, Virginia, June 2, 2006, and interviews on July 27, 2006 and February 21, 2007; quotes from Frank Ledee are from interviews on July 28, 2006 and February 20, 2007.

10. Deborah A. Osborne and Susan C. Wernicke, *Introduction to Crime Analysis: Basic Resources for Criminal Justice Practice* (New York: Haworth, 2003), 1.

11. Deborah Dash Moore, *To the Golden Cities: Pursuing the American Jewish Dream in Miami and L.A.* (Cambridge, MA: Harvard University Press, 1994), 25–26.

12. Moore, *To the Golden Cities,* 35.

13. Alex Stepick, Guillermo Grenier, Max Castro, and Marvin Dunn, *This Land Is Our Land: Immigrants and Power in Miami* (Berkeley: University of California Press, 2003), 35.

14. U.S. Bureau of the Census, "Miami-Dade County, Florida," *State and County QuickFacts,* http://quickfacts.census.gov/qfd/states/12/12086.html.

15. U.S. Bureau of the Census, "Miami (city), Florida," *State and County QuickFacts,* http://quickfacts.census.gov/qfd/states/12/1245000.html.

16. U.S. Bureau of the Census, "Hialeah (city), Florida," *State and County QuickFacts,* http://quickfacts.census.gov/qfd/states/12/1230000.html.

17. Joan Didion, *Miami* (New York: Vintage, 1988), 17.

18. Didion, *Miami*, 57–58.

19. Samuel P. Huntington, *Who Are We? The Challenges to America's National Identity* (New York: Simon and Schuster, 2004), 249.

20. Stepick et al., *This Land Is Our Land*, 10.

21. Patricia Nelson Limerick, *The Legacy of Conquest: The Unbroken Past of the American West* (New York: W. W. Norton, 1987), 191.

22. Didion, *Miami*, 64.

23. Didion, *Miami*, 67.

24. This discussion of the early Cuban youth gangs is based on J. Bryan Page, "Vulcans and Jutes: Cuban Fraternities and Their Disappearance," *Free Inquiry in Creative Sociology* 25, no. 1 (May 1997): 65–73.

25. Page, "Vulcans and Jutes," 69.

26. Page, "Vulcans and Jutes," 72.

27. Hector Alfonso, "Strategic Assessment of Gang Enforcement in Miami-Dade County" (paper written for Florida Department of Law Enforcement Analyst Academy Class, n.d. [probably 2003]), available at http://www.tallahassee infragard.org/FCJEI/Analyst_Info/Analyst%20Academy/Assessments%20Class%201/Hector %20Alfonso%20Assessment.pdf.

28. "Final Report of the Grand Jury: Fall Term A.D. 1984," Circuit Court of the Eleventh Judicial Circuit of Florida, May 14, 1985, available online at http://www.miamisao.com/publications/.

29. "Final Report of the Grand Jury: Fall Term A.D. 1984," 8.

30. "Final Report of the Grand Jury: Fall Term A.D. 1984," 13.

31. "Final Report of the Grand Jury: Fall Term A.D. 1984," 17.

32. "Final Report of the Grand Jury: Fall Term A.D. 1987," Circuit Court of the Eleventh Judicial Circuit of Florida, May 11, 1988.

33. "Final Report of the Grand Jury: Fall Term A.D. 1987," 1.

34. "Final Report of the Grand Jury: Fall Term A.D. 1987," 3.

35. "Final Report of the Grand Jury: Fall Term A.D. 1987," 7.

CONCLUSION

The epigraph is a statement made by an anonymous gang member quoted in S. Lynne Walker, "Gang Members Deported from U.S. Take Deadly Culture to Their Home Countries," Copley News Service, January 18, 2005.

INDEX

Abramoff, Jack, 42

"Ace" (Fernando King), 244, 245

"Adrian" (Adrian Covarrubias), 250, 251–52, 253

African American gangs. *See* black gangs

age cohorts, early gangs organized by, 66

agribusiness: in California, Great Migration and, 53–56; growth in South Florida of, 268–69; in Midwest, Mexicans drawn to, 234–36; seasonal workers needed for, 63, 64–65

Aguilar, Tiburcio "Tibs," 148, 149, 150, 153, 157

AIDS epidemic, start in 1980s of, 103

Air Force, U.S., trauma surgery training center in Baltimore, 20

AK-47 semiautomatic assault rifles: in bus attack in Honduras, 165–66; Comandari arrested for possession of, 202–3; emergency room treatment of wounds from, 19; Houston gangsters posing as FBI with, 2; murder of unnamed man and woman in 1994 and, 120, 121, 132–33; Rivera Paz arrested

for possession of, 167; use by drug dealers and gang members, 20, 104–5, 266

Alfonso, Hector J.: on denial of gangs, 273; on gangs in Miami, 265–66; as head of multiagency task force, 275; on MS-13 in Central America, 162, 163; on weed and seed program to deter gangs, 267

"All for Crime" (AFC) gang, Los Angeles, 59

Almaguer, Tomas, 46–47

Almighty Latin Charter Nation, Connecticut, 234

Almighty Latin King and Queen Nation, New York, 234

Almighty Latin King Nation, Chicago, 232. *See also* Latin Kings

Alpine Street gang, Los Angeles, 66

al Qaeda terrorists, 13, 177, 209

America Me (gang movie), 37

American Psychiatric Association (APA), on post-traumatic stress disorder, 17

American Spectator, 34

anchor babies, 107. *See also* second generation

Anglo-Saxon culture/"race": Cubans in Miami and, 270–72; fears about Latin American culture and, 34–35; fears about Latino gangs and, 89; Manifest Destiny, Mexican-American War and, 48; pachuco culture as assault on, 71

"Arana" (Ismael Cisneros), 186, 187

Arbenz Guzman, Jacobo, 261

Arizona State Prison, New Mexican Mafia and Cisneros Organization in, 216–18

Army, U.S.: pathfinder units in World War II of, 215–16; trauma surgery training center in Miami for, 20

Arroyo, William, 16, 17, 18–19, 20–21

Aryan Brotherhood, Eme joining with, 128

Ashcroft, John, 159, 209, 217

Asian organized crime, Carwile and Justice Department program on, 228

ATF. *See* Bureau of Alcohol, Tobacco, and Firearms

attorney general, U.S., on gang statistics, 9. *See also* Justice Department, U.S.

Ayres, Edward Duran, 77

Ayres Report (1942), 77–78

Aztecs (Cuban gang in Miami), 272

Aztlan, Mexico, 47

"Baby King" (Raul Gonzalez), 244

Bachman Lake, Texas, Calzada murder in or near, 175–76

Baghdad, Iraq, FBI in, 158–59

Baird, Lourdes, 140–41

Baires, Fredie "Travieso" (Mischievous), 184

Baker, the. *See* Ochoa, Daniel "Panadero"

Baltimore: MS-13 clique in, 171; U.S. Air Force trauma surgery training center in, 20. *See also* Maryland

"Bam Bam" (José Souffront), 256–57

Barr, William P., 90, 99

Barrera, Angel "Maldito" (Cursed), 184

Barrio 18 (Dieciocho), Guatemala, 80, 260, 262, 263

Barrio Mojados (BMS), 59

barrios and barrio culture: absence in Miami of, 267; Anglo migration to California and, 53; attraction for Mexicans coming to Los Angeles, 63–64; in Chicago, 238; conflicts of LAPD's proactive policing with, 83–84; early gangs organized around, 66; history of American West and, 35; off-season agribusiness workers in, 56

Bauman, John, 198, 206

Bautista, Juan Antonio, 3

Benjamin Franklin Branch Library, Los Angeles, books in languages of cultures served by, 39–40

Bennett, William J., 104

betabeleros (Mexican migrant workers in Midwest), 235

Big Gangster Locos Salvatrucha clique, 178

Bird, the (Juan Bautista Jimenez Mejia), 167–68

black gangs: in Chicago, 233–34, 237, 240; crack cocaine in Los Angeles and, 85; FBI's investigation of, 143; federal anti-gang effort in 1992 against Latino gangs vs., 102; homicides in Washington, D.C., and, 223–24; Justice Department on drug trafficking by, 105; in Miami-Dade County during 1980s, 274; start in Los Angeles of, 14–15. *See also* blacks; gangs

Black Gangster/New Breeds, Chicago, 234

Black Guerrilla Family, Nuestra Familia and, 128

Black Panther Party (Compton), 109

Black P. Stone Nation (Chicago), 234

blacks: LA communities, conflicts of LAPD's proactive policing with, 83–84; locations of LA communities, 64; murder clearance rate in Chicago for, 248; murdered male, crack cocaine, semiautomatic weapons and, 105. *See also* black gangs

Bloods, 14–15, 85, 102, 105

body art, minimal, as new MS-13 style, 3. *See also* tattoos

Border Patrol. *See* U.S. Border Patrol

Born in East L.A. (movie), 37

Bowron, Fletcher, 76

colonias, 53. *See also* barrios and barrio culture

Columbia Lil' Cycos (CLCS): Eme interlopers poaching on, 132; Eme's control of *renta* system and, 130; extortion scheme success for, 135–36; fallout after Garcia raid within, 156; innovations under Termite as chief shot caller, 133–34; location and areas controlled by, 118–19; murder of unnamed man and woman in 1994 and, 120, 121–22, 132–33; *renta* (tax collection) system for street dealers, 127–28; Riordan and Sandford hear references to, 146; search for Greedy Tape by, 123; tensions over disrespect by Cazales, 134–35; testimony on criminal work of, 125–27; Valerio on Eme drug trafficking and extortion system and, 123. *See also* 18th Street Gang

Columbian drug trafficking organizations, 125

Comandari, Alfredo "Fredi," 201–2

Comandari, Antonio, 202

Comandari, Emilio, 201

Comandari, Nelson Martinez (Agustin) Varela: arrested in El Salvador as head of gang, 202–3; arrested in Houston in 2005, 206; Clifford's BOLO on, 198; eludes FBI in 1999–2000, 157; family of, 201–2; as FBI and LAPD fugitive in 2001, 14; FBI wiretap on Termite and information on, 203; jailed on federal drug-trafficking charge, 200–201; lying low in El Salvador mid-2001, 204–5; Morales's information about, 199–200, 203–4; as refugee from Salvadoran civil war, 29–30; as stalled case, 206–8; Termite's first contact with, 156

Comandari family, of Palestinian Tarajmeh clan, 25, 201

combat fatigue, 17–18. *See also* post-traumatic stress disorder

Coming to America (movie), 140

commerce, global: criminals and terrorists' use of, 193; Latino gangs and, 5–6. *See also* economy, U.S.

communications, global, criminals and terrorists' use of, 193

Compton, California: gangsta rap and

demographics of, 108–9; poverty in 1960s in, 110

Compton Police Department, Los Angeles Metropolitan Task Force on Violent Crime and, 99

Compton Varrio Tres (gang), 109

"Conejo." *See* Rivera, Denis "Conejo"

Congress, U.S.: on crack cocaine, 103; estimates of gangs in hearings by, 10; McClellan's Senate committee, 225; restraints on FBI due to, 195; Wolf's subcommittee, 161–62

Connecticut, Almighty Latin Charter Nation in, 234

Contreras, Donatilla, 120, 123, 133

Cook, Glenn, 172

corporatism, in El Salvador, 24

Correctional Services Division, LASD, 112–13. *See also* Los Angeles County Sheriff's Department

corruption, LAPD and, 75–76

Corvette Summer (1978 movie), 94

countersurveillance, in MS-13 operation in Houston, 2

court reports, facts on gang activities in, 57–58

courts, PTSD as defense to criminal charges in, 18

Covarrubias, Adrian, 250, 251–52, 253

crack cocaine: demand for and epidemic in, 102–5; FBI's Safe Streets Violent Crimes Initiative and, 90; federal anti-gang effort in 1992 against black vs. Latino gangs and, 102; gang violence and trafficking in, 124; and industrial economy demise in early 1970s in Los Angeles, 111–12; in Los Angeles, 85; Smiley Hauser clique and, 146

CRASH (Community Resources against Street Hoodlums) unit, LAPD, 15, 84, 115

Creative Associates International, 263–64

crime: Ayres's comments on Mexican Americans and, 77–78; by gangs, as predestination, 42–43; by gangs, statistics on, 9–10; gangs and public discourse about, 278; and immigration, commentators on, 44. *See also* drive-by shootings; homicides; violence

Latino barrio, 64; poverty in 1960s in, 110; Sleepy Lagoon case and, 62. *See also* Los Angeles

East Side Stories: Gang Life in East LA (Rodriguez and Martinez), 39, 43

Economic Opportunity Act (1964), 110

economy, U.S.: drugs and drug trafficking and, 124; immigrants to Southern California and, 31; industrial, in California, gangs and, 111–12; industrial, in California, Salvadorans and, 31; Mexican migration to Chicago and, 234–36; Puerto Rican migration to Chicago and, 236–37; support for, as gang suppression, 281–82. *See also* commerce, global; Great Migration

Edmondson, Randy, 241–42, 249, 251–52

education: civil war/violence in Guatemala and, 261–62; Salvadoran community in Los Angeles without, 31; in the United States, gang prevention and, 280

18th Street Gang: bad blood between MS-13 and, 86; cliques across the United States in 2007 of, 162; deportation from United States, 163; estimates on proportion of illegal immigrants in, 106, 107; Gates on problems at end of 1980s caused by, 115–16; illegal immigrants to United States in, 116; and leaders of, RICO case against, 146–47; MS-13 National Gang Task Force and, 80, 230; as muscle and mules for Mexican DTOs, 194; Riordan assigned to, 141–42; Riordan's use of RICO against, 102; Sandford's study of, 143; start in Los Angeles of, 14–23; as transnational criminal enterprise, 34, 124; Valerio's protective custody and relationship to, 123. *See also* Columbia Lil' Cycos; Smiley Hauser clique of 18th Street Gang

"El Culiche." *See* Rivera Paz, Ever Anibal "El Culiche," "El Little Baby," "the Tapeworm"

"El Jefe" (Gustavo Colon), 231–33, 244, 246, 254, 255–57

"El Little Baby." *See* Rivera Paz, Ever Anibal "El Culiche," "El Little Baby," "the Tapeworm"

"El Magnate" (Gustavo Colon), 231–33,

244, 246, 254, 255–57

El Monte Flores (EMF) gang (Los Angeles), 58–59

"El Pajaro" (Juan Bautista Jimenez Mejia), 167–68

El Rukn street gang (Chicago), 99, 138–39

El Salvador: bipartisan U.S. policy on military aid for, 27–28; civil war in, 26–27; (Fredi) Comandari and prisons in, 201–2; (Nelson) Comandari's arrest staged in, 203; income inequities in, 24, 25–26; military governments in, 26; population density, 24–25; PTSD in children from, 21; refugee children from, MS-13 gang and, 23; refugees in Los Angeles from wars in, 19; refugees to the United States from, 28–29; undocumented aliens in LA gangs from, 115–16; U.S. criminal aliens deported to, 164; U.S. deportees re-creating LA gangs in, 34; U.S. military establishment and, 12–14, 287n53; wars between MS-13 and 18th Street Gang in, 164–65

Eme. *See* Mexican Mafia

Encinas, Louie, 74

enforzador (enforcer), in Latin Kings' hierarchy, 245

enganchistas (Mexican migrant workers on railroads), 235

English language: Mexicans in the Great Migration and, 65; nonspeakers, in Chicago, 236–37; nonspeakers, in East LA and Boyle Heights, 37

English-only movement, Cubans in Miami and, 271–72

Enlightenment thought, racial superiority theory and, 48

enterprise theory. *See* federal enterprise theory

Escobar, Wilfred, 256, 257

Eth, Spencer, 16–17, 18, 20–21, 22

Europe, gangs in, 6

Evergreen gang, of East LA, 38

Fairfax Village Crew, Washington, D.C., 223–24

fair fights, early gang rules on, 67

Falfurrias, Texas: geography and demographics of, 168–69; Rivera Paz captured at checkpoint in, 170–71

false flagging, Mateo murder and, 252
Farabundo Martí National Liberation
  Front, El Salvador, 26–27, 202
Fast Times at Ridgemont High (movie),
  88–89
Federal Bureau of Investigation (FBI): accelerating transnational threats vs. core
  mission of, 193; constitutional and legislative restraints on, 195; criticisms on
  crack cocaine epidemic handling by,
  104; documenting informant debriefing
  by, 150; on 18th Street Gang, 80; on
  federal enterprise theory, 101;
  GangTECC and, 229–30; Houston
  sting operation November 2005 and,
  1–3; on ICE's criminal alien sweeps,
  213–14; investigational methods,
  145–46; investigatory agents for, 255; in
  Iraq, 158–59; jurisdiction in Southern
  California, 90; LA field office in Santa
  Monica, 89; on LA street gangs, 88,
  90–91; Latino gangs and, 86; Los Angeles Metropolitan Task Force on Violent
  Crime and, 99; on Miami gangs, 266;
  power struggle with Justice Department, 209; Special Division for Organized Crime, 225–26; Special Operations Division and, 205; stalled
  Comandari case and, 208; support for
  gang squads after *Los Angeles Times*
  series, 148; as Truchon career goal, 16;
  Varela and Comandari clans of El Salvador and, 14; Wolf's subcommittee
  and, 161; on writing about Comandari,
  200
federal enterprise theory: elements of,
  100–102; as shared and interactive enterprise, 136–37. *See also* RICO antiracketeering law
federalization of law enforcement: black
  gangs and drug trafficking as focus of,
  102, 105; investigative techniques and
  tools for, 100–101; after Rodney King
  Riots, 97; statutory basis for, 100;
  transnational drug-trafficking networks and, 277–78
federal witness protection/security program: Paz's ineligibility for, 184–85; as
  tool in organized crime investigations,
  101; Valerio and, 157. *See also* witness

intimidation
"Feo." *See* Lopez Romero, Juan Manuel
  "Termite," "Feo"
field interrogations, by LAPD, 81, 84
fighting gangs, of Los Angeles, 66–67, 68
Fitzgerald, Patrick, 245
Flagler, Henry Morrison, 268
Florencia 13 (Los Angeles gang), 59, 106
Flores, Frank: on 18th Street Gang start,
  80; on gangster choices, 126; on his sin-
  gle-parent household, 38; on illegal im-
  migration and gangs, 41–42; as LAPD
  detective and MS-13 gang expert, 39;
  on life choices, 36, 40–41; on public
  perception of East LA, 37; on respect,
  41
Flores Parada, Juan Ramon "Junior,"
  175, 182–83, 185
Florida East Coast Railroad, 268–69
Ford, Gerald, 227
Foreign Miners' License Tax, California
  (1850), 50
Four Corner Hustlers (Chicago), 234
Four Kings (Los Cuatro Reyes) case,
  Chicago, 233, 254–57
Fourteen Families, of El Salvador, 24, 202
Freeh, Louis, 209
French Connection (heroin conduit from
  Turkey), 247
Fricke, Charles William, 62
Fulwood, Isaac, Jr., 223

*Gang, The: A Study of 1,313 Gangs in
  Chicago* (Thrasher), 233
gang nicknames, 38–39
gang prevention programs, 7, 267, 280
Gang Prosecution Unit, Miami-Dade
  County State's Attorney's Office,
  267–68
gangs: in California, horizontal structure
  of, 129; in Chicago, in early twentieth
  century, 237; in Chicago, since early
  twentieth century, 233–34; in Chicago,
  vertical structure of, 243–44; cooperation with Mexican Mafia, 129–30;
  Cuban, in Miami, 272, 281; denial of
  problem with, 6, 272–73; escalation in
  violence during 1940s of, 68; fighting,
  66–67, 68; historical documentation
  difficulties for, 237; identification with

and loyalty to, 67; and industrial economy demise in early 1970s in Los Angeles, 111–12; in LA barrios in the 1940s, 56; in Los Angeles, Salvadoran refugee kids and, 32; in Los Angeles County jails, Valdemar's introduction to, 113; in Los Angeles of the 1920s, characteristics of, 65–66; law-and-order approach to, 42; as organisms, 15; organized crime in western United States and, 228; peak violent periods since 1988 by, 84–85; signs thrown by, 58; statistics on, 9–10; transnational, Clifford on MS-13 as, 208; transnational, cliques across the United States in 2007, 162; transnational, criminal, and drug-trafficking organizations and, 123–24; in United States, alliances with Guatemalan Zetas, 261; Vigil on multiple marginality and, 43–44; after World War II, barrio kids' perception of, 79. *See also* Mafia; *specific gangs*

Gang Squad, of U.S. Justice Department, 229

gangsta rap, Compton as birthplace of, 108–9

Gangster Disciple Nation (Chicago), 234

gangsters: character and values of, 4; imprisonment as rite of passage for, 79–80. *See also* clothing

Gang Strike Force, Miami-Dade County State's Attorney's Office, 266

gang suppression, in United States, 6–7, 280–81

GangTECC, 229–30

Garcia, Janie Maria "Mom": conviction and sentencing of, 157; FBI's focus on, 150–51; information from wiretap on, 152–54; on murder of Cazales, 134–35; as Puppet's conduit to CLCS, 132, 133; search warrant for house of, 154; on Termite as a snitch, 156

Garcia, Juan "Drac," "Vamp," 250, 251–52, 253–54, 258

Garcia, Michael J., 171

Garcia, Mickey, 70

garment industry, in California, Salvadorans in, 31

Gates, Darryl: on beating of Rodney King, 298n17; iron-fisted reaction to

Latino gang wars under, 86; on LAPD antigang CRASH program, 115; on proactive policing, 81, 84; retirement after Rodney King Riots, 98; on TRASH unit, 15; on undocumented aliens in LA gangs, 115–16

Giuliani, Rudolph W., 104

globalization, Latino gangs and, 5–6, 193

Golden, Michael, 249–50, 253

Gold Rush, 49, 50

Gomez, Maria, 186

Gonzales, Alberto, 209, 218–19, 228–29, 311

Gonzales, Manuel: on Manifest Destiny, 47–48; on Mexican population in California after Mexican-American War, 45–46; on Mexican resistance to California's discriminatory laws, 52–53; on social class and massiveness of Latino immigration, 65

Gonzalez, Raul "Baby King," 244

Gotti, John, 207

graffiti: 18th Street Gang, 120; gang-related, absence in Miami of, 267

Grande, Oscar Antonio, 187

Grape Street Crips (Los Angeles), 117

Gravano, Sammy "the Bull," 207

Gray, William P., 139–40

Greaser Act (California, 1855), 52

greasers, Anglos on Mexicans as, 46, 291n32

Great Depression, 64

Great Migration, 47, 53–56

Great Society, Johnson's, 110

Greece: Clifford assistance with N-17 terrorists in, 196–97; November 17 (N-17) terrorist group in, 193

Greedy Tape, 123, 135, 154. *See also* Valerio, Ramiro "Greedy," "Ojos"

Greedy Valerio. *See* Valerio, Ramiro "Greedy," "Ojos"

"Green Light Club," Riordan's, 147, 148–49

green light(s): assigned by prison-based Mexican Mafia, 129; on Paz, 185; gang definition of, 119; on Valerio, 118–19, 122; paperwork on snitches and, 123

Guadelupe-Hidalgo, peace treaty of, 45, 49

Guatemala: civil war in, 260–62; gangs in, 165; Los Angeles gang culture exported to, 262; MS-13's smuggling routes through, 194; Ochoa's presentation at Washington embassy of, 259–60; population density, 25; U.S. deportees recreating LA gangs in, 34

Guatemalans, incarceration rate in United States for, 44

Gunfight at the O.K. Corral, 93–94

gun(s): civilian market in, explosion in 1980s of, 104–5; commercially made, White Fence gang as first to use, 68; increased gang homicides in 1970s and, 85; in Mateo murder, 252–53; owned by gangs, Rodriguez on, 59; semiautomatic "wonder nines," 86; smuggled by gangs, democratic governance and, 278–79; stolen after Rodney King Riots, 98. *See also* AK-47 semiautomatic assault rifles; M-16 assault rifles

gunshot wounds, multiple, as LA-USC hospital specialty, 19

Gutierrez, Juana, 121

hairstyles, of pachuco culture, 69. *See also* clothing

Haitian criminal gangs, in South Florida, 266

Hamill, Mark, 94

Hamilton, Olga, 154–55

hard candy, gang definition of, 119

Hawks (Cuban gang in Miami), 272

Hayworth, Rita, 62

Henry, O., 284n2

heroin, Los Angeles as distribution center for, 125

Heroin Highway, 247

herpes epidemic, of 1980s, 103

Herrera-Nevares, Jaime, 246

Herrera organization, drug trafficking by, 246

Hess, Jason, 198–200

Heston, Charlton, 89

Hialeah, Florida: grand jury report on gangs in, 274; Latino population of, 270

Hickory Street gang (Los Angeles), 114

Hill and Barlow (law firm), 190

Hinson, Edward T., 222

Hispanic, use of *Latino* vs. as generic term, 8–9

Hittner, David, 172

Hogan, William, 99, 101–2, 138–39

Holder, Eric, Jr., 190–91

Holliday, George, 95

Hollywood Gangsters (HGs), 128, 130, 146–47

Holmes, Brian, 249–50, 253

homicides: gang-related, in California, 18, 19, 20; gang-related, in California vs. United States, 84–85; gang-related, escalation during 1950s, 79; gang-related, semiautomatic guns and, 86. *See also* drive-by shootings; violence; *specific cases*

Honduran *mayoristas,* CLCS's *renta* system and, 133–34

Honduras: Christmas bus attack in, 165–68; U.S. deportees re-creating LA gangs in, 34

Hoover, J. Edgar, 11, 225

Houston, Texas, sting operation November 2005, 1–3

Houston Chronicle, on Rivera Paz escape, 172–73

Hunter, Gregory T., 180, 181, 185, 186, 187

Huntington, Samuel P., 271, 279

Ice Cube, 109

illegal immigrants to United States: estimated proportions in street gangs, 106–7; Flores on choices for, 41–42; in gangs, deportation of, 115–16, 117, 162–63, 164, 171–72. *See also* immigrants to United States

Illegal Immigration Reform and Immigrant Responsibility Act (U.S., 1996), 162–63

immigrants to United States: for agribusiness in California, 63, 64–65; backlash against, Cubans in Miami and, 271–72; Cuban, in Miami, 267–68; during Great Migration to California, 53–56; large-scale immigration, gangs and, 65–66; Mexican, to Chicago and Midwest, 234–36; Puerto Rican, to Chicago and Midwest, 236–37. *See also* illegal

immigrants to United States; second generation
Immigration and Customs Enforcement (ICE), U.S.: authority for deporting criminal aliens by, 117; deportation of criminal aliens by, 163; on MS-13 smuggling operations, 194; Operation Community Shield sweeps by, 212–14; on Rivera Paz disappearance, 172–73; Special Operations Division and, 205
Immigration and Naturalization Service (INS), U.S., 116, 117, 163
immigration laws, U.S., 5, 29, 34, 117, 278
immigration raids, law enforcement investigations of stranger-to-stranger homicides and, 248
incarceration rates: in California and United States, 6–7; among Latinos, 44. See also prisons
Incas, in Latin Kings' hierarchy, 245
Indians, as obstacle to Anglo western expansion, 271
informant(s), confidential: Justice Department's use of, 101; keeping control of, 181; Lopez Romero as, 157; Paz as, 180–83; Riordan on management of, 150; stalled Comandari case and potential for, 207; Valerio as, 122–23, 133, 149–50; Varelli as, 14, 30
Inglewood Police Department, Los Angeles Metropolitan Task Force on Violent Crime and, 99
Internal Revenue Service, U.S., 205, 226
Interperimeter Office, of Almighty Latin Kings, 232
intervention programs, 7. See also gang prevention programs
investigador (investigator), in Latin Kings' hierarchy, 245
Iran/Hezbollah Unit, FBI's International Terrorism Section, Clifford as head of, 196
Irish immigrant gangs, in Los Angeles, 66
Italian Mafia. See Mafia

Jackson, Curtis, 114
Jackson, Terry, 233, 244, 254–55

jails, Los Angeles County: Mexican Mafia in, 113, 129–30; Morales escapes from, 200; Valdemar's tour in, 112–13. See also prisons
James, Harry, 60
James, McElroy, and Diehl (law firm), 221–22
jamming techniques, of CRASH antigang units, 84
jazz culture, gangs and, 68
Jews, in Miami, 269
Jimenez, Ismael "Loner," 126
Jimenez Mejia, Juan Bautista "El Pajaro" (the Bird), 167–68
Johnson, Lyndon B., 22, 110, 226
Joint Terrorism Task Force, FBI's, 94
Jolley, Laurie, 233, 255, 256
Jordan Downs neighborhood (Los Angeles), black gangs in, 19–20
Juarez, Mexico, 37–38
jumping in, as admittance to a gang, 67, 179
"Junior" (Flores Parada), 175, 182–83, 185
Justice Department, U.S.: Carwile and Organized Crime Section, 223–24; Clark's organized crime strike forces of, 226–27; GangTECC and, 229–30; Kennedy on lack of Mafia intelligence, 225–26; LA gang investigations and, 150; Latino gangs and, 86; Los Angeles Metropolitan Task Force on Violent Crime and, 99; Organized Crime and Racketeering Section, 101, 225–27; organized crime strike forces of, 226–27; power struggle with FBI, 209; report on nation's drug problem (1989) by, 105; on special antigang effort, 218; Special Operations Division, 205; stalled Comandari case and, 208; wiretap application process of, 151–52; Wolf's Subcommittee and, 161; on writing about Comandari, 200
Jutes (Cuban gang in Miami), 272

Kaibiles (Guatemalan counterinsurgents), 261
Kennedy, John F., 225, 226
Kennedy, Robert F., 225–26
King, Fernando "Ace," 244, 245

King, Rodney: acquittal of officers in beating of, 88, 95–96; incident leading to beating of, 94–95. *See also* Rodney King Riots

knives, homemade, in California prisons, 130

Koon, Stacey, 95, 98, 298n17

KTLA television, King beating video on, 95

La Cosa Nostra (LCN). *See* Mafia

La Eme. *See* Mexican Mafia

Laguna Duck Club, 72

La Matanza (the Slaughter) in El Salvador (1932), 26

Lancaster, Burt, 93–94

language, of pachuco culture, 69. *See also* English language

"La Pantera" (the Panther) (Juan Carlos Miralda Bueso), 167, 168

Lassar, Scott R., 233

Latin American culture, fears about Anglo-Saxon culture and, 34–35

Latin Counts, 238, 240, 250–51

Latin Kings: ATF investigation of, 255–57; attempts to form in Miami, 267; in Chicago, 234; in Chicago, Puerto Rican vs. Mexican factions of, 232; drug trafficking by, 245–46; formation in Chicago, 238; leadership after top leaders arrested, 245; vertical leadership structure, 243–44; YMCA program in Chicago for, 239–40. *See also* Motherland

Latino gangs: as challenge to national security, 278–79; changes in United States and, 5; in Chicago (*see* Mexicans; Puerto Ricans); federal antigang effort in 1992 against black gangs vs., 102; heartless violence of, 4; larger, more sophisticated criminal networks and, 193–94; in Los Angeles (*see* Los Angeles); Mara Salvatrucha and national notoriety of, 33; marking territory in Chicago as focus of, 240; megagang potential among, 278; Mexican Mafia mass meetings with leaders of, 130–31; in Miami, 265–67; in Miami-Dade County during 1980s, 274; moral panic about, 10–11; myths and stereotypes

about, public policy and, 33–34; reluctance to admit existence of, 11; return to streets of imprisoned members in late 1980s, 85–86; Wolf's subcommittee and, 161–62. *See also* 18th Street Gang; gangs; Mara Salvatrucha

Latinos: gangs as small percentage of, 7; gender role changes during World War II among, 68; migrating to United States, fractured families among, 31–32; murder clearance rate in Chicago for, 248; use of *Hispanic* vs. *Latino* as generic term, 8–9; U.S. immigration policies on, 279–80

law-and-order approach to gangs, 42

law enforcement: Anglo, communicating/understanding Latino gangs by, 6; in California, gang problem for, 22; character and values of, 4; on Comandari's vision and capabilities, 203–4; debate on gang involvement in larger criminal organizations within, 194–95; federal, Latino gangs and, 86; federalization and internationalization of, 5; gang suppression and, 280–81; immigration raids and murder investigations by, 248; interagency politics, MS-13 National Gang Task Force and, 211; *Los Angeles Times* on 18th Street Gang and failures of, 147–48; Sleepy Lagoon episode, Mexican American community and, 75–79; supporting role of gang analysts, 265–66; transnational drug-trafficking networks and, 277–78. *See also specific units*

LCN. *See* Mafia

Ledee, Frank, 267–68

"Lefty" (Javier Cazales), 119, 134–35

Legion of Fire: Killer Ants (TV movie), 24

Lench, Lisa, 141

Leon, Antonio Carreto, 58–59

Lil' Cycos. *See* Columbia Lil' Cycos

Limerick, Patricia Nelson, 82, 271

Little Aztecs, in Miami-Dade County, 274

little brown brother, use of term, 284n2

Littles, Larell and Larnell, murder of, 223–24

Little Village neighborhood, Chicago, 238, 240, 245

"Loner" (Ismael Jimenez), 126

Long Beach Police Department, Los Angeles Metropolitan Task Force on Violent Crime and, 99

Lopez, Carlos Alberto "Truco," 120, 122, 123, 132, 133

Lopez Romero, Juan Manuel "Termite," "Feo": on acceptance by CLCS, 126–27; CLCS attempt to murder, 156; Comandari in FBI wiretap of, 203; on discussions about murder of Cazales, 134–35; as FBI informant, 157; FBI learns of delivery of $9,000 to Janie by, 154; innovations as chief CLCS shot caller, 133–34; murder of unnamed man and woman in 1994 and, 120, 121, 122; pen registers and trap-and-trace devices on phone calls of, 151; shot caller for Columbia Lil' Cycos, 119; Truco hit and, 132–33

"Lord Gino" (Gustavo Colon), 231–33, 244, 246, 254, 255–57

Lorena gang (East LA), 38

Los Angeles: as center of nation's drug problem in 1989, 105; crack cocaine in, 103; democracy among Latino gangs in, 114; early gangs in, multiple ethnicities of, 66; as epicenter of America's gang problem, 14–23; gang-related homicides in, 18, 19, 20; Great Migration and barrios of, 56; industrial economy demise in early 1970s in, 111–12; interests in stalled Comandari case vs. Justice Department, 207–8; Mexican population in mid- to late-nineteenth century, 49; Project Safe Neighborhoods in, 229; RICO cases against MS-13 in, 230; significance as illicit drug distribution center, 125. See also East Los Angeles; Los Angeles Police Department; Salvadorans

Los Angeles County: Great Migration and growth of, 56; increased gang homicides in, 85

Los Angeles County Sheriff's Department (LASD): contracts by Los Angeles County's cities with, 109; East LA and, 37; Los Angeles Metropolitan Task Force on Violent Crime and, 99; Operation Safe Streets (antigang unit), 106;

rivalry with LAPD, 105–6; television coverage of, 94; Valdemar on patrol duty for, 113–14; Valdemar's tour in jails of, 112–13. See also law enforcement

Los Angeles County–University of Southern California Medical Center (LA-USC), 18–19

Los Angeles Metropolitan Task Force on Violent Crime, 99, 143

Los Angeles Police Department (LAPD): acquittal of officers in beating of King and, 95–96; buy-bust operations in Smiley Drive area, 145–46; Comandari as fugitive in 2001 from, 14; CRASH unit of, 15, 115; on drive-by shootings, 32; investigating Cazales murder, 135; Los Angeles Metropolitan Task Force on Violent Crime and, 99; Morales's confession, importance for, 200; negative aspects to proactive policing by, 82–84; officers living outside the city, 88; proactive policing by, 81–82; reforms of 1930s, 76–77; rivalry with Los Angeles County Sheriff's Department, 105–6; South Central unit, Truchon as head of, 19–20; television coverage of, 94; World War II emergency officers, 71–72; Zoot Suit Riots and, 78–79. See also Bub, Robert; Gates, Darryl; law enforcement

Los Angeles Riots (1992), 90. See also Rodney King Riots

Los Angeles Times, 59, 119–20, 147–48

Los Cuatro Reyes (The Four Kings) case, Chicago, 233, 254–57

Lost Dutchman Gold Mine, 92–93

Lou Dobbs Tonight, 10

Lozano, Balde, 169

"Lucifer" (Andy Salinas), 184

lynchings, in California, 51–52

Maduro, Ricardo, 170

Mafia (La Cosa Nostra [LCN]): difficulties in quantifying problem of, 11; FBI's expertise against, 90–91; Hoover, Kennedy, and, 225; as model for Mexican Mafia, 129; respect in prisons for, 80; RICO antiracketeering law used against, 99. See also Mexican Mafia

law enforcement and, 75–79; social estrangement of working-class youth, 68–69; Zoot Suit Riots and, 78–79; zoot suits and, 70. *See also* 18th Street Gang; Latino gangs; Mara Salvatrucha; Mexicans; pachuco culture

Mexican-American War (1846–48), 45, 47

Mexican Mafia (La Eme, Eme): Comandari's deal with, 204; on conquest story and "political resistance," 47; FBI's RICO case against, 141; green light on Valerio by, 119, 122; independence of New Mexican Mafia from, 217; in Los Angeles County jails, 113; mass meetings with Latino gang leaders, 130–31; power in prisons and beyond of, 80, 128–30; Riordan's use of RICO against, 102. *See also* New Mexican Mafia

Mexicans: feudal ranchero society in Alta California in mid-nineteenth century and, 46–47, 50–51; Great Migration of, 53–56; as illegal aliens in LA gangs, 116; as immigrants to Chicago and the Midwest, 234–36; as immigrants to Southern California, 31; incarceration rate in United States for, 44; old elite vs. mixed-blood mestizos, racial pecking order among, 48; as racially inferior in California and the United States, 49. *See also* Mexican Americans

Mexico: cohorting tradition of, 66; drug-trafficking organizations based in, 5; gangs in, 6; land grants in California of, 50–51; Latino gangs spreading across, 162; MS-13 and 18th Street Gang consolidation in, 164; MS-13 control of smuggling stash houses in, 194; transnational 18th Street Gang and drugs from, 124–25

Miami: Alfonso on Latino gangs in, 265–66; crack cocaine in, 103; Cuban gangs (fraternities) in, 272, 281; gang suppression in, 275; grand jury report on gangs in, 274–75; Jewish population in, 269; railroads, agribusiness, and growth of, 268–69; U.S. army trauma surgery training center in, 20

Miami-Dade County, grand jury reports on gangs in, 273–75

Miami-Dade County Police Department, 82, 266

Miami-Dade County State's Attorney's Office, 266, 267–68

Miami Herald, 269, 270

microgangs, in Chicago, 234

minority neighborhoods, conflicts of LAPD's proactive policing with, 83–84. *See also specific groups*

Minutemen at Arizona-Mexico border, 108

Miralda Bueso, Juan Carlos "La Pantera," 167, 168

mob, the. *See* Mafia

"Mom." *See* Garcia, Janie Maria "Mom"

Moore, Joan, 64, 65, 67, 76, 79

Morales, Erick, 198–200, 203–4

moral panic: over crack cocaine, 103; in United States, about Latino street gangs, 10–11

Morgenthau, Robert M., 104

Motherland, 234, 245. *See also* Latin Kings

motorcycle gangs, violence of, 10–11

movies/films: army ants as basis for, 24; on battle of Rorke's Drift, 137–38; on life in East LA, 37; on mythical and romantic Spanish mission period, 53; on only human survivor of a biological war, 89; Truchon's love of, 93–94; on Valley girls, 88–89; zoot suits in, 70

MS-13. *See* Mara Salvatrucha

MS-13 National Gang Task Force: 18th Street Gang added to mandate of, 80, 230; FBI focus on, 23; formation within FBI of, 3; funding for, 208; gang suppression and, 281; international arrest sweep (2008), 214; in Los Angeles, Comandari interrogation and, 203; Swecker hires Clifford for, 197–98

M-16 assault rifles, 19, 20, 165–66

M-18, 80. *See also* 18th Street Gang

Mueller, Robert S.: Attorney General Gonzales and, 209; Carwile prosecuting black gang homicides and, 222–23; early life and influences, 189–90; national gang task force and, 190–91, 197; Wolf's call about gangs in Virginia to, 188–89

Original Mexican Mafia, 217. *See also* Mexican Mafia

Orozco (Chicago police officer), 249

orthopedic surgeons, in Los Angeles, as multiple gunshot wound specialists, 19

Oseguera, Rick, 181–82

Ottoman Empire collapse, Middle Eastern Arabs in Central America and, 201

Pachuca, Mexico, zoot suits and, 70

pachuco culture: confrontational dress and mannerisms of, 69; gangs and, 68; tensions with LAPD and, 76; war emergency officers and, 71–72; zoot suit symbolism for, 70–71. *See also* Mexican Americans

Pagan, Eduardo Obregon, 63, 74

Page, J. Bryan, 272, 273

palomillas, 66

"Panadero." *See* Ochoa, Daniel "Panadero"

Pancho Villa, 108

"Papa King" ("Papa Santos"), 244

paperwork, gang definition of, 123

Parker, William H., 81

Parker Center (LAPD headquarters), 81, 96

Partnership for Public Service, 192

Party People (Chicago), 241, 242–43

Patton, Alan, 176, 181–83

Paz, Brenda "Smiley": on Calzada murder, 181–83; Cisneros, Grande, and Rivera's trial for murder of, 187–88; on Daingerfield Island murder, 183–84; Daingerfield Island murder and, 177; defiance against rules, 179–80; early life and influences, 178–79; green light on, 185; as informant on MS-13, 180–81; McNulty memo on MS-13 cases linked to, 218; murder of, 187; questioned in Calzada murder, 176; in safe houses, 184–86

PCP, Los Angeles as distribution center for, 125

peasant uprisings, in El Salvador, 25–26

pen registers, 151, 257. *See also* wiretaps

People v. Leon (2005), 59

Phoenix, Arizona, Truchon and Latino gang case in, 216–18

Pillsbury, Madison, and Sutro (law firm), 190

Pilsen neighborhood, Chicago: Latin Counts of, 238; smaller gangs in, 240. *See also* Mateo, Ana

Pino, Juan Antonio, 3

Piru Bloods, 109

Piru Street Boys, 109

police. *See* law enforcement

Ponce de Leon, 268

Porter, John Clinton, 64

post-traumatic stress disorder (PTSD), 17, 20–23, 261

Post-Traumatic Stress Disorder in Children (Eth and Pynoos), 21

poverty, in Los Angeles County of 1960s, 110. *See also* economy, U.S.

Powers, Scott, 183–84

predestination, for gang membership or crime, 42

preventive (police) patrols, of LAPD, 81. *See also* gang prevention programs

prisons: Arizona, Latino gangs in, 216–18; California, administrative segregation in, 130; California, dispersal of Eme leaders throughout, 129; California, gang mythology about, 79–80; gang-controlled, in El Salvador, 164–65; gang-controlled, in United States and Central America, 164; Illinois, Colon's control of, 231–33; rehabilitation vs. warehousing in, 280; tapes of phone calls from, 151, 257; U.S., gangs in, 7. *See also* Correctional Services Division, LASD; incarceration rates; jails, Los Angeles County

Project Safe Neighborhoods, ATF's, 229

Proposition 13, California's, 22, 109

protective custody, gang suspicions about, 123. *See also* federal witness protection/security program

public opinion, on Latino gangs, formation of, 33–34. *See also* news media

Puerto Ricans: in Chicago, Division Street riot and, 239; conflicts of LAPD's proactive policing with, 83; as immigrants to Chicago and the Midwest, 236–37

Puerto Rico, Valdemar at international conference in, 110–11

States, 171–72; disappearance details sealed from public eye, 208; escape from U.S. prison, 172–73; explanations for disappearance of, 173–74; press releases on apprehension of, 206

Rivera Paz, Lester, 172

Robleto, Sergio, 131

Rodney King Riots (1992), 19, 88, 90, 95–99

Rodriguez, Joseph, 39, 59. See also *East Side Stories: Gang Life in East LA*

Rojas, Sergio "Smoke," 249

Romero, Juan, attack on, 57, 58–59, 75

Romero, Oscar Arnulfo, 26

Ronald Reagan Presidential Library, 87

Roosevelt, Franklin D., 79

Rorke's Drift, Riordan's appreciation of battle at, 137–38

Rowan, J. Patrick, 191

Ruchhoft, Robert, 116, 117

Rudolph, Eric, 159

Rumsfeld, Donald H., 12–14

rural drug markets, Columbia Lil' Cycos and, 125

Rush Town Crew, Washington, D.C., 223–24

Russian immigrant gangs, in Los Angeles, 66

Safe Streets Initiative, FBI's, 117, 215, 230

Safe Streets Violent Crimes Initiative, FBI's, 90–91

Sagal, Boris, 89

Sagato, Vevesi "Vesi," 130

Salazar, Chuck, 122

Salgado Pineda, Guillermo, 165

Salinas, Andy "Lucifer," 184

Salvadorans: as illegal aliens in LA gangs, 116; incarceration rate in United States for, 44; in Los Angeles, changes in immigration status of, 29; in Los Angeles, number of illegal refugees among, 30; in Los Angeles, youth joining and not joining gangs, 35–36; in Los Angeles before 1980 without gangs, 23; refugees in Los Angeles, gang membership among, 86. See also El Salvador

salvage surgery, U.S. Navy training for, 20

Sanchez, George, 74

Sandford, Carl: on Comandari's background, 156, 198; on discovery documents as gang paperwork, 135; early life and influences, 143–44; on Garcia wiretap, 154; Garcia wiretap application and, 151–52; on *Los Angeles Times* article on 18th Street Gang, 148; orientation on street gangs for, 143; partnership with Riordan, 137, 142; partnership with Wines, 154; planning to bring down Lil' Cycos, 136; raid on Garcia's home and, 154–55; Valerio's testimony on Eme's operations and, 123; on Valerio, 122

San Fernando Valley, California, as white community, 64

San Salvador, El Salvador. See El Salvador

Satan Disciples (Chicago), 241, 242–43, 249, 251

Saunders, Stephen, 197

Scheper, Dave, 141

Schwarzenegger, Arnold, 140

Schwein, Rick, 196

scientific criminology, Ayres Report (1942) and development of, 78

Scotland Yard, 197

second generation (children of immigrants): continuous waves of immigrants and, 65; Latino gangs and, 5; marginalization of, 44; political assertiveness in 1930s and 1940s of, 68; social networks after Great Migration among, 66. See also anchor babies

secretario (secretary), in Latin Kings' hierarchy, 245

Senate Select Committee on Improper Activities in the Labor or Management Field (1950s), 225

service economy, in California, Salvadorans in, 31. See also economy, U.S.

Sessions, William B., 90, 91

shell shock, 17. See also post-traumatic stress disorder

Shevardnadze, Eduard, 224–25

shot callers: for Columbia Lil' Cycos, 118, 119, 120; role in gangs, 4. See also specific gangs

Sibaja, Harold, 263–64

signs thrown by gangs, 58

White House Office of National Drug Control Policy, 104

"white power" hate gangs, violence of, 10–11

whites: elite business and political class in Miami, 269; gangs of, in Chicago, in early twentieth century, 237; murder clearance rate in Chicago for, 248

Williams Ranch, 60, 72. *See also* Sleepy Lagoon

Wines, James "Jim": assigned to 18th Street Gang investigations, 148; Carcamo arrest by, 157; on Comandari's background, 156, 198; on illegal aliens in Latino gangs, 107; raid on Garcia's home and, 154–55; search warrants for Garcia raid, 154

Winthrop, John, 288n66

wiretaps: for Colon case, 257; difficulties in application process, 151–52; international, NSA and SOD's mission and, 206; on Janie Garcia's phone, 152–54; as tool in organized crime investigations, 101. *See also* pen registers; trap-and-trace devices

witness intimidation, 120–21, 217. *See also* federal witness protection/security program

Wolf, Frank: on budget for national gang task force, 208; call to Mueller about gangs in North Virginia, 188–89; FBI's focus on criminal street gangs and, 228; on FBI's mission vs. accelerating transnational threats, 193; national gang task force and, 197; observes gang gathering in North Virginia, 160; on special antigang effort, 218; as Virginia's Tenth Congressional District Representative, 160–61

Wolfman Jack (DJ), 243–44

"Wonder nines" (semiautomatic pistols), 86, 104

World War II, 61, 71–72

Youth Alliance Program, Guatemala, 264

youth gangs. *See* gangs

Yutes (Cuban gang in Miami), 272

Zappa, Frank, 88

Zaragosa, Anthony "Coco": on associating with 18th Street Gang, 126; calls to Janie Garcia from prison by, 151; conviction and sentencing of, 157; Garcia wiretap and, 153; murder of Lefty Cazales and, 135; murder of unnamed man and woman in 1994 and, 120, 121–22; as shot caller for Columbia Lil' Cycos, 119; tensions with Lefty Cazales, 134; on Termite as a snitch, 156; Truco hit and, 132–33

Zetas (U.S.-trained Mexican special forces), 261

Zoot Suit Riots, 78–79, 109–10

Zoot Suit Riots (television documentary), 73–74

zoot suits, 68, 70. *See also* pachuco culture

Zorro, 52–53

Zulu (movie on battle of Rorke's Drift), 137–38

Zulu army, battle of Rorke's Drift and, 137–38

ABOUT THE AUTHOR

Tom Diaz is a lawyer, author, and public speaker who conducts research on gun policy and violence for the Violence Policy Center, a D.C.-based think tank. During his former career in journalism, he covered national security affairs for the *Washington Times*. He also served as counsel to the U.S. House Subcommittee on Crime and Criminal Justice from 1993 to 1997. His previous books include *Lightning out of Lebanon: Hezbollah Terrorists on American Soil,* with Barbara Newman (New York: Random House, 2005), and *Making a Killing: The Business of Guns in America* (New York: New Press, 1999).

Printed and bound by CPI Group (UK) Ltd, Croydon, CR0 4YY

09/06/2025

14685639-0005